ROGER TORY PETERSON

The Bird Watcher's Anthology

HARCOURT, BRACE AND COMPANY • NEW YORK

COPYRIGHTS AND ACKNOWLEDGMENTS The publishers and Roger Tory Peterson thank the following for their permission to use the selections reprinted in this book. The permissions are listed in the order of their appearance in the book.

DODD, MEAD & COMPANY, INC.—"The Spark" adapted from *Birds Over America* by Roger Tory Peterson, copyright © 1948 by Roger Tory Peterson. AUDUBON SOCIETY OF THE DISTRICT OF COLUMBIA, INC. and CONSTANCE SMITH—"The Meaning of Birds" by Charlton Ogburn, Jr. HOUGHTON MIFFLIN COMPANY—"The Invitation" from *Wake Robin* by John Burroughs. DOUBLEDAY & COMPANY, INC. and JOHN KIERAN—"The Nuthatch" from *Footnotes on Nature* by John Kieran, copyright 1947 by John Kieran. A. D. PETERS—"The Green Woodpecker" from *Bird Watching and Bird Behaviour* by Julian Huxley, published by Chatto & Windus Ltd. COUNTRY LIFE LIMITED and PETER SCOTT—"The Aura" from *Morning Flight* by Peter Scott. ALFRED A. KNOPF, INC., MARIE F. RODELL and JOAN DAVES, INC., and SIGURD OLSON—"Wild Geese" from *The Singing Wilderness* by Sigurd F. Olson, copyright 1956 by Sigurd F. Olson. DODD, MEAD & COMPANY, INC.—"The Lure of the List" adapted from *Birds Over America* by Roger Tory Peterson, copyright © 1948 by Roger Tory Peterson. HOUGHTON MIFFLIN COMPANY—"The Lure of the List" adapted from *Wild America* by Roger Tory Peterson and James Fisher. MARY B. DEVOE—"The Birds I Used to See" by Alan Devoe. HARPER & BROTHERS and FLORENCE PAGE JAQUES—"The Big Day" from *Birds Across the Sky* by Florence Jaques, copyright 1942 by Francis Lee Jaques and Florence Page Jaques. SPORTS ILLUSTRATED and JOHN O'REILLY—"The Biggest Bird Watch" by John O'Reilly, © 1957 by Time Inc. MCCLELLAND AND STEWART LIMITED and RICHARD M. SAUNDERS—"Winter Birds" from *Flashing Wings* by R. M. Saunders. NATIONAL AUDUBON SOCIETY and MAURICE BROOKS—"Let the Dummy Do the Work" by Maurice Brooks. ROYAL SOCIETY FOR THE PROTECTION OF BIRDS and BRUCE CAMPBELL—"Birdsmanship" by Bruce Campbell. G. P. PUTNAM'S SONS, GEORGE T. BYE AND COMPANY, and GEORGE ALLEN & UNWIN LTD.—"Return of the Birds" from *Almanac for Moderns* by Donald Culross Peattie, copyright 1935 by Donald Culross Peattie. DODD, MEAD & COMPANY, INC.—"Salute to a Brown Bird" from *Pageant in the Sky* by Raymond S. Deck, copyright © 1941 by Dodd, Mead & Co., Inc. DUELL, SLOAN & PEARCE, INC.—"Feathered Good Neighbors" from *High Jungle* by William Beebe. DODD, MEAD & COMPANY, INC., EYRE & SPOTTISWOODE (PUBLISHERS) LTD., and EDWIN WAY TEALE—"A Hundred Miles of Warblers" from *North with the Spring* by Edwin Way Teale, copyright © 1951 by Edwin Way Teale. THE UNIVERSITY OF MINNESOTA PRESS, OXFORD UNIVERSITY PRESS (LONDON), and H. ALBERT HOCHBAUM—"Patterns of Local Movement" from *Travels and Traditions of Waterfowl* by H. Albert Hochbaum, copyright 1955 by University of Minnesota. DODD, MEAD & COMPANY, INC. and MAURICE BROUN—"Red-Letter Day on Hawk Mountain" from *Hawks Aloft* by Maurice Broun, copyright © 1948, 1949 by Maurice Broun. E. P. DUTTON & CO., INC. and J. M. DENT & SONS LTD.—"Migration on the Pampas" from *A Hind in Richmond Park* by W. H. Hudson, copyright 1922 by E. P. Dutton & Co., Inc. Renewal, 1950, by The Royal Society for the Protection of Birds. CARRIE M. BRANDT—"Migration on the Bering Sea" by Herbert Brandt. THE ARGUS & AUSTRALASIAN LTD.—"Arrival of the Mutton-Birds." COWARD-MCCANN, INC. and CURTIS BROWN LTD. (LONDON)—"Migration in France" from *Why Birds Sing* by Jacques Delamain, copyright 1931 by Coward-McCann, Inc. NATIONAL AUDUBON SOCIETY—"A Night in a Channel Lighthouse" by Roger Tory Peterson. AUDUBON SOCIETY OF THE DISTRICT OF COLUMBIA, INC. and PAUL BARTSCH—"A Pet Carolina Paroquet" by Paul Bartsch. HENRY BEETLE HOUGH—"A Bird That Man Could Kill" by Henry Beetle Hough. NATIONAL AUDUBON SOCIETY and CARL KOFORD—"Condors Feeding" by Carl Koford. DODD, MEAD & COMPANY, INC. and ROBERT P. ALLEN—"Upflight of the Spoonbills" from *The Flame Birds* by Robert Porter Allen, copyright © 1947 by Dodd, Mead & Company, Inc. APPLETON-CENTURY-CROFTS, INC. and HODDER & STOUGHTON LTD.—"Flamingos of Andros" from *Camps and Cruises of an Ornithologist* by Frank M. Chapman, copyright 1908 by D. Appleton and Company. THE MAC-MILLAN COMPANY and BASIL BLACKWELL & MOTT LTD.—"Flamingos of the Camargue" from *Flamingos of the Camargue* by Etienne Gallet. THE MACMILLAN COMPANY and HELEN G. CRUICKSHANK—"The King's Bar Rookery" from *Flight into Sunshine* by Helen Cruickshank. CARRIE M. BRANDT—"Wild Turkeys at Bedtime" by Herbert Brandt. THE VIKING PRESS, INC. and LOUIS J. HALLE—"Man-o'-War" from *Birds Against Men* by Louis J. Halle, Jr., copyright 1938 by Louis J. Halle, Jr. JOHN MURRAY (PUBLISHERS) LTD.—"Adélie Penguins" from *Edward Wilson—Nature Lover* by George Seaver. NATIONAL AUDUBON SOCIETY—"The Great Bustard" by Roger Tory Peterson. HARPER & BROTHERS, A. M. HEATH & COMPANY LTD., and DILLON RIPLEY—"The Bower Bird" from *The Trail of the Money Bird* by Dillon Ripley, copyright 1942 by Dillon Ripley II. THE MICHIGAN STATE UNIVERSITY PRESS and ANGUS & ROBERTSON LTD.—"Lyre Bird Revels" from *Bird Wonders of Australia* by Alexander Hugh Chisholm. RINEHART & COMPANY, INC.—"Sea Birds on the Beach" from *The Outermost House* by Henry Beston, copyright 1928, 1949 by Henry Beston. APPLETON-CENTURY-CROFTS, INC. and GEORGE G. HARRAP & CO. LTD.—"Birds of Skokholm" from *I Know an Island* by R. M. Lockley. HOUGHTON MIFFLIN COMPANY—"The Dry Tortugas" from *Wild America* by Roger Tory Peterson and James Fisher. A. W. BOYD and WM. COLLINS SONS & CO. LTD.—"Lake of the Swans" from *The Country Diary of a Cheshire Man* by A. W. Boyd. OLIVER & BOYD LTD. and COLONEL R. MEINERTZHAGEN—"The Lammergeier" from *Birds of Arabia* by R. Meinertzhagen. H. F. & G. WITHERBY LTD.—"Birds at the Victoria Falls" from *Wanderings of a Bird Lover in Africa* by Madeline Alston. A. D. PETERS—"A Voice in Africa" from *Bird Watching and Bird Behaviour* by Julian Huxley, published by Chatto & Windus Ltd. G. P. PUTNAM'S SONS—"The Guanay—The Most Valuable Bird in the World" from *Bird Islands of Peru* by Robert Cushman Murphy, copyright 1925 by Robert Cushman Murphy. UNIVERSITY OF OKLAHOMA PRESS and GEORGE M. SUTTON—"Faisán Real" from *Mexican Birds: First Impressions* by George Miksch Sutton, copyright 1951 by University of Oklahoma Press. MICHAEL JOSEPH LTD.—"The Bush" from *Birds and I* by Leslie Brown. NATIONAL AUDUBON SOCIETY—"Voices of Tropical Birds" by Louis Agassiz Fuertes. APSLEY CHERRY-GARRARD—"The Weirdest Bird-nesting Expedition" from *The Worst Journey in the World* by Apsley Cherry-Garrard. MACGIBBON & KEE—"The Wandering Albatross" from *The Wandering Albatross* by L. Harrison Matthews. SCIENTIFIC AMERICAN—"Sonar in Birds" by Donald R. Griffin. THE BOBBS-MERRILL COMPANY, INC.—"Flamingo Hunt" from *Flamingo Hunt* by Paul A. Zahl, copyright © 1952 by Paul A. Zahl. NATIONAL AUDUBON SOCIETY—"Last of the Louisiana Whoopers" by Robert Porter Allen. THE ATLANTIC MONTHLY and GEORGE M. SUTTON—"An Adventure with a Turkey Vulture" by George Miksch Sutton. HAROLD PENROSE and COUNTRY LIFE BOOKS—"Peregrine Saga" from *I Flew with the Birds* by Harold Penrose. WILLIAM BEEBE—"Asiatic Adventure" from *Pheasants, Their Lives and Homes* by William Beebe. JAMES CHAPIN—"The Congo Peacock" by James Chapin. THE NATIONAL GEOGRAPHIC MAGAZINE—"The Curlew's Secret" by Arthur A. Allen. OXFORD UNIVERSITY PRESS (NEW YORK)—"Sky Dance" from *A Sand County Almanac* by Aldo Leopold, © 1949 by Oxford University Press, Inc. CHARLES SCRIBNER'S SONS and CHRISTY & MOORE LTD.—"Dance of the Prairie Chickens" from *Trail of an Artist-Naturalist* by Ernest Thompson Seton, copyright 1940 by Ernest Thompson Seton. ALFRED A. KNOPF, INC. and CHATTO & WINDUS LTD.—"The Crested Grebe" from *Essays of a Biologist* by Julian Huxley, copyright 1923 by Alfred A. Knopf, Inc. UNIVERSITY OF CALIFORNIA PRESS—"The Territorial Instinct" from *Lifelong Boyhood* by Loye Miller. UNIVERSITY OF CALIFORNIA PRESS—"Uphill Planters" from *Philosophy of Nature* by Joseph Grinnell. LEWIS WAYNE WALKER—"Vital Struggle: Elegant Tern vs. Heermann's Gull" by Lewis Wayne Walker. METHUEN & CO. LTD.—"Swifts at Night" from *Swifts in a Tower* by David Lack. ALEXANDER F. SKUTCH—"Montezuma Oropéndola" from *Life Histories of Central American Birds* by Alexander F. Skutch. THOMAS Y. CROWELL COMPANY and METHUEN & CO. LTD.—"King Solomon's Ring" from *King Solomon's Ring* by Konrad Lorenz, copyright 1952 by Thomas Y. Crowell Company, New York. THE YALE REVIEW and WILLIAM VOGT—"Will and Kate" by William Vogt from *The Yale Review,* copyright Yale University Press.

Library of Congress Catalog Card Number: 57-10067

Lithographed by The Murray Printing Company in the United States of America

Atlantic Puffins

To the National Audubon Society, the Royal Society for the Protection of Birds, and all other groups dedicated to preservation of the bird watchers' way of life

FOREWORD

IT HAS been stated by James Fisher that in Britain an average of one new bird book sees publication every week. The number of titles published in America is comparable if one includes the specialized volumes issued by the university presses. A hundred new bird books in the English language every year is indigestible fare to all but the most voracious readers. Even among professional ornithologists few can keep abreast of the literature of ornithophily. True, a third of the books should never have been published, a second third are adequate, and only the remaining third are significant.

In building this anthology I did not set out to read every book on the library shelves of the National Audubon Society or of the American Museum of Natural History. Nor did I attempt to bring together another treasury of great nature literature. Calling on my memory of more than thirty years of reading I selected those pieces that reflected the brighter light of direct observation, reports of firsthand experiences by bird watchers "who had been there." Some selections have less literary distinction than others, but all, I think, convey the author's enthusiasm for his science or his hobby.

After this initial phase in which my mind roamed over the many books I had previously enjoyed, I set out to investigate those that I had neglected. This discipline, which forces the anthologist to catch up on his reading, is perhaps his greatest reward.

To give continuity to the eighty-five selections, I have organized this book into seven sections. These trace the classic progress of the bird watcher from the first spark of his interest through the discovery and listing stages to the thoughtful observations of the mature student. The short introductory paragraphs are not so much biographical sketches as they are program notes, which introduce the author in some instances or tell a bit about his subject matter.

In some cases, because of the limitations of space, I have been compelled to condense essays. In doing this I have seldom changed sentences but, rather, have omitted entire sentences or paragraphs that were digressive. In no instance has the author's style been altered.

An anthology, of course, should reflect the anthologist, but in order not to overlook anything important, I carefully considered many suggestions made by friends. One evening at the Savile Club in London, Julian Huxley became very enthusiastic when I told him of my project. He immediately jotted down a dozen titles for me to think about. James Fisher, on his second visit to the United States, spent half an evening at my home systematically recalling from memory significant items out of his many years' reading of the ornithological literature. With many of his suggestions I concurred. Other items with a specialist appeal did not fit well when lifted out of their context. I could have built a book double this size easily, but publishing costs dictate practical limitations. If some of your own favorites have been omitted, forgive me.

In addition to Dr. Huxley and Mr. Fisher, I have had thoughtful suggestions and help from Robert Porter Allen, Elisha Atkins, Irston Barnes, François Bourliere, Maurice Brooks, Maurice Broun, Amy Clampitt, Roland Clement, William Cottrell, Helen Cruickshank, Monica de la Salle, David Garrison, C. A. Harwell, Florence Jaques, Joseph Hickey, P. A. D. Hollom, Sigrid Lee, C. Russell Mason, Rosario Mazzeo, Guy Mountfort, Charlton Ogburn, Jr., Fred Packard, Barbara Peterson, John O'Reilly, Alexander Sprunt, Jr., Edwin Way Teale, William Vogt, and Richard Westwood. To all these and to an understanding and generous publisher I am grateful.

ROGER TORY PETERSON

April, 1957

CONTENTS

CONTENTS

xii

CONTENTS

CONTENTS

xiv

BIRD DRAWINGS *by Roger Tory Peterson*

1 *The Spark*

Many have tried to explain this pastime of bird watching. Joseph Hickey writes: "By some, it is regarded as a mild paralysis of the central nervous system, which can be cured only by rising at dawn and sitting in a bog. Others regard it as a harmless occupation of children, into which maiden aunts may sometimes relapse." James Fisher, the British ornithologist, comments: "The observation of birds may be a superstition, a tradition, an art, a science, a pleasure, a hobby or a bore; this depends entirely on the nature of the observer."

Doctor Frank Chapman used to say: "Everyone is born with a bird in his heart." But I wonder. Why will a dozen boys in a classroom become mildly absorbed when their teacher starts a bird club, but only one or two really take hold? Many older women are enthusiastic bird watchers, but how is it that so few teen-age girls go in for ornithology? And why the exceptions? On the whole, however, birding is more of a boy's hobby.

How does it happen that so many of our best ornithologists started at the age of ten or eleven? Some of the top men—John James Audubon, Frank Chapman, Alexander Wetmore and Ludlow Griscom—began even earlier than that. Professor Arthur Allen, of Cornell, sent a questionnaire to the fellows of the American Ornithologists' Union a few years ago and found that every last one of them was launched before he was out of his teens, and ninety percent by the age of ten. Often it is a particular bird that sets off the chain reaction that makes an ornithologist. In the selections to follow we learn that a scarlet tanager was the spark that fired the imagination of Elliott Coues. For John Burroughs it was a black-throated blue warbler, for Julian Huxley a green woodpecker, and for John Kieran an ordinary white-breasted nuthatch.

A few years ago, on a Tuesday night, during a meeting of my old bird club, the Linnaean Society of New York, I sat in the back of the room where I could see everyone present. There were boys not yet seventeen, men past seventy; several housewives; a man who lived in a hall bedroom in lower Brooklyn, and at least two millionaires. There was one banker, a publisher, a cartographer, two lawyers, at least three physicians, a playwright, two artists, assorted businessmen, and at least one man with no visible means of support. A lad of particularly dull intellect sat near John Kieran, paragon of quick wit and fabulous memory. What is the common denominator? Here is a challenging opportunity for a group survey by some analyst. Instead of a behavior study of birds, why not a behavior study of bird watchers?

Would symbolism be the key? And what do birds symbolize? As with all symbols they probably represent different things to different people. Certainly the Linnaean Society or the American Ornithologists' Union or the Audubon Society or any large group seems to be a representative cross section of humanity. Kings, presidents, princes, prime ministers, secretaries of state (at least four), generals, admirals, members of parliament, governors, senators, motion picture stars, and all manner of glamourous folk have been interested in birds. So have unnumbered people without particular distinction, right down to the maladjusted souls in mental wards and prisons. (But very few of the latter. I once received a letter from a lifer who asked for a checklist of American birds so he could give appropriate monickers to his fellow "jailbirds.")

Every state has a state bird. These, chosen as they often are by garden clubs, school children, and popular vote, usually favor such familiar birds as meadowlarks, bluebirds, goldfinches and chickadees. They are seldom the birds the ornithologist would choose as his personal favorites.

If a questionnaire were sent to all the members of the American Ornithologists' Union, asking each to name his favorite three species, we might through the association of ideas gain some clues to the emotional appeal of birds. To say that people are attracted to birds because of their color, music, grace, and vivacity is superficial rationalization. I suspect a more fundamental reason is that birds suggest freedom and escape from restraint. They can fly where they please, when they please—or so it seems to us, who are earthbound.

I have been astonished, on putting my friends to the test, how often the peregrine falcon, the fastest of all birds, is indicated. Even more suggestive is the symbolic similarity of those birds that take second or third place. If a man's favorite is the peregrine, the chances are his second choice will be a hawk, too—perhaps a red-tail. Asked to name a bird that is not a hawk, to my surprise several replied "pileated wood-

4

pecker." What do the dashing peregrine and this big wild woodpecker have in common?

If a gentleman from Georgia tells me his favorite bird is the mockingbird, I know that his second choice will be the cardinal, and his third—you might guess—the Carolina wren, of course! All these stable, dependable garden birds represent the same thing: the gracious living of the old South. For a similar reason, in Ohio, the song sparrow and the cardinal are likely to share the honors.

Granted there are special reasons why some individuals like birds, there is far more general interest in birds now than there was at the beginning of the century. In those days a man who scouted around the woods for "dickey birds" felt self-conscious about it, almost apologetic. Today so many people are taking to the out-of-doors that a man who does not watch birds or grow flowers, collect minerals, study the stars, or show a little interest in at least one of the natural sciences is likely to feel uneasy about it and offer his excuses.

Why this flood-tide? It has swept across the land from East to West; and even in the Northwest, the nearest thing to a frontier we have left, people are taking time out to look at birds.

Life is becoming more and more complicated; but it seems that the more artificially complex man's affairs become the more he yearns for the fundamentals, the things of the earth. There has been a tremendous Renaissance in nature study since the beginning of the recent war, not only here, but also in Europe, particularly in England, Holland, Germany, and Scandinavia. Bird clubs are swamped with new members. Peoples of the warmer parts of the world—and the colder—closer to nature perhaps, show little interest (other than gastronomic) in birds. Bird watching as we know it is indigenous to the populous temperate regions.

Some would say it is a form of escapism and perhaps it is, in a way— but not an escape from reality; rather a flight from the unreal things— from the "somnambulism of the hive" as Louis Halle calls it. In this gadget civilization which man has built to insulate himself against the world, he finds himself entrapped, not knowing whence he came or where he is going. Halle observes that "it becomes necessary, occasionally, simply to throw open the hatches and ventilate one's psyche, or whatever you choose to call it. This means an excursion to some place where the sky is not simply what you see at the end of the street."

We invent systems, Socialism, Fascism, Communism, and Capitalism. Each despises the other. Yet, as Professor Aldo Leopold of the University of Wisconsin pointed out, they all espouse one creed: *salvation by machinery*. Is it any wonder that when these systems prove faulty and men detect the synthetic nature of the civilization of their devising they turn to nature? In an artificial world is it any wonder birds have such appeal? Birds are, perhaps, the most eloquent expression of reality.

Massachusetts can be called the cradle of American ornithology, although Philadelphia could make just claim by pointing out that both Wilson and Audubon once lived there. Bird watching became a respectable pursuit in these centers long before it was countenanced elsewhere. It is a hobby that seldom thrives where men are pushing frontiers; it takes hold when life has settled down to the civilized complexities. The appeal of birds seems to be greater the more life is restrained.

As frontiers dissolved and communities weathered, the center of ornithological interest moved westward, until now we find the more progressive work (ecological studies, behavior studies and the like) being turned out in such states as Ohio, Michigan, Wisconsin, and California. Massachusetts still has more bird watchers per square mile and probably produces more expert field observers than any other state, with the possible exception of New York.

In large cities like Cleveland, St. Louis, and Detroit, bird clubs that numbered scarcely a hundred members twenty years ago now have more than a thousand. As an Audubon Screen Tour lecturer I have been astonished at the size of the audiences that filled some of the halls —twelve hundred in Omaha, Nebraska; sixteen hundred in Kansas City. In Toronto the lecture is repeated on successive evenings to fifteen hundred people. In Detroit they do not publicise the lecture until the day after, for the hall holds only a thousand; otherwise three thousand would turn up! Two hundred cities are now on the Audubon Screen Tour circuit and the total yearly audiences are estimated at more than 750,000.

The number of children in Junior Audubon Clubs is climbing, too. Since the inception of the idea nearly fifty years ago, more than ten million juniors have been enrolled. Enrollment has exceeded four hundred thousand in a single school year. The influence of these clubs is widening like the ripples on a pond. In addition, the Boy Scouts of America with three million members and the Girl Scouts of the U.S.A.

6

with two million make bird study an integral part of their programs.

Several statisticians have tried to estimate the number of bird watchers in the United States. Roger Barton, an advertising executive puts his guess at close to ten million. This estimate is based partly on readership of his weekly bird column for the *Newark Sunday News*. By taking a conservative 22 percent interest factor and applying it to the 45,900,000 readers of all the nation's Sunday newspapers he has arrived at the potential of ten million. I suppose it depends on what one means by "bird watcher." Certainly those who go outdoors for the specific purpose of watching birds, or who supply seeds or suet for them at the kitchen window, or who take at least a casual interest, must number millions.

Unlike the twelve million sportsmen who buy hunting licences and the fifteen million who buy licences to fish, the bird watchers, who need no licences, cannot be accurately counted. Ten years ago I wrote that we as a nation were still a generation behind some of the countries of western Europe—England for example—in per capita bird interest. Since then, I believe we have caught up, and if the sales of the *Field Guides* are an index, we are actually a bit ahead of England. (Both American and British *Field Guides* have comparable competition from other guides.) However, Holland, if publishers' statements are an indicator, seems to lead all countries in bird interest.

Not long ago, when Bausch and Lomb made a survey to determine who bought their binoculars, they discovered to their astonishment that the chief customers were not the sportsmen, race-goers or boatmen, but the bird watchers. Although the "balscope" is much in vogue among the higher ornithological brass, particularly in Massachusetts where it is not unusual to see a dozen of these handy telescopes focussed on a single rarity, the 8 x binocular is the principal badge of the bird watching fraternity. Anyone sporting a pair and looking searchingly toward the horizon can be approached confidently on the basis of friendship. Louis Halle in *Spring in Washington* is reminded of the relationship of Picts and Romans beyond Hadrian's Wall:

" 'Thirty feet high is the Wall, and on the Picts' side, the north, is a ditch, strewn with blades of old swords and spear-heads set in wood, and tyres of wheels joined by chains. . . . On one side heather, woods and ruins where Picts hide, and on the other a vast town.' . . . This was a frontier that, while it was manned, even a rabbit could not slip across. The centurion of the Thirtieth soon learned on the Wall to 'take heather,' this being his way of escaping the noisy and sordid life of the town. 'Taking heather' means 'going out hunting in the Pict country with a tame Pict. You are quite safe so long as you are his guest, and wear a sprig of heather where it can be seen.'

"This custom of taking the heather I can understand, since it is my custom too. Granted, the scene has changed in its details. Instead of the heather in my cap, a pair of binoculars is my badge. . . . I know how Parnesius the centurion felt, escaping from the uproar and stench to follow the trail of the dog wolf across the bogs, or of the 'great red deer with horns like Jewish candlesticks.'

"There is as you might expect, a freemasonry among those of us who take the heather. We already know the badge when we meet, and enter into conversation without introduction, talking like old friends of our common preoccupation. More than that, we trust one another like brothers and constitute a mutual-aid society. Take the example, which I cherish gratefully in memory, of the lonely soldier who arrived for a week-end leave at Chapel Hill, N.C., after an unremitting month of drill on the barren fields of Fort Bragg. Having no acquaintance in the entire state of North Carolina, I entered the first bookstore I came to and asked the proprietor who there was in town who professed an interest in birds. He immediately put me in touch, by telephone, with a Mrs. Jensen, who, as soon as she knew I was a stranger and of the brotherhood, invited me to dinner at her home in the outlying country-side. At the kindly hands of the Jensen family I enjoyed the most un-reserved and spontaneous hospitality, so that within an hour of arriving at Chapel Hill I was no longer a stranger and, before the evening had passed, felt myself at ease among old friends, in a circle of acquaint-ance that widened with repeated visits. That badge bespeaks mutual trust, as between Pict and Pict, Roman and Roman, or Pict and Roman. It is one brotherhood the country over, and I daresay the world over."

(Adapted in part from *Birds Over America*)

CHARLTON OGBURN, JR.

The Meaning of Birds

Charlton Ogburn, Jr., like many Americans of his generation, was introduced to birds through the writings of Ernest Thompson Seton and Frank M. Chapman. The emotional fires stirred by these writers in the boy of twelve have never burned out. In his early twenties, in search of wilderness and new birds, he made a trip up the Amazon. This satisfied him for a while, but ten years later, while in the army, he volunteered for special operations in jungle country, as did other adventurous ornithologists. At the close of the war he joined the Department of State where he has been engaged in Asiatic problems. This fits the pattern too, for in no department of our government (with the exception of the Fish and Wildlife Service, of course) will one find so many bird watchers. This is, I suppose, partly because the work demands a certain quality of mind, but also because of the lure of distant places.

T HE APPEAL of birds is not something one may expect to sum up succinctly. In a sense, the whole literature of ornithology is addressed to the problem of explaining this appeal. Perhaps, however, the essential clue is afforded by the circumstances in which we become interested in birds in the first place—for I imagine that with most of us the circumstances are not too dissimilar.

To begin with, there is something stirring in the very idea of birds, of the freedom that mastery of the air allows, of the exalted perspective that flight affords of the mountain-wrinkled, river-ribboned earth, of the vast distances birds travel. In the mere contemplation of such

9

beings is to be found a vicarious release from the limitations to which mortal man is sentenced.

What makes the appeal of birds immediate and real to us for the first time, however, is likely to be an encounter with a particular bird. By chance or because someone points it out to us, our attention is drawn to a towhee—let us say—in the sense that we really see it. There it is, with its tidy, contracting pattern of black, white, and chestnut. There it is, self-contained and complete in its own universe. All at once it strikes home with us. This is not an abstraction in a painting or a zoo, a trivial background figure for man's activities. In all its individuality and perfection, it was produced without any particular intention that mankind should ever even see it. Its intense dedication to towhee-ism, with which its red eyes are bright, would remain unruffled by the subtraction from the scheme of things of the entire human race. And it is one of myriads of equally individual and perfect species that populate the forests and the seas.

There is suddenly disclosed to us the whole tide of life, limitless in its scope, scrupulous in its attention to the tiniest detail, that lies beyond our smoke-hung cities, beyond the expressionless façades of masonry, glass, and steel with which we have surrounded ourselves, and—more than that—beyond our rationalistic reckoning of things. For what, in the materialistic concepts our age entertains, can explain why there should be this jewel of a towhee?

I like to think that the appeal of birds lies in their incomparably vivid representation of life. It is as if the essential principle had been isolated in these creatures to display its attributes most pointedly and most movingly. Consider the cedar waxwing's refinement of sculpture and creamy-consistency of hue. Could a conscious artistic inspiration have wrought with greater sureness? Picture the fire in the Blackburnian warbler's throat, the cascades of gold and silver in the hackles of the pheasants, the torpedo-purpose in the forms of the diving birds, the heraldic grandeur of the condor, the reckless lines of the frigate-birds, the war mask of the harpy eagle. What an incomparable display is this! Motionless as the trogon watching from its branch, violent as the jaegers in the chase, birds seem always to manifest a matchless vitality of purpose. It encompasses the rocket-energy of the swifts, the exuberant, assertive vivacity of the jays, and the concentrated virility of the hawk, glaring unmoving and unmoved out of the solitude of his soul.

Birds are translators for us, the intermediaries between the vast

10

world beyond us and our own emotions, expressing in their notes, in tones within our spiritual register, the nature of our common setting, voicing in the lost, falsetto cries of the gulls the mood of the beckoning, dangerous sea, in the whiplash calls of the chuck-will's widow (crouched round-eyed, black-eyed, frog-mouthed) the nighttime witchery of the southern woods, in the cathedral-singing of the thrush an intimation of a transcendent purpose in the universe.

It is the effect of birds to quicken our loftiest compulsions. Who can hear the mockingbird in the moonlight, the veery in the corridors of the forest without experiencing that yearning to be at one with what is universal? And who can watch the flight of birds without feeling within himself an echo of that impulse to try his strength against the infinite that is the meaning of liberty? There in the tripping, swinging flight of the swallow, in the soaring of the tip-tilting hawk, in the skyward climb of the kingbird, in the buoyant rise of the gull to the windward of the ship, are the symbols of our aspiration to freedom. What wonder that the nobleman of centuries past acknowledged no keener satisfaction than to unhood his falcon and send her winging toward the sky! For there was more than sport in the spectacle; the sport, we may suspect, was only the excuse. In the falcon's release from the darkness of the hood and her hurtling ascent of the open air was the allegorical depiction of the liberation and ascension of what is inmost to us, the imagination, the soul—whatever we may call it.

Above all, there is the migration of birds.

When we think of that tremendous spectacle there is apt to come to mind a succession of images. For me the migration means a string of Arctic terns winging northward past South Georgia and the Horn, setting their course for the top of the world with less concern for the magnitude of our globe than for the sparkle of a fingerling fish in the waves below. It means the first purposeful stirrings of the golden plovers in the valley of the Plata, of the bobolinks in the grasses of the Gran Chaco, then of the tanagers, grosbeaks, and warblers in the forests of the Amazon, Orinoco, and Magdalena, as they feel the thin edge of the impulse to set forth that must be like the rise of the wind in a new quarter when the season changes. It means a jangling flock of red-wings coming in between a still-frozen northern lake and a gray northern sky, and then that liquid burble of song, like bubbles of music escaping up from the thawed swamp, that I have waited, single-minded, all through a northern winter for the sound of.

11

The images crowd upon one another. There are the processions of geese passing by night across the city to make your hair stand on end with the sound of their baying as they beat for the cloud-choked passes of the Appalachians. There are the phalanxes of warblers coming in by dark over the low coast of Louisiana after crossing the Gulf of Mexico. There are the nights of the flood tide in May when your imagination depicts for you the small forms scattered across the lower sky, anonymous in the uniform instinct that drives them forward, dusted above with the white powder of the moonlight, perhaps catching on their underparts an unnatural tinge of red from the neon lights of Atlanta or New York. Then there are those May mornings when we awaken to a countryside that has been transformed and rings to the singing of a triumphant army that has raised the siege of winter and brought life back from the south.

Perhaps some day a writer may be able to set down in an all-encompassing perception a vision of this mighty progression. What a vision it would be! What a comprehension we should have of the force and scope of life if we could really conceive of these streams of birds across the skies, of the vast river-system of the migration that has the pattern of a tree with roots in Patagonia, Peru, and Brazil, a bole of a trunk blanketing Central America and the Gulf, and branches reaching into every valley of our continent to terminate finally upon the coast of Greenland, the shores of the Arctic Ocean, and the marshes of Siberia!

The meaning that birds have for us increases with the depth and precision of our knowledge. It makes all the difference to know that the red-eyed vireo whose somewhat oriental face (an effect of the line through the eye, no doubt) peers at me from the tupelo on summer days very likely peers during the winter with equal impartiality at the Indians of the lowlands of Colombia. To know the accelerating swiftness with which the gray-cheeked thrush migrates northward through the Dakotas, Saskatchewan, the Northwest Territory, and Alaska adds to the significance the species and birds in general have for us. It is important for us to know why the young of robins are spotted and the young of gulls are dark and what it signifies with respect to the evolution of the herons that the young of the little blues are white. It is important for us to know the effect of climate on the size and color of a species across its range and to understand as well as we can the effect of all the factors of environment upon all the characteristics of birds. If

12

we know that an emperor penguin can hatch its eggs when the temperature is sixty degrees below zero and that the poor-will is capable of hibernation, we shall have a truer conception of the range of avian potentialities.

It is equally important to recognize the limitations of birds, to learn that the maternal instinct of some birds is so mechanical that it will embrace stones; to learn from the case of the mallards that remained too long in Montana (and perished) that when birds interrupt their migration they may not be able to resume; to learn that a kingfisher trapped in its nesting burrow by an earth-slip will die because the instinct that causes it to dig into a bank will not activate it to dig its way out. It cannot fail to be meaningful that while a kingbird will attack a crow in the vicinity of the nest with consuming fury, some of the herons will stand by indifferently while crows make off with their eggs.

We shall never finish acquiring the kind of knowledge that adds to our understanding and appreciation of birds for what they are. If we knew how an albatross, encircling the globe in its wanderings, can return—apparently unerringly—to the speck of land in the emptiness of the ocean on which it will nest, if we knew what caused the successive flocks of passenger pigeons observed by Audubon to repeat in turn the evasive movement executed at that particular spot by a preceding flock that had been assaulted by a falcon, we should know a great deal more than we do about birds and about much else besides. Meanwhile, I should be gratified enough to discover why different species behave as they do at the windowsill feeding tray—why the tufted titmouse comes and goes like a flash, in a panic, while the ruby-crowned kinglet will tarry a full minute, although constantly flicking its wings and tail, and the Carolina wren will remain indefinitely, crawling methodically the full length of the crack between the tray and the sill (it is a great one, besides, for exploring the motor of the tractor and disappearing up under the car); why the white-breasted nuthatch alights on the top of the hopper (with the sound of a French taxi horn and the grace of a wooden toy) and works down to the seed while other birds alight below and fly up to it; and why, when most birds fly off from the tray, the mockingbird habitually drops over the side with legs dangling, like a schoolboy jumping off a raft. Indeed, without knowing why any of them behave as they do, it is no small satisfaction to know *how* they behave.

13

We who have birds as an avocation owe an immeasurable debt to the ornithologists who have opened this world up to us. We are in their debt not only for the information and understanding they have gained for us through long devotion and much hardship and not only because they have infused the literature of their field with the sense of exhilaration that birds in the field arouse in us, but that could so well be lost among the desiccated collections and dispassionate records from which the truth must be excavated. Perhaps above all we may be thankful that they have imposed a discipline upon the study of birds—a standard of verifiable truth. They have rescued it from a quagmire of sentimentality.

Birds for some reason, as we are all only too well aware, have provided the occasion for some of the most saccharine outpourings adult human beings have been capable of. In speaking of the rescue work done by ornithologists I do not mean to imply that the battle with the sentimentalists has been won. It is a continuing one. We still must contend with popular conceptions of birds as coy, bonneted little housewives—monstrosities that are not even caricatures of birds, which above all else are clean, impersonal, and direct. The pursuit of birds still attracts some individuals whose distinguishing characteristic is that they have never grown up. We still have the tendency among popular writers on natural history to wax flirtatious with their subject and endow birds with all manner of human traits. We are still subjected in magazines with some technical pretensions to references to "Mr. and Mrs. Cardinal. . . ."

Having acknowledged our obligations to the scientific point of view, we may now, it seems to me, be entitled to express some concern over the direction that the study of birds is tending to take in the hands of the serious practitioners. Believing as I do that it is because we find the mechanistic aspect of our world repugnant that we find birds appealing to begin with, I, at least, find it odd that as we progress in knowledge of birds we seem more and more to force a mechanistic interpretation upon the subject of our enthusiasm. This mechanistic interpretation influences both the nature of our research and our conception of what birds are.

On the first score we are now going in heavily for what we might call the statistical approach. We are becoming omnivorous collectors of facts and figures. For example, in a study of a given species of bird, it seems today to be imperative for the observer to put himself in a

14

position from which he can record the circumstances of every visit to the nest by the parents, day after day. We read: "Female alighted on northeast side of adjacent silver maple, *Acer saccharinum,* at 2:05 PM bearing the larva of a moth (sp?) about 2.50 cm. long in her bill. At 2:06 she flew to the edge of the nest and fed nestling no. 3. Half a minute later the male sang one complete song from a perch about 5 m distant from and slightly above the nest." And so on. Another example is the proliferation of censuses of one kind or another. In the past few years breeding-bird censuses have become one of our main preoccupations. These tabulations, as we all know, record the number of nesting species in an "Immature, Storm-Damaged, Climax, Flood-Plain, Mixed Oak-Maple-Hickory Forest located 10 miles southeast of Centreville, West Virginia, on Route 15. Size, 19.35 acres. Coverage: May 10, 11, 17, 18, etc., etc."

One thing may certainly be said of these statistical studies that are coming increasingly to pre-empt the literature of bird study. They are remarkably dull. Whatever else they may be is a matter of opinion. Manifestly, knowledge can be advanced only on the basis of truth, and facts are an essential part of truth. Breeding-bird censuses can give us a far more accurate idea of the changes in our bird life than can unorganized observation. But let us not imagine that the amassing of facts is an end in itself. A man could spend his whole life counting the leaves on white oak trees and at the end tell you how many leaves the average white oak is adorned with. The figure would be futile.

The collection of data forms so vital a part of the scientific process that it is easy to forget that abstract facts are meaningless unless they contribute to a significant principle. Unless they extend or refine for us the pattern of an ordered universe they do nothing. Or they do worse than nothing; they make for chaos. Living among unrelated facts is as demoralizing as inhabiting a house full of bric-a-brac.

It is, I suspect, our preternatural determination to be unswervingly scientific that exposes us to the danger of merely compiling data for its own sake. (Human laziness may also play a part; collecting facts demands nothing of us but persistence.) I recall that in my teens I would have protested hotly had anyone averred that my interest in birds was other than scrupulously "scientific."

When we come to the current conception of what birds *are,* we again, as it seems to me, find ourselves espousing a mechanistic view out of defensiveness. . . .

15

It is painful to read some of the effusions about birds that get into print, and to be identified with them is enough to make one writhe. Still, there must be some more satisfactory response than to demonstrate our bedrock realism by denying birds the possession of any attributes not shared by a piece of clockwork.

No doubt there is a great deal of warrant for maintaining that male birds sing as a means of posting claim to a certain territory. But I do not believe that the singing of birds is exclusively a mechanical response. That theory leaves too much unaccounted for. It does not explain why, from the higher birds, we hear intricate melodic passages and tones of surpassing purity that have moved men for thousands of years.

What causes man to compose symphonies, sail the chartless ocean to unknown shores, trail the mysteries of the universe? So long as we bear in mind that it is something *extra,* not strictly demanded by the requirements of survival or of perpetuating the species, it does not matter what we call it. Each of us (who believes in it at all) will have his own designation for this extra something of the spirit. But do not tell me it is found in man alone. I have seen it in birds, too. I have seen it in a black eagle diving and tossing up for sheer sport two thousand feet above the plains of Java. I have heard it in the voice of a mountain tailorbird striving in tones of unutterable sweetness and rarity to reach and then exceed the upper ceilings of audibility, lost to all other concerns in the mists of his forest home on the high slope of a volcano. I have seen it among a flock of ravens chasing one another in a pattern of feints and passes above the Blue Ridge Mountains. I have seen it in the swoop and glide and towering of gulls as they encircle a ship. I have heard it in the spiraling glissandos of an olive-backed thrush as he alternately sang and listened at the summit of a spruce in Vermont, and in the challenging hooting of the barred owls in Virginia.

It is a spirit inherent in life and manifest in birds. To me it is the consciousness of the individual that he lives. It is the living being exulting in his powers. It is his determination to make his presence known, to make himself felt. It is the proclamation, "See! I am here!"

As for why male birds are adorned in some cases with plumage that makes us gasp, perhaps here again we might allow ourselves to range a little farther in our speculation than the competition over territory and the struggle for existence. There are also the moths and butterflies and their larvae that will stand comparison with the boldest, deftest master-

16

pieces of the lapidary or the artist in enamelwork, and there are flowers —"born to blush unseen" though they may be—with corollas figured in hues of such richness, so precise and harmonious in their symmetry, that one can become lost in contemplation of them, drawn, as it were, into a vortex of wonder. And why are these things? Is it not conceivable that there is such a thing as an aesthetic principle in the universe? Science can tell us nothing about beauty because beauty is something science cannot identify to begin with, let alone measure.

It is for these reasons that I am not greatly concerned to think that the study of birds may never have such prestige among the sciences as, say, metallurgy. The study of birds is to me like the study of man. It demands more than one faculty, and the end is not so much the elucidation of great laws, such as we may expect to derive from examination of the physical universe, as the delineation of character. What man is and what birds are, collectively and individually—that seems to me to be the ultimate object of inquiry for the student of mankind and the student of birds. What is required are the apprehensions both of the scientist and the artist, objectivity of observation and intuitive perception, a feeling for fact and a feeling for relevance. It is notably these faculties that are joined in those whose works in the natural sciences we find most rewarding and that are most likely to endure: the best of Charles Waterton, Gilbert White, Henry David Thoreau, W. H. Hudson, the Huxleys, John Muir, John Burroughs, William Beebe, Robert Cushman Murphy, Donald Culross Peattie, Louis J. Halle—and, of course, others. What makes their books live is that they wrote about life. It is life they evoke in their pages. By all means let us collect facts and let us explain the behavior of birds, so far as we can, uncompromisingly in terms of physical cause and effect. But let us also remember our ultimate objective, which is the characterization of life that birds so vividly represent to us, that is something more than a pyramid of facts and that perhaps is not wholly encompassed in systems of mechanics.

The living force in man has been vastly complicated by the element of self-consciousness. This fruit of the tree of knowledge as I suppose it is, has produced the richness and the splendor of our culture and our civilization, but it has also brought with it uncertainty and malaise. So far from glorifying life, it sometimes seems that man is coming to feel a fascination in extinction. There is such a thing as the impulse to death, psychologists tell us, and in this perhaps we may believe them.

17

Certainly our race, for whatever motives, is reaching out for the means of its own extermination. Already we have alienated ourselves by our armies of appliances, our high degree of specialization, our huge cities, our air-conditioning, from our earthly setting—from nature, or reality, whatever you please to call it. And history tells us that mankind can only at its peril thus uproot itself.

In these circumstances, in which we seem to be drifting ever farther from the source of life, what I say is—here's to the pursuit of birds! Here's to the ivory gull in the pale, pitiless glare of his Arctic wilderness. Here's to the lammergeyer, looking down on the transport planes from his eyrie in the Himalayas. Here's to the winter-dauntless chickadee that tempers the widow's loneliness. Here's to the ghoul-white neophron that fed on death before the Pharaohs had been born. Here's to the winter wren that is lost to sight at the top of a balsam yet with the thin, clear cadences of his song tears our hearts more devastatingly than the eagle tore the vitals of Prometheus. Here's to the killdeer with the questing, doubtful notes it sounds at night from the misty sky. Here's to the scoters whose dogged flocks butt headlong into the Atlantic's winter gales. Here's to the peregrine whose cannon-ball descent evokes the wonder of the German falconer, the Alaskan Eskimo, the observant Manhattanite, the Javanese, and the Caboclo on the Amazon. Here's to birds and here's to life!

(From *Atlantic Naturalist*)

18

JOHN BURROUGHS

The Invitation

When John Burroughs was a boy, books on birds were almost non-existent. However, there was Nuttall's two-volume *Manual of the Ornithology of the United States and Canada* in which he could have found a color plate of the black-throated blue warbler, the bird which sparked his lifelong interest. There were also, of course, the ponderous works of Audubon and Wilson, but these were not available to the country boy. Today the road to bird recognition is paved with dozens of fine illustrated books, and a score of bird artists as well as the color camera are continually turning out new portraits. We admire the old-timers who, lacking these crutches, set out to fashion their own. A half century ago the identification of a bird was usually confirmed by the use of a shotgun. John Burroughs was one of the first to put aside the fowling-piece and watch the living bird. Modern ornithologists, appraising his contribution, are more likely to classify him as a "naturist" rather than as a naturalist, insisting that his writings were more notable for their appreciation of birds than for their contribution of new facts. Many of us still remember this picturesque patriarch with the white beard who died in 1921. His memory is perpetuated by the John Burroughs Memorial Association, which each year presents a medal to an author who has distinguished himself in the tradition of fine nature writing.

Y EARS AGO, when quite a youth, I was rambling in the woods one Sunday with my brothers gathering black birch, wintergreens, etc., when, as we reclined upon the ground, gazing vaguely up into the trees, I caught sight of a bird that paused a moment on a

19

branch above me, the like of which I had never before seen or heard of. I saw it a moment as the flickering leaves parted, noted the white spot on its wing, and it was gone.* How the thought of it clung to me afterward! It was a revelation. It was the first intimation I had had that the woods we knew so well held birds that we knew not at all. Were our eyes and ears so dull then? There was the robin, the blue jay, the bluebird, the yellowbird, the cherry bird, the catbird, the chipping bird, the woodpecker, the highhole, an occasional redbird, and a few others, in the woods or along their borders, but who ever dreamed that there were still others that not even the hunters saw and whose names no one had ever heard?

When, one summer day later in life, I took my gun and went to the woods again in a different though perhaps a less simple spirit, I found my youthful vision more than realized. There were, indeed, other birds, plenty of them, singing, nesting, breeding, among the familiar trees, which I had before passed by unheard and unseen.

It is a surprise that awaits every student of ornithology, and the thrill of delight that accompanies it, and the feeling of fresh, eager inquiry that follows can hardly be awakened by any other pursuit. Take the first step in ornithology, procure one new specimen, and you are ticketed for the whole voyage. There is a fascination about it quite overpowering. It fits so well with other things—with fishing, hunting, farming, walking, camping out—with all that takes one to the fields and woods. One may go a-blackberrying and make some rare discovery; or, while driving his cow to pasture, hear a new song or make a new observation. Secrets lurk on all sides. There is news in every bush. Expectation is ever on tiptoe. What no man ever saw before may the next moment be revealed to you. What a new interest the woods have! How you long to explore every nook and corner of them! You would even find consolation in being lost in them. You could then hear the night birds and the owls and, in your wanderings, might stumble upon some unknown specimen.

In all excursions to the woods or to the shore, the student of ornithology has an advantage over his companions. He has one more resource, one more avenue of delight. He, indeed, kills two birds with one stone and sometimes three. If others wander, he can never go out of his way. His game is everywhere. The cawing of a crow makes him feel at home, while a new note or a new song drowns all care. Audu-

* Black-throated blue warbler. (Ed.)

20

bon, on the desolate coast of Labrador, is happier than any king ever was; and on shipboard is nearly cured of his seasickness when a new gull appears in sight.

One must taste it to understand or appreciate its fascination. The looker-on sees nothing to inspire such enthusiasm. Only a little feathers and a half-musical note or two, why all this ado? "Who would give a hundred and twenty dollars to know about the birds?" said an Eastern governor half contemptuously to Wilson, as the latter solicited a subscription to his great work. Sure enough. Bought knowledge is dear at any price. The most precious things have no commercial value. It is not, your Excellency, mere technical knowledge of the birds that you are asked to purchase but a new interest in the fields and woods, a new moral and intellectual tonic, a new key to the treasure house of nature. Think of the many other things your Excellency would get— the air, the sunshine, the healing fragrance and coolness and the many respites from the knavery and turmoil of political life.

(From *Wake Robin*)

JOHN KIERAN

The Nuthatch

The mass medium of radio broadcasting has made the name of John Kieran known to more of America's millions than that of any other bird watcher. During the 1940's he became the bright star of *Information Please;* he was "the man with the answer" to questions ranging from Shakespeare to baseball. Bird questions were a snap for him. In fact, I myself was asked to appear on the program one night to imitate seven birds for Kieran to guess. He got four; he failed on the other three mostly because I am such an atrocious mimic.

After his retirement as a sports reporter, "perhaps the greatest of our time," as one of his colleagues put it, he was able to give much more of his time to rambles in Van Cortlandt Park and along the Hudson. In *Footnotes on Nature,* published in 1947, he records with bounce and Irish wit some of these walks with The Artist (Fred Nagler), The Astronomer (Clyde Fisher), The Magician (Herman Foster), The Drama Critic (probably Brooks Atkinson), and others. No one knows the natural history of the great city of New York more intimately than he. Whereas most dyed-in-the-wool bird watchers of the male sort start in their early teens, Kieran caught the germ a bit later; and not through a spectacular bird, as we shall see, but a commonplace one.

OUT OF a clear September sky I was asked by the chairman of the District School Board to undertake the task of teaching the six pupils who would attend the district school that year. The school building was a little unpainted shack in a fringe of woods just east of the railroad cut above Anson's Crossing, which was a "whistle stop" on

22

the Newburgh, Dutchess & Connecticut Railroad, now defunct, not "its irised ceiling rent, its sunless crypt unsealed," but its rails and ties removed and its right of way returned to the wild state. Under the shingled roof of the shack that served as a school there was an entrance hallway that was used to hold hats and coats and to store firewood for the chunk stove that stood in the middle of the schoolroom into which the hallway opened. There were half a dozen rows of desks for pupils, one raised desk at the front for the teacher, and a blackboard on the front wall.

By virtue of being a college graduate, I was allowed a "temporary license" to teach there, and I went to work at it for the sum of forty dollars a month, less 1% for some retirement fund of which I never took advantage. It was then that the hand of the law was laid upon me, and I was compelled by "statoot made an' perwided," in the words of Mr. Weller, to buckle down and really learn something about birds. I discovered that rural teachers in that area had to give a Nature Study Course in a small way to their pupils. Part of this program in my term of office included teaching the pupils to recognize four common birds of the region. Colored pictures of the chosen birds, with some pure reading matter attached, were provided by the Department of Education. When it came time to teach this subject, I picked up the first leaflet and saw on it a picture of an odd-looking bird in what seemed to me to be an utterly impossible position. It was a stumpy-tailed bird about six inches long, white underneath, gray and black on top, and it was pictured apparently going down an old fence post headfirst. I never had seen any bird proceed in that topsy-turvy fashion and, furthermore, the bird of the picture was a total stranger to me. I glanced at the pure reading matter under the picture and it ran something like this:

"The White-breasted Nuthatch. This common bird is known to every farm boy and girl . . ."!

I looked at the picture again in astonishment. No, sir; never before in my life had I seen anything that looked like that bird, and I had been outdoors in that area for a dozen summers and many weeks at other seasons of the year. Not only that, but the confounded bird was shown *walking down* a fence post, a most irregular procedure in my view. There was no lesson in Nature Study that day. The bird leaflet went quietly back into the drawer of teacher's desk and I took up some subject I could handle with greater confidence: spelling. I decided that

23

the bird problem could go over until the next morning. I would sleep on the mystery. *La nuit porte conseille.*

As usual, I slept outdoors. My cot was on an open porch facing the east. It was October, with consequent cool weather, and the next morning when I awakened I lingered under the blankets a few minutes before getting up. About ten feet away on the lawn there was a cultivated Black Cherry tree. As I lay there I noticed something moving on the trunk of the tree. The moving object was, to my utter amazement, the mysterious bird "known to every farm boy and girl," the aforesaid White-breasted Nuthatch of the Nature Study leaflet—*and it was moving down the tree headfirst!* I reared up on my cot to have a better look at this phenomenon and my sudden movement caught the bird's attention so that it paused in its downward journey to twist its head to stare at me, which put it momentarily in the exact pose of the bird in the picture that the Department of Education had forced upon me.

This experience was a stunner and gave me furiously to think. I never had suspected the existence of any such bird until I had seen its picture and a few printed words about it the previous day. But the first thing that met my eyes the next morning was a live specimen of this type not ten feet from the end of my nose! I decided to begin to look into the matter immediately. It was nearly a mile from our farmhouse to the school and, on the way that morning, I kept my eyes open with astonishing results. I saw four more of these birds going up or down the trunks of trees! By the time I reached the school I realized that I had been practically blind for twenty years. While looking for White-breasted Nuthatches on this morning walk, I noted that there were odd-looking sparrows in the undergrowth. They had white lines on the sides of their heads and white patches under their throats. That was my introduction to the White-throated Sparrow, though I did not know its name. I saw other birds I never had noticed before, but what they were I couldn't guess. I determined to keep my eyes open and investigate further.

(From *Footnotes on Nature*)

JULIAN HUXLEY

The Green Woodpecker

Julian Huxley, whose distinguished grandfather, Thomas Huxley, was the great interpreter of Darwin, is one of the leading biologists of our time. When U.N.E.S.C.O. was created he acted as its first director.

But all biologists—certainly all ornithologists—start off on the emotional level. They may profess a purely scientific interest in birds, but pin them down and they will admit that their boyhood interest was one of open-mouthed wonder. Julian Huxley credits a green woodpecker with igniting the spark that made him a slave to the lamp of ornithology.

I HAD been fond of birds since a child; but it was when I was about fourteen that I became a real bird-watcher. The incident which precipitated the change was this. One morning of late winter, crossing the laundry-yard of my aunt's country house, I saw a green woodpecker on the grass only a few yards from me: I had just time to take in the sight of it before the bird was off to the wood beyond the hedge. The green woodpecker is a common bird enough; but I had never seen one close. Here I saw every striking detail: the rich green of the wings, the flash of bright yellow on the back when he flew, the pale glittering eye, the scarlet nape, the strange moustache of black and red; and the effect was as if I had seen a bird of paradise, even a phoenix. I was thrilled with the sudden realization that here, under my nose, in the familiar woods and fields, lived strange and beautiful creatures of whose strangeness and beauty I had been lamentably unaware.

(From *Bird Watching and Bird Behaviour*)

25

ELLIOTT COUES

The Scarlet Tanager

In the tropics where nearly every bird is brightly colored—and therefore commonplace—few people seem interested in them. Bird watching is indigenous to the more temperate parts of the world. In northern latitudes, where gaudy pigment has been used sparingly, a vision of a brightly colored bird glimpsed by a youngster may burn in his memory forever. Doctor Elliott Coues, writing in 1878, recalled that a scarlet tanager ignited the tinder of his long career as a distinguished ornithologist.

MORE YEARS have passed than I care to remember since a little child was strolling through an orchard one bright morning in June, filled with mute wonder at beauties felt, but neither questioned nor understood. A shout from an older companion—"There goes a Scarlet Tanager!"—and the child was straining eager, wistful eyes after something that had flashed upon his senses for a moment as if from another world, it seemed so bright, so beautiful, so strange. "What is a Scarlet Tanager?" mused the child, whose consciousness had flown with the wonderful apparition on wings of ecstasy; but the bees hummed on, the scent of the flowers floated by, the sunbeam passed across the greensward, and there was no reply—nothing but the echo of a mute appeal to Nature, stirring the very depths with an inward thrill. That night the vision came again in dreamland, where the strangest things are truest and known the best; the child was startled by a ball of fire, and fanned to rest again by a sable wing. The wax was

soft then, and the impress grew indelible. Nor would I blur it if I could—not though the flight of years has borne sad answers to re-iterated questionings—not though the wings of hope are tipped with lead and brush the very earth, instead of soaring in scented sunlight.

(From *Birds of the Colorado Valley*)

PETER SCOTT

The Aura

"Make the boy interested in natural history if you can; it is better than games. . . . Above all, he must guard and you must guard him against indolence. Make him a strenuous man."

These words were written by Captain Robert Falcon Scott to his wife as he lay dying, immobilized by blizzards and swirling drifts, on his struggle back from the South Pole.

Peter Scott has fulfilled his explorer-father's hopes. Everyone in Britain knows him, for attention was focussed on his affairs almost at birth. To many, mention of his name means wild geese. He is undoubtedly the world's first authority on waterfowl, but he could have been almost anything he chose. He has been junior doubles ice-skating champion of England, an Olympic contender in sailboating, a national naval hero in battles of the North Sea, a telecaster, directing one of England's most popular TV programs, a portrait artist of ability, an explorer, a writer of charm and an artist whose bird canvasses bring a greater price on New York's 57th Street than any American bird artist can command. Today, as the Director of the Waterfowl Trust he spends much of his time on scientific research. In only one venture has he ever failed—his short sally into British politics.

In the following selection from *Morning Flight,* Peter Scott attempts to explain his obsession with wild geese.

THERE is a peculiar aura that surrounds in my mind anything and everything to do with wild geese. That I am not alone in this strange madness, I am sure; indeed, it is a catching complaint, and I hardly know any who have been able to resist its ravages, when once

29

they have been exposed to infection. It is difficult to know just why this should be so. It is perhaps a matter both of quality and quantity.

I wish it were possible accurately to estimate numbers after they have reached the thousands.

I remember an afternoon at the end of September when a great gathering of geese were sitting on a big grass marsh. All day we had watched them straggling in in bunches of half a dozen to a dozen—tiny specks in the sky suddenly hurtling downward to settle on the marsh. They had done it all the day before, and the day before that too —arriving from Spitzbergen and Iceland and Greenland.

Some of them flew out and settled on the sand, and we tried to estimate their numbers. We counted and multiplied, counted and multiplied, starting first at one end and then at the other. Eight thousand was our estimate after half an hour of eye-straining through a field glass.

And then suddenly behind us a roar broke out, and the whole surface of the marsh seemed to rise into the air. A black cloud of geese, which conveyed just the same oppressiveness as an approaching rainstorm, moved out over the sand where sat the ones we had been counting. They did not settle with them, however, but stretched away down the crest of the high sand until those that pitched farthest were only visible as they turned to head the wind; fully two miles of solid pinkfooted geese.

It was idle to return to our futile estimates. We could only gasp and murmur that our 8,000 were but a quarter of them.

Is it possible that 20,000 geese made up that black line which stretched as far as the eye could reach along the high sand?

Perhaps there were half of the pinkfooted geese that exist in the world here before us. Nearly all of them winter in England and Scotland, except for the few flocks which go to Holland. They breed in Spitzbergen and Greenland and a few in Iceland, and although it is possible to see vast numbers together, yet in their world distribution the pinkfeet are a tiny species of probably no more than 50,000 individuals, possibly much less.

When they first come south on migration, they collect on this particular marsh, but after about a fortnight they split up and go to other marshes and estuaries to spend the winter.

However many there may have been on that September afternoon, it was a sight and sound that must have thrilled the hardest heart. In this

30

case perhaps it was their very numbers, or the volume of sound, or the mystery of their arrival from Arctic regions on the very date upon which they had arrived every year for who knows how long; perhaps it was the thought of so many great birds together, for pinkfeet are more than 5 feet from wing tip to wing tip; or the thought that, although the flocks are so big, yet the places they come to are so very few—or perhaps it was a combination of all these things.

But probably the chief reason why wild geese hold such a peculiar fascination is because of their wariness. They are so difficult to be near, that being near them itself is thrilling, whether one is painting them or shooting them or photographing them, or catching them alive in a net. If you have been within 5 yards of unsuspecting wild geese you have achieved something, and that achievement alone has its special thrill. It is the knowledge that you have outwitted, not one, but perhaps a thousand *very wily creatures*. And there is another thing that makes wild-goose chasing so good. If you go after wild geese you will assuredly go into beautiful wild places at the most beautiful times of day —at dawn, or dusk, or moonrise—and, best of all, you will hear them call.

I have been many hundreds of times on a certain marsh in Norfolk, but I see it now as I have only seen it once or twice each season. And I hear the geese calling—a music of indescribable beauty and wildness, and fitness for the flat marsh which is their home. The moon has just risen, very large and orange over the sea, and the tide is high, half covering the salting, and filling the creeks right up to the sea-wall. There are a few wigeon calling as they fly along the shore, and away to the west a big pack of knots and dunlins twitter incessantly. Just an occasional call note reminds one that the geese are there waiting for enough light to come in and feed on the potato fields over the bank.

Suddenly there is a little burst of calling—the first ones are up— they're coming.

(From *Morning Flight*)

SIGURD OLSON

Wild Geese

Like many another boy, Sigurd Olson was initiated into the ways of the wild by hunting and fishing. Outgrowing his Daniel Boone period, he put aside the gun and has matured into one of our most articulate spokesmen for the wilderness. As President of the National Parks Association he is staunch in the defense of these national treasures, so mercilessly sniped at by private interests, and so easily eroded by too heavy public use. The Quetico-Superior wilderness area was set aside largely because of his efforts. Sigurd Olson's writings have a strong nostalgic undertone; only a Minnesota Viking could write with such feeling about the land of lakes and the north-woods.

IT WAS November and I was on top of a high birch-covered ridge. The air was rich with the smell of down leaves and the ground was covered with bronze and tarnished gold. Far below was a blue lake with a rice-filled river flowing into it. Where the river met the open water, the rice fanned out like a golden apron, solidly colored at the gathered waist, flecked with blue toward its fringes.

Suddenly out of the north came the sound I had been waiting for, a soft, melodious gabbling that swelled and died and increased in volume until all other sounds were engulfed by its clamor. Far in the blue I saw them, a long skein of dots undulating like a floating ribbon pulled toward the south by an invisible cord tied to the point of its V.

I have never killed a goose and now I never intend to, the sight and the sound of them is enough. But there was a time when, more than anything else in the world, I wanted to bring one of those high wanderers down to earth. The sound of wild geese on the move haunted me and I felt that somehow I must capture some of their mystery, some of their freedom and of the blue distances into which they disappeared. The idea grew into an obsession, and I used to lie awake at night, dreaming and planning how I would bring it about. I never went hunting without a handful of shells loaded with buckshot, never heard the grand music without praying that the birds would come close. I do not believe that there was ever a boy who wanted a goose as badly as I did. It was not just a case of being able to say: "I killed a goose," though in my country, well out of the main flyways, that would have been something to boast about. It was far more than that; it was involved with the way I felt and with the wonder of listening to them as they came year after year and wove their way into space.

There was a time when a flock of them alighted in an open field and I crawled on my belly for a mile, praying every foot of the way that the birds would not see the waving of the stubble, that they would keep on feeding until I was within range. That day there were other flocks in the air and the wind was alive with their calling. I can still hear those geese gabbling softly to themselves as they fed on the down grain, still see the long necks, the outstretched heads of the sentinels as I drew near. Then just when I was at the limit of range, a crow flew over, cawing its find to the world. They took to the air with a thunder of wings and I lay there a bare hundred yards away, watching them disappear over the horizon.

Another time when the sun was setting over the marshes of Totogatik Lake, the wild gabbling came out of the north and the birds were silhouetted against a flaming sky. That time they caught me in the open between the rice and the tall grass near shore, but it was dusk and the canoe blended into its background. That instant is burned into my memory: the water like wine, the approaching flock, black spruce etched against the sky. Then they came, down—down—down out of the gloom until I could feel the measured beat of their wings. As they swung to land, a hunter fired from the far shore. They swerved and went out the way they had come.

A third time, in the hills during deer season, I heard a flock circling and circling, looking for a spot of open water. I knew a man who had shot one with a rifle; I had talked to him and wondered enviously if I

33

would ever have such luck. The birds were big, their flight slow, and if you held right, your chances were good; but when the flock finally swung over that day in the hills, though they were well within range, nothing happened. Only a lone wing feather floated down, spiraling lazily out of the cold November sky.

Then one year my great chance came. I had been following a trail through a black spruce swamp on my way to the river, where I hoped to find a few last mallards feeding in the rice. It was in the very center of the bog that I heard them—just the merest hint of melody, but enough to stop me in my tracks. The flock was far away and almost instantly the sound was gone. Mallards were forgotten, everything else in the world but the geese circling the bend in the river. I reloaded my gun with buckshot, checked and rechecked my safety, placed the duck loads where I could not possibly make a mistake. Nothing must go wrong now. This was the time I had been praying for.

I stood there straining to catch the music again, but the moss-hung spruces and the soft cushion of muskeg seemed to absorb it. Suddenly the sound grew louder, changed in a moment from a vague, blended harmony to the clear, joyous clamor of birds coming in to feed. As yet I could see nothing, but the music rose and fell as the flock dipped between the hills and valleys looking for a place to land. Then they were overhead and their bugling filled the trees, and I ran madly for the closest ridge where I might have a chance of seeing them as they came by. I plunged through the tangle of heather and sphagnum beneath the spruces, scrambled up the rocks to the crest of the ridge. They had seen the patch of rice in the river, had spotted the blue open water, and would have to circle close to the ledge in order to land. Wild, impossible thoughts were mine that day, but nothing was impossible then.

I was breathless when I reached the top. From where I stood, I commanded a clear view of the swamp, the winding blue of the river, the golden spot of rice in the mallard hole. The din of their calling grew louder and at last was so deafening that the rocks themselves seemed to bounce back the sound. Then they were directly above and I could see the outstretched necks with their white chin straps, the snowy undersides of the wings.

Straight overhead now in a wavering V, still just out of range. I crouched against a boulder and prayed that they would swing back. For a moment they disappeared behind a ridge, and as the calling died

34

I was sick at heart, knowing I should have taken my chance and fired.

Then they were back, and as they sailed over the spruce tops I knew this was the moment I had been waiting for. They were much bigger than I had ever imagined. I could not only hear the beat of their wings and the rush of air through them, but could actually feel it. At that moment they seemed almost close enough to touch and I could see their eyes, the wary turning of their heads, their outstretched feet. Then they saw me there against the rock and pandemonium broke loose. The flock climbed into the sky, beat the air desperately to escape. Not until then did I remember my gun and what I had come for, and now it was too late. The birds were out of range.

After that boyhood experience I never tried to kill a goose, and now that I am older and a little wiser, I think I know the reason why. As I look back, I could comfort the boy I was. I could tell him that one should never try to capture something as wild and beautiful as the calling of geese, that it is better to wait and listen as they go by and wonder where they have gone. But, knowing that boy, I realize that he would not believe me. Only many years could heal the wound of that October day.

The long skein of dots was fading into the horizon and the calling grew fainter and fainter. Then for a moment it was gone and I heard it almost as a remembered sound. Once more it came and I caught the lift of the flock just before it was swallowed in the blue. There was the lake far below me and the rice-filled golden river running into it, and the air was rich with the smell of down leaves.

(From The Singing Wilderness)

11 *The Lure of the List*

B IRD LISTING or just plain "birding," not to be confused with serious bird watching, is basically a sport rather than a science. Many boys go in for it, but so do many professional men who have only Sundays to spare. They cruise the roads, scan the lakes, investigate new places, and keep a year-to-year record of what they find. Housewives, more confined, keep lists of what they see in the back yard.

Guy Emerson, a New York financial expert who always engineered his business trips so that he would catch the spring migration of warblers in Texas, the shorebirds in California, and the ducks in Utah, in 1939 ran up a grand total of 497 species (no subspecies included). For thirteen years this record stood unchallenged as the greatest number of species seen by an observer in a single year in North America, north of the Mexican border. In 1953, when James Fisher and I made our grand tour around the perimeter of Wild America, we set out to top Emerson's score. The critical bird—number 498—came shortly after we stepped from the plane at Anchorage, Alaska. Flying overhead near the airport was a short-billed gull. We sent Guy Emerson a telegram informing him that he had been dethroned as champ of the bird listers.

Fisher pulled off a deft bit of gamesmanship in Anchorage. While I stayed in the hotel to work on a drawing he went into the mountains and came back with five new birds on his list. He retained this margin until he returned to England; and so, for a month, an Englishman held the record list of birds seen in one year in North America. It was not until I returned across the continent in August that I caught up.

Incidental information: my year's list at the end of 1953 was 572 species (not counting an additional 65 Mexican birds). This record, however, stood for only two years. In 1956, a young Englishman, Stuart Keith, who had read *Wild America,* retraced our path and amassed a total of 594.

To make these top scores we traveled to the far corners of the country, but local lists of 250 species or more are made every year by

39

birders who live close to salt water, particularly around such cities as Boston, New York, Philadelphia, Washington, Charleston, San Francisco, and Los Angeles. Inland, 150 to 200 is a good year's total.

As in any other sport, "scores" seem exciting chiefly to those who play the game. If, in this section I seem to be placing too much emphasis on sheer collecting or listing, it is because I have an academic interest in these games men play with birds, and believe the phenomenon should be recorded.

Ludlow Griscom, now in his late sixties, has garnered scientific prestige enough to satisfy any museum man, but he has always found time to play the game of his boyhood for all it is worth. Over the years I watched with fascination his acceleration of pace. Three decades ago, when he was at the American Museum, he made the statement that it was physically impossible for one man to see 250 species of birds in the New York City region in one year. On the very last day of that year, Frank Watson, an entomologist in the American Museum, saw his 250th bird, a razor-billed auk. Griscom, after duplicating the feat himself, moved to Cambridge, Massachusetts, where reputedly there were leaner pickings. In due time he was getting lists of 250 there, and eventually 290! Later, he developed a state-wide grapevine. His friends telephoned him immediately when they discovered anything rare. They tipped him off to all the strays: birds from Europe, the far north, the south, and the far west. Thus, he did not have to travel outside the state to get his birds. The world came to his door; the mountain came to Mohammed. In 1941, he attained a list of 304, all in Massachusetts. Then he wrote: "The war and the tire shortage will make a repetition of 1941 impossible for some years to come. I trust this will be written up in some detail as a record of a way of life and a technique of bird study, so that it will have historical rather than purely passing interest . . . I shall never again even try to duplicate 1941." This is what he wrote, but, in 1945, the very year the war ended, his year's total was 307. Then post-war inflation set in. In 1946, his personal list soared to such heights that he refused to publish it! When I asked Griscom, late the following year, whether it was a secret, he said no, but he had felt, at the time, that publishing it would emphasize unduly a relatively unimportant side of ornithology. Be that as it may, Griscom's list for 1946 was 317. I said, surely that would be his top record for all time. With a wry smile, he informed me that he had just that week reached 318, with two months of 1947 still left to go. His latest bird was a painted redstart! I thought he said painted bunting, and I was not too impressed, but then it dawned on me that he meant the gorgeous butterfly-like warbler with the red belly and white wing patches that lives in the mountains of southern Arizona, the most stunning of all the warblers, bar none!

Two women, Mrs. de Windt and Mrs. Searle, newcomers to bird watching, were scanning the trees on Marblehead Neck when they made their incredible discovery. The bird flitted among the branches overhead like a vision. They could not find it in their eastern *Field Guides,* so they called up Russell Mason at the Massachusetts Audubon Society. He could think of nothing that fitted their description but suggested it might be a towhee. The ladies were indignant. They knew towhees. Then Mason had a hunch. He called up Griscom and the following morning they both went to Marblehead Neck. Within two minutes after their arrival they found the bird—a painted redstart—2400 miles from its home in the desert mountains. During the day this rare visitor was seen by 100 to 150 observers from all over the state, including a busload of Massachusetts Audubonites on a scheduled trip. Even kodachrome movies were taken for the record.

Every state in the Union has its quota of rarities, stray birds out of their normal range. Joseph Grinnell once remarked that, given enough time, every North American species would be recorded in California.

What makes a good field-man? I once knew a guide at Barnegat who could identify the ducks as they rose in a smoky cloud on the horizon, so distant that we could scarcely distinguish what they were with our binoculars. "There go your cannies," Oscar would say, "and them's broadbills over on the end." He was always right. Of course, he went partly by location. He was out on the bay every day so he knew approximately where to expect things. I knew another guide on Great Salt Lake who could tell the different ducks by the murmur of their wings. Without hesitation, one night, he called pintails, redheads, teal, shovelers, and mallards. I believed him, even though the sky was so black I had no way of checking.

There are many, like Oscar, the Barnegat bayman, who, on familiar ground, can call off the birds before anyone else; but I think the test of a good field observer is how quick and accurate he is away from home. I am sure you could put George Sutton, the bird artist, anywhere on the continent and he would know immediately what to look for in that

41

particular area. Sutton has a technique all his own. He doesn't stick to the paths the way most of us do, but wanders off into the dark thickets and makes squeaks on the back of his hand. In this way he turns up a lot of things, little obscure warblers and the like, that most of us would miss.

Ludlow Griscom has been called the "virtuoso of field identification." He knows hundreds of birds by their flight alone, and 500 or more by their songs. Very few North American birds have eluded him, and his world life list is well over 2500. After 10,000 field trips he has learned to call off birds in a split second—so quickly and surely that his scientific colleagues sometimes have their doubts. But when they check, he is almost invariably right. What gives Griscom this edge? Let us look at his early background. Brought up in a family with a tradition of international diplomacy, he crossed the Atlantic fifteen times before he was twenty-eight. He spoke French and German, not as an American speaks them, but like a European. All told, he learned to speak five languages fluently, can read ten easily and can translate up to eighteen with a little help. As a youngster, he played the piano so proficiently that by the time he became a young man he had to make a choice between the career of a concert pianist and that of an ornithologist. There came a time when he could further his art only by devoting eight hours a day to the keys instead of four, and this meant he would have to give up the birds. Although he still plays Chopin beautifully, ornithology won out. Languages and music both demand the control of great masses of detail, so organized that they can be sorted out with unconscious speed. Griscom's achievements in these fields undoubtedly conditioned his way of thinking, and, in addition to his training as a first-rate botanist and museum ornithologist, helped make him the field-man he is.

The mind of a good field observer works just like a kaleidoscope, the gadget of our childhood, wherein loose fragments of colored glass fall quickly into symmetrical patterns. We see a bird. With an instinctive movement we center it in our glass. All the thousands of fragments we know about birds, locality, season, habitat, voice, actions, field marks, and likelihood of occurrence flash across the mirrors of the mind and fall into place—and we have the name of our bird.

Guy Emerson insists that his lists are of purely secondary importance. Birds, he says, give him a closer tie with America than any other medium, for through them he meets people in walks of life with which he would otherwise have no contact—people with long vistas before their eyes. And he sets foot in places that are untrod by the multitude—from remote groves in our National Parks, the most beautiful places this side of heaven, to city garbage dumps.

Even the seamy places appeal to some birds and to the men who pursue them. One day, Geoffrey Carleton of New York set out in his rattletrap of a car to see a rare gull that had been reported on one of the city dumps. He became lost, and, chugging up to the nearest policeman, called out over the asthmatic sobbing of his engine:

"How do I get to the dump?"

The policeman, visibly indignant, replied, "Sorry—you can't leave that old hack there. It's not a junk yard, you know."

Mr. Carleton, an inveterate bird-lister, has become callous to such brushes with his uncomprehending fellow man. Even the scientific ornithologist is not too sympathetic and often looks down his nose at such goings on. "So you broke a hundred today!" he taunts. "What does that prove?" He forgets that he went through the same stage himself and that the "lure of the list," as Guy Emerson calls it, came first, before the science. Scratch a fellow of the American Ornithologists' Union and you will find, beneath, a boy who stood open-mouthed when he first heard a thrush sing; a boy who made lists for years before he put his hobby on a more intellectual basis. Many of the leaders of American ornithology, men like Robert Cushman Murphy of the American Museum and Alexander Wetmore of the Smithsonian, are not ashamed to enjoy a good day's birding whenever they can, even if it adds not one scrap to science. Arthur A. Allen, Professor Emeritus of Ornithology at Cornell, still keeps lists, and even goes out for an exhausting "Big Day" once in a while.

The field-glass amateurs need not apologize to the professionals. To the beginner, advanced ornithological research seems as dull and pointless as bird listing seems to some biologists. Yet they blend, one with the other. There is no reason why the bird lister should justify his hobby on scientific grounds any more than should the sportsman. Still, he inevitably adds something to our knowledge of birds. To the rank and file of field-glass observers we owe much of what is known about the sweep and movement of migration, of invasions, distribution, extension of range, and periodic increases and declines.

But the game of listing pays smaller dividends the longer it is played. Rare birds no longer seem rare when you have seen them a dozen times. After a few years, even the most fanatical bird chaser takes things easier. He no longer gets up at the crack of dawn on every field trip. I remember how the rest of my party once despaired of me when near Cobb's Island, Virginia. They got up at daybreak to see what they could find before breakfast. I stayed in bed. In the two hours they were gone they listed forty-two species. My own list when I came downstairs was forty. I had heard them all from my pillow and only once did I raise my head to look out the window—when a flock of curlew flew by.

It used to take a lifetime to learn to identify all the birds; now it can be done in several years. That does not mean that bird study stops when you can no longer add new birds to your list. Some expert field-men, like John Baker, plunge into conservation work; he is now president of the National Audubon Society. Others, like Allan Cruickshank, transfer their interest from seeing new birds to photographing them. The thoughtful person may graduate from Christmas counts to breeding-bird censuses, and from there on to life histories, or studies of song, territory or whatever strikes his fancy. If he wishes to become really profound, he might even probe into bird psychology.

The vistas of bird watching stretch out to the horizon.

(Adapted from *Birds Over America*
and *Wild America*)

ALAN DEVOE

The Birds I Used to See

Many years ago, when I was fifteen or sixteen, four of us, all teen-agers, started a nature correspondence club. Soon we had fifty or sixty members in seventeen states and even a mimeographed publication, *The Passenger Pigeon*. When our editor, Russell Walp, went away to college, this short-lived journal became as extinct as its namesake. Soon our club followed it into oblivion, but not some of its members. Gustav Swanson of Minnesota was to become one of the country's leading wildlife technicians and is now head of the Department of Conservation at Cornell University. Alan Devoe, who saw his words in print for the first time in *The Passenger Pigeon* became a writer so successful, in fact, that he joined the staff of the *Reader's Digest,* to which he contributed many articles on natural history. His career ended abruptly when he died at his Connecticut farm at the age of forty-five. For years he had been a regular contributor to *Audubon Magazine*. His "Life of the Chipmunk" is a classic of nature writing but would not fit into this anthology. An off-beat article, one of his best, was entitled "The Birds I Used to See." It struck a bell with bird watchers of my generation, for we all had seen scissor-tailed flycatchers fifteen hundred miles from their normal range, and we all swore by our little Reed bird guides.

M Y GRANDFATHER, who lived to be ninety-two, used to spend a good deal of time in his later years complaining bitterly of the fact that people no longer spoke up so that a body could hear what they were saying. In his young days, it seems, people had been perfectly audible; but now they had taken to mumbling and practically whispering, so that he could scarcely catch a word. It used to annoy and puzzle the old gentleman immensely.

I feel the same way about what has happened to the birds I used to see.

Back in the glorious early days of my life as a bird-enthusiast, it used to be nothing at all for me to go for a short walk in the countryside within twenty miles of New York City, and easily see a scissor-tailed flycatcher or perhaps a chestnut-collared longspur. Prowling the fields and thickets with boyhood's rapt attentiveness, I was constantly coming upon some bird that was obviously no common species but must be a great ornithological rarity. Perhaps (who could be sure?) it might be a species hitherto unknown. And so I would watch very closely, through my binoculars, and I would note every detail of coloring and feathering and eye-ring or eye-stripe or throat-patch and all the rest of it; and I would put it all tremulously down in my field notebook. Then, at home in the evening, there would be the magical delight of thumbing through Chester A. Reed's "Bird Guide," in search of the identity of the bird I had seen. And presently—sure enough!—there it would be. A scissor-tailed flycatcher, to the life. Unmistakable. There would be a fresh excitement in going out for the next bird-walk, for there was always a chance that a similar piece of good luck might come my way again. Indeed it virtually always did.

There were *birds* in those days, I tell you. A zealous young ornithologist could look out of the window on almost any propitious winter day and perceive, stuffing itself with seeds at his bird feeder, a gray-crowned leucosticte. (I understand there is an absurd movement afoot nowadays to have this bird called simply the gray-crowned rosy finch, but I want nothing to do with this prosy modernism. Chester A. Reed, in my beloved 1909 edition of his "Bird Guide," said that the bird's name is leucosticte, and that is what I say its name is.) There used to be a small area of woods a mile or two from where I lived in the days of my boyhood ornithologizing. I don't suppose these woods were more than ten or twelve acres in extent, but they were able to produce more than one Acadian sparrow, innumerable warblers of such striking kinds as the cerulean and the prothonotary, and, on one forever-memorable morning, a pyrrhuloxia. I remember the exact spot where the pyrrhuloxia presented itself to me, startling and fascinating me so exceedingly that I could scarcely keep my binoculars focussed on the

46

bird. I remember, too, the renewal of excitement in the evening, after I had identified my specimen in Mr. Reed's pages, when I was able to record in my notebook that I was probably one of the very few observers who had ever seen a pyrrhuloxia elsewhere than in southern Texas, Arizona, or Mexico. Those were the areas, Mr. Reed said, in which the bird ordinarily might be found.

And so it went, all during the days of my first burning enthusiasm for ornithology. My hikings and huntings were done in a glorious cloud of dickcissels, pauraques, and Sprague pipits. There was some *fun* in being a bird-man in those days. Not only fun, but a sense of high scientific achievement and discovery. For in those days not only were the rarest specimens of our native avifauna discoverable by a sharp watcher, and the western and mid-western species given to turning up excitingly in the east, but also there was a wonderfully high incidence in this country of foreign "strays" (as Mr. Reed called them). The Greenland wheatear, for instance, often used to show up in my territory. I never found its nest (made, surprisingly enough, according to Mr. Reed, of "any rubbish obtainable"), but I often saw the bird itself feeding in the snow in my yard. It had a remarkable resemblance to one of our own common winter birds, such as perhaps the junco or the tree sparrow, but of course I could tell the difference. Any enthusiastic young ornithologist could. Then again, I remember, there used to be the occurrence of European goldfinches and Lapland jays. The Lapland jay was distinguishable from the Canada jay, which has a more southerly range, by the fact that "the black on the head is deeper." These were the "Bird Guide's" words. I cannot recall that, as a young man, they ever gave me any trouble.

Well, as I say, that is the way things used to be. By my late teens, as I recall it, there was already a certain slight dwindling and dulling in our bird-life; but it was nothing sufficient to give an ornithologist any real dismay. The dismay did not start until a few years later. By the time I had reached my majority, I had decided pretty clearly that what I wanted to be was a writer-naturalist. And so, not very long afterwards, I moved to an old farmstead, way out in the country, where I could have a piece of land that would serve me permanently as a sort of living laboratory, and I settled down to watch it closely.

I have been watching it ever since. With my fortieth birthday coming up, I continue to go out daily, with the binoculars slung around my neck, and prowl through the hemlock woods and across the open up-

47

land fields and down along the winding brook, looking for birds. Never once, by any chance, does a pyrrhuloxia pop up. In all the great sweep of the meadow, no wheatear sounds its cry, tinkling with the icy music of Greenland. The Labrador jay, its head a blacker black than that of the Canada jay, avoids my acres utterly. Oh, I find a lot of birds, of course. But all so commonplace, so expectable, so—if I may thus express it—so *native*. I love my phoebes and barn swallows dearly, and have been happy in making intimate studies of their lives in the way in which I used to promise myself I would some day study birds, but still, somehow, bird-study is not the adventure that it used to be. It isn't like the old days when the European goldfinch used to be so much commoner than it is now. I have an ideal farm here for European goldfinches, but they just don't come. I don't know where all the pauraques can have gone, but they have certainly gone somewhere. I see a lot of birds these days; I can't complain of their quantity. But what a carload of them I would trade for the blazing excitement of seeing just one chestnut-collared longspur. Just *one* would content me. When I was starting out in ornithology, they used to be as thick as the flying autumn leaves.

Where are the birds I used to see? Could it be—could it just possibly be—that they have gone where the days of my youth have gone? No; it is too sad a thing to think about; I cannot admit it. I prefer to think that the trouble is just that many years ago I lost my copy of the 1909 edition of the "Bird Guide" by Chester A. Reed.

(From *Audubon Magazine*)

FLORENCE PAGE JAQUES

The Big Day

When Florence Jaques met her husband, the famous bird artist Francis Lee Jaques, he was just starting his distinguished career as preparator of habitat groups in the American Museum. He was to travel to many bird-rich places—the Bering Straits, the bird islands of Peru, the Swiss Alps, and Panama. On two or three of these expeditions Florence was able to accompany her husband, but no trip to far places made as much impression on her as her first "big day" in Dutchess County, only two hours by train from New York City. The big day has become a tradition among bird watchers everywhere. The scheme is to pick a day in May when migration is at its peak and to go all out for a record list. One professional ornithologist, with just a hint of scorn, has called it "bird golf." But like other games, bird listing needs no apologies. No one would want to engage in one of these dawn-to-dark endurance tests every week end, but once or twice a year it is great sport, a test of the skills acquired by months and years of bird watching.

WHEN I married a bird artist, I had not realized how continually I was to flock with birds. But now, I said to myself in slight alarm, wings seemed to be closing in all about me. Here was a whole week end approaching, threatening me not only with birds but with bird lovers; for Maunsell Crosby had asked us up to Grasmere, his place in Rhinebeck on the Hudson River, to share in one of his famous birding week ends.

I felt wary about this, as well as delighted. I remembered suddenly how, as an undergraduate, I had laughed to myself at the little groups of birders standing intently beneath the trees of our university campus. Early worms, with binoculars like black eye-stalks and campstools for extra legs—such oddities, I had thought blithely, as I dashed by.

Now—having lived all my life in a university town, scientists in cubbyholes seemed natural enough to me. But scientific birders, ranging freely through the landscape—they were different. Outdoors had always meant a release to me—it was an aesthetic pleasure. I kept that emotion when I went out with Lee; the bird angle had not changed the focus, since it was still an artistic emphasis. But *science* in a holiday— wouldn't that dull its brightness? I didn't know . . .

However, I was certainly going to find out, I told myself, on this bird-haunted week end.

Our host, Maunsell Crosby, was one of the most gifted of field ornithologists, Lee said. His vision was as keen as a hawk's; his hearing even more exceptional, both in its long range and its ability to distinguish between similar sounds. His interest in birds was intense and unvarying. For many years he had kept careful census lists of the birds which appeared at Grasmere, month by month, and he thought nothing of traveling a hundred miles to attend an ornithological meeting.

He kept open house for ornithologists, and every week end in the spring and fall he filled his house with guests who went with him on his all-day field trips. These week ends were famous, both because of his hospitality and because even in the notable gatherings that he collected he was outstanding in his expert and enthusiastic leadership in the field. I was excited about being included in one of these expeditions, but I felt slightly out of place, like a cocker joining a pack of wolf-hounds.

When the day arrived and we sped out from our New York apartment, I forgot my qualms, for it was early May and spring had captured the countryside. Lee was full of anticipation too; he had been in Rhinebeck the winter before, to make sketches for a duck painting, but he had never seen the place in fair weather.

Maunsell, a big man full of life and cordial charm, met us at the station and drove us through country roads bright with new-hatched leaves and drifts of blossoms. A lane led us through an orchard where tilted garlands, as delicate as ivory and frail coral, made my heart sing. I was sure no bird, however sprightly, could move me as those windy petals did.

50

Soon we came to a pleasant old mansion surrounded by thorny locust trees, whose trunks were veiled in pale green. On the steps we met the other guest, Ludlow Griscom, a noted ornithologist from Boston. He was a square man with black and silver hair, strong decided features and equally decided opinions. Lee told me, as we went into the house, that Mr. Griscom was supreme in identifying birds in the field, "all known sub-species at ultimate range."

I felt a little sorry for any birds who tried to evade him; they could not be stern and rockbound enough to stand against him, I was sure. I also felt a little sorry for myself. I had wanted to see an expert bird-identifier in action, to be sure, but two such superhuman ones were overpowering.

Maunsell and Mr. Griscom were evidently intimate friends, and their railleries, humorous and easy on one side and caustically witty on the other, sparkled like fireflies through their tales of trips taken together through Florida, Texas, Panama and Guatemala. But it was easy to see that in spite of the interest Maunsell had in far places, it was Dutchess County which he passionately loved.

After dinner, we had coffee in a yellow drawing room and Mr. Griscom played Bach for us, while our host showed us his daughter's poetry. A little after ten, Maunsell suggested that we might like to get some sleep. "We get up frightfully early, you know, Florence. I hope you won't mind."

"Oh, I won't mind at all." (What statements we do make for courtesy's sake!) "When do we start?"

"Half past two."

I hope my eyes didn't get as round as they felt; my worst fears had skirted half past five. "We get the night birds that way, do you see? We are taking the northern part of Dutchess County and another group covers the south half. We'll meet them tomorrow night and compare our lists."

I walked upstairs with one look at Lee. This was like learning to swim by being thrown into Niagara Falls—*this* as an introduction to a bird walk!

It seemed to me I had only been asleep a minute when a knock on the door awakened us.

"Right!" Lee answered, in a festive voice that made me want to throw my pillow at him. He is as bad as a bird for liking to get up early.

"—middle of a night—all black—" I muttered.

51

"Awake?" boomed Mr. Crosby. "Turn on your light, Jaques." It was evident he had learned to put no trust in cheery voices. Lee got up.

"All set."

"—Meet you downstairs in ten minutes."

I staggered around the room in a weak-kneed manner. "Quarter after two," I grumbled. "What do you wear at a quarter after two?"

When I had collected myself and my apparel, I followed Lee downstairs. In the dining room was Maunsell and a midnight lunch, sandwiches on a tray and thermos bottles of coffee. I woke up a little. This was rather fun. Mr. Griscom appeared and after coffee we gathered up our field glasses.

Out in the black night the car stood waiting. We moved swiftly down the drive, past the pale blurs of the orchard.

"By these woods we might get something," Maunsell said after a time. He stopped the car. A moment of silence in the dark. The woods were bulky against the dark gray sky. "HOO—Hoo—hoo—" far off. That was an owl.

"Barred owl. Our first count." Mr. Griscom made a note.

"Now we'll hurry to the pasture road and get the whip-poor-will."

Whip-poor-will—*Whip*-poor-will—it came faint but very clear through the night air. I thrilled at that curious half-human sound. Two birds now.

I have no recollection of the order of our next discoveries, partly because I had a relapse into sleepiness again and partly because I had never heard of such birds. I only remember the cold and the dark lessening inch by inch, a morning star brilliant in the pallid east, a few chirps, then bird songs rising here and there like stray Roman candles. At last a radiant rosiness and bursts of song like sky rockets all about us.

"Shall we take the marsh before breakfast?" Maunsell asked.

"Early morning is a great time," said Lee. "Let's go."

By a green frog-haunted stream, still veiled in fog, we left the car and climbed a sandbank. It was chilly in the mistiness and only a muffled croaking broke the silence. Mr. Griscom made me jump by clapping his hands sharply together and then to my astonishment Maunsell drew a pistol from his pocket and fired it into the air.

"No rails," he said as the echo died away. "They are sure to cry out at a shot if they're here."

"Do you carry that pistol just to fire it for the rails?" I asked.

52

"Yes, it means one more bird for our list. In this way you have a chance to hear a rail, but it's a rare thing to see one. They run through the dense reeds and no matter how closely the stems grow they seem to slip between."

"Oh, that's it," I said comprehending.

"What do you mean, 'that's it'?" Lee asked.

"I always thought 'thin as a rail' meant a rail from a fence. It's the bird," I murmured.

Lee and I went down along the sand to see what we could discover; the others splashed along a boggy brook. "This is a very *odd* occupation for three grown men," I said dreamily. "Nonsense, but nice enough, if it wasn't so long between breakfasts."

The air was faintly fragrant, the colors all about us were Botticelli's own. Delicate willow boughs, amber green, trailed against the quiet water and a meadowlark sang from a fence post. Walking in the new grass, each sharp green blade sheathed in dew, while mist swirled waist-high, was like ethereal wading, and on the long hills behind the meadows the beginning leaves made an airiness of pale green and gray and silver.

I could hardly refrain from out-singing the meadowlark. But just then Lee decided he hadn't been generous enough with his field glasses and forced them on me.

I hated those field glasses. They were too heavy for me and they jiggled. I could never succeed in locating anything through them. Lee was so anxious for me to see that he grew frantic if I fussed with the lens and missed his bird, and I couldn't use his focus. So my method was to take a quick look at the bird with my own eyes—I could generally see it reasonably well—look blindly through the glasses and say, "Oh, yes!" and then look with my own eyes again.

But I missed many birds by that method. I missed a bittern that morning. I was sorry, for Lee had startled a subway crowd one night by imitating a bittern's guttural pumping for me, and I had a desire to see the creature.

To cover my failure—"What's that big dark bird, Lee?"

"A crow, darling," he said, far, far too patiently. "You ought to know a crow." But just then a loon flying across the pond surprised him. Loons mean northern Minnesota to him, and in his pleasure at the sight of one he forgot my shortcomings.

"And there is another bittern, just by that grass clump." I saw that

53

one. What a grotesque object! Its head pointed vertically upward with the beak high in the air so that the whole bird looked like a crooked stake—no wonder it used to be considered sinister. A bittern is a hermit, Lee told me; its only amusement seems to be its mimicry of pumping and driving stakes, and it contrives to look so much like a post you wonder why it doesn't drive itself down into the marsh with its own imitations.

When it is frightened it often "freezes" with its head stretched erect in this manner. A party of birders following a boardwalk through the Troy meadows passed a bittern within arms length and not one of them noticed it until the last man, spying it, reached down and picked it up by the bill.

But Maunsell was calling us in. We hurried back to the car. "We'll try these hills," he said, "and stop on the other side at an inn for breakfast."

So after a brisk run up a steep meadow, where we found doves, I think, we came to a sunny room with purple lilacs outside the windows, and ordered mammoth breakfasts.

"But you seem to go to a certain spot and find the exact bird you want!" I said to Maunsell. "I thought birds went their own sweet ways, here, there, and everywhere."

"Not at all. Birds are closely tied to their special environment," Mr. Griscom said. "Just as you'll find a banker in a bank and a mechanic in a garage, you'll find a jacksnipe in a boggy field and an oriole in an orchard." He proceeded to tell me about bird distribution in North and South America. I was flattered by his casual use of Latin names when I didn't know half the English ones I've heard, but—

"There's a big bird now," I interrupted excitedly.

"It's a crow," Lee said. "We've counted it." I kicked him under the table.

Strengthened by our repast, we started out again, my spirits rising higher after my hot coffee. We ranged over hill and dale, popping in and out of the car like cuckoos from a clock. Swans on a reedy pond (it surprised me to find that introduced swans had become wild in this country); sandpipers on a sandy curve with cliffs of translucent azure, lilac and heliotrope beyond the blue Hudson; orioles in bright orange flashing across the little roads—we discovered odds and ends everywhere. . . .

But it was really amazing to me to see how many kinds of birds we

54

found. I began to watch the list with a wild pride in every addition. I watched Lee too—I knew how much the day was meaning to him, after our city barriers. When I first knew him, his quiet demeanor had seemed almost indifference; now I knew it was a shield for any degree of intensity.

And Maunsell Crosby's enthusiasm was a joy to see. You would have said that this day was the one chance in his lifetime to find birds from the way he reveled in each new foundling. Mr. Griscom was as keen and his erudition continually astonished me. So did his organization, for in his zest he was marshaling us in companies, dividing us in columns, sending scouts here and there, and otherwise making the most efficient use possible of what force we were.

Later in the morning a small but violent thunderstorm pounced suddenly at us, and we hastened back to the house, where we had luncheon on the porch with the rain making murmuring curtains down the leaf-green tracery around us.

"This is as exciting as golf or tennis," I said. "I had no idea it would be so exhilarating."

"And valuable besides," Maunsell said. "You see, this data which we are collecting may really extend ornithological knowledge. All these details may give us new ideas about bird behavior and distribution, or help in migration problems; perhaps in some manner which we don't yet realize."

"Maunsell has notebooks by the score," Mr. Griscom told us. "Graphs and tabulations and histories. Each day has its temperature and climatic condition written down, as well as what birds it offers. He can tell you all about this particular day of the month, for years back."

"How does our list stand now, Maunsell?" Lee asked.

"Seventy-three species. We aren't up to last year's list," Maunsell said, consulting his notebook. "But it was a good morning, wasn't it?"

"Of course we've seen the less difficult birds this morning; we'll have harder work this afternoon," Mr. Griscom warned. "We'd better concentrate on the warblers first, don't you agree?"

So forth we went to another estate, the Franklin Roosevelt one. Rather *lèse majesté* to hunt warblers here, I thought, but Maunsell had free range on all these places. We walked up a grassy lane, shadowy under boughs. It was hot and steaming even there, after the short rain, and I felt so drowsy that it was hard to see the landscape clearly. Birds were quite obscure.

55

But Maunsell had praised me for coming—he said that most women were silly enough to lose the afternoon's fun by taking a nap. How reprehensible! oh, how comfortable that would be, I thought longingly. But I couldn't disgrace Lee by withdrawing now.

So I trotted faithfully after the fanatics, trying through my stupor to remember the birding etiquette I'd learned that morning, trying to see the warblers the men saw. I never succeeded. Small things bobbed like popcorn among the twigs, but if they ever stopped an instant it was always behind a leaf. If I had found these warblers when my enthusiasm was highest, between breakfast and lunch, I would have been enchanted by their diminutiveness. But now I was too dazed to bother with such trifles.

Trying to locate them with the field glasses made them seem more nervous still. Occasionally I could see that a flitting bird had some yellow feathers. But when I announced this discovery, Lee crushed me by informing me that warblers in general were yellowish. Well then, it was just hopeless.

And they all squeaked. Simple and unattractive little squeaks, practically alike, sounded from far and near, but I could never see what was making them. Maunsell and Mr. Griscom were congratulating each other ecstatically. "We have never had the first great wave of warblers at such an early date, I am sure."

"*What* is a wave of warblers?" I asked Lee.

"Numbers of warblers fly north together. They'll come through one day, then there will be several days without warblers, and then another wave will come by."

"*You* can't tell which squeak is a black-throated blue warbler and which is a chestnut-sided, can you?" I asked apprehensively.

"Lord, no—I can't be bothered with warblers and sparrows," he said cheerfully.

I felt a glow of tenderness. "Can *they* really tell?" I asked confidentially. I apologize for that question—I did not realize at the time what a deadly insult it was.

I should have appreciated the Crosby-and-Griscom tour de force I was seeing. Not many novices have the privilege of witnessing such feats of identification as I saw that hour in the wood. But the men were so big and the birds were so small and I was so hot, I felt, I regret to say, scornful.

If they had a Blackburnian and a Cerulean, why was there a Parula

56

and not a parulean? Prothonotary as a name for a bird an inch long was pure ostentation. And Kentucky, Nashville and Maryland warblers were so unfair they wouldn't even give you a color clue by their names. I felt exasperated at warblers.

The sun shone hotter and hotter; in the ravine we were following no wind stirred. Much later we did get out on an open hillside, but the spaces were wider there, and we had to run more to keep up with our wayward midgets. I took to sinking on the grass as I struggled to focus my binoculars on them. Oh, for a fine *large* feathered friend. And there was one!

"Oh, look!" I cried. "A huge black—"

"It's simply a *crow!*" Lee hissed in anguish at me. I blushed, but it didn't show; I was far too hot.

Now we were boarding the car again. All day we had been darting out of that car like imps out of hell; I did not want to do it *any more*. And I had seen so many birds they had mobbed my mind. I could remember no individual. Even without those incoherent warblers, there were veeries and vireos, nuthatches and sapsuckers, killdeers and redstarts—I couldn't remember which was where or what. Even hawks; I had thought a hawk was a hawk. But no, it had to be a sharp-shin or a red-tail or a Cooper's—Maunsell interrupted my brooding.

"We've time for this one more pasture and the wood," he reassured us, "before we meet the others at Brickyard Swamp."

The pasture was a relentlessly sunny one. All day I had been very docile, obeying orders like a well-trained lamb, but here I became a rebel. Ignoring Mr. Griscom's instructions to scout along a fence, I made an abrupt sortie of my own. Up on the hill I could see streaks of shade.

There in the wood it was suddenly blissfully cooler. A golden sheen fell softly on the fields below me, shadows were lengthening blue wings. Far down the gentle slope the trees stood serenely in the mild air. I sat down and happiness swept me, in spite of myself.

Under the green shelter of a hawthorn that tilted against the hill, crooking its lowest branches to the grass, I lay back, grateful for this chance to relax. I forgot the discomfort just past. My mind was utterly occupied with the spring around me, the restless shimmer of the tiny leaves just touched by the faint wind, the frail tangle of briers that deepened the forest edge, the irregular scrolls of clouds curling across the sky.

57

Before me was an opening in the wood, with grass of luminous green under a starriness of white flowers, and space for the wind to follow. Miniature leaves of velvety rose and shining buds added to the green intricacy about me. So clearly drawn and so young, this beauty—there is never enough of May! . . .

The others came up the hill. They looked as if they needed to lie down on the grass too, in the cool shade. They looked a little cross. With a great effort I sat up and spoke pleasantly.

"The birds are beginning to sound sleepy," I mentioned. "They aren't singing as they did this morning. They just chirp."

"And your laugh," Mr. Griscom observed in a detached way, "has become a titter."

Titter! I sat on the grass in a fury. Of all *mean* words! How horrid, how unfair! Here I had been staggering around all night and all day, as bright as a dandelion, looking on gently instead of scornfully at this ridiculous behavior, and then I was accused of tittering!

I remained silent and aloof on my grass tuft. And later in the car I looked as grim as I could in my exhausted state. Sixteen hours of birding had undone me.

But when we reached Brickyard Swamp and met the other party—all four men and looking extremely hot and tired, I was glad to see, even if they were not tittering—we discovered that they had one hundred and fifteen birds on their list and we had one hundred and twenty-one. So in our triumph I forgot to sulk and dinner was a great success, though we had to miss an enticing dessert and part of a discussion about the difference between personality and individuality, to catch our train back to town.

On the way home I pondered the day's events. "Most of the time," I said dejectedly to Lee, "I couldn't even see those little bits of birds they were discussing."

"Never mind," he told me, "the difference between warblers and no warblers is very slight."

This lofty viewpoint made me shout; I have found warblers enchanting instead of maddening ever since.

I was completely exhausted the next day, but in spite of that I liked the feeling that I had assisted, even in a microscopic way, in adding to ornithological data! And then I found that I was remembering the long-extended hunt from dark to dark, and its spangles of birds, with the greatest joy.

The periods of personal discomfort faded like dew, but the whip-poor-will call in the night, the grotesque bittern of the marsh, the fire-flash of the oriole remained as vivid as when they were happening. Even, I thought, some time in the distant future, when I had recovered from such avalanches of bird information and had had time to look up a few species quietly myself, when I was rested and longing for out-doors—I *might* like to do it again.

(From *Birds Across the Sky*)

JOHN O'REILLY

The Biggest
Bird Watch

To many bird watchers the Christmas Count is the high point of the year. This ornithological field day has been reported by many national publications, including *Time, Life,* and *The New Yorker,* but perhaps the best account to date is this one by John O'Reilly who covered the 1955 count for *Sports Illustrated.*

O'Reilly is perhaps the most satisfying natural history reporter among American newsmen. Whereas the press too often takes the view that unnatural history is more palatable than natural history, O'Reilly has always insisted that the straight unretouched version makes the best reading.

NORTH AMERICAN birds, from chickadees to sand-hill cranes, got their greatest going-over in 56 years during the Christmas-New Year holidays. The country's most ardent bird watchers, 8,000 strong—men and women, boys and girls, experts and neophytes—turned out in scientifically organized groups, setting records for bird watching which would have been considered impossible only a few years ago.

This army of birders, marshaled into more than 575 groups, combed their favorite birding spots in nearly all the states and Canadian provinces. Their aim was to see as many as possible of the continent's several billion land birds and of its legions of sea birds along the coasts. No single birder or group could hope to spot as many as 200 of the 650 or more recorded species. But each group was out to establish a record.

Bird watching has been described as a hobby, a sport and a scientific pursuit. Whatever it is, the birders proved that it is big doings. This was no haphazard, leisurely observation of the feathered fauna of America, but the highly organized 56th Annual Christmas Bird Count under the aegis of the National Audubon Society and in collaboration with the U.S. Fish and Wildlife Service. The rules were strict and the competition keen. Foul weather couldn't hold the watchers back. Task forces were deployed in military style. Predawn blackness found them deep in the woods hooting up owls. Noon saw them gnawing sandwiches while keeping an eye out for just one more species. And in the darkness, long after nightfall, they were still huddled over their lists, checking their totals and gloating over rare finds they had made during the long day.

Top honors for the entire nation went to the group at Cocoa on the east coast of Florida. There 42 watchers, under the leadership of Allan D. Cruickshank, ran up the phenomenal total of 184 species, the greatest number ever attained on a Christmas Bird Count. With this total, Florida nosed out its chief competitor, San Diego, Calif. Despite an all-out effort the California birders couldn't do better than 168 species, although they had won the previous year with 175.

Cruickshank, determined that Florida would shade California, planned his campaign long in advance. The rules state that the count must be taken within one 24-hour period from December 24 to January 2 in an area not greater than a circle with a 15-mile diameter.

Several years ago he had carefully chosen the best bird-watching spots in his area. Then calipers and maps were put to use to make sure that the birdiest locations fell within the required circle. Dr. Cruickshank's region is rich in birds, and he selected the cream of it. For weeks before December 27, the day of the count, Cruickshank and a corps of trained local observers studied the chosen area thoroughly, noting the movements of such rare species as avocets, white pelicans and scissor-tailed flycatchers so they would be able to spot them on the big day. . . .

Cruickshank had announced that he was out to win. To increase his chances he imported some of the country's best bird watchers. . . . Roger Tory Peterson flew down from his home at Old Lyme, Conn. Other imports included Miss Farida Wiley, bird-trip leader of the American Museum of Natural History; Dr. Joseph Howell, professor of

61

zoology at the University of Tennessee; and Henry Bennett, supervisor of the Corkscrew Sanctuary. These, plus a contingent of sharp-eyed local birders, gave Cruickshank a phalanx which he divided into task groups.

Cruickshank had the manpower, and he drove his groups unmercifully. Each party was assigned to a specific area and given a typewritten route annotated with locations of roosts, favorite feeding grounds and other pertinent data. At noon they rendezvoused on a lonely back road, where they gobbled their lunches while watching unsuccessfully for the seldom-seen western kingbird and the scissor-tailed flycatcher. Then they plunged back into woods and marshes with orders to get certain species missed during the morning. . . .

All told, the Cocoa group spent over 500 man hours in the field, covered more than 1,000 miles by foot and car, saw almost 78,000 birds in achieving the record count. . . .

Their record was made despite murky weather. Before dawn their flashlights could barely pick out canvasbacks and pintails through a dense fog. They missed for the most part the spontaneous burst of sound and color as thousands of herons, ibis, and pelicans poured out of their rookeries at the first peep of the sun.

But when the fog lifted in midmorning they were gratified at the vast numbers and varieties of ducks spreading out over the tidal lagoons as far as their 60-power Balscopes could reach. Further inland, Henry Bennett stumbled upon 77 sand-hill cranes in one field, and in the pinewoods Peterson astonished even the other veterans by his remarkable ability to identify little-known birds by their calls alone. . . .

In late afternoon a sudden cold drizzle blew in from the Atlantic, but it turned out to be a blessing. Two parties parked their cars facing the surf and trained their binoculars through rainswept windshields at a fleet of 26 fishing boats making for the harbor under a canopy of screaming sea birds. They spotted over 100 gannets, a duck hawk and, perhaps the best catch of the day, three parasitic jaegers, swift hunters of the deep, offshore seas which snatch their food from the other birds. . . .

All day long Cruickshank had been barking orders like a general dispatching crucial missions—"Get the old squaw"—"Honk up some fat geese"—"Tie down the avocets." And when his crew assembled at his home at Rockledge that night, his eyes were still bright with the eagerness of the chase. Party leaders phoned in their tallies and the

63

totals mounted. By 10 p.m. it became evident that their group had broken all Christmas Count records, and Cruickshank's grin was wider than ever.

Tougher conditions were encountered by 53 members of the Delaware Valley Ornithological Club who invaded the historic birding grounds at Cape May, N. J. Here Dr. Ernest A. Choate, a Philadelphia high school principal, was the general in command of the bird-watching troops. Twenty-five birders arrived at Dr. Choate's summer house at Cape May Point wearing boots and binoculars and swathed in many layers of clothing. The others stayed at motels.

Even though a mockingbird sat in a bush in front of the house when the first watchers arrived, Dr. Choate and his crew were dubious over their prospects because a prolonged cold spell had frozen the marshes and fresh water ponds. Sitting around an iron stove, they received their assignments, and party leaders went into separate huddles with their aides. Their ages ranged from 12 to 73, but they all had the same enthusiasm.

It was early when they crawled into bedding rolls spread on the floor. They had to be afield at dawn. They had a long tradition to uphold, for Cape May's first Christmas Bird Count was made in 1903.

The first man abroad was Edward Reimann, a chiropodist, who had the assignment to hoot up some owls. He began by hooting up three great horned owls and by the end of the day the list included the barn, screech and short-eared owls. Some owls are not too hard to hoot up, answering even a poor imitation of their call. Another way to interest an owl is to squeak like a mouse. . . .

By 6 a.m. the task forces were deployed in the woods, along the beaches and out on windswept rock jetties. Some checked feeding stations in towns while others cruised the fields for meadowlarks. When they reached the wide marshes of the Delaware they found they could walk out on the ice, a slippery trip which netted a killdeer, an American egret, and various hawks.

One party was easing into some woods to investigate an odd sound when a woman emerged from a nearby house and advanced with the obvious intent of chasing them off her property.

"We're looking for birds. We're making the Christmas Bird Count," Philip A. Livingston, a publisher, hurried to explain.

"Oh, I thought you were hunters," the woman said. "You can look

64

all you want to." Then she added helpfully, "Say, I've got a Peterson's guide up at the house."

This brought smiles, and they assured her they were well equipped with bird guides. There was a time when birders were looked upon with greater suspicion. During World War II many a bird watcher was hauled in and given a hard time by the police.

The high point of the day at Cape May came when Dr. Dale R. Coman, professor of experimental pathology at the University of Pennsylvania, spotted a European woodcock, a rare visitor to these shores. Dr. Coman insisted that credit for adding this rarity to the list should go to his seven-month-old setter pup, Huckleberry, which had flushed the bird.

That night all the watchers assembled in a restaurant for dinner while the party leaders gave their reports to Dr. Choate. The results showed 144 species, seven less than last year's record for the Cape May Count. This disappointment was offset by the European woodcock and the fact that they had also seen two barn swallows, a white-crowned sparrow and a European black-headed gull, all good birds for the region. Bird watchers are never crestfallen for long.

Across the country from Cape May, 60 bird watchers conducted the Portland, Ore. count on January 2nd in a heavy rain, showing up in all sorts of foul-weather gear, including World War II gas capes. Despite the heavy going, they ran up a total of 93 species and 67,123 individuals, both records for the area. . . .

Farther down the West Coast, Dr. James E. Crouch, professor of zoology at San Diego State College, led the watchers on the San Diego count. Well aware of Dr. Cruickshank's vow to beat the San Diego crowd, they made a valiant effort to repeat or better their performance of last year when they rang up the highest count in the nation, 175 species. But the best Dr. Crouch and his birders could do this year was 168 species and 38,038 individuals. . . .

All this business of counting birds at Christmas time was started in 1900 by the late Dr. Frank M. Chapman, a great and kind man who was the father of popular American bird watching. Twenty-seven persons took part in the first Christmas Count. Their numbers increased steadily, but in recent years the sport took on a real spurt. There were almost twice as many participants this year as five years ago. . . .

The bird-watching bug is spreading faster than ever, striking people of almost all ages and occupations. There is no question that it is deeply infectious. For example, Bill Shelton, SI's Florida correspondent who covered the Cocoa count as his first bird-watching assignment, attached the following note to his dispatch:

"This was a fascinating assignment. Incidentally, I spotted the first white pelicans (with 9-foot wingspreads) seen on the count. Think I'll join these birders myself."

(From Sports Illustrated)

RICHARD M. SAUNDERS

Winter Birds

Some bird watchers just watch birds. Others, gratifying a suppressed desire to collect something, collect the names of birds, ticking them off as they see them on the little white check lists now so popular. The "listers" are legion; and in Boston, where—as Will Cuppy once remarked—"the ability to tell one sparrow from another is hereditary," a grapevine system has been developed which has no equal anywhere else in the ornithological world. By lifting the receiver and dialing KEnmore 6-4050, one may hear a voice which informs:

"This is the voice of Audubon. A cardinal and two bald eagles are in Marshfield Hills. A Bullock's oriole is present at a bird feeder in Cohasset," etc.

In Toronto where there are fully as many bird watchers per square mile as there are in Boston, the Field Naturalist's Club keeps its members posted by means of a newsletter. Its editor, Dr. Richard Saunders, an amateur ornithologist who never misses a Sunday afield, has conscientiously kept a journal for years. To those of us who live south of the border the entries of greatest interest are the days in winter when powdery snow lies deep and erratic boreal finches are seen.

THIS LAST Sunday a party consisting of Dr. and Mrs. L. E. Jaquith, T. R. Murray and I started out in a blinding snowstorm. You would have said it was the last day in the world to go looking for birds, even winter birds. But wait! Just as we turned from Route 7 into the road to Maple and King things began to happen. The snow was swirl-

ing out of the west, whipping across the road, and forcing up collars
and scarves, but Murray had spied a large flock of buntings in the
field, feeding on the seeds of weeds that still topped the snow. Five
hundred of them spiralled into the air as we entered the field, whirling
about like a great gust of vaster snowflakes in the midst of the storm,
settling down but a short distance off to go on with their busy feeding.
Again and again we came upon such flocks, large and small, as we
went along. One farmer's yard had a hundred or more of them right
up by the house. We stood within ten feet of this flock and watched as
long as we wished, their rich tawny marking emitting a pleasant glow
through the falling snow. Always as a flock swept into the air it filled
the crannies of the storm with merry sprightly music, gentle and
canarylike in quality. Why should they fear the snow? Even in summer
they live close to it. They are born near it, live with it, and die in it. So
they sing in it.

Four miles west of Maple we came to our destination, a large bush
of evergreens and mixed hardwoods. The wind had much abated, and
only a few large flakes circled lazily down through the quieter air. In
the woods all was still. The powdery snow lay in a heavy blanket,
almost hiding the hemlocks in a thick down, and etching the lines of
the deciduous trees in sharp relief. We had not penetrated far into this
fairyland before a large bird burst so unexpectedly from the midst of
a snowy hemlock that it got away before we could identify it in the
midst of the falling snow which it had dislodged. In all probability it
was a horned owl, but all we could record was an explosion. It was as
if the owl had pronounced an "open sesame" for now the woods came
to life.

A cottontail scurried from a bush in bounding escape, the story of
its frightened hurry being written in the snow. The sound of heavy
tapping spurred us to an eager hunt, for these woods are filled with the
fresh work of pileated and three-toed woodpeckers. . . . A band of
chickadees whistled from the depths of some pines and hemlocks and,
as we have learned always to follow the chickadees in winter, we
scanned them all carefully until Murray found a busy little bird searching a pine limb, making no noise at all, but travelling along with the
chickadees, a red-breasted nuthatch. As we walked along, the sharp
call of the pine grosbeaks sounded overhead, and as we came to the
edge of the woods, and fields stretched away, a large flock of redpolls
swept by, following the boundary of woods and fields, and settling not

68

far away in an alder bog. Two ruffed grouse burst from a cedar and sailed across the fields to another line of evergreens. In the evergreens too, were, in all likelihood, the birds we had come to see. Sure enough, in a deep little ravine we first heard the calls we wanted so much to hear—the soft chatter of the crossbills.

As we gazed high up, a flock of thirty or so eddied into the tree tops and settled first in a large oak, then in a hemlock. We were delighted, especially when a few of this flock proved to be red crossbills which, though they are called "common," are really very rare in this region. Their presence had been suspected before we saw them, for the soft *cha-cha, cha-cha* of the white-winged crossbills had been punctuated by several high-pitched clearer, *kip-kip* notes which are characteristic of the red crossbill. This sight was gratifying but rather disappointing as they were too far off to see the bills and the feeding operations. But now as we wandered about we heard the crossbills, almost all white-winged, everywhere. The woods had become filled with them. Flock after flock was seen. And then all at once we entered a glade where hemlocks the size of large Christmas trees stood in ranks around the edge, mantled in snow. Abruptly we came to a halt, warned by the soft chatter ahead. Not twenty feet away scores of the lovely birds were feeding on the seeds of these Christmas evergreens. They did not fly, but, unafraid and trusting, they let us stand and watch. They were intensely busy, fluttering from one cone to another, chattering and working all the time, but not fighting, as there were cones for all. Like little parrots they hung on with one foot or the other, or even by their bills, as they moved about, head up, or head down, no matter to them. Their queer crossed bills, very white on most of the birds, were inserted quickly into cones, the cones spread open with a motion like opening a scissors, and the seeds, then exposed, picked up with the tongue. Most of the birds, to our surprise, were males, brilliantly plumaged. Deep rose and black and white marked the white-wing, and brick or orange-red all over, the red crossbill. The females and immatures showed softer tones of green and grey and yellow. All, as they busied themselves with feeding, dislodged the soft mantle of snow from the trees, so that constantly a powdery veil hung before the scene, softening all colours to the delicacy of pastel.

(From *Flashing Wings*)

MAURICE BROOKS

Let the Dummy Do the Work

His friends often think of Professor Brooks as "Mr. Appalachia." No one knows these ancient hills more intimately than he, for his home in West Virginia lies in that puzzling halfway zone where north meets south and influences mingle and contradict.

It is as difficult to label Maurice Brooks accurately as it is to classify some of the plant and animal associations of the central Appalachians. Bird men know him as a leading ornithologist; herpetologists would claim him for their ranks, while botanists admire his scholarly work with ferns and other groups. He is really an ecologist, one who interprets nature as a whole through her many parts.

W<small>E LEARNED</small> that almost any methods would attract some birds, but that some *finesse* was required in bringing others close to our home. Too frequently food was provided, but that other essential, cover, was forgotten. In the bushes and trees at the edge of the yard were to be found birds that never seemed to reach our feeding places, and naturally these unattainables seemed to us the most desirable of all. Finally, a shelf was mounted on a sharpened stake and placed near the bushes about fifty feet from one of the kitchen windows. An abundant food supply was provided, and we presently found that six or eight species of birds which had refused to come to our window shelves were here feeding regularly.

70

After about two weeks this shelf was moved ten feet nearer to the house; the birds were a bit confused for a time, but presently grew accustomed to the new location. Another move brought the shelf still nearer, until, by successive steps, we had tolled to a point just outside the window all the birds which had been feeding at a distance.

This is the point, perhaps, at which most bird feeding stops. One day, however, it occurred to us that a dummy hand might be constructed in such a lifelike manner as to fool the birds. An old leather glove was selected, stuffed full of paper and rags until it was forced into the semblance of a cupped human hand, and nailed to a stick about fifteen inches in length. An old coat sleeve was pulled over the stick and the whole device was fastened to the window sill in such a manner that it extended almost to an established feeding shelf on the sharpened stake. In this cupped hand black walnuts were placed, and the banquet invitation was left to the pleasure of the birds.

At first they were quite shy, coming hurriedly to the regular feeding shelf, but frequently flying away nervously without taking any food. Just here we began cutting down on the supply of food placed in the regular container, until within a day or two only the dummy hand offered the food which the birds wanted so badly. It was not until the third day that we saw a bird, a Tufted Titmouse, tentatively light on the glove. Evidently he did not like the feel of the leather under his claws, for he flew away quickly. Presently he, or another of the same species, returned, and after a few ventures of this nature, a kernel of the walnut was seized and carried away. This seemed to break the ice, for before the day had closed a number of Titmice were coming regularly, a few Chickadees had made the venture, and just at dusk a Carolina Wren actually fed from the glove for several minutes. Our black walnut kernels were disappearing almost as fast as we could put them out.

During succeeding days we found that other species were gaining confidence, and we made it a point to spend much time near the window nearest to the dummy hand. Here again I must anticipate in order to keep the record straight. We learned that our presence at the windows was not necessarily alarming to the birds so long as we made no abrupt motions. Neither were normal sounds objectionable, and we came to consider these movements and sounds an integral part of the birds' training. Another point we found to be very important. The birds became used to a closed window, and when we first opened it they were

71

so alarmed and nervous that they refused for some time to come to the stuffed glove. Noting this, we made it a rule to raise the window to varying heights whenever the weather permitted, and in this way they became used to its different appearances. I am convinced that without this training they would not have come to our hands at all readily.

After a few days of such preparation, our next step seemed obvious. Selecting a winter day when the temperature was not severe, we took the dummy glove and its stick down, pulled a similar glove onto one of our own hands, cupped up the fingers to hold black walnut kernels, and placed an elbow on the sill, the hand extending the invitation and the feast. I shall never forget with what excitement I took my turn at the new game. Hardly had I gotten settled before a Titmouse dropped quickly onto my hand, seized a piece of walnut, and was gone, only to make way for another visitor of his own species. Within fifteen minutes I was reasonably certain that at least six Titmice and four Chickadees were coming regularly, and when I withdrew my hand to replenish the walnut supply they seemed to be waiting impatiently for its reappearance.

During this first experience I had my share of "beginner's luck." Only a few minutes after I had extended my hand, a Cardinal flew to it and, without any apparent nervousness, took a kernel. This seemed almost too good to be true, and it was! Since that time not a single Cardinal has ever voluntarily come to my hand to take food. Some of my friends have had better luck, but it was denied to any member of my family.

For some days following I am afraid that work suffered around our home. Turns were taken at the favored position by the window, and we found our visitors increasing steadily in numbers and variety. The White-breasted Nuthatches were next to develop confidence, and, once they had learned to come at all, they did what the Titmice and Chickadees would not—stayed on the hand for some seconds or even minutes as they inspected all the walnut kernels present. Their "instinct" for the biggest kernel was almost infallible. Occasionally also a Carolina Wren would spend some time on the hand, particularly if the walnuts were left in the shells where the bird had to work to extract them. Downy Woodpeckers found the food acceptable on our terms after a while, and we soon learned to facilitate their approach, as well as that of the Nuthatches, by placing dead branches near enough our hands so that the birds could reach the food without leaving the familiar and reassuring wood and bark on which they preferred to alight. Juncos and Tree Sparrows made tentative calls, but we never felt that we had completely won their confidence.

A few weeks of such experience as is detailed above convinced us that the dummy idea had further possibilities. It seemed a natural step to use a dummy man in place of a mere dummy hand, so we set about securing some fairly convincing human replica. At first we tried local clothing stores, thinking that they might have stored away some place one of those hideous wax men, heavily mustached, which used to adorn show windows. We finally located one, but the owner felt that it would require fifteen dollars to salve his conscience in making the separation, so we decided that it would be cheaper to construct our own model. From Dr. Robert T. Morris, my father had got the idea of growing gourds for possible bird homes, and although we had not found the birds rushing to build in our gourds, we did finally find an ornithological use for these vegetables.

Selecting one of about human head size, we pulled over it an old white stocking. This was the basis for our dummy's face. The curved handle of the gourd made an excellent Roman nose, and pieces of coal were inserted to represent eyes. A mouth and chin were added, and some frayed-out burlap sacking made a convincing suit of hair. A cross-piece nailed to the top of a sharpened stake furnished the framework of the body and over this we draped an old black coat. The head was attached, collar and tie added to give a touch of style, and an old black hat placed over the burlap hair. As a final touch, a corncob pipe was placed in the dummy's mouth, the bowl hollowed out to hold walnut kernels. Our Frankenstein was now ready to go to work.

Ten or twelve feet from our established window feeding shelf the dummy was set up, the sharpened stake facilitating the operation. As was to be expected, the birds were much alarmed, and for several hours we did not see a visitor to our shelf. Finally a few individuals made the venture, and within a few days we found them coming about as freely as before. The dummy was now moved nearer, with another nervous period resulting, but it was not long until he stood a scant three feet from the shelf. Soon there came one of those evenings when birds feed desperately, the beginning of a snowstorm, with the first big flakes drifting down. Apparently forgetting the strange visitor, dozens of birds, Juncos, Tree Sparrows, Titmice, Chickadees, Cardinals, and the rest, flew to the shelves and the ground below, and from that time on they seemed to come without hesitation.

Presently we filled up the bowl of the corncob pipe, crushed down the crown of the dummy's hat until it would hold walnuts, and began to cut down on the feed placed on the shelf. Quickly enough most of the birds learned to visit the hat or the pipe.

As before, our next step seemed clear. One day, when the weather was not too severe, the dummy was taken down, placed out of sight, and the familiar hat and pipe assumed by a human being who stood where the scarecrow had been. We never quite knew whether or not it was complimentary to us, but most of the birds seemed to detect little difference in the situation! Without hesitation they came to hat, pipe, and hand, relieving us of walnuts almost as fast as they could be supplied. Slow movements did not frighten them, and we soon got in the habit of talking to them ("baby talk," and some of it pretty silly, I am afraid).

It happens that my father was somewhat on the spare side, while I am more given to enbonpoint, so we decided that both of us should have dummies, each after his own likeness. With two such robots available, we found that we could place them in different situations, and that the birds soon came to associate them with food. After a time they made the association with human beings who stood still for a few moments, and presently we found that some of them were following us about the place, begging for food, and taking it whenever and wherever offered. At last we felt that we had pretty well won their confidence.

Only the Chickadees, Titmice, and Nuthatches came to us freely; it took a long wait for a Downy Woodpecker or a Carolina Wren. Once, greatly to my father's surprise, a Red-bellied Woodpecker alighted on his hat as he stood quite still. Such ground-feeding species as Juncos and Tree Sparrows were never at home on our hands or hats, although they did make infrequent visits. Cardinals fed regularly on the dummies, but no amount of patience would bring them to us when we substituted. From this we derived a grain of comfort, for it looked as though at least these birds could discriminate between the animate and inanimate bodies!

(From *Bird Lore*)

74

BRUCE CAMPBELL

(with acknowledgment to the Master Potter)

Birdsmanship

The British humorist Stephen Potter is the chief protagonist of an art at which most civilized Britons seem peculiarly adept—"intimidation by conversation." Potter's first book, *Gamesmanship,* is subtitled *The Art of Winning Games without Actually Cheating.* His second work, *Lifemanship,* lays down the various methods by which the full-blown ignoramus can take the field successfully against highly placed experts in travel, art, literature, typography, and military affairs. It was inevitable that "Birdsmanship" should be developed. Although Potter himself is a good birdsman, and has written on this theme in *One-upmanship,* I have decided to present Bruce Campbell's version.

I know one practitioner who rapidly rose to the vice-presidency of his local natural history society by employing this subtle form of bluff. But you cannot deceive the real pundits for long. I remember, on one of my many trips to England, being accused of this borderline practice. James Fisher and I were driving to Scotland when we saw, perched against the sky, a hawk. Jamming on the brakes, we brought binoculars to bear on the silhouette. Now, in America, we usually say *"Buteo," "Falcon,"* or *"Accipiter,"* narrowing the bird down to its group, and then we pronounce it a red-tail, red-shoulder, or what-not. In this instance, I quickly announced, "It's a *buteo.*" Fisher replied, "Good bit of birdsmanship." Shamefacedly I recalled that in England they have only one *buteo,* the common buzzard (*Buteo buteo*). I should have simply called it a buzzard in the first place.

A$_N$ INTEREST in birds is to-day almost *de rigueur* in the more cultured parts of these islands, and the success of S. Potter's courses in Lifemanship and Gamesmanship have led me to try to put together for the benefit of my fellow bird-watchers (hereafter: birdsmen) some hints which they may find of use when attempting to establish their dominance in the ornithological pecking order, in the field, in the meeting-room and (where we shall begin) in the hurlyburly of a social gathering.

1. THE BIRDSMAN IN SOCIETY

One of three questions is inevitably asked of the birdsman following the stock introduction by his hostess: "Oh, Mabel, I do want you to meet Mr. Er; he's a great authority on birds."

(a) "Oh, how interesting, do tell me, is this a good place for birds?"

Provided the questioner is not outstandingly pretty, and it is not desired to prolong the conversation for other reasons, the correct answer here is a flat "No place is bad for birds, you know." Unless Mabel is a real trier, there will be no come-back to this and an escape can quickly be made.

(b) "Oh, how interesting, do tell me, do you know Peter Scott?" Answer: "Well, I saw him when I was at the New Grounds the other day." This is what C. E. Montague called paying the truth the homage of equivocation, since it does not stress the fact that you were one of a coach party from your local natural history society and that all you saw of the Director was the top of his head as he talked to two admirals and a bishop at the far end of the Rushy Pen.

From this it should be easy to lead on to an account of your own observations on wildfowl, which should play out time successfully.

(c) "Oh, how interesting, do let me tell you about my robin!" This is superficially the easiest of the three to meet, since it initially requires from you only a listening rôle, but as the inevitable anecdote (the bird is sometimes a blackbird, occasionally a chaffinch, and it always does one of three things: taps on the window, builds two nests on top of each other, or seems *really* to recognize her) winds to its end, you realize that some fitting comment is needed.

76

By far the best is: "Most interesting: of course, there's something just like it in the Dutch literature." The beauty of this is that your questioner probably does not know the specialised meaning of "literature," and will credit you with uncanny omniscience; in any case the fact that many Dutch papers have English summaries or are abstracted in the *Ibis* will almost certainly be unknown to her.

2. THE BIRDSMAN IN THE FIELD

But birdsmanship is not all social cut and thrust; sooner or later the birdsman must come into the open and show his mettle, probably at a field outing of his local society. Here the preliminary build-up is of great importance, so we will consider first

(a) *Equipment:* It is essential that the successful birdsman should be the *worst-dressed* man in the party. The remains of (preferably) two ancient plus-four suits form an admirable base, on which should be superimposed as many bits of leather as possible. The more unusual their location, e.g. the small of the back, the seat of the plus-fours, the more deadly their effect, and the whole should be topped by a tweed cap on which birds have paid numerous tributes (a couple of nights in a chicken-house should do the trick). Just because most bird-watchers now wear wellingtons, the birdsman should sport an enormous pair of boots liberally larded with a revolting preservative and brought to notice if necessary by some such comment: "Go anywhere in these y'know; wellingtons are no good in brambles." . . .

Now we come to the vital question of optical aids, and the birdsman may have to show considerable skill if he is to take a trick here. Three usual situations present themselves.

(1) You have an old and battered pair and your chief potential rival has a large, new pair of binoculars. Attack is the best defence in this situation, with the opening line: "Nice little toy you've got there; but can you *see* with them?" Then, for you have picked the moment carefully, you flick your ancient pair to your eyes and say: "Gosh, that juvenile foxed me for a second; I thought it was a female. Oh, sorry, didn't you get on to them in time?" Your rival, who is still unlimbering his pair, is thus caught at a disadvantage and not only feels that he is guilty of ostentation in the eyes of the rest of the party, but that he has probably wasted £40.

Your advantage can be rammed home later in the day if he lags behind at any point, by suggesting that the weight of the glasses is holding him back.

(2) Reversed position to (1): You have the new pair and your rival has an old pair. This needs greater aplomb to carry off, and the recommended line is to wave them about merrily, saying, "Well, there's my wife's winter coat, *and* our summer holiday, but I simply had to have them—one owes it to the birds, if you see what I mean." Carry on in this vein, prattling ingenuously about their illumination, and periodically offer to lend them to your rival just as he has focused on some object of interest.

(3) You both have large pairs. There is nothing for it now but to go into a technical huddle, making much play with exit pupil diameters, and await your chance to gain advantage in another opening altogether.

The same general rules guide the birdsman in dealing with telescopes. If he doesn't use one, he should say loftily, "After all, they're not much good for passerines," thus implying that he has only come on this particular wader-watching expedition as light recreation, and then, as soon as his rival has got ensconced with his telescope, stage a diversion some way off to look at a meadow-pipit. . . .

(b) *Identification:* The first task of the birdsman in the field is to show his superior skill in bird recognition, and while his opportunities will to some extent depend on the co-operation of the birds themselves, it is possible to engineer certain favourable situations in advance.

The rival should be trapped early on into offering to show the party a particular species, e.g. a Curlew-Sandpiper. Then, when his attention is held elsewhere, remark casually but briskly: "There's your Curlew—with that pack of Dunlin. Oh, sorry, I'm afraid they're out of sight now." This is a development of the Binocular Play (1) already described, but note the use of "your" to convey that you have had to find his bird for him. If by any chance he doesn't know the birdsmannish omission of the "Sandpiper," he will be even further outplayed; in fact this species is the ideal birdsman's bird.

In the case of a not readily identifiable bird that stays put, the birdsman must combine patience and a sense of timing to an unusual degree, for, after a prolonged and silent inspection, he *must* be the first to ask, "Well, what do you think?" which gives him the chance of trapping an unwary diagnosis from his rival. Should this agree with

78

his own private opinion, he jumps in with: "Of course, but the super-ciliary stripe (or absence of superciliary stripe) was a bit unexpected, wasn't it?"

If he disagrees, then he must use an enigmatic smile, directed to the most receptive member of the party, and make some more entries in his field note-book. This stalling enables him to come out on top whether his rival's identification is confirmed by others, in which case he must convey that he knew all the time but was just giving the rest a chance; or whether it isn't, which puts him at an obvious advantage, clinched by such moral remarks as "I never think it's safe to diagnose at this time of year unless one can see the wing-pattern." The phrase *At this time of year* should be noted, as it indicates easy familiarity with all phases of the bird's plumage.

(c) *Tally-hunting:* The principles underlying previous advice also rule in this important aspect of field birdsmanship: find out your potential rival's line, and play the opposite for all you're worth.

Thus, if he is an acknowledged tally-hunter, you must use the scientific gambit, "After all, it's only the common birds that really count, isn't it?" and continually hold up the party by calling their attention to Robins or Hedge-Sparrows sitting in huddled attitudes on the vegetation. If after five minutes observation the Robin gives a perfunctory peck at its plumage, you murmur "Ah, an intention movement!" make profuse notes, and add, to the air in general, "I must write to Tinbergen about this." A slight hesitation before the Tinbergen should make it clear that among your real associates you would say "Nikko."

On the other hand, if your rival is a serious ornithologist you follow the line already suggested in Binocular Play (2), cry "I'm frankly pot-hunting today; leave the sparrows alone for once, old chap and come and see some real birds! Tally-ho! Yoicks!" By incessant remarks you should manage to scare away any of the commoner species at which he may wish to look, and if you can keep up your flow, and have the luck to see one or two scarce birds, you should manage to convince the party that your rival is an introverted spoil-sport living in an ivory tower.

(d) *Field Investigations:* The birdsman should not let himself in for any real field studies until he has worked his passage in Identifications and Tally-hunting. By then he should know what he is up to, and can take part in, for example, a winter census of titmice in rather

79

rough woodland, with good prospects of enhancing his reputation in return for the minimum expenditure of energy. Indeed, his goal should be never to take his hands out of his pockets either to use his glasses (strung apparently purposefully round his neck) or to make notes. This will be more easily achieved if the observers on either side of him are reasonably painstaking, by playing on their anxieties with such leads as "You got that Blue Tit, I hope? It was definitely off my line;" or "Longtails coming over: 1, 2, 3, 4—oh, awfully sorry, I'm poaching: they're yours now." Difficult country can be avoided by a deft change of direction. "Sorry, I'm off my line; that big bramblebush is yours now, I think. Nearly always a Willow-Tit in it." At the end of the drive, the birdsman saunters up with a rueful smile, "You people have all the luck; I only got one Great Tit. By the way, you did get that Marsh-Tit I heard calling just at the end, didn't you?" It is also a good plan to insinuate, by well-timed aposiopeses, that everyone else is going too fast and probably missing birds.

3. THE BIRDSMAN AT MEETINGS

The greatest test of the birdsman comes when he takes part in an ornithological discussion. Silence and a billowing pipe between them make a useful build-up and literal smoke-screen, out of which, when the speaker makes any assertion not backed by a mass of evidence, should be jerked in a tone indicating apparent sympathy overridden by devotion to truth (admittedly not very easy) and with equal emphasis on each monosyllable: "do we know that?"

This line . . . is guaranteed to throw all but the toughest out of their stride at the first application, and may even bring their contribution to an early and humiliating end.

In the event of a convincing reply, however, the birdsman must make a quick decision. If he feels that his opponent really knows his subject, he can still sign off without losing face by saying: "Exactly, thanks very much, but I wasn't quite sure if everyone (inclusive-exclusive wave of the pipe-stem round the gathering) here knew of Blobsch's work on substratal stimuli." But if he decides a counter-bluff is being attempted, then he should simply nod and try the line again at the next opportunity. If a third use of the gambit is successfully met, there is nothing for it but to have trouble with the pipe until interest is focused elsewhere.

80

Should the birdsman ever be trapped for prestige reasons into speaking himself, he must—short of actually mastering his subject—rely on two things: first, immediate acknowledgement of his indebtedness to the work of his most likely critics; and secondly, a rigid refusal to come to any conclusions whatever. The work should always be in progress, as indicated by such a parry and riposte to a questioner: "That's just what I'd like to know; perhaps by this time next year, if all goes well, we'll have some more data to help us."

In this way the adept birdsman may succeed in dining out for two or three years as the guest of ornithological societies up and down the country before equipping himself with a new, and perpetually unfinished, problem.

(From *Bird Notes*)

III *Migration*

MIGRATION, perhaps more than any of the other mysteries of life, has stirred the imagination of men. Joseph Hickey once estimated the number of published items about migrating birds in the United States at not less than 750,000. Now, with the passing of fifteen more years, he would probably revise this figure upward to 1,000,000; for since the war a great upsurge of research and inquiry has been directed at this facet of ornithology, both here and in Europe. We are coming closer to an understanding of the mechanics of bird navigation but are still far from its ultimate secret.

It is their incredible journeys that make these "all-of-a-sudden" creatures so impressive. The five-inch warbler singing amongst the new leaves of the big oak may have just arrived from Venezuela or Brazil, without the benefit of complicated instrument panels which make this same flight possible for Pan American skyships. It will probably travel another thousand miles before it puts down at its own private airport somewhere in Canada.

The appreciation of warblers, as Louis Halle points out, is a slow acquisition, since most of the species—those en route to the north woods—are to be seen only for a few days each year, and the rarer ones, such as the mourning or the Connecticut, may be seen in some localities only at intervals of several years. Jaques, the bird artist, shrugs them off with the quip that "the difference between warblers and no warblers is very slight," but most migration watchers take their *Parulidae* more seriously. The warblers, at least the males, are well-marked in the spring but even a musical ear has its problems separating the *chees, churrs, sees, sirs, tews, tweets,* and *zips* of their various songs. The *witchity, witchity, witchity* of the yellowthroat and the *teacher, teacher* of the ovenbird are distinctive enough, but the songs of the others, learned one spring, must be learned again the next, and still again the next, until they become fixed.

The rush of warblers is the high tide of migration, but other weeks also have their drama; the ducks which follow the breakup of the ice,

85

the shorebirds in late May, the hawks on the October ridges. There is scarcely a month when some migration is not taking place; the last northbound shorebirds in mid-June almost meet the first sandpipers returning late the same month.

Bird migration as we know it—a north-and-south-movement—is mainly a phenomenon of the northern hemisphere. In fact, only about 15% of the world's birds indulge in this kind of travel, although in southern lands many species make local seasonal journeys, from high country to low or from wet country to dry. In eastern and middle North America, because of the climatic gulf between hot summers and cold winters, migration is more dramatic than it is in the far West where birds come and go without fanfare over a longer period of weeks. In the Pacific states there is none of the bombshell effect of a good migration wave in New England or on the shores of the Great Lakes; birds drift seasonally from the mountains into the valleys and back again. Spring, therefore, does not mean as much to a bird watcher who lives near Portland, Oregon, as it does to one who has been snowed in all winter near Portland, Maine.

If naturalists had their way, they would not begin the calendar year in January when the world is asleep. They would follow the ancient Jews, Egyptians, and Greeks, all of whom started their year in March. March is the month when life begins—when sap flows, buds swell, and birds return. It is the month when the bird watcher, who perhaps has not taken his binoculars from their case since the Christmas Count, goes out to see if the redwings are back in the cattail swamp or if the meadow-larks and killdeers are on the pasture-lands. Actually, the fall—September and October—with its wind-drifted strays and lost juveniles, is a better season for rarities; but for every bird watcher abroad in autumn there are perhaps five in the spring. The annual re-awakening and the return of the birds must be examined, for these are signs of eternity.

DONALD CULROSS PEATTIE

Return of the Birds

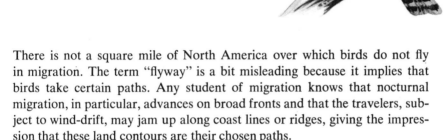

There is not a square mile of North America over which birds do not fly in migration. The term "flyway" is a bit misleading because it implies that birds take certain paths. Any student of migration knows that nocturnal migration, in particular, advances on broad fronts and that the travelers, subject to wind-drift, may jam up along coast lines or ridges, giving the impression that these land contours are their chosen paths.

The bird watcher may wonder about the mechanics of this annual miracle, but more likely he will leave these problems for the pundits to ponder while he simply enjoys the spectacle, finding pleasure in sorting out the different kinds. Donald Culross Peattie, in his *Almanac for Moderns* which was awarded the Limited Editions Club gold medal as a modern classic, records two spring "waves."

April Tenth:

After the long spell of bad weather the birds, who were banked up, I fancy, somewhere in the Carolinas, are coming through in a torrent. There are so many that I can keep but the most delirious count of them. My records are carried away in fluttering confusion, like a wind gauge in a hurricane. Every time I approach the marsh I hear the warning cries of the herons, like the drop of an old chain on its own coils, and from beyond the cat-tail lances the snaky neck and archaic head of the bittern is turned to look at me, with the astonished and disapproving gaze that archaeopteryx might have turned on an anachronistic human.

87

In the wet maple woods, where the skunk cabbage leaf is expanding in its unabashed ugliness, the grackles are already quieting, and in their place I hear, morning and evening, the first sounds of mourning doves. Along the runs and rills kingfishers are setting up their riparian claims with loud cries, like the whirling of a boy's wooden rattle. I have simply lost all account of the order of arrival of the sparrow tribe, of the swallows, vireos and warblers and wrens. There is no order; they all seemed to come on the same day, and continue to arrive in increasing numbers every day.

Now is the moment when the novice at bird-gazing needs a friend. Flowers are best identified, if one is a neophyte, by one's self. The mere exercise of tracking them to their names will fix them in the memory. But with the birds, a guide, a friend by the side, to point out what you ought to have seen, to pass you the binoculars and whisper eagerly in your ear, is worth a shelf of books.

May Fourth:

On this fine May morning, at about six o'clock, I took up my station in a convenient tree, where I could make my long limbs comfortable, and lifted my binoculars. At my first coming I created the usual exodus and silence that a human being's presence always brings in the wood. After a time I ceased to be noticed—after far shorter an interval than would have been possible at any other season. But the birds were so intent upon their hurried affairs, every tree in the glade was so occupied, and the fresh arrivals were so many, that there simply was not time to give me more than a glance.

Catbirds and brown thrashers and thrushes and mourning doves and robins and wrens seemed to pour through like rain blowing horizontally. They came, they teetered, they ate if they could find anything, and sped on. Everywhere about me the chorus arose—the whistling, the alarm calls, the anger calls, the rapture and the loud demand for mates, mates! Of these I saw as yet but very few. As a general thing the males arrive before the females, no doubt to stake their local claims and drive off rivals.

No one who has not lived in the subtropics can imagine what the effect of the spring migration is there. To us here it brings returning joy, a sense that the world is full of brilliant and cheerful friends. But in the South it means the falling of a silence, a long sad monotony. I recall, like a caesura in melody, those days by the Mediterranean, in

88

July, when the nightingale had ceased to sing, the little European robin with his bright red vest was flown away, and gone were the chaffinch and the blackbird. Even the gulls deserted the harbor, where the fishing town lay burning beside the stagnant sea.

(From *Almanac for Moderns*)

RAYMOND S. DECK

Salute to a Brown Bird

Every bird that flies to the West Indies, to Mexico, or to South America and back, is made of championship stuff. There are no unfit birds. The inept are weeded out; nature's realistic bookkeeping is concerned only with percentages—the strong, successful percentages. It seems tragic when one of these small fliers completes the long flight only to dash its life out on something as prosaic as a wire or a window. It is as though an intrepid explorer, on his return from far adventures, slipped on the stairs of his own home or killed himself while cleaning his rifle. Raymond Deck himself died in one of these home accidents shortly after the publication of his book *Pageant in the Sky*. "Salute to a Brown Bird" is the prelude to this book on the modern sport of bird watching.

J EAN AND I were sitting quietly in a wood the first time the child heard a northern Veery sing. We already had marked a dozen bird songs, I remember, for all New England was flooded with birds on that morning in May. Now a Grosbeak with a red escutcheon on its breast was brightening the blue sky with cheery roundelays. Ovenbirds, drunk with spring, fluttered high above the woodland roof to shower the earth with silky song. And Catbirds chanted. Somewhere behind us a Yellowthroat whistled of *witchery!*

Then the Veery sang, and a hush seemed to fall on the land like the

90

still in a church, for the song of that little brown bird is an other-worldly thing. Like the chiming of golden bells the song wavered through the trees. It swelled from a whisper into a frosty, ringing thing, then vanished among the black trunks. I cannot tell you where the soloist hid to sound that beautiful cool anthem, for the Veery, like the Mockingbird and a handful of other gifted singers, is an able ventriloquist. I cannot even describe the song so that you would recognize it. Maybe Jean can, though.

"It sounds," Jean said, "like spirals of white gold."

Yes, if she really wanted, I answered her question, perhaps we could manage a look at a Veery or two. Not more than a glimpse, though, for the bird is shy and furtive. It never will sit unafraid on a limb and let you watch it at its singing the way its cousin the Wood Thrush will. Softly, softly, we would have to walk in damp ferny places to catch a glimpse of a Veery.

All we could hope to see then would be the whisking flight of a dusky brown bird smaller than a Robin. It would flit out of a spice-bush maybe, or up from a mossy boulder by the creek. There would be a flash of wings which always looked like silver in the shadows where brown Thrushes dwell; and a strange throaty *churrp* of alarm. That was all we could expect for a lot of searching. But Jean wanted to see the bird that sang white gold spirals so we backed the car into a little woods-road and struck off among the trees.

We tramped around a long time. We heard Towhees sing; and Orioles, and a host of jewelled Warblers. In the trunk of a dead silver birch we found the brood of a Chickadee pair. But we had no glimpse of the bird that strikes chimes, and we heard no Veery sing.

I told the child, I remember, that if these birds were not uncannily timid perhaps there would be no golden-bell songs for people to hear. For Veeries, like most other birds, fly south every fall; only they go farther than most, and consequently face more dangers. Jean remembered flocks of Bluebirds in southern peach orchards on mid-winter days. She knew that many birds, like them, journey five or six hundred miles every fall to find sanctuary from northern blizzards. But Veeries, I knew well, fly on and on over Dixie to wilderness places.

"Just before your second birthday, Jean," I said as we trudged along, "I left on an expedition. . . ."

Then, oddly, the whole scene changed, though I went on talking to my daughter. The oaks and birches vanished. Great purple orchids

91

shimmered above me on the branches of kapok trees. Parrots and red Macaws streamed through the sky. And I was standing with my Indian boy on a Christmas Day, in the ageless, beautiful forest that is Brazil. There were birds all about, as there are in the Maytime woods at home, only more birds and brighter ones. There were Tanagers, blue, yellow and crimson; big fluffy Trogons gayer than the bravest canvas in the world; and Parrakeets which fairly glittered as they flew chattering through the trees.

But I had no eyes for these tropic-hued dandies, for I had spied a dusky Thrush on the jungle floor. This was not the plump gray bird which called *oomp,* in the jungle at twilight in such sonorous tones that I called it the Organ Thrush. It was no one of the dozen other native Thrushes which filled the air with rich music at dawn and dusk. The bird that I saw beside the Amazon on that blazing Christmas Day was a Veery—perhaps from New England.

No doubt it will seem silly to you that I did not shoot the thing so that its stuffed skin might be resting today in a museum case. But all that I did was to say "humph," which to the Indian meant that this bird was too commonplace to kill. But to me it meant: "You will see Connecticut again long before I will, even if you do have to fly by night over leagues of steamy jungle, even if you must cross five hundred miles of naked ocean by yourself. I know there are a hundred snakes and ocelots here, a hundred Hawks and foxes to the north, which will try to kill you, but you will manage to get through all right because you are so uncannily wary.

"When you get back to the land where cool breezes blow, where Old Glory waves in majesty against the sky, . . ." the *humph,* went on to mean, ". . . perhaps you will drop down briefly for me in a certain ferny wood. A strain from those rolling golden bells of yours should say to Jean and her mother, 'All is well.' "

Jean liked the idea of any bird's being strong and brave enough to fly thousands of miles to tropical jungles and back. She said that it must be a great relief to Veeries to know, now that May was here, that their worst dangers were over—until the return journey started in August, anyhow. She was sure they all felt very happy to be safely back or they would not sing as beautifully as they did. Jean hoped she would hear a Veery sing again. And especially she wished she could see what these birds looked like, that had faced so many perils and come through.

92

We had sat down in a maple glade as we discussed these things. It was a lovely place, with sunlight sifting through baby leaves in the gayest manner imaginable. Birds were singing all around. Then the sky clouded over of a sudden, as must happen sometimes, even in North America in May. The ostrich-ferns and other tender green things about became almost luminous when that happened, just as they always do. Ground-Robins left off calling *twee-cher-lee!* A Wren, perched eloquently close to a hollow stump, quit his rollicking serenade.

Then the Veeries sang with abandon in the false dusk, as they do in the half-light of dawn and coming night. They had been everywhere about us all the time. Like the chiming of bells or the gentle sobs of organs—I never have decided which—their fairy spirals floated through the air. It is an exalting thing to hear a dozen Thrushes sing in chorus! This experience was such that even after the sun shone out again, and the last whorl of song trailed off among the trees, Jean did not think of tracking down one song to see the singer.

"Just think," was all she said, "every one of those birds has flown clear to South America and back! I'm glad they are so shy and careful!"

We wandered back to the car soon after that. We were late for dinner already. Jean was a few paces ahead of me when we reached the little woods-road. She gave a start, I thought, as she put her foot on the running-board and turned to wait for me.

"Look daddy," she said, and pointed to the ground.

A dusky brown bird the size of a Wood Thrush was lying there. It was quite dead though its body was still warm. Jean said she was very sorry, and I was sorry too, that after a Veery had lived all winter in primeval jungles it should have been killed by flying against the window of a car parked in Connecticut in May.

(From *Pageant in the Sky*)

93

WILLIAM BEEBE

Feathered Good Neighbors

For more than forty years William Beebe, acting as Director of Tropical Research of the New York Zoological Society, has been one of the tropical world's most articulate interpreters. More than a score of books have come from his gifted pen—*Jungle Peace, Edge of the Jungle, Pheasant Jungles, Half Mile Down,* and others—rich by-products of his scientific studies which were to be presented in more formal attire in the Society's technical bulletins. For three years he concentrated on a square kilometer of cloud jungle around the Rancho Grande laboratories in the Venezuelan Andes, and this resulted in *High Jungle,* published in 1949. The story of the night-migrating blackpoll warblers, the closing chapter, is a device by which Beebe prepares us for our return home after our South American adventure.

T HIS IS the story of the northward migration of a blackpoll warbler which nests in the northern United States, Canada, and Alaska, and then, like the author of this volume, flies thousands of miles southward to spend six months of the year in Venezuela. These tens of thousands of migrant birds are the best kind of Good Neighbors, for in all countries in which they live they devour hosts of harmful insects, and at the same time, with their beauty, they delight the eyes of both Venezuelans and *Norte Americanos.*

At seven-thirty in the evening of the twenty-first of April we sat at our tables in the laboratory of Rancho Grande with the ceiling lights

94

ablaze. A spider, a bird, a frog and a painting held us individually absorbed. The fog swirled through the area of illumination outside the windows, and soon there was a steady drumming of rain. Another sound increased in volume, one difficult to describe, and no wonder, for it was the soft impacts of the heads and wings of moths against the three hundred square feet of glass. It had something untropical about it—exactly the sound of thousands of snowflakes against the panes. Again and again our eyes disillusioned our ears.

Small moths and those of medium size were the first to arrive, and then came sharper raps, often repeated, and we saw the whirring wings of sphinx moths, the hummingbirds of the insect world, whose strong swift flight hurled them against the invisible barrier. Their heads were most resistant, for we saw a single moth keep it up for an hour, a definite individual marked by a conspicuous tear in the wing edge.

After the rain began I was startled by a really loud thud, and on the ledge, gazing full at me was a male blackpoll warbler in full breeding plumage. He was joined by a female, then another male and next by a gray-cheeked thrush. All stood quiet, apparently confused, or strove to push against the invisible glass which prevented further approach to the source of light; light which exerted to the full its mysterious power, a pull as inexplicable to us as gravitation.

If we turned off the ceiling lights for five minutes, the birds became restless, hopped to the edge of the window ledge and finally launched out into the wind, blinding fog and rain—a third incredibly impelling attraction taking possession of the little bodies, the pull toward the north and home. . . .

As a bird would fly, from our laboratory to the adjacent shore of the Caribbean Sea is only about six miles. When deflected by the hypnotic power of our electric lights, the birds were headed direct for the neighboring pass, through which they would funnel down to the sea, the beginning of their great voyage. They gave evidence of careful preparation, perhaps begun as long as a month ago. It was a preparation as unconscious as each breath or heartbeat. But some trigger in their bodily make-up was pulled, some change in glands occurred, some shift in chemistry of blood resulted in the slow piling up of fat. No migrant which we examined had anything in its stomach, but the body, even the neck and upper thighs, was lined and padded with golden fat.

Instead of sufficing for daily needs, part of the food was precipitated

95

as nutrient oil. This was probably somewhat of a handicap; the activity of daily routine must have been slightly slowed down. In a captive bird such accumulation of fat would result in death. By means of this slight addition of weight and increase of stored food, the black-polls filled their little holds with cargo and crowded their decks with fuel for the great effort. From what we know I doubt whether this ghastly weather delayed them a moment. Another preparedness was the abstinence from a recent meal. Neither stomach nor intestine contained a single leg, wing, or body of gnat or other insect. At the zero hour of taking off, digestion would have a rest; a stomachful would be supercargo.

As the birds disappeared I tried to project myself into their place and a cold horror came over me. It was the feeling of the absolute unknown, plus the certain knowledge of being at the mercy of the primeval elements of the planet, where only a rare combination of favorable conditions of avian energy and cosmic forces would spell success and ultimate safety. My feeling for the migrant birds was the same that came over me, many years ago, as I was slowly sliding down a slope of ice-glazed snow toward a Himalayan half-mile drop. I was stopped at the brink by the frozen hollows of a snow leopard's track. In that case, however, before my Tibetans reached me I peered over the edge and had the additional anti-climactic shock of seeing a soft, snowy ledge a few feet below.

Perhaps the blackpoll warbler could fight his way up through low-lying neblina and higher rain clouds into the clear sky, but even there, there would be only the sheerest silver sliver of a last quarter Easter moon. We must deny him the reasonable orientation of Scorpio and the Southern Cross blazing behind him, and the Pole Star beckoning from the northern horizon. Without compass or sextant, map or chart, the boreal pull is steady and unceasing, both upon him and his uncountable fellows beating along the sky. Now and then they wasted a bit of energy in a friendly (let us be momentarily anthropomorphic and say an *encouraging*) chirp through the blackness of the tropical night.

Little by little the blackpoll's store of surplus fat is drawn upon, drop by drop going to fortify the beating of the wings and the rhythm of delicate muscles, to counter the fatigue of hour after hour, mile after mile. The final gamble is a race between the last stored golden food and the final aerial lap before the landfall of a Florida haven. Looking out from the warm, bright laboratory of Rancho Grande, I

96

could imagine no mitigation of this terrible ordeal by water, wind and night, with the additional handicap of weather such as swallowed the bird from my sight.

Every blackpoll, of the thousands upon thousands living on our planet, spends the winter in South America. So even if my particular bird had never been south of Rancho Grande, he still had twenty-five hundred miles ahead with an ultimate goal, even at the southernmost limit, of nesting trees in Vermont. If by chance, he wintered in Brazil and called northern Alaska home, his small wings must carry him five thousand miles at a speed, from Florida north, of thirty to two hundred miles a day. These are almost unbelievable facts, yet well sustained.

We looked through the window at our fellow North American in his neat black and white. Moths buffeted him. Once he was neck deep in the fluttering dust of scales. He pecked angrily at a large owl moth which banged against him. He tried to find a quiet place where he could rest and gaze into the laboratory whose lights held him prisoner as would a cage of wire. I saw that he was injured, so I caught him and wondered anew at his smallness and frailty. The blackpolls I had taken and studied on New England southward migrations were just other warblers. This one was a precious personality which held my deepest interest because he made me visualize the vital fight for existence which he and his fellows must wage. From beak to tail-tip he was only five and a half inches, and with his full Caribbean cargo of fat he weighed only eighteen grams, three-fifths of an ounce.

Night after night more blackpolls and other warblers arrived and departed in safety, going through the same routine, bewilderment, hypnotic disregard of all danger in striving to reach the light, a reluctance again to give themselves to the darkness behind them and the down-pouring rain. But in the end not a single bird held back. The last flutter of white in the darkness was the start toward the latitude, country, state, township, grove, the spruce, and often the very branch on which the little bird had been hatched a year or more ago. The chance of a successful return to the natal bough and the finding of the same or a new mate is a desperate gamble against loaded dice and nicked cards, yet the general population of blackpolls remains the same. This means that the equivalent of the four young birds reared each season is eliminated, or half the young and both parents. Against talons of hawk or owl and all the migration hazards we have visualized, the odds against life are three to one, no more, no less.

97

Later in the evening I took a last look at the quartet of blackpolls peering in the window, and as I turned off the lights for the last time, I wished them *"Bon voyage, Dendroica striata."*

(From *High Jungle*)

EDWIN WAY TEALE

A Hundred Miles of Warblers

In 1948, Edwin Way Teale explored the natural history of a season. On a seventeen-thousand-mile journey with his wife Nellie, he accompanied the eastern Spring from the Everglades to the Canadian border. His report, *North with the Spring,* published in 1951, immediately became a best seller and was the first of a four-volume series on the American seasons. Halle's *Spring in Washington* accents the vernal season's breadth in time—as a series of events covering three months in one locality. Edwin Teale's book, on the other hand, deals with its linear movement in space, its northward surge through half a continent.

Perhaps no manifestation of spring is so spectacular as the rush of warblers. Bird watchers are everywhere on the alert for "waves" during late April and May when conditions favor the concentration of these bird-butterflies. Edwin Teale tells of his encounter with the myriad *Parulidæ* during his spring journey.

FOR HOURS that April Friday we went in and out of spring.

Our road led through mountain country, over a long series of ridges. It rose and fell, climbed and tobogganed down again like a roller-coaster a hundred miles in length. Each time the road lifted us to a new summit we found ourselves amid trees with buds hardly opened. Then, like a swimmer diving downward into foaming surf, we would swoop into a world of white dogwood, of fruit trees clouded with blooms, of grass freshly green. Spring would be all around us in some valley fragrant with flowers.

The season was advancing swiftest along the valleys; its high-water mark was lifting little by little up the mountainsides. Like floods of water, the floods of spring follow a lowland course. They race ahead down the long valleys, climb slowly, as though struggling with gravity, up the slopes. In the mountains the streams, the highways and the railroads go through the gaps together. And with them goes spring.

We had awakened early that morning in a cabin beside a rushing mountain brook, 20 miles east of Asheville. It was still dark when we heard, high overhead where the flying bird was already touched by the sunrise, the wild, lonely voice of a killdeer. Then the valley lightened and wood thrushes, mocking birds, and cardinals sang all up the slope of the mountain that climbed steeply behind us. Their notes descended in varying volume. Those of the topmost singers reached us in fragments during lulls in the lower chorus, as mere fairy songs, whisper songs, echoing down the slope. These were the first of innumerable birds we heard that day.

During the night a great warbler wave had poured over the Appalachians, spilling its gay, colorful migrants down the ridges that, in gigantic waves of granite, descended toward the east. The fluttering wings that had carried them from islands of the Caribbean, from Central or South America, from Mexico, had lifted them over the barrier of this ancient range. Before we had started our trip, Ludlow Griscom, Harvard's famed field ornithologist, had told us:

"Be near Asheville, North Carolina, the third week in April and you will see the warblers pour across the mountains."

This was the third week in April. And these were the warblers he had promised. Nearly one-third of all the species of warblers found east of the Rockies were about us that day.

We never knew whether we were in the beginning, the middle, or the end of the wave. We drove for more than a hundred miles, from east of Asheville south to Hendersonville and west to Highlands, and there were warblers, pockets of warblers, trees swarming with warblers, warblers beyond count, along the way. These rainbow birds of spring, like other manifestations of spring, increased and decreased as our road tobogganed or climbed. They were most numerous in the valleys; absent almost entirely on the higher summits. Wood warblers come north as the leaves unfold. They feed on the forest caterpillars that feed

100

on the new green leaves. Their northward flight keeps pace with unfolding bud and expanding leaf. The sequences of nature, the timing of the tides of migration, are exact. Buds burst, new leaves unfurl, larvae hatch, and warblers appear.

South of Asheville the road descended a long decline with climax forest on either side. For an hour we swept the hardwoods with our glasses, watching the warbler show.

No other family of North American birds travels more in mixed companies than do the wood warblers. Redstarts darted among the branches, fanning their brilliant tails. Ovenbirds called from the woodland floor. Prairie warblers endlessly went up the scale in the thin "zee-zee-zee-zee-zee-zee" of their song and chestnut-sided warblers ended on a whip lash "switch you!" As they appeared and disappeared among branches and bushes, we saw the rich lemon of yellow warblers, the black raccoon masks across the faces of Maryland yellowthroats, the flash of yellow rump patches as myrtle warblers swooped and rose. . . . And every bird was in perfect plumage. This was the season of the new and unmarred leaf, the time of the bird at its best. This was the unblemished world of the spring.

A little later we pulled up near a huge tulip tree. Its billowing cloud of pale-green new leaves was a world of succulent plenty for larva and warbler alike. Magnolia warblers and black-throated blues and parulas and redstarts and myrtles swarmed through this arboreal land of plenty. Nothing in the world is more alive than a warbler in the spring. Surely it must have been a warbler that James Stephens described in *The Crock of Gold* as being "so full of all-of-a-sudden." All of a sudden a warbler starts and stops. All of a sudden it flashes from branch to branch, peers under leaves, snaps up small caterpillars, darts on again.

One black-and-white warbler, a little striped mouse of a bird, left its caterpillar hunting to hawk after a pale-brown moth gyrating beyond a lower branch. It fluttered, hovered, spurted ahead, missed the moth in its erratic course time after time. In the end it became discouraged and suddenly zoomed upward, back to the trunk among the gray-green leaves of the tulip tree. By the time we drove on, our necks ached from looking up at the strenuous little treetop birds.

In the White House, in Washington, D. C., on May 4, 1906, Theodore Roosevelt wrote to John Burroughs, at Slabsides, that he had just come in from walking around the White House grounds and had wished heartily that Burroughs had been there to tell him what the

101

various warblers were. Most of the birds had been in the tops of the trees and he could not get good glimpses of them. But there was one with chestnut cheeks, with bright yellow behind the cheeks and a yellow breast thickly streaked with black, which had puzzled him.

This same warbler that perplexed the twenty-sixth President of the United States at the White House danced among the upper branches of a maple near the cemetery at Fletcher, North Carolina, where Bill Nye, the humorist, is buried. It was a Cape May warbler, the only one with chestnut cheeks. This warbler, incidentally, has little to do with Cape May, New Jersey. It does not breed there. I have never seen one there. Its name resulted from the fact that, during migration in 1809, the individual from which it was described happened to be shot on Cape May. Breeding almost as far north as the Great Slave Lake of northern Canada, these warblers concentrate in winter in the West Indies, especially on the island of Haiti. The path of their migration is wide at the top and funnels down to form, roughly, an inverted pyramid.

In contrast, the redstart—the "firetail," the warbler the Cubans call the "little torch"—has a particularly broad front throughout both its southward and its northward movement. As these warblers near their southern wintering grounds, their flyway still has a width of more than two thousand miles, extending all the way from Mexico on the west to the Bahamas on the east.

Near Druid Hills, North Carolina, we pulled up beside an apple orchard in bloom. The trees descended a long slope in tumbling clouds of white. Bees hummed. The air was fragrant with the perfume of the apple blossoms. Sunshine filtered among the branches, where a myriad white petals glowed, luminous in the backlighting. And here warblers —myrtles, magnolias, Maryland yellowthroats, prairies, and black-and-whites—darted amid blossom-laden boughs or flicked, in flashes of living color, from tree to tree.

There were other moments of especial beauty that day. Where a mountain road turned sharply on the way to Highlands, a black-and-white warbler flitted past us over a shining, glittering waterfall of mica that streamed down an embankment from decomposing rock. Then there was the hooded warbler we saw, singing with face lifted to the sunny sky, beside an upland pasture blue with bird's-foot violets. Once we came upon a prairie warbler, its yellow breast edged with streakings of black and its tail bobbing about, balancing itself on the fiddlehead of a cinnamon fern. Another time a long finger of sunshine descending through a treetop spotlighted a Maryland yellowthroat, brilliant in contrasting yellow and black, swinging on a low cluster of red maple keys.

John Burroughs thought the yellowthroat's song said: "Which way, sir? Which way, sir? Which way, sir?" In a less genteel modern day it is usually set down as: "Wichity, wichity, wichity, witch." And so it sounds in the North. But here some of the birds seemed substituting an "s" sound; seemed to be singing: "Seizery, seizery, seizery." We wondered if this was a warbler dialect, a local accent given by birds that originated in the same area. Several times on our trip we encountered regional variations in song. . . .

Later, as we drove north, we were tantalized by a ringing bird call from the woods. It was a monosyllabic "Teach! Teach! Teach!" It immediately suggested the ovenbird. But it was so different from the rounded "Teacher! Teacher! Teacher!" of the northern ovenbird that we thought it must be made by a different species. Finally, near Lynchburg, Virginia, we saw the singer in the act of singing. It was unmistakably an ovenbird. Through the southern part of its range, below the Mason and Dixon Line, the warbler drops the final syllable from its song. Roger Tory Peterson has noted that along the old canal that by-passes the Falls of the Potomac, near Glen Echo, Maryland, he can distinguish the resident from the migrant ovenbirds, when they return together in the spring, by this difference in their song.

Each time we crossed a brook among the wooded ridges, on that day of warblers, we stopped. For there we were sure to find a pocket of migrants. The trees beside such streams were always filled with the song of the spring woods, the small and varied music of the warblers.

During one such stop we were impressed by the way the bright yellow rump patches of the myrtle warblers disappeared almost instantaneously when they alighted, leaving only grayish plumage that blended with the tree bark behind it. The effect was similar to that produced by the sudden disappearance of the brightly colored underwings of an alighting *Catocala* moth. This swift eclipse of the yellow rump patches produces the impression of watching a creature vanish into thin air.

During another stop, beyond Lake Toxaway, we fell into conversation with a native of the region. He had noticed the swarms of birds

103

that day. But he assured us that migration had nothing to do with it. Why? Because there is no such thing as migration.

"The birds are here all the time," he said.

"Why don't we see them in the winter?"

"That's simple. They're just farther back in the woods."

Surrounded by uncounted migrants, standing on one of the great, immemorial flyways of the East, he was unalterably convinced that migration did not exist. . . .

Somewhere near Frozen Lake we stopped for half an hour where ancient hemlocks receded into gloom beside the jumbled boulders of a mountain torrent. The trees were hoary with usnea lichen. In small gray beards, like lesser Spanish moss, it waved from branches and the rough bark of the tree trunks. Usnea is the chief nesting material of the parula warbler. And, appropriately, here we found half a dozen parulas. They danced from limb to limb, alternately in sunshine and shade, the males singing their buzzy little trill that has been aptly described as resembling the winding of a watch.

Perhaps for these warblers the hemlocks were home, the goal of their northward migration. Driving among migrating birds along the Gulf we had assumed, before we thought about it, that the earliest flocks contained the birds with the farthest to go; that those with only a short flight ahead of them would wait until last. The reverse is true. As spring moves northward, birds return home behind its advancing front. Each bird, as Ernest Mayr so well expresses it, seems attached to its breeding area by a rubber band. No matter how far the autumn migration stretches the band, when spring comes it draws the bird back home again. Georgia birds return to Georgia and Maryland birds to Maryland. The farther south their breeding ground, as a rule, the earlier they come home. Conditions are right for the return of the songbirds in Virginia weeks before they are in Massachusetts. Thus, returning migrants leapfrog up the map. Banding has shown that the successive waves in the tide of migration carry birds over and beyond those already at home.

Late starters in the migration parade tend to catch up with the spring. The yellow warbler, for example, winters in the tropics and reaches the Gulf coast about the first week in April. Some of these warblers nest as far north as Manitoba. During the last fifteen days of their journey they traverse an area that spring requires thirty-five days to cross. The average progress made by all species of spring migrants

104

ascending the Mississippi flyway is said to be 23 miles a day. Black-poll warblers, one of the last warblers to come north, exceed this rate by a dozen miles a day. Between Louisiana and Minnesota they average as much as 35 miles every 24 hours. Beyond Minnesota the blackpolls that nest in western Alaska increase their speed as they follow the Mackenzie Valley until they are making 200 miles a day. They require only half the time consumed by the initial 1,000 miles to cover the final 2,500.

As the road climbed nearer to Highlands, among these ancient ridges that are a relic of the early paleozoic continent, snowdrops were in bloom beside the mountain road. Riding west we seemed transported north. Hardwoods and open meadows set among dark evergreens were around us. The Low Country of the coast had the charm of the exotic; the High Country of North Carolina had the attraction of the familiar. The forest openings might well have been in Maine. But the sun was the sun of the South. Through the clear air of the heights, unhindered by vapor, its rays beat down with full intensity. This same clear atmosphere, when we came to vantage points above the valleys, enabled us to see for immense distances across the green panorama that spread away to the east.

In the dawn of that morning, what a host of warbler eyes had glimpsed that very scene!

During the hours of the night, with tiring muscles, with consumption of stored-up fat, the little birds had followed, in the dark, the sky highway of their ancestors. They had threaded through gaps, climbed over ridges, mounted to cross the continental hump of the Appalachian range. Rocks untouched by glaciers, plants of older lineage than any in the North, had passed unseen beneath their wings. Their aerial trail had cut across the path of the early Spaniards who in 1567—so many warbler generations ago—had pushed northward among the mountains. Some of the migrants, perhaps, had passed in the night above the very spot on Bear Camp Creek, near Highlands, where in 1886, Charles S. Sargent, of Harvard, rediscovered Michaux's *Shortia,* a flower that had been lost for a century.

Now the little birds were scattered over the descending ridges, feeding, resting, regaining their strength, just as their ancestors had done in pre-Columbian springs. We wondered how many times in each bird's life it stopped at the same spots while journeying from its winter

105

quarters to its summer home. . . . Do the birds tend to come down at regular stopping places, at way stations along the route?

So far as I know, no final answer is available. The area of migration is so great, the number of migrants so astronomical, the percentage of individuals banded so infinitesimally small, the chances of recovery so slight that exact and accurate information is difficult to obtain. But it seems logical to conclude that the eastern slope of the Appalachians in North Carolina is an ancient annual resting ground of the songbirds, offering sanctuary after strain. And of this we were sure; the descending ridges for many miles that day were providing food and rest and shelter and new strength for a host of homegoing warblers.

(From North with the Spring)

ALBERT HOCHBAUM

Patterns of Local Movement

If Peter Scott, the celebrated English wildfowl expert, has a counterpart on this side of the Atlantic it is Albert Hochbaum. As a matter of fact, the two are firm friends and each watches with intense interest the researches of the other. Hochbaum—a talented naturalist, writer, and artist—is director of the Delta Waterfowl Research Station in Manitoba. Years of observation in the vast prairie marshes when the wild ducks, geese, and swans are in passage, and long months of reflection between flights have crystallized much of this thinking about migration. Unlike those who would explain everything with the vague word *instinct,* he believes there are also *traditions,* and that these may be acquired and transmitted. The following passages are the opening paragraphs in his latest book, *Travels and Traditions of Waterfowl.*

L ISTEN! . . . No, it's only the wind.

"*But listen!* Quiet, Tim, you fool hound-dog." No, it is only the children at their game.

"*Listen!* . . . No, it is nothing at all." A heavy black cloud hangs in the west; through a rift the sun bathes the marsh in gold. The evening flight has begun; small parties of ducks lift from the bay, flying into the northwest. The tall poplar by the channel is dark with a thousand blackbirds creaking and tinkling.

"*Listen, listen!* . . . Yes, it *is* the swan! The Whistling Swans are back!"

107

Our eyes scan the purple east. There they are: fourteen great white birds halfway across the bay, coming straight toward us, their high-pitched voices yodeling loud and clear. They swerve, moving north to the lake. They turn again, swinging wide; now they are coming back, the south wind on their breasts. Now they are overhead. What a sight to behold! They are dropping, dropping. A dozen yards above the water their necks arch, they set their wings, spreading feet wide like Canvasback. Then softly they alight near Archie's Point. Another leg of their northward journey is completed.

A band of Whistling Swan seen in the evening light of the first day of spring stirs the heart and soul of a man so that, for a moment, his communion with the wilderness is complete. Yet tonight I feel more than the beauty of the scene itself. Here, mind you, in the fading day when you or I might lose ourselves in the maze of marshland, this band of swan has come from far beyond the horizon to a place they have not visited since last spring. There was no faltering; they came unerringly to this small corner of marsh that has been the April rendezvous of Whistling Swans for at least forty years. Tomorrow there will be more, and more again on following days, until the chorus of their multitudes will not let us sleep. Then, sometime in mid-May, they will be on with their journey and Archie's Point will be swanless until next April. . . .

Saturday night! For those who live in the country, this is the big event of the week: early supper, hurry with the dishes, change to best clothes, and off to town for three hours of shopping and small talk. Last evening Joan and I crossed the marsh at sunset on our way to Portage la Prairie. We had just slipped past Slack's Bluff when Joan touched my arm and I brought the car to a stop. "There, over toward Portage Creek. What are they, ducks or geese?" Far to the southeast there hung a thin line above the horizon, a frail whisp of thread, barely visible. We watched in silence as it grew until finally we could make out its components. "Geese!" Then, of a sudden, their voices drifted to us on the south wind. "Wavies!" We stepped from the car to stand in the gathering dusk as the birds passed. Most were Blue Geese, but their lines were punctuated here and there by lesser Snow Geese. They flew in a wide line from which sprouted small branches, the whole forming a great blunt "V." As the mass moved it rose and fell as if riding a rolling swell, the individuals within the flock ever shifting position so that the pattern changed constantly. The geese were in full and constant voice, a guttural gabbling accented by high, nasal shouts, by no means as rousing as the whoop of swans or the bark of Canada Geese, but sweet music, nevertheless, over the April prairie.

The flock held steady course; then at a point near Slack's Bluff it turned sharply toward the annual lakeshore stopping place at the mouth of the Whitemud River. As their voices faded, there came a louder clangor from the southeast. As far as we could see came the geese, one broad "V" after another. It was a great moment in my life, and I removed my hat in unconscious response to some inner urge of respect as they passed.

Each flock followed the same route as the first, and as the second group approached Slack's Bluff it turned sharply to the west. Every successive band held a steady course until it reached the turning place where the bend west was made. Not only were these birds moving toward a destination, but their trailway was marked by some special pattern which they followed. Maybe it was Slack's Bluff. Maybe it was the arrangement of the fields or the plan of the marsh and lake beyond or some other features of the landscape near or far. Whatever it was, these geese moving in the boundless prairie skies followed some cue that held them to their route. . . .

The sun has dropped into the lake. It is an April evening not of one day or of one year, but of at least three hundred April days of sixteen years. I am standing at the bayside. Before me is the vast expanse of marshland still frozen except at the edges, where a black moat of water separates ice from tules. Behind, to the north, is the narrow ridge of woodland that marks the south shore of Lake Manitoba. Beyond that, far past the northern horizon, are the marshes of Winnipegosis, of the Saskatchewan, of the Mackenzie.

The setting sun is the signal for Mallards and Pintails to leave these dark waters and move to other marshlands. Paired drakes and hens in company with their kind rise from the bays and go directly into the northwest. I am impressed by their precision, for, although their numbers are scattered far and wide over the marsh, the departure is not along a solidly broad front. Instead, as the bands leave the bays, the flight resolves into well-defined lanes of travel. The movement over the lakeshore is not in a wide sweep. The crossings are at passes. From where I stand I can see a flight over the village of Delta; there is another over Dr. Cadham's garden, and still another not far to the east. It has been so for countless springs—the trails to the northwest cross the lake ridge at the same places year after year. Are these passes cues

109

to orientation, each a step in the long journey from the wintering grounds to the breeding marshes far beyond?

The annual return of the Whistling Swan to their April rendezvous, the turning of the wavies at Slack's Bluff, the lakeshore crossings of the Mallard and Pintail are examples of the avian reaction to the pattern of landscape. These movements are not indiscriminate, nor are they directed primarily toward the final destination somewhere beyond. Here is an awareness of special plots of terrain along the way, responses to mere pinpoints on the map of total migratory movements. Here are the resting places and local crossings that are just as incidental, yet just as important, to the over-all journey as a Chicago transfer is to a transcontinental railway passenger.

(From *Travels and Traditions of Waterfowl*)

MAURICE BROUN

Red-Letter Day on
Hawk Mountain

When cool drafts from the Northwest add *finis* to summer and the first frosts
turn the green of the countryside to red and gold, thousands of week-end
bird watchers grasp the steering wheel and head toward Hamburg, Pennsylvania. "Going to Hawk Mountain" is now a tradition to thousands who
live within a day's drive. On some days the hawk watchers on the top of
the mountain outnumber the migratory birds of prey, but if the wind is
right—particularly if it is in the northwest—hawks and other migrants
string past in an astonishing aerial parade. Although vulnerable elsewhere
along the ridges they are safe at this point, because the mountain-top is inviolate sanctuary. The most spectacular flight, that of the broad-wings,
goes through in a body, usually within the period of a day or two or three
during the second week of September. Maurice Broun, Curator of Hawk
Mountain, who has seen more hawks than any other living man—nearly a
third of a million in twenty years of observation—tells of his number one
broad-wing day.

Thursday, September 16, 1948

AND NOW for the miracle day, when the sky was literally
darkened by broad-wings, giving us a glimpse of the way it must have
been any mid-September day a couple of centuries ago. Some sixth
sense forewarned me of this flight. John and Grace Prest, of Wilming-

111

ton, Delaware, were visiting the Sanctuary. They had a week on their hands, enjoying excellent birding with us. I said to the Prests, "Better hang around until Thursday—*that's* the big day." They hesitated, but departed at last to visit some relatives in New Jersey. You can imagine their chagrin when later they heard all about it.

The morning looked hopeless for good hawking. A dull sullen sky, and a fresh easterly wind—the worst possible wind for a flight—chilled us in body and spirit. But not for long! At exactly 8 o'clock an adult bald eagle circled above Schaumboch's, followed by 50 broad-wings. Then came a continuous movement of broad-wings, on both sides of the ridge, and at moderate elevations, many of the birds so close we could have hit them with stones. There was nothing remarkable the first two hours—only 1,396 broad-wings, and a sprinkling of ospreys and sharp-shins. An additional 1,371 broad-wings were tallied in the next hour. But soon after 11 o'clock a swirling mass of broad-wings boiled over the mountain, and they soon filled the southern sky in a seemingly interminable, densely straggling line, moving rapidly. My 18-power binocular revealed a level sheet of moving birds as far to the south as I could see. It was impossible to count, and I found myself making estimates, for the first time in all my years at Hawk Mountain. My tally for that last hour of the morning was 7,587 plus broad-wings. My companions on the Lookout, making independent counts, found my figures extremely conservative. Many more birds went by. The handful of observers who were present are not likely to see such a sight again. In the more than 7,200 hours that I have watched birds atop Hawk Mountain, there has never been anything remotely comparable to this avalanche of hawks. In that one hour before high noon, we saw more broad-wings than we usually see in an entire season. Only a thousand odd hawks passed the rest of the day; and the day's count was 11,392 plus hawks. This historic migration was witnessed by Donald Bieber and Walter Listman, both of Rochester, New York, Theodore Hake of York, Pennsylvania, Mabel and Ralph Lutz of Philadelphia, and my wife.

Apparently the broad-wings had been pent-up somewhere along the ridge. But why? During the five days prior to this mass exodus, the weather had been favorable for migration, and indeed the collective broad-wing count for September 11th to 15th was 1,530 birds. In any event the birds moved south in a body on this fabulous September 16th. At noon of this same day, George Pyle observed 1,500 plus

112

broad-wings over Riegelsville, along the Delaware River, and about 18 miles south of the nearest part of the ridge. In the days following the 16th we recorded only 1,140 broad-wings.

(From *Hawks Aloft*)

W. H. HUDSON

Migration on the Pampas

Much of the best nature writing is nostalgic. William Henry Hudson, leaving South America at the age of twenty-eight, left behind him the most joyous years of his life, years that he constantly tried to recall while writing in the dingy back room of his London boarding house. The greater the time-lapse from his boyhood on the pampas, the more clearly the visions returned. The following passages, reflecting his most mature style, actually were written shortly before his death at the age of 81.

Hudson was saddened by the knowledge that the Eskimo curlew was close to extinction and that the other three North American shorebirds of his youth, the golden plover, buff-breasted sandpiper, and upland plover, were in danger of disappearance from the Argentine plains. The curlew is probably gone, but since Hudson's death the others—at least the golden plover and the upland plover—have made a partial comeback.

SOUTH AMERICA can well be called the great bird continent, and I do not believe that any other large area on it so abounded with bird life as this very one where I was born and reared and saw, and heard, so much of birds from my childhood that they became to me the most interesting things in the world.

It was not only the number of species known to me, but rather the incalculable, the incredible numbers in which some of the commonest kinds appeared, especially when migrating. For it was not then as,

114

alas! it is now, when all that immense open and practically wild country has been enclosed in wire fences and is now peopled with immigrants from Europe, chiefly of the bird-destroying Italian race. In my time the inhabitants were mostly the natives, the gauchos, descendants of the early Spanish colonists, and they killed no birds excepting the rhea, which was hunted on horseback with the bolas; and the partridge, or tinamu, which was snared by the boys. There was practically no shooting.

The golden plover was then one of the abundant species. After its arrival in September, the plains in the neighbourhood of my home were peopled with immense flocks of this bird. Sometimes in hot summers the streams and marshes would mostly dry up, and the aquatic bird population, the plover included, would shift their quarters to other districts. During one of these droughty seasons, when my age was nine, there was a marshy ground two miles from my home where a few small pools of water still remained, and to this spot the golden plover would resort every day at noon. They would appear in flocks from all quarters, flying to it like starlings in England coming in to some great roosting centre on a winter evening. I would then mount my pony and gallop off joyfully to witness the spectacle. Long before coming in sight of them the noise of their voices would be audible, growing louder as I drew near. Coming to the ground, I would pull up my horse and sit gazing with astonishment and delight at the spectacle of that immense multitude of birds, covering an area of two or three acres, looking less like a vast flock than a *floor* of birds, in colour a rich deep brown, in strong contrast to the pale grey of the dried-up ground all round them. A living, moving floor and a sounding one as well, and the sound too was amazing. It was like the sea, but unlike it in character since it was not deep; it was more like the wind blowing, let us say, on thousands of tight-drawn wires of varying thicknesses, vibrating them to shrill sound, a mass and tangle of ten thousand sounds. But it is indescribable and unimaginable.

Then I would put the birds up to enjoy the different sound of their rushing wings mingled with that of their cries, also the sight of them like a great cloud in the sky above me, casting a deep shadow on the earth.

The golden plover was but one of many equally if not more abundant species in its own as well as other orders, although they did not congregate in such astonishing numbers. On their arrival on the

115

pampas they were invariably accompanied by two other species, the Eskimo curlew and the buff-breasted sandpiper. These all fed in company on the moist lands, but by-and-by the curlews passed on to more southern districts, leaving their companions behind, and the buff-breasted sandpipers were then seen to be much less numerous than the plover, about one bird to ten.

Now one autumn, when most of the emigrants to the Arctic breeding-grounds had already gone, I witnessed a great migration of this very species—this beautiful sandpiper with the habits of a plover. The birds appeared in flocks of about one to two or three hundred, flying low and very swiftly due north, flock succeeding flock at intervals of about ten or twelve minutes; and this migration continued for three days, or, at all events, three days from the first day I saw them, at a spot about two miles from my home. I was amazed at their numbers, and it was a puzzle to me then, and has been one ever since, that a species thinly distributed over the immense area of the Argentine pampas and Patagonia could keep to that one line of travel over that uniform green, sea-like country. For, outside of that line, not one bird of the kind could anywhere be seen; yet they kept so strictly to it that I sat each day for hours on my horse watching them pass, each flock first appearing as a faint buff-coloured blur or cloud just above the southern horizon, rapidly approaching then passing me, about on a level with my horse's head, to fade out of sight in a couple of minutes in the north; soon to be succeeded by another and yet other flocks in endless succession, each appearing at the same point as the one before, following the same line, as if a line invisible to all eyes except their own had been traced across the green world for their guidance. It gave one the idea that all the birds of this species, thinly distributed over tens of thousands of square miles of country, had formed the habit of assembling, previous to migration, at one starting-point, from which they set out in successive flocks of a medium size, in a disciplined order, on that marvellous journey to their Arctic breeding-grounds.

The autumnal migration, which was always a more impressive spectacle than that of the spring, began in February when the weather was still hot, and continued for three long months; for after the departure of all our own birds, the south Patagonian species that wintered with us or passed on their way to districts further north would begin to come in. During all these three long months the sight and sound of passage birds was a thing of every day, of every hour, so long as the light lasted, and after dark from time to time the cries of the night-travellers came to us from the sky—the weird laughter-like cry of rails, the shrill confused whistling of a great flock of whistling or tree duck; and, most frequent of all, the beautiful wild trisyllabic alarm cry of the upland plover. . . .

It is a charming bird, white and grey with brown and yellow mottlings on its upper plumage, beautiful in its slender graceful form, with a long tail and long swallow-like pointed wings. All its motions are exceedingly graceful: it runs rapidly as a corncrake before the rider's horse, then springs up with its wild musical cry to fly but twenty or thirty yards away and drop down again, to stand in a startled attitude flirting its long tail up and down. At times it flies up voluntarily, uttering a prolonged bubbling and inflected cry, and alights on a post or some such elevated place to open and hold its wings up vertically and continue for some time in that attitude—the artist's conventional figure of an angel.

These birds never flocked with us, even before departing; they were solitary, sprinkled evenly over the entire country, so that when out for a day on horseback I would flush one from the grass every few minutes; and when travelling or driving cattle on the pampas I have spent whole weeks on horseback from dawn to dark without being for a day out of sight or sound of the bird. When migrating its cry was heard at all hours from morning to night, from February till April: and again at night, especially when there was a moon.

Lying awake in bed, I would listen by the hour to that sound coming to me from the sky, mellowed and made beautiful by distance and the profound silence of the moonlit world, until it acquired a fascination for me above all sounds on earth, so that it lived ever after in me; and the image of it is as vivid in my mind at this moment as that of any bird call or cry, or any other striking sound heard yesterday or but an hour ago. It was the sense of mystery it conveyed which so attracted and impressed me—the mystery of that delicate, frail, beautiful being, travelling in the sky, alone, day and night, crying aloud at intervals as if moved by some powerful emotion, beating the air with its wings, its beak pointing like the needle of the compass to the north, flying, speeding on its seven-thousand-mile flight to its nesting home in another hemisphere.

(From *A Hind in Richmond Park*)

117

HERBERT BRANDT

Migration on the
Bering Sea

Perhaps the most bird-rich tundra in the Arctic world is that which lies around Hooper Bay, Alaska, between the mouths of the Yukon and Kusko-quim Rivers. Here, in 1953, as recounted in *Wild America,* our party found three of the world's four species of eiders nesting and hatching their young. That was late in June. To see the spectacular arrival of these seafaring ducks we would have had to fly in six weeks earlier at the breakup of the ice floes. Herbert Brandt made his epic trip to Hooper Bay in 1924 before planes were commonplace in Alaska and, to reach the coast in time to witness the spring arrival, he traveled by dog sledge.

Dr. Brandt, a successful Cleveland businessman, financed his own ex-peditions and published his own sumptuously illustrated books. A great ad-vocate of the amateur status, he once suggested that I should go into the business world, maintaining that anyone—even I—could make money, and that by budgeting nine months of the year to business and three to orni-thology, I could enjoy many more expeditions to far places than most pro-fessional ornithologists who are closeted in their museums and institutions by lack of funds for travel. Herb Brandt, an elective member of the Ameri-can Ornithologists' Union, followed this scheme himself and looked for-ward to three or four months of exciting field work every year until his death early in 1955, when his heart gave out after a strenuous day in the Everglades.

By THE morning of May 7 the gale had subsided, and the ice floes sparkled brilliantly, reflecting the sun from their millions of crystal facets. We were perched on a high block of ice at the edge of the open water, enjoying the sight of the flocks of ducks passing north. Far away on the southern horizon a line of dusk-like specks appeared against the snow. We all crouched low behind an ice cake to make ourselves as inconspicuous as possible. The specks grew rapidly larger, and took the form of a thin, wavy black line, which undulated, expanded, and contracted, like a rubber band, as it came along the open lane of water. On it came, with the speed of an express train, one of the many flocks of birds of passage that we saw fly over Point Dall on that morning. The Pacific Eider flight was on, and it was one of the most impressive ornithological sights that I have ever seen. These beautiful big black and white birds made a noise like a roaring waterfall as they rushed close overhead in their hurried flight to the land beyond. They flew in groups of from a pair to forty birds, and often alighted on the water nearby, the males giving forth their mating calls—which sounded like the labored cooing of large pigeons—to their beautiful big brown mates.

Much more plentiful than the eiders were those sea clowns, the talkative Oldsquaws, which passed in long, strung-out flocks like those of some shore birds. They are swift and light of wing, the long tail adding to their easy elegance, whereas the eiders' powerful flight seems heavy and almost gooselike. As they traveled they kept up a continual musical chatter, different from any bird that I know, and, because of its tones, almost indescribable. . . . Among the Oldsquaws that we saw, the males and females were rather evenly divided, but among the eiders the males outnumbered the females by more than five to one. The Oldsquaw is very hardy, and according to native information many of them spend the winter here in the open water among the ice floes.

We saw two King Eiders heading a flock of Pacific Eiders, and there were occasionally a few of them in the flocks of the latter. Murres were often seen flying with the Oldsquaws, but not with the eiders; while two flocks of about thirty murres each passed north. As they went

119

over they seemed to stir up a lot of atmosphere, making a loud noise as the air rushed through their stiff, pointed pinions, whereas the streamlined Oldsquaws made more of a musical whistling sound. Pelagic Cormorants, very striking with their reddish faces and green crests, passed in scattered flocks, their twinkling wings seemingly set far back on their iridescent, elongated bodies.

Well out of gun range, large white gulls were calling continuously, but were most wary, and we could never attract them to our lower strata. Never once did they fly direct, but always soared in great, advancing circles, after the manner of certain migrating hawks. What peculiar volant logic have these air masters, to fly more than twice the direct distance of their long journey? Yet theirs is a soaring honeymoon, one that utilizes the rarer currents and eddies of the air high aloft, instead of the laborious wing propulsion of the fast-flying flock formations that skim the sea's surface. The gliding method of the gulls is due perhaps to the much greater proportion of wing surface, compared to their weight. In all kinds of weather the great white fleet sailed northward, screaming and graceful, its units dancing their wide, clockwise minuets in the sky.

On May 8 the temperature moderated to a little above freezing, and an easterly wind coaxed the higher moss-covered ridges to peep coyly here and there on the face of the white tundra. Spring was in the air again, and our first east breeze was gentle, as we made our way to Point Dall. High overhead against the clear sky, five gray specks appeared, flying in triangular formation, headed toward the open sea. They proved to be the first White-fronted Geese, and they seemed to be weary as they slackened their speed, looking for a place to alight. We had no sooner gotten over the excitement of this new record—our first goose—than we had the big thrill of the migration, the stirring occasion we had long awaited, the annual epochal event in the lives of the natives; the coming of the first Whistling Swans. They flew high and leisurely, snow white in the sunlight against the blue sky, like phantom ships wending their way north. Both geese and swans were silent as they passed.

Offshore the easterly wind and the tides had driven the ice out so that the water lane between the floes had changed again to open sea. The water was of a cold deep blue, studded here and there with glistening white blocks broken off from the anchored shore ice. Perched on our high, limbic cake of ice, fifteen feet above the water, we were fearful lest at any moment the ebbing tide would take us out. In the distance against the white ice rim and the slaty Arctic sky the wavy lines again appeared. From their irregularity we knew that they were made up of eiders but we did not have to wait long to see, for they came fast, and the deep quacking of the birds was soon audible. As before, there were many more males than females. The air trembled with the heavy rush of their wings as the eiders came straight toward us, only fifteen or twenty feet above our icy station, but we let them pass, as we had sufficient specimens for scientific study.

Another big flock of birds, this time Oldsquaws, came chattering and cackling, flying lightly and speedily, not in the regular breast-to-breast formation of the eiders, but strung out in an irregular manner and with the elevation of the course often changing so that a side view of the flock presented a wavy line. Thus it continued during the big flight, single birds, pairs, or flocks of almost any size appearing every few minutes, onward bound for the great north.

A large flock of Pacific Eiders alighted in the water among the scattering ice cakes, almost within gun range, and drifted toward us with the tide, which was running past at the rate of perhaps six miles an hour, carrying with it the brilliant drift ice. They exhibited the traits of our more familiar ducks, often, as it were, standing on the surface of the sea, fanning the air vigorously with their wings, or throwing water over themselves with a rapid bobbing of the head, their continuous cooing, meanwhile, causing one to imagine he was near a cote of giant, deep-voiced pigeons. The flight of the previous two days had been largely of this species, but occasionally a few of the smaller, more graceful King Eiders passed, the yellow knobs on the foreheads of the males showing distinctly. Later we noted two pairs of American Pintails, the first of these birds that we had seen. High above us the Little Brown Cranes announced themselves, "garooling" in a lively manner, as if happy to be back. Two species of gulls were calling continuously, and the labored flight of the iridescent Pelagic Cormorant invariably attracted the eye.

The sun was warm and the air clear; it was a perfect day in an ornithologist's paradise. The romance of sitting among the wild, drifting floes and watching myriads of the rare northern birds of passage will always remain among my happiest recollections. During each lull in the migration all was silent except the continual lapping of the small waves against the ice, and the voices of the children chanting in the

122

Eskimo village half a mile back across the snow-covered beach. These sounds were soon drowned out again by the thundering wings of another wave of migrants; and so the colorful procession continued all day until about four o'clock in the afternoon, when the movements seemed to abate.

(From *Alaska Bird Trails*)

Arrival of
the Mutton-Birds

In the late fall and early winter, after the sooty shearwater has diminished in numbers, another dark shearwater, the slender-bill, can sometimes be spotted scaling over the waves off our Pacific shores. These wayfarers are thought to be strays thousands of miles off their normal path down the Asiatic side of the Pacific en route to Australian waters where they are known as mutton-birds. In the year 1839 John Gould estimated the flock approaching their nesting colony on Green Island in Bass Straits to number 150,000,000 birds. And these millions, converging on their home island each year arrive almost precisely within the same hour of the same day— or so we are told—reminding us of the legend of Capistrano's swallows. At Phillip Island in Westport Bay, Victoria, a similar horde of mutton-birds arrives with equal punctuality, as reported in *The Melbourne Argus*.

FAR ON THE eastern horizon a black patch could be discerned. It grew in size, until finally it could be distinguished as a flight of fast-moving birds. Outdistancing the rest, a dozen reached the cliff at exactly 8 o'clock. There—wheeling, swooping, circling, and diving —they uttered strange unmusical cries, as though rejoicing to be home again. The return of the Mutton-Birds had begun. For some time they came in singly—here a bird and there a bird. Gradually their numbers increased until the sky was covered with them. Swiftly they hurtled in from the sea, by tens, by twenties, by hundreds, by thousands; but not to land at once. There seemed a spirit of unrest about the birds, as if, having reached their objective after long wandering,

124

they were too overjoyed to be still, but must be darting and poising, rushing and gliding, wheeling and circling, all the time screaming discordantly till the semi-darkness was filled with their cries. Now distant against the sky, now lost in the darkness of the land, the birds might be thought to have no aim in their manoeuvres, but closer watching showed that each was most nearly touching the earth at one particular breeding burrow. At first the velocity with which the spot was traversed scarcely indicated any desire to land, but after many gradually narrowing loops had been described, there came a time when the speed decreased, and the wings flickered somewhat. On the next circle the bird poised, and then alighted as softly as snow at the very mouth of the burrow—not even then to rest until darkness was complete. Cape Woolamai was as busy as a bargain sale, new arrivals running hither and thither, inspecting, rejecting, visiting, courting, fighting, and singing their deep sea chanty. By half-past 8 it seemed that fully 100 acres of the cape was a mass of excited birds. Angry squawks here and there denoted that fights were in progress in some of the burrows. Now and then a bird could be seen hastily emerging, while his successful rival screamed with harsh triumph. Similar scenes had been enacted simultaneously on a dozen minor rookeries around the island. Altogether they represented a line of breeding burrows six and a half miles long, and the birds must be numbered in millions. The birds, which have come in from the sea to breed, will remain until late in April. During all this time similar stirring fights may be witnessed every night. Silence at last returned; birds which had found no burrows, or had been ejected from those which they considered theirs, were walking awkwardly up and down, muttering in what might be taken to be sullen resentment. At the mouth of one burrow one unmistakably proud householder was sending forth to the skies an unmusical paean of sheer delight. So another great problem has been solved. For the past week everywhere one has gone on this pleasant island one has been informed that the Mutton-Birds return to the day, to the hour, to the minute, each year; on that, all those who are not hopeless disbelievers in the Mutton-Birds legend have agreed. The only point has been that nearly everyone has named a different day, a different hour, a different minute. Let all doubts be resolved. The Mutton-Birds returned to Phillip Island at 8 o'clock on November 23.

(From *The Melbourne Argus*)

JACQUES DELAMAIN

Migration in France

A delightful little book entitled *"Pourquoi les Oiseux Chantent,"* published in 1932, is largely responsible for the modern revival of field ornithology in France and the book was awarded a prize by the *Academie Française.* The author, Jacques Delamain, here describes the pageantry of migration in the vicinity of Paris.

L̲ONG BEFORE their departure, on the edge of the Mediterranean basin and as far away as the other side of the Equator, the migratory instinct by species and in successive waves, now calm and regular, now slowed up and disjointed by stormy weather, has slowly put into motion our summer visitors who are going to populate our woods and gardens. By stages, traveling for weeks, especially at night or in the early morning, shortening the sea-crossings by way of the peninsulas, Spain and Italy, they face the long voyage, the perils of tempest and birds-of-prey, the traps of men. This is the supreme trial of endurance, clearing up the ranks, eliminating the weak and bringing on hand for the reproduction of the species only the strong, the dexterous or the fortunate. Almost always the males have departed first, about ten days in advance. This is because yonder in the native land to the north the choice of the place where the couple will settle must already have been made when the females arrive. . . .

The first summer visitor to arrive from the Mediterranean coasts is a little warbler with green-brown plumage, the Chiff-Chaff. On a sunny

126

day in February, on the border of the wood or in the lilacs, whose buds are already swelling in the shelter of the garden wall, this tiny somber bird lightly explores the bare twigs. His only song, "Zip-zip-zap," the syllables well detached and endlessly repeated, has caused him to be nicknamed the "money-counter." The year is still new, with the trees so bare and the wind so cold that one can scarcely see in him a harbinger of spring. A little later, his cousin, the Willow-Warbler, lighter colored, more slender, mounts after him toward the forests of Ile-de-France, repeating on the way that song begun on a joyful note and terminated in a tired plaint which will resound all summer in the copses. Then there is another Warbler, the Blackcap, so sober of color in her ashen dress, so bright in her pure light voice which will cheer up little gardens even in the midst of towns.

One morning at the end of March, between two tufts of heather, on the cool sand which he crosses with a solemn step, a strange bird with a long curved bill suddenly spreads out, if you surprise him, the fan of his reddish tuft which he was keeping lowered on his head, and two wonderful wings with wide alternating bands of black and white. This is the Hoopoe, who has fled the African lands which the sun is going to harden, to ask our damp soil for the worm or larva that he seeks under the moss or in the ground.

Finally, in the first days of April, as if to confirm the tidings which the showers were still making us doubt, one after another two great messengers arrive—the Chimney-Swallow and the Cuckoo. The first Swallow! The first Cuckoo! Ever since humanity, from the shelter of caves, has wanted to scrutinize the horizon for signs of the weather, it has made of these two harbingers emblems of joy, light and plenty, at the departure of cold and night. The Swallow travels in daily stages from the heart of the black continent and from India, followed closely by her white-rumped sister, the House Martin, who will construct the closed cup of her mud nest under the eaves of our roofs. The Cuckoo, parasite bird of equivocal loves, distant migrant from Africa and Asia, fond of hairy caterpillars, the processionnaries, who are just leaving their silky nests in the pines in long files, throws out on arriving in the gray morning, his double mocking note, repeated by the little shepherds. And at the same period, the White Stork, in pairs or in weak flocks, ascends from equatorial marshes toward the Lorraine country.

Other migrants hasten on and each day a new surprise, a new delight awaits the one who can see the furtive flight of brown, tawny, or

127

gray wings in the hedges turning green, who can listen and recognize the familiar calls. One morning it is the Nightingale, and all the songs which have delighted us until now seem shrill or jerky beside this voice, though it is still only stammering; then the Redstart, in sumptuous nuptial plumage, copper breast and back, gray-blue coat, black throat and pure white forehead. His cousin, the Black Redstart, who lets drop from the heights of the old stones of the churches and from the village walls devastated by war, his song like a cascade of crashing glass, has preceded him by several days. Tomorrow, the Yellow Wagtails, with their incessant tail-wagging will steal in between the green tufts of grass in the riverside meadows; the Tree Pipit will let himself drop like a parachute from the isolated tree in the clearing, singing until out of breath, his wings opened out. The White-Throat will whisper, invisible in the thickness of the hedgerow. Then, very high in the sky, a black bird will appear—the Swift, whose noisy bands will circle round buildings until August; the powerful flier whose slender wings carry him without effort toward our countryside from the Cape of Good Hope and Madagascar; the true king of the air, the only one among all the birds, perhaps, who can, like the queen bee, perform the nuptial rite in full flight.

Then, toward the end of April, as if he were awaiting the sudden bursting forth of the first copper colored oak leaves to hide among them his too glittering tropical plumage, the Oriole, warm yellow and deep black, hurls out his triumphal fluted call.

Others will come in crowds—Shrikes, soft of color and fierce of attitude, Warblers, of copses, gardens and reeds, and Flycatchers; then the Nightjar, strange somber bird with his velvety summer twilight flight, and the Turtledove. Finally a belated flock of Sandpipers hurrying toward the extreme north, flies over our estuaries and announces to us that up there, in the Arctic lands, the sun has made the ice retreat to limits from which it no longer wants to yield. But none of these last comers, in the already toughened foliage, can make us forget the arrival of our first harbingers of spring among the still bare twigs, nor the golden dart of the Oriole's flight among the black oak tree trunks.

(From *Why Birds Sing*)

128

ROGER TORY PETERSON

A Night in a
Channel Lighthouse

For years I had wanted to spend a night in a lighthouse when the birds were flying; to see the small travelers pouring out of the darkness into the dazzling beams. Guy Mountfort, with whom I had been collaborating on *A Field Guide to the Birds of Britain and Europe,* based on the system in my American Field Guides, was an old hand at lighthouses where he often went on bird-banding expeditions. He said that St. Catherine's Light on the English Channel should be at its best about the third week in April. Keith Shackleton, the bird artist, and his pretty young bride offered to fly us in their plane to St. Catherine's.

WHEN WE took off from Fairoaks, an aerodrome not far from London, our four-seater crammed with gear seemed like a flying sardine tin. The bird nets, which we planned to use for banding, would not fit inside, so the long bamboo handles were left to project through the open window. This created a rattle and a turbulence which made the small craft rather difficult to handle.

The green English countryside with its hedgerows, coppices, and old castles was like a terrain model below us; we crossed the Solent with its backwaters and tortuous estuaries on which swans rested like little white specks. Thus fascinated by the moving panorama, time slipped by as quickly as the miles until we found ourselves over the white chalk cliffs at the edge of the English Channel.

129

St. Catherine's Light stands on a bold headland of the Isle of Wight, a lonely light of a style which might be called "Railway-station Gothic," to use Shackleton's words. We carried with us a document from Trinity House in London which stated that the "Elder Brethren" (whoever they may be) had granted us permission "to visit St. Catherine's Light on the 19th April, 1952 for the purpose of observing bird migration." This we presented to the head lightkeeper, who showed us into the tower and up the winding steps to the lofty chambers where the huge rotating lenses magnified the relatively small light to something like 6,000,000 candle power. Formerly, the keeper told us, when the light boasted 15,000,000 candle power, the destruction of birds was much greater. In fact, he had seen no great numbers of birds on any night so far this season. We had timed our visit, however, to coincide with the absence of a moon which would otherwise illuminate the shore. A small front was due to arrive and the fair warm breezes from France would probably be blocked by cooler air. Conditions seemed right.

At eight o'clock the light went on and the long beams, revolving in a clockwise direction probed the increasing darkness. Although we knew it would take at least three hours for a small bird to make the channel crossing, we were impatient. We started our vigil at once. At 9:03 a swallow fluttered briefly before the lenses but, being normally a day migrant, it must have left the coast of France before dark. Shortly after 11:00 P.M. a fine rain descended in a silky drizzle across the bright beams of the light and the foghorn down toward "the needles" lowed like a lonely bull. Then we caught sight of our first real night migrant. Flickering and ghostly, it darted toward our high catwalk and swept over the top of the tower into the darkness. Soon another came in and another, like moths to a street lamp. During the next two hours there must have been hundreds. Several which came close enough to be caught in our hand-held clap nets proved to be white-throats (not like our American white-throats, but warblers with gray caps and white chins). We also caught two or three willow warblers—little olive-drab fellows which, incidentally, are the most numerous summer visitors to northern Europe. Another swallow was identified and one skylark. But this was the big night for white-throats—their mass arrival. At least 80 per cent of the birds were of this one species. Most got past the light safely and we ringed with little aluminum leg bands those few which fell to our nets. As they flew by, not a sound did they make (European night migrants are not as vocal as ours), and I was deeply impressed

130

with the silent drama that was taking place in this world of blackness, revolving white light and rain. Weighing less than an ounce, these tiny mites had crossed sixty to eighty miles of water by dead reckoning to be met by head winds, turbulence, and rains. So tired were they when we scooped them from the air that they closed their eyes and fell asleep in our hands. This was the second sea crossing they had made on their northward pilgrimage from Africa. They had crossed the much wider Mediterranean and some would continue on across the North Sea. We hand laurels to channel swimmers, yet every bird is a champion—an Olympic champion. It would not survive if it were anything less.

At one o'clock the stars came out, the shoreline was darkly visible against the lapping waves, and the birds no longer streamed in. I descended to the control room where I tried to get an hour's sleep on the cement floor while the huge grinding cogs rotated the ponderous lenses above. When I returned, refreshed, the mist had thickened again and a second great wave of birds was pouring in; a thousand birds, no less, must have passed during the night.

For some reason our American lighthouses—most of them, at any rate—do not seem to take the toll of tiny travelers that the European lights do. I believe there is a good reason for this. In the spring there is no really great movement of migrants up our Atlantic coastal plain other than those birds which nest there. The big waves from the tropics to Canada are up the Mississippi Valley and along the Appalachian ridges. In the autumn, however, when cold boreal winds from the Northwest blow across the lanes of travel many birds are drifted toward the coast, like swimmers in a strong current. It is then that they jam up at coastal points such as Cape May, Cape Charles, and Hatteras. Such a wind from the Northwest brings clear blue skies and starlit nights. It takes an easterly wind from the sea to bring the fogs which obscure the shoreline and cause bewildered birds to seek the beams which penetrate the mist and beckon them to their destruction. In short, the mists and the birds seldom coincide on our side of the Atlantic. On rare occasions there is a catastrophe such as the one which took the lives of 5,000 myrtle warblers at the Barnegat Light in New Jersey on a foggy autumn night some years ago. But these were undoubtedly the birds which normally wintered along the barrier islands. Myrtle warblers were decidedly scarce on the Barnegat strip for several years thereafter.

131

Europe, with its more complicated coastlines, is another matter. Some of the lighthouses along the channel, the North Sea, and in the Baltic, take a great toll of birds, so great that racks of perches have been erected about the huge lenses to give weary birds resting places.

In the old days of fixed beams the mortality was much greater. On some mornings the rocks below certain lighthouses would be littered with thousands of birds, from tiny gold-crests to large waders, dead and dying, to be devoured later by the ever-hungry jackdaws and gulls. The revolving beams of today are less lethal. However, some Europeans contend that many birds follow the revolving shafts of light round and round until they fall exhausted, but this is not so. The beams rotate faster than the birds can fly.

We were relieved to note that during our visit no birds killed themselves against the screen-covered glass. Under different wind conditions, when the eddies are strong, it might have been otherwise. Occasionally a bird rested momentarily on the perches which I calculated would accommodate two thousand birds. Some might have hit the unlit tower above where there were no perches. The keeper told us that the perches above had never been replaced after the war—after the day at the close of spring migration in 1945 when the racks were being stored for the season. A Nazi dive bomber, one of the last hit-and-run raiders, swooped across the channel, blew up the powerhouse and the shed where the perching racks were being stored and killed all three lightkeepers. As the first light of dawn streaked the sky our informant pointed out the spot where the tragedy occurred.

And now for the unexpected sequel to our all-night vigil. At dinnertime the following day Keith Shackleton called up so excited as to be almost breathless. After leaving us at Fairoaks he had flown to another airfield, Biggleswade (about one hundred miles north of the Isle of Wight). There, while taking the afternoon sun in a grassy meadow he noticed two little birds working down the hedge toward him. He focussed his binoculars on them. They were white-throats, both of them, and one wore a shiny new band!

(From *Audubon Magazine*)

H. GÄTKE

The Heligoland Light

Thirty miles off the German coast in the North Sea is Heligoland, a fortress island that has become synonymous with migration. Here the student of migration, Gätke, found unheard-of numbers of migrant birds, for this speck of land is just small enough, and just far enough from other landfalls, yet just close enough to the general stream of continental migration, to concentrate the maximum number of small travelers. There are other islands, such as Fair Isle off northern Scotland, which drain huge areas of the ocean of their wind-drifted strays, but Heligoland is the most famous of such islands. Gätke reported immense diurnal flights, climaxed by hundreds of thousands of starlings in a single October day, but our imagination is stirred more by his description of the mass assault upon the island at night.

WE MUST not omit to mention those nocturnal migration flights which, revealed by the light of the lighthouse, proceed on so stupendous a scale as to form one of the most characteristic and attractive phases of the whole phenomena of Migration as displayed on this island. They reach their grandest development during the later half of the month (October), especially towards its close. Predominating in numbers among these night travellers are the Skylarks; next come the Starlings and Thrushes, always accompanied by the many different forms of the great Snipe Family. Strange to say, the Golden-crested Wren occasionally, though rarely, makes its appearance in such migratory flights, as in the night from the 28th-29th October

133

1882, during which those tiny creatures swarmed round the lighthouse like so many snowflakes, while every square foot of the island literally teemed with them.

The landscape, which forms the background of so rich an unfolding of animal life, possesses in and for itself an extraordinary fascination. An equable calm dark night, without moon or stars, and attended by a very light south-east wind, are the conditions necessary for the grandest possible development of a migration of this nature; the presence in the atmosphere at the same time of a considerable quantity of moisture powerfully augments the intensity of the phenomena.

The darkness, equally dense on all sides, amid which the lighthouse appears to float like some great luminous body; the broad beams which radiate from it in all directions, and in the dim air seem to stretch into infinite space; the consciousness of the near presence of the great sea around, and the complete absence of every sound in surrounding Nature,—all these combine to form a picture of the utmost solemnity and grandeur.

This wide silence is first broken by the solitary low "Zeep" of the Song Thrush, and perhaps here and there the clear call-note of the Lark. Then again silence reigns for a minute or two, only to be once more suddenly broken by the far-sounding "Ghük" of the Blackbird, soon followed by the manifold "Tir-r-r" of a swiftly-passing flock of Sandpipers. The calls of the Skylark rapidly increase in number, smaller and larger flocks of the birds being heard approaching and disappearing near and far. The hoarse "Etsch" of the Snipe is accompanied by the clear "Tüth" of the Golden Plover, the clear, loud "Klü-üh" of the Grey Plover, the wild, far-sounding cry of the Curlew, the manifold "Schack-shack-shack" of the Fieldfare, the long-drawn "Zieh" of the Redwing. Next, by the sound of hundreds of rapidly-ejaculated cries, "Tütt-tütt--tütt-tütt--tütt-tütt," we recognise a long-extending swarm of Knots hastily pursuing its journey. . . .

The whole sky is now filled with a babel of hundreds of thousands of voices, and as we approach the lighthouse there presents itself to the eye a scene which more than confirms the experience of the ear. Under the intense glare of the light, swarms of Larks, Starlings, and Thrushes career around in ever-varying density, like showers of brilliant sparks or huge snowflakes driven onwards by a gale, and continuously replaced as they disappear by freshly arriving multitudes. Mingled with these birds are large numbers of Golden Plovers, Lap-

134

wings, Curlews, and Sandpipers. Now and again, too, a Woodcock is seen; or an Owl, with slow beatings of the wings, emerges from the darkness into the circle of light, but again speedily vanishes, accompanied by the plaintive cry of an unhappy Thrush that has become its prey.

(From *Heligoland as an Ornithological Observatory*)

IV *Glamour Birds*

G LAMOUR BIRDS," a useful term I think, usually suggests egrets and the other long-legged birds of Florida—the roseate spoonbill, the ibises and the flamingo—birds publicised by the National Audubon Society's campaigns of protection. But this is too narrow a category. To the dedicated bird watcher nearly every bird is glamourous, even Lincoln's sparrows and other plain little brown jobs.

Most glamourous of all are the birds we shall never see, the extinct ones. Until a few years ago many a mourning dove was transmogrified into a passenger pigeon, but finally *Ectopistes migratorius* has been allowed to remain extinct. But some of us still dream fitfully of Carolina paroquets. However, ten generations hence men will still see the endless aerial river of wild pigeons, hear the rush of their wings and witness their slaughter through the pages of Audubon's writings. They also will know the noisy flocks of paroquets and see them come into the fields of cockleburs through the careful prose of Alexander Wilson. A pity that the Labrador duck was denied similar immortality for lack of documentation by one of these able biographers.

For every ornithologist in Audubon's day there are now a thousand, and those birds which are close to the shadow of extinction—the ivory-billed woodpecker, California condor, and whooping crane—all have their Boswells. Each of these three species now has an exhaustive monograph to perpetuate its memory. In fact, the whooping crane, currently down to a scant two dozen individuals, has caught the imagination of the man in the street as no other bird has before. The press keeps us informed and should two cranes more or three cranes less make the journey from Wood Buffalo Park in Canada to their winter home in Texas it becomes national news.

These rarest of the rare are so carefully guarded that the average watcher can only hope—but never expect—to see them. In fact, no one knows exactly where the last ivory-bills are, if indeed they are still with us. The sixty condors in their mountain fortress in California are on restricted ground and so are most of the Texas whoopers.

139

But there still are more than 650 species north of the Mexican border for the watcher to see, and 450 in Europe. If he makes the world his province there are 8600. Many of these, a great many, have glamour, whether it be the awkward loon with its lightning dives and maniacal laughter, or the magnificent quetzal with emerald plumes.

What experience of my own do I remember most vividly—what was my most glamourous bird?

Was it the wall creeper that Charles Sibley and I found on a Swiss mountaintop? Or the herd of flamingos, watched from behind a dyke in the Camargue? Wonderful as they were, I think the pack of fourteen great bustards Guy Mountfort and I saw on the plains of Andalusia easily top them, but even they do not head the list.

Was it the whooping crane—the last of the Louisiana whoopers—that Bob Smith and I pursued by plane one New Year's Day? Or California condors riding the thermals over the Sespe? When I saw these it seemed as though I had been granted a glimpse of the Pleistocene.

Or was it the quetzal that Eddie Chalif and I found after long search in the cloud forest in Chiapas—the resplendent trogon whose plumes Cortez wore in his helmet when he subjugated Montezuma? Very nearly, but not quite.

Was it, then, the ivory-billed woodpecker? Yes. The last of the Louisiana ivory-bills, the two females that roamed the Singer Tract in 1941. I felt strangely as though I had stepped back a century into the boots of Audubon himself.

JOHN JAMES AUDUBON

The Passenger Pigeon

If we are to credit Audubon and Wilson, both of whom estimated single flights of passenger pigeons at more than 1,000,000,000, this one species must have made up a very large part of the entire population of North American birds. According to one authority, there were probably 5,000,-000,000 pigeons in the three states of Kentucky, Ohio, and Indiana alone. Compare my own estimate (1948) of between 5,000,000,000 and 6,000,-000,000 breeding land birds—*of all species* in the United States. Doctor Herbert Friedmann of the National Museum suggests that the wild pigeons may have kept down some of the other birds, for where the great flocks went they ate up all the food.

Note Audubon's closing remarks: "I have satisfied myself, by long observation, that nothing but the gradual diminution of our forests can accomplish their decrease." How wrong he was. Less than a century later, on September 1, 1914, the last survivor of these astronomical hordes died in the Cincinnati Zoo.

THE MULTITUDES of Wild Pigeons in our woods are astonishing. Indeed, after having viewed them so often, and under so many circumstances, I even now feel inclined to pause, and assure myself that what I am going to relate is fact. Yet I have seen it all, and that too in the company of persons who, like myself, were struck with amazement.

In the autumn of 1813, I left my house at Henderson, on the banks of the Ohio, on my way to Louisville. In passing over the Barrens a

141

few miles beyond Hardensburgh, I observed the pigeons flying from north-east to south-west, in greater numbers than I thought I had ever seen them before, and feeling an inclination to count the flocks that might pass within the reach of my eye in one hour, I dismounted, seated myself on an eminence, and began to mark with my pencil, making a dot for every flock that passed. In a short time finding the task which I had undertaken impracticable, as the birds poured in in countless multitudes, I rose, and counting the dots then put down, found that 163 had been made in twenty-one minutes. I travelled on, and still met more the farther I proceeded. The air was literally filled with Pigeons; the light of noon-day was obscured as by an eclipse; the dung fell in spots, not unlike melting flakes of snow; and the continued buzz of wings had a tendency to lull my senses to repose.

Whilst waiting for dinner at YOUNG's inn, at the confluence of Salt-River with the Ohio, I saw, at my leisure, immense legions still going by, with a front reaching far beyond the Ohio on the west, and the beech-wood forests directly on the east of me. . . . I cannot describe to you the extreme beauty of their aerial evolutions, when a Hawk chanced to press upon the rear of a flock. At once, like a torrent, and with a noise like thunder, they rushed into a compact mass, pressing upon each other towards the centre. In these almost solid masses, they darted forward in undulating and angular lines, descended and swept close over the earth with inconceivable velocity, mounted perpendicularly so as to resemble a vast column, and, when high, were seen wheeling and twisting within their continued lines, which then resembled the coils of a gigantic serpent.

Before sunset I reached Louisville, distant from Hardensburgh fifty-five miles. The Pigeons were still passing in undiminished numbers, and continued to do so for three days in succession. The people were all in arms. The banks of the Ohio were crowded with men and boys, incessantly shooting at the pilgrims, which there flew lower as they passed the river. Multitudes were thus destroyed. For a week or more, the population fed on no other flesh than that of Pigeons, and talked of nothing but Pigeons. The atmosphere, during this time, was strongly impregnated with the peculiar odour which emanates from the species.

It is extremely interesting to see flock after flock performing exactly the same evolutions which had been traced as it were in the air by a preceding flock. Thus, should a Hawk have charged on a group at a certain spot, the angles, curves, and undulations that have been described

142

by the birds, in their efforts to escape from the dreaded talons of the plunderer, are undeviatingly followed by the next group that comes up. . . .

It may not, perhaps, be out of place to attempt an estimate of the number of Pigeons contained in one of those mighty flocks, and of the quantity of food daily consumed by its members. The inquiry will tend to show the astonishing bounty of the great Author of Nature in providing for the wants of his creatures. Let us take a column of one mile in breadth, which is far below the average size, and suppose it passing over us without interruption for three hours, at the rate mentioned above of one mile in the minute. This will give us a parallelogram of 180 miles by 1, covering 180 square miles. Allowing two pigeons to the square yard, we have one billion, one hundred and fifteen millions, one hundred and thirty-six thousand pigeons in one flock. As every pigeon daily consumes fully half a pint of food, the quantity necessary for supplying this vast multitude must be eight millions seven hundred and twelve thousand bushels per day.

As soon as the Pigeons discover a sufficiency of food to entice them to alight, they fly round in circles, reviewing the country below. During their evolutions, on such occasions, the dense mass which they form exhibits a beautiful appearance, as it changes its direction, now displaying a glistening sheet of azure, when the backs of the birds come simultaneously into view, and anon, suddenly presenting a mass of rich deep purple. They then pass lower, over the woods, and for a moment are lost among the foliage, but again emerge, and are seen gliding aloft. They now alight, but the next moment, as if suddenly alarmed, they take to wing, producing by the flappings of their wings a noise like the roar of distant thunder, and sweep through the forests to see if danger is near. Hunger, however, soon brings them to the ground. When alighted, they are seen industriously throwing up the withered leaves in quest of the fallen mast. The rear ranks are continually rising, passing over the main-body, and alighting in front, in such rapid succession, that the whole flock seems still on wing. . . .

On such occasions, when the woods are filled with these Pigeons, they are killed in immense numbers, although no apparent diminution ensues. About the middle of the day, after their repast is finished, they settle on the trees, to enjoy rest, and digest their food. On the ground they walk with ease, as well as on the branches, frequently jerking their beautiful tail, and moving the neck backwards and forwards in the

143

most graceful manner. As the sun begins to sink beneath the horizon, they depart *en masse* for the roosting-place, which not unfrequently is hundreds of miles distant, as has been ascertained by persons who have kept an account of their arrivals and departures.

Let us now inspect their place of nightly rendezvous. One of these curious roosting-places, on the banks of the Green River in Kentucky, I repeatedly visited. It was, as is always the case, in a portion of the forest where the trees were of great magnitude, and where there was little underwood. I rode through it upwards of forty miles, and, crossing it in different parts, found its average breadth to be rather more than three miles. My first view of it was about a fortnight subsequent to the period when they had made choice of it, and I arrived there nearly two hours before sunset. Few Pigeons were then to be seen, but a great number of persons, with horses and wagons, guns and ammunition, had already established encampments on the borders. Two farmers from the vicinity of Russelsville, distant more than a hundred miles, had driven upwards of three hundred hogs to be fattened on the pigeons which were to be slaughtered. Here and there the people employed in plucking and salting what had already been procured, were seen sitting in the midst of large piles of these birds. The dung lay several inches deep, covering the whole extent of the roosting-place, like a bed of snow. Many trees two feet in diameter, I observed, were broken off at no great distance from the ground; and the branches of many of the largest and tallest had given way, as if the forest had been swept by a tornado. Every thing proved to me that the number of birds resorting to this part of the forest must be immense beyond conception. As the period of their arrival approached, their foes anxiously prepared to receive them. Some were furnished with iron-pots containing sulphur, others with torches of pine-knots, many with poles, and the rest with guns. The sun was lost to our view, yet not a Pigeon had arrived. Every thing was ready, and all eyes were gazing on the clear sky, which appeared in glimpses amidst the tall trees. Suddenly there burst forth a general cry of "Here they come!" The noise which they made, though yet distant, reminded me of a hard gale at sea, passing through the rigging of a close-reefed vessel. As the birds arrived and passed over me, I felt a current of air that surprised me. Thousands were soon knocked down by the pole-men. The birds continue to pour in. The fires were lighted, and a magnificent, as well as wonderful and almost terrifying, sight presented itself. The Pigeons, arriving by thousands,

144

alighted everywhere, one above another, until solid masses as large as hogsheads were formed on the branches all round. Here and there the perches gave way under the weight with a crash, and falling to the ground, destroyed hundreds of the birds beneath, forcing down the dense groups with which every stick was loaded. It was a scene of uproar and confusion. I found it quite useless to speak, or even to shout to those persons who were nearest to me. Even the reports of the guns were seldom heard, and I was made aware of the firing only by seeing the shooters reloading.

No one dared venture within the line of devastation. The hogs had been penned up in due time, the picking up of the dead and wounded being left for the next morning's employment. The Pigeons were constantly coming, and it was past midnight before I perceived a decrease in the number of those that arrived. The uproar continued the whole night; and as I was anxious to know to what distance the sound reached, I sent off a man, accustomed to perambulate the forest, who, returning two hours afterwards, informed me he had heard it distinctly when three miles distant from the spot. Towards the approach of day, the noise in some measure subsided, long before objects were distinguishable, the Pigeons began to move off in a direction quite different from that in which they had arrived the evening before, and at sunrise all that were able to fly had disappeared. The howlings of the wolves now reached our ears, and the foxes, lynxes, cougars, bears, raccoons, opossums and pole-cats were seen sneaking off, whilst eagles and hawks of different species, accompanied by a crowd of vultures, came to supplant them, and enjoy their share of the spoil.

It was then that the authors of all this devastation began their entry amongst the dead, the dying, and the mangled. The pigeons were picked up and piled in heaps, until each had as many as he could possibly dispose of, when the hogs were let loose to feed on the remainder.

Persons unacquainted with these birds might naturally conclude that such dreadful havock would soon put an end to the species. But I have satisfied myself, by long observation, that nothing but the gradual diminution of our forests can accomplish their decrease, as they not unfrequently quadruple their numbers yearly, and always at least double it.

(From *Ornithological Biography*)

ALEXANDER WILSON

Ivory-billed Woodpecker

Alexander Wilson, "Father of American Ornithology" and contemporary of
Audubon, started out as a minor poet. He knew nothing of ornithology.
After the failure of his third love affair he was persuaded by the Philadelphia naturalists William Bartram and George Ord to take up the study of
birds as an antidote to his melancholia. His career seems an exception to
the general rule that great ornithologists are born (or inspired by the age of
11), not made.

Although Wilson met Audubon in Louisville, Kentucky, one March day
in 1810, they did not get on well. It must have been a stunning blow for the
itinerant poet who had dedicated himself to portraying all the birds of the
American wilderness to find a back-country merchant whose drawings were
obviously superior to his own. Wilson lacked the flair of the Kentucky
woodsman, but his writing was more dependable, free of Audubon's ebul-
lient blunders.

During his travels he carried on his shoulder a live Carolina paroquet, a
bird now extinct. He tried to make a similar pet of an ivory-billed woodpecker, but with no success.

IN LOOKING over the accounts given of the ivory-billed
woodpecker by the naturalists of Europe, I find it asserted, that it in-
habits from New Jersey to Mexico. I believe, however, that few of
them are ever seen to the north of Virginia, and very few of them even
in that state. The first place I observed this bird at, when on my way
to the south, was about twelve miles north of Wilmington in North
Carolina. There I found the bird from which the drawing of the figure
in the plate was taken. This bird was only wounded slightly in the wing,

146

and, on being caught, uttered a loudly reiterated, and most piteous note, exactly resembling the violent crying of a young child; which terrified my horse so, as nearly to have cost me my life. It was distressing to hear it. I carried it with me in the chair, under cover, to Wilmington. In passing through the streets, its affecting cries surprised every one within hearing, particularly the females, who hurried to the doors and windows with looks of alarm and anxiety. I drove on, and, on arriving at the piazza of the hotel, where I intended to put up, the landlord came forward, and a number of other persons who happened to be there, all equally alarmed at what they heard; this was greatly increased by my asking, whether he could furnish me with accommodations for myself and my baby. The man looked blank and foolish, while the others stared with still greater astonishment. After diverting myself for a minute or two at their expense, I drew my Woodpecker from under the cover, and a general laugh took place. I took him up stairs and locked him up in my room, while I went to see my horse taken care of. In less than an hour I returned, and, on opening the door, he set up the same distressing shout, which now appeared to proceed from grief that he had been discovered in his attempts at escape. He had mounted along the side of the window, nearly as high as the ceiling, a little below which he had begun to break through. The bed was covered with large pieces of plaster; the lath was exposed for at least fifteen inches square, and a hole, large enough to admit the fist, opened to the weather-boards; so that, in less than another hour he would certainly have succeeded in making his way through. I now tied a string round his leg, and, fastening it to the table, again left him. I wished to preserve his life, and had gone off in search of suitable food for him. As I reascended the stairs, I heard him again hard at work, and on entering had the mortification to perceive that he had almost entirely ruined the mahogany table to which he was fastened, and on which he had wreaked his whole vengeance. While engaged in taking the drawing, he cut me severely in several places, and, on the whole, displayed such a noble and unconquerable spirit, that I was frequently tempted to restore him to his native woods. He lived with me nearly three days, but refused all sustenance, and I witnessed his death with regret.

(From *American Ornithology*)

147

PAUL BARTSCH

A Pet Carolina Paroquet

Dr. Paul Bartsch, now well along in his eighties, is a living link with the great naturalists of the old school—Ridgway, Coues, Mearns, and the others—who built the framework of American ornithology after Audubon and Wilson had laid its foundations. Although Bartsch's great field is mollusks (he is one of our two foremost authorities) he can rightfully be called the father of modern bird banding. Nearly a hundred years had elapsed since Audubon placed the silver wires on the legs of nestling phoebes beside the Perkiomen when, in 1902, Bartsch ringed twenty-three night herons in the District of Columbia with sections of aluminum tubing bearing the inscription "Return to Smithsonian Institution." At least eight million American birds have been banded since that historic experiment.

During his lifetime Paul Bartsch has seen the passing of three or four North American birds into the void of extinction. He must have been one of the last to see a live Carolina paroquet—his own pet—which died in 1914, the year the last captive passenger pigeon died. There are only two accredited records in the literature of wild paroquets seen after this date.

D OODLES WAS the son of Jack and Jackness, a pair of Carolina paroquets. We had first christened him Jackanapes, and how that came to be perverted to Doodles is a mystery to me even now.

Mr. Robert Ridgway, the famous ornithologist, on his collecting trip to Florida in 1896 brought home the parent birds, which he housed in

148

a cage at his home. They rewarded him by setting up housekeeping and producing a family.

When I came to Washington to work in the Division of Mollusks in 1896 my office occupied the southeast balcony of the main hall of the Smithsonian Institution while Mr. Ridgway and Mr. Charles W. Richmond, his assistant, and the Division of Birds were housed in the southwest balcony.

In 1902 Mr. Ridgway came to our gallery and said, "Bartsch, how would you like a Carolina paroquet?" I replied, "Shame to tease me so cruelly." But said he, "I mean it. My paroquets are neglecting one of their young and the poor fellow will die if he hasn't some one to take care of him." (Mrs. Ridgway was on a visit in Illinois at the time. Had she been home Doodles would not have become a member of our household.)

Doodles was in poor shape, a neglected mite who had been cast out by his parents. So I had to tease him to open his bill to accept soft food, bread soaked in milk, bits of meat and many things as well as water. It was then and there that he adopted me as a parent. While he also displayed affection for Mrs. Bartsch, there never was a question as to who was his favorite. Within two days I persuaded him to use the pecking method to pick up food and shift for himself.

Doodles was a member of the family and like the other members had the run of the house. He shared our meals, was well behaved, and stuck to his own plate almost always.

He was a mischief, and rings and pins with stone settings were irresistible objects to him. I am confident that no jeweler could have competed with him in the speedy removal of a setting. Such things had to be kept under cover. His favorite perch was the top of a door, and from such a vantage point he would sally forth to a bureau top in quest of gems. If I shouted, "DOODLES!" he would return to his perch and croon and talk paroquet fashion (Doodles never learned to use English) until he thought I had forgotten his sally. He might fly to the floor and amble in his pigeon-toed way, steadily heading back for the bureau, and slyly climb to the top only to be intercepted with another "DOODLES!" which usually caused him to return to his door perch. Doodles enjoyed playing with marbles and would roll them over the floor and chase them about. He also enjoyed being petted and frequently came to me practically asking to be mussed up.

149

For sleeping quarters he selected the furnace room, which contained the furnace, coal bin and many odds and ends. He probably chose that because it was a little warmer at all times than the rest of the rooms. His favorite daytime habitat was the window in the dining room facing the street, which gave him a conspicuous perch from which to watch the passersby.

In the morning Doodles would fly up two flights of stairs, come to my room, fly up on my bed, push his pointed tail down under the covers near my neck, place his cheek against mine, purr for a while and then take a nap with me. And woe betide anyone who would dare disturb us.

Several times Doodles managed to get out. He seemed fascinated with the pigeons that frequented the neighborhood and tried his best to be friends with them. But the pigeons would have none of his company. As the bunch flew away he would give pursuit, and he could outfly them. Fortunately they always returned to the neighborhood and I was eventually able to recover him by climbing out of windows on roofs in pursuit until he finally grew weary of the new sport and waited for me to gather him in. Later, when he was on such escapades, I would whistle the bob-white assembly call and he would answer in his own language and come to my hand.

One big scare he gave me was on an occasion when Mrs. Bartsch was sick in the hospital, and I returned home late, called to Doodles, and received no reply. I turned over every thing in the furnace room thinking that he might have fallen down, as he sometimes did when he missed his perch, and had hidden away shamedly. No Doodles! Then my heart sank with fear—did the little red squirrel which was also a pet kill him and drag him into his lair? Looking for the squirrel's quarters, I found that one of a group of empty trays stacked upside down had a hole in its side. Shaking this caused the squirrel to pop out, followed slowly by Doodles, who had wanted companionship and had gone to sleep with the squirrel.

I might continue to tell stories about Doodles, but perhaps these are enough to show what a wonderful companion the only known real pet Carolina paroquet was.

It only remains to say that Doodles followed the pattern set by his parents in Mr. Ridgway's cage. Mr. Ridgway believed that something had frightened them and scared them to death. I do not believe so, for Doodles had several strokes of apoplexy before his final demise. In his

150

final passing he dropped from his favored perch on the top of a door, and when he was picked up and held gently, slowly closed his eyes and stiffened. Thus passed one of the last members of his species.

(From *Atlantic Naturalist*)

HENRY BEETLE HOUGH

A Bird That Man Could Kill

Somewhere in the brushlands of Martha's Vineyard in the fall of 1931 the last heath hen lived out its life.

In efforts to save this seaboard race of the prairie chicken at least $100,-000 had been spent, $70,000 by the Massachusetts Department of Conservation alone. This relict colony of the Vineyard was built up from less than a hundred at the beginning of the century to about two thousand in 1916. Then in May a great fire swept the island, burning the brooding birds and reducing the population to a hundred and fifty, mostly males. Hard winters, interbreeding, and finally poultry disease brought the number down to thirteen by 1927; the following fall only two birds were seen and by December only one. This lone bird, intensively watched, survived three years more before it too disappeared.

The following editorial which appeared in the Vineyard Gazette on April 21, 1933, is an eloquent statement of the meaning of extinction.

Now we know there are degrees even in death. All around us nature is full of casualties, but they do not interrupt the stream of life. When most living things die, they seem only to revert to the central theme of existence from which they were temporarily detached. There is a spirit of vitality everywhere which enfolds the dead with a countenance of consolation, and bestows upon the living races more than has been taken away. But to the heath hen something more than death has happened, or, rather, a different kind of death. There is

152

no survivor, there is no future, there is no life to be recreated in this form again. We are looking upon the uttermost finality which can be written, glimpsing the darkness which will not know another ray of light. We are in touch with the reality of extinction.

It is written in scientific works that the heath hen had ceased long ago to be of economic importance, and that it could never have been of economic importance again. It follows, therefore, that preservation of this bird was a matter of sentiment alone, since between economic usefulness and sentiment our world knows no middle ground. The heath hen was a curious creature, an actor out of place, surviving beyond its appointed days, simply because there happened to be a bit of scenery fortuitously at hand for the playing of a last dramatic act and a sentimental epilogue. The bird we are speaking of was the prairie chicken of the east, and the contradiction in terms is clear, for where in the east is there a prairie, or any suitable environment for a bird not of the forest nor of the sea nor of the air, but of the open range? By chance there is a great plain on Martha's Vineyard, and despite the fact that the island is relatively small, it has never been considered amiss to speak of the vastness of this great plain of scrub oak, sweet fern, alder, blasted pine—and of the heath hen. Here, then, in sound of the roaring surf, amid such great and monotonous distances all encompassed in small space, the prairie chicken of the east lived a century beyond its time and then died, a single specimen making an end of the race, somewhere alone in the brush.

The heath hen failed to adapt to changing conditions and fell a victim to the laws of natural selection. This is a curious thing, for until the white men took over the land, the heath hen had achieved an admirable adaptation, embodying such fine distinctions of nature that scientists appreciate their nicety and would like to understand them better. Even if you knew where a heath hen was, against a background of twigs and brush, you could not see it unless it moved. Failed to adapt! Why, no creature was ever more at home, more nicely adjusted to place and time than the heath hen on the Vineyard plains! The whole trouble lay in the fact that the heath hen was a bird man could kill, and so it had to die. A wild bird in a thicket and a man in a house cannot be neighbors, for cats will be turned loose and forced to forage, fire will burn over the landscape time and time again, and there are even diseases of the domestic poultry yard to menace wild things.

In recent years an impression has gone forth that man has learned

153

to withhold his hand and to let things about him grow and multiply. The gospel of conservation, it is said, has won the day. We know this is not true. May the death of the heath hen serve to bring us nearer a time of realization and fulfillment! Until now, saving only the imperious grace of economic importance and sometimes not even that, a creature that man could kill has had to die.

Is nothing to follow the extinction of this bird except one more lesson in conservation for school books, and a sentimental mourning? On the Vineyard, certainly, there is more. What an awe and fascination have been written into the theses of scientific men who came to observe the heath hen on the great plain! What accents of mystery, beauty and the eternal rites of life the heath hen, in spring, has given to this strange region! At first sight a visitor has thought the seemingly limit-less miles of plain both dreary and uninteresting. But not for long. The most prosaic scientist, full of a passion for metric measurements of feathers or Latin labels, has lain among the black scrub oak in the white mists of a chill April morning, and has returned to write poetry. The meticulous observations and Latin terms appear modestly, softened by a cloak of mystery. We read of birds appearing "as if by magic." We are told that the call of the heath hen did not rise or fall, but "ended in the air like a Scotch ballad." And a naturalist who is also a writer has heard in the peeping of the pinkletinks the voice of Ariel, and in the witch dances and goblin cries of the heath hen the grosser spirits of the island.

And so it is that the extinction of the heath hen has taken away part of the magic of the Vineyard. This is the added loss of the island. There is a void in the April dawn, there is an expectancy unanswered, there is a tryst not kept. Not until the great plain has grown again a forest of tall pines and cedars, such as that which wooded the level acres a few centuries ago, will the loss of the heath hen be forgotten. One turns to Prospero's promise that he will abjure his charms:

> ". . . I'll break my staff,
> Bury it certain fathoms in the earth,
> And, deeper than did ever plummet sound,
> I'll drown my book,"

So deeply, so irrevocably is part of the island's magic buried and drowned; so before our eyes is Prospero's promise perversely carried out.   (From *Vineyard Gazette*)

CARL KOFORD

Condors Feeding

America's third rarest bird (and its largest) is no longer as accessible as it was in 1936 when I first visited its stronghold in the Séspé Range forty miles north of Los Angeles. There are still about the same number of California condors that there were then—about fifty or sixty. That is the belief of Carl Koford, who spent three years living in caves and camps in the back country while studying this giant relict of the Pleistocene. But the reason that the bird is no longer as accessible is because the Séspé country has been declared a refuge—forbidden ground, even to the field glass fraternity. In Koford's monograph (Research Report No. 4, of the National Audubon Society) he describes the feeding habits of the condor.

W<small>HEN A</small> group of condors appears to be foraging, they scatter in various directions over a large area and occasionally gather in small groups or, more rarely, in one big group. These groups soon break up and the birds scatter again. Often a single bird flies straight to a circling group. The whole action suggests that condors are aware of one another and that they may find food by cooperative effort. . . .

Fighting, chasing, and other evidences of social dominance are more common near carcasses than near roosts or water. One condor often gives way to another at a choice portion of a carcass. On the ground immature condors may be chased by adults, but I did not observe the reverse. Adults chase other adults but immatures chase only immatures, frequently chasing those which are obviously younger. Rather

155

than one bird trying to keep all others from the food, the attacking bird seems to dislike certain individuals and pursues them. One condor may walk 50 or even 100 feet away from a group at a carcass in order to chase another. Once I saw an adult walk 30 feet from a carcass toward a standing group of six. Half of the group started away when the attacker arrived several feet from them. The attacker, wings flapping and neck outstretched, ran at one bird. This bird then jumped, flapping, into the air and the pursuer reached up toward the flying bird with its bill.

Some chases on the ground continue for 10 or 20 yards including one or two sharp turns. Often the chase continues into the air. The pursued bird may commence walking back toward the carcass as soon as the attack ceases. Immatures are especially persistent in returning. Most encounters result in no actual contact. However, John Storer told me that he saw two adults fight vigorously near a carcass, one hanging onto the skin of the neck of the other with its bill, and both kicking, flapping, and rolling on the ground.

The feeding of a large group of condors in a vigorous scramble is not their usual method. When this action occurs, the birds are especially hungry or the carcass is particularly choice. Generally an eagle or coyote has kept the condors from the carcass for an hour or more. Pemberton photographed 30 condors feeding on a single sheep in Cuyama Valley on October 8, 1938. His helpers had toured the vicinity and picked up all the carcasses except Pemberton's bait. An eagle kept the condors from feeding for most of the day but it was finally crowded off the sheep by 14 condors. I watched a flock of 28 condors feed all at once on a deer carcass. A pair of eagles kept the condors from the carcass until late afternoon. Then the eagles departed and the condors commenced to feed. Adults and young mixed in the melee as the struggling and flapping group of condors moved down the slope at a steady rate. Occasionally one which had been crowded away from the carcass walked around the group as if looking for an opening and then rushed in again.

When one of a feeding group jerks a scapula or other large piece from a carcass, this bird may scramble away followed by several others. A few then feed on the separated part, sometimes having a brisk tug of war. These actions explain the numerous feathers and scattered bones which mark the route along which a carcass is dragged.

(From *The California Condor Report*)

157

WILLIAM BARTRAM

King Vulture

Just before the American Revolution, in 1774 and 1775, the wandering botanist, William Bartram of Philadelphia, was roaming the Florida wilderness. No one knows exactly where he encountered the king vulture, but it is quite certain that he knew the bird; his detailed description leaves no doubt of it. Although he believed it to be new to science, Linnaeus had already described it, presumably from Mexico, in 1758. Another new vulture, first mentioned by Bartram, turned out to be the black vulture, and he is given credit for its discovery in the A.O.U. check-list. No mention, however, is made of his rarer find in the fourth edition (1931), even in the hypothetical list, but the new check-list (fifth edition) will give him belated acknowledgment.

Plainly this spectacular scavenger disappeared early from the American scene and today there is evidence of a further decline in tropical Mexico. Recently, while on a camping trip in southern Vera Cruz, we looked in vain for its white figure among the high wheeling black and turkey vultures.

THERE ARE two species of vultures in these regions, I think not mentioned in history: the first we shall describe is a beautiful bird, near the size of a turkey buzzard, but his wings are much shorter, and consequently he falls greatly below that admirable bird in sail. I shall call this bird the painted vulture. The bill is long and straight almost to the point, when it is hooked or bent suddenly down and sharp; the head and neck bare of feathers nearly down to the stomach, when the feathers begin to cover the skin, and soon become long and of a soft texture,

158

forming a ruff or tippet, in which the bird by contracting his neck can hide that as well as his head; the bare skin on the neck appears loose and wrinkled, and is of a deep bright yellow colour, intermixed with coral red; the hinder part of the neck is nearly covered with short, stiff hair; and the skin of this part of the neck is of a dun-purple colour, gradually becoming red as it approaches the yellow of the sides and fore part. The crown of the head is red; there are lobed lappets of a reddish orange colour, which lie on the base of the upper mandible. But what is singular, a large portion of the stomach hangs down on the breast of the bird, in the likeness of a sack or half wallet, and seems to be a duplicature of the craw, which is naked and of a reddish flesh colour; this is partly concealed by the feathers of the breast, unless when it is loaded with food (which is commonly, I believe, roasted reptiles), and then it appears prominent. The plumage of the bird is generally white or cream colour, except the quill-feathers of the wings and two or three rows of the coverts, which are of a beautiful dark brown; the tail, which is large and white, is tipped with this dark brown or black; the legs and feet of a clear white; the eye is encircled with a gold coloured iris; the pupil black.

The Creeks or Muscogulges construct their royal standard of the tail feather of this bird, which is called by a name signifying the eagle's tail: this they carry with them when they go to battle, but then it is painted with a zone of red within the brown tips; and in peaceable negotiations it is displayed new, clean, and white: this standard is held most sacred by them on all occasions, and is constructed and ornamented with great ingenuity. These birds seldom appear but when the deserts are set on fire (which happens almost every day throughout the year, in some part or other, by the Indians, for the purpose of rousing the game, as also by the lightning): when they are seen at a distance soaring on the wing, gathering from every quarter, and gradually approaching the burnt plains, where they alight upon the ground yet smoking with hot embers: they gather up the roasted serpents, frogs, and lizards, filling their sacks with them: at this time a person may shoot them at pleasure, they not being willing to quit the feast, and indeed seeming to brave all danger.

(From William Bartram's *Travels*)

ROBERT PORTER ALLEN

Upflight of the
Spoonbills

Robert Porter Allen knows more about the long-legged waders than any other man in the world. Thirty years of association with the National Audubon Society, first as sanctuary director, later as research associate, have given him an intimacy with herons (and the other birds which look vaguely like herons) which no other ornithologist can match. A behaviorist as well as an ecologist, his first serious investigation, made simply to satisfy his own curiosity, was the breeding behavior of the black-crowned night heron. This project was carried out in a cedar grove rookery not far from his home on the south shore of Long Island. I remember, with amusement, the gaudily painted wooden blocks with which he tested the birds' visual responses. The birds accepted these "eggs" in place of their own (providing they were in the right place) and even brooded square ones! Better known than his early night heron studies are Bob Allen's research assignments for the National Audubon Society. Three arduous years in the field preceded the publication of each of his now famous monographs: *The Roseate Spoonbill, The Whooping Crane,* and *The Flamingos.*

I N THE shallow waters on the far side of the island stood rows of pink birds, motionless against the coffee-colored bay—coffee with cream in it. The light breeze ruffled wing coverts here and there, but the birds themselves seemed scarcely animate. They looked like painted lawn ornaments lined up for inventory. Or improbable char-

160

acters in a new *Alice* that had been set to ballet music by Stravinsky. In spite of the warm April sun and the shrill, earthy whistles of the great-tailed grackles, the scene was drowsily unreal. I looked down the rows of pink birds and thought, "Take an attitude not too stately" . . . what was the rest of it? "Still . . . still sufficiently dignified." What in the world was that from?

A reddish egret a few feet in front of the opening in my blind bristled his stiff, mane-like head and neck feathers and scolded an unabashed grackle that had darted close to his favorite thorny perch. In the fresh blue sky the clouds were small and fragile and their motion was like feather down. Across the low, brushy mainland, a mile to the north, a vague heat haze was beginning to form long, indistinct lines that wavered like visible ribbons of sound. The Spoonbills faced the breeze, which was from the south, a soft breeze from the wild, scrubby sands of Matagorda Island and the open Gulf out beyond. Row upon row of Spoonbills. From east to west there were sixteen in the first row, facing south; twenty-one in the second row; eighteen in the third. I counted almost one hundred Spoonbills and there were more beyond the heavy brush to my left, probably many more. And they all appeared to be exactly alike, all colored the same pinks and carmines and saffron yellows; greenish heads, broad, incredible-looking bills. All were facing the same direction, all in the same posture and position, each bird seemingly an exact counterpart of all the others.

But I knew that this was an illusion of the moment, a picture of the mind. For here before me was a flock made up of males and females, more or less evenly divided by an imponderable and provident Nature. Here were the beginnings and the endings, the vital fluids and fibres, the hidden purposes and destinies of the Spoonbill race. When the rhythm of heredity, like a great clock, struck the hour and ticked off each successively requisite minute, these astounding creatures would move unfalteringly into the drama that was their own individual part of the Universe. Theirs and only theirs. No one had ever observed this spectacle; there were countless difficulties and numberless barriers in the way of any except the most fortunate and determined observer. It was as if a creature of such extraordinary beauty was more perfectly guarded than most wild things from the prying eyes of casual, disinterested Man. I suffered once more from the feeling that I was an interloper, an intruder. That my presence was a desecration. This may seem very foolish but I assure you that it did not seem so to me, there under

161

the strange spell of that ageless and definitely awesome scene. If I had not had a responsibility to an employer, as well as a family to feed, I might have responded to an almost irresistible urge to step quietly away, replete with unspoken and somewhat mystic wisdom, perhaps, but no wiser by a whit in matters of Science.

This experience taught me that scientists may not look it but they are, of necessity, a very hard-boiled lot. As I continued my vigil I did my best to think and act and to be, in fact and in deed, as hard-boiled as possible!

But like most spells this one shortly ran its course. One can become extremely realistic on an empty stomach and, after several hours, with hunger came impatience and then exasperation, both rather down-to-earth emotions. For more than an hour there had been a subtle change taking place in the silently gathered flock, a shifting and withdrawing of row upon row, until only four Spoonbills were visible. The others, I thought with growing impatience, were still on the oyster shoal, but out of sight beyond the brush of the adjacent island. They won't *do* anything, I grumbled, and now they won't even stay in view.

In this mood I was less intent than I had been through the morning hours, so that the explosion that took place, without warning, was more startling than it might have been earlier. It wasn't a powder explosion but it might as well have been. It shook me quite as much. Actually, it was an eruption of the entire pink flock, a mass ascent, three hundred pairs of pink and carmine wings. The sound was indescribable, overpowering. It was like a blow between the eyes and I was literally stunned by it. The great flock swept before me in a mad rush of swishing, flashing wings, outstretched necks and heads, rigid legs. In an instant the visible world was filled with a confused, careening mass of pink birds; in another the roar of sound had ceased, the hurtling bodies, the confusion of wings had disappeared.

As I flopped about on all fours awkwardly trying to get my head outside the blind the flock suddenly rose again, from a reef not one hundred yards away, and sailed by, almost without sound, ghostly, baffling, unbelievable! When they settled down a half minute later, they were farther to the north and completely beyond my range of vision. I lay back on the ground cloth exhausted and bewildered! Again I felt the urge to quit the whole thing, but as I tried to think clearly of just what had happened I recalled a vaguely similar behavior on the part of the less spectacular but distantly related night herons I

162

had watched some seasons before. I remembered the herons gathering in compact and apparently irresolute flocks just prior to pairing off. Instead of an exposed oyster bar they had sought the budding upper branches of maple trees on the edge of the Long Island cedar swamp in which they were subsequently to nest. And without explanation that entire flock had risen *en masse* and moved headlong into another group of maples a half mile away. Eventually one of these bewildering moves had landed them in the heart of the cedar swamp and the next thing we knew the mystic rites of the pairing ceremony were under way. Taking courage from these thoughts, I smiled grimly (or perhaps it was sheepishly) and sat down once more to the business of watching.

What I had witnessed was indeed the beginning of the Spoonbill's complex reproductive cycle. Subsequently I termed this explosive behaviorism an *up-flight,* and what may be a similar outburst has been described by Kirkman for the black-headed gulls that he observed at Scoulton Mere and Twigmoor in England. The night heron flights were far less spectacular than those of the Spoonbills, but, like them, resulted from no visible stimuli. As a spectacle these up-flights are one of the most thrilling sights in all Nature, a vivid and breath-taking ritual that would be magnificent in any large bird. With the Roseate Spoonbill as the principal, it is a drama of unequalled beauty.

(From *The Flame Birds*)

163

FRANK M. CHAPMAN

Flamingos of Andros

In one of the upper hallways (now closed) of the American Museum of Natural History there is a diorama of a flamingo colony, an exhibit prepared by Frank M. Chapman after his historic expedition to Andros in the Bahamas in 1904. The great Andros rookery, denied protection during the war years, exists no longer. Robert Porter Allen in his Flamingo Report (Research Report No. 5 of the National Audubon Society) is of the opinion that five unsuccessful nesting seasons in succession mean *finis* to a flamingo colony.

In natural history museums around the world the "habitat group" is today the standard way of presenting animals and plants to the public. These dioramas, a deceptive amalgamation of painted background and carefully reproduced plant and animal material which draws upon the skills of a team of artists, taxidermists, carpenters, metalworkers, masons, electricians, and other preparateurs, have reached their highest development in the American Museum. To Dr. Chapman, who for many years was curator of birds at that great museum, is given the credit for devising the first habitat groups half a century ago. Although dedicated to the science of ornithology he had a flair for elucidation and his eleven books have enjoyed a sale of more than 250,000 copies. Younger readers of *Audubon Magazine* perhaps do not know that the name of the magazine originally was *Bird Lore* and that Dr. Chapman was both editor and owner. More than any other ornithologist of his time he spread the gospel of bird watching.

For THE first time since leaving Florida, wind and tide favored us. A distance which, on a former voyage, had consumed four days was now covered in one, and the next morning we reached the nearest point to which the schooner could approach the rookery. Peter's assurance that it was "not too berry far, sir," to the Flamingos, convinced us, in the light of past experiences, that they were distant at least ten miles, possibly more. . . .

Without loss of time, our outfit was embarked in the schooner's two boats which, with two of the crew and Peter, we rowed or poled against the wind, and dragged over muddy shoals and marly bars hour after hour, until, though coming from the west, we arrived at an islet of large mangroves, occupied by Reddish Egrets and Louisiana Herons, which I recognized as a landmark we had reached from the eastern side of the island in 1902. Though no chart showed the route, it was evident, therefore, that Andros could here be crossed from east to west. Still we continued and when after a trying day's work Peter said we were "there," we had no feeling of having arrived anywhere. All day we had been following broad, shallow creeks, which, meeting other creeks, widened at intervals into lagoons, while, on every side, the country spread away into the low, flat swash, neither land nor water and wholly worthless for everything—except Flamingos. So, when Peter announced that our journey was ended, we looked over this hopeless country in search of a camp-site, to find that the narrow, somewhat sandy shore of the creek was the only available place where one might pitch a tent. At the moment, however, we were more concerned about Flamingos than with the details of camping. When for the second time I asked Peter, "But where are the birds?" he replied, "Dere dey are, sir," and pointed across the swash to a thin pink line, distant at least a mile, but showing plainly against the green of the mangroves. Flamingos, surely; but were they nesting? We lost no time in speculation but started at once to investigate. Ten minutes wading through the mud and shallow water, brought us so near the now much enlarged pink streak that, with a glass, the birds could be seen unmistakably seated on their conical nests, and with an utterly indescribable feeling of exultation, we advanced rapidly to view at short range this wonder of wonders in bird-life.

165

At a distance of about three hundred yards, the wind being from us, toward the birds, we first heard their honking notes of alarm, which increased to a wave of deep sound. Soon the birds began to rise, standing on their nests, facing the wind and waving their black, vermillion-lined wings. As we came a little nearer, in stately fashion the birds began to move; uniformly, like a great body of troops, they stepped slowly forward, pinions waving and trumpets sounding, and then, when we were still one hundred and fifty yards away, the leaders sprang into the air. File after file of the winged host followed. The very earth seemed to erupt birds, as flaming masses streamed heavenward. It was an appalling sight. One of the boatmen said, it looked "like hell," and the description is apt enough to be set down without impropriety.

The birds were now all in the air. At the time, I should have said that there were at least four thousand of them, but a subsequent census of nests showed that this number should be halved. This was a tense moment. Knowing, through many disappointing experiences, how excessively shy Flamingos are, I feared that even the lately aroused parental instinct might not be sufficient to hold them to their homes and that, after all, I should be denied the fruits of victory,—the privilege of studying these birds on their nesting ground. Imagine, then, a relief I cannot describe, when the birds, after flying only a short distance to windward, turned abruptly and with set wings sailed over us, a rushing, fiery cloud, to alight in a lagoon bordering the western edge of the rookery.

Soon we were among the apparently innumerable, close-set mud nests each with its single white egg, while two held newly hatched Flamingos! Not only were these the first young Flamingos ever seen in the nest by a naturalist, but their presence was an assurance that this rookery was not composed of the birds whose homes had been flooded by the storm of May 17, but another colony and one which had not suffered a similar catastrophe. I should not therefore have to wait at least three weeks for the eggs to hatch, but had arrived at the most favorable period it would have been possible to select.

While we were standing, half dazed by the whole experience, the army of birds which had gathered in the lagoon rose, and with harsh honkings bore down on us. The action was startling. The birds in close array came toward us without a waver, and for a few moments one might well have believed they were about to attack; but with a mighty

166

roar of wings and clanging of horns, they passed overhead, turned, and on set wings again shot back to the lagoon.

On every one of the hundreds of occasions when, in fancy, I had entered a city of Flamingos, I had devised some plan for a place of concealment from which the birds might be observed and photographed. Should they occupy a site on a flat far from vegetation, similar to that of the abandoned rookery visited in 1902, I had proposed to sink a barrel in the marl, fringing it about with small mangroves; but should the growth be near enough, I had decided to place my umbrella-blind in the bushes. But the sight of the birds over the swash, as we landed, had banished from my mind every thought but the desire to know whether they were nesting; the blind was forgotten, and fearing now to keep them too long from their homes, I erected around a small bush, some thirty feet from the border of the rookery, a shield of branches behind which the blind might be placed the following day.

We now returned to the boats, seeing, with immense satisfaction, the Flamingos go back to their nests when we were but half across the swash. The claim had been located; it promised nuggets at every step, and our next move was to prepare to work it. I have never camped in a less suitable place, but if we had been beneath hemlocks with a dashing mountain stream at our threshhold, we could not have pitched our tent more cheerfully. At once it was discovered that the sand barely covered the limestone. To drive a tent-pin effectively was out of the question, and our tent was stayed to roots and bushes and to one of the boats, which was hauled ashore to windward, as an anchor for both tent and fly. Incidentally, it proved a capital tank. The daily rains (we had over twenty inches during the month) soon filled it, and beyond a few gallons brought from the schooner, it proved the only and an unlimited supply of fresh water during the eight days we were in camp.

The prospects of the morrow were fatal to sleep, and at an early hour preparations were made for the second invasion of the rookery. As with blind and cameras we now approached, the birds left their nests with the same orderly sequence of movement shown the preceding afternoon, gathering in a densely massed flock in the lagoon. The blind was quickly set in the place arranged for it, and hung with mangrove branches and palmetto leaves. I entered it and Mrs. Chapman at once started for camp.

This was a moment of supreme interest. Would the birds return to

167

their nests, the nearest of which were about thirty feet from me, or would the blind arouse their suspicions? Twice they rose in a body and swept over the rookery, each time alighting again in the lagoon. It was a reconnaissance in force, with evidently satisfactory results. No signs of danger were detected in the rookery, and, in the absence of ability to count, the retreat of one figure across the swash was as reassuring as the approach of two figures had been alarming.

Without further delay, the birds returned to their homes. They came on *foot,* a great red cohort, marching steadily toward me. I felt like a spy in an enemy's camp. Might not at least one pair of the nearly four thousand eyes detect something unnatural in the newly grown bush almost within their city gates? No sign of alarm, however, was shown; without confusion, and as if trained to the evolution, the birds advanced with stately tread to their nests. There was a bowing of a forest of slender necks as each bird lightly touched its egg or nest with its bill; then, all talking loudly, they stood up on their nests; the black wings were waved for a moment, and bird after bird dropped forward upon its egg. After a vigorous, wriggling motion, designed evidently to bring the egg into close contact with the skin, the body was still, but the long neck and head were for a time in constant motion, preening, picking material at the base of the nest, dabbling in a near-by puddle, or perhaps drinking from it. Occasionally a bird sparred with one of the three or four neighbors which were within reach, when, bill grasping bill, there ensued a brief and harmless test of strength.

In some instances a bird was seen adding to a nest in which an egg had already been deposited. Standing on the nest, it would drag up mud from the base with its bill, which was then used to press the fresh material into place. The feet were also of service in treading down the soft, marly clay.

The nests at this side of the rookery were below the average in size. Few of them reached a height of eight inches, while nests in the older part of this city of huts measured thirteen inches in height, with a diameter of fourteen inches at the top and twenty-two at the bottom. The depression forming the nest proper was never more than an inch in depth, and was without lining of any kind. . . .

The bird on the nest was relieved late in the afternoon and early in the morning. The one, therefore, which incubated during the day, fed at night, and his or her place was taken by another which had been feeding during the day. Or as Peter put it: "I do t'ink sir, dat when de lady Fillymingo leave de nest, den de gen'leman Fillymingo take her place, sir; yes, sir."

Morning and evening, then, there was much activity in the rookery. Single birds, or files of as many as fifty, were almost constantly arriving and departing, coming from and radiating to every point of the compass.

Flamingos in flight resemble no other bird known to me. With legs and necks fully outstretched, and the comparatively small wings set half-way between bill and toes, they look as if they might fly backward or forward with equal ease. They progress more rapidly than a Heron, and, when hurried, fly with a singular serpentine motion of the neck and body, as if they were crawling in the air.

As noon approached, the birds disposed themselves for sleep. The long necks were arranged in sundry coils and curves, the heads tucked snugly beneath the feathers of the back, and, for the first time, there was silence in the red city. Suddenly—one could never tell whence it came—the honking alarm-note was given. Instantly, and with remarkable effect, the snake-like necks shot up all over the glowing bed of color before me, transforming it into a writhing mass of flaming serpents; then, as the alarm-note continued and was taken up by a thousand throats, the birds, like a vast congregation, with dignified precision of movement, gravely arose, pressing their bills into the nests to assist themselves.

Under circumstances of this kind the birds rarely left their nests, and it was difficult to determine the cause of their alarm. Often, doubtless, it was baseless, but at times it was due to a circling Turkey Vulture, the gaunt ogre of Flamingodom, which, in the absence of the parent birds, is said to eat not only eggs but nestlings. Possibly some slight sound from my tent, where, with ill-controlled excitement, I was making photograph after photograph, may have occasioned the deep-voiced, warning *huh-huh-huh*.

I had so often fruitlessly stalked these wary birds across the swash, that I was tempted to step out from my blind and address a word of triumph to the assembled multitude; but so sudden an alarm might not only have caused the destruction of many eggs, but might have resulted in the birds deserting their homes. Consequently, several hours after entering the blind, Mrs. Chapman, by arrangement, returned; the birds retreated to the lagoon, and I left my hiding place without their being the wiser.　　　　　(From *Camps and Cruises of an Ornithologist*)

ETIENNE GALLET

Flamingos of the Camargue

The flamingo of Europe differs from our own West Indian bird in that it is pale, almost whitish. Only its wings are crimson; our bird is flame-pink throughout. Today the flamingos of the Camargue at the mouth of the Rhone are known throughout the world. Although the colonies are jealously guarded by the French who ration the visits of ornithologists, I have had the privilege of three such expeditions and count them among the high points of nearly four decades of bird watching. It was Etienne Gallet of Arles who held the secret of the Camargue flamingos for many years. He discovered their unsuspected colonies, and under the pitiless sun in the vast salt lagoons devoted himself to their photography and study.

W̲E SHALL never forget the feelings with which, for the first time, we observed, far off, as in a mirage, the exquisite rose-red tint of the flamingo. Our eyes were dazzled by this mass of plumage, these groups of white and pink and black, all blended against a background of shimmering mother-of-pearl. From this enchanted scene of prismatic brilliance arose a fiendish clamour like the ravings of a maddened crowd. We could now discern each bird erect upon its nest, beating its wings and trumpeting. We seemed to be spying upon unknown and virgin ground, and treading the sandy shores of tertiary seas when the world was young. Closer to, the din was terrifying and insupportable. It was the clamour of thousands of birds who screamed

170

and splashed and beat their wings, preparing for flight. Suddenly the horizon seemed alight and the sky afire. The red of their wings was like a flame, mounting up in a twisting, crimson spiral. Some of them rushed into the sea, beating their wings, leaving a trail of glittering spray amid the din of falling water. We were amazed at the sight, feeling that we had stumbled upon something that man was never meant to see. We mastered our excitement and approached the nests which were dappled with white and fringed with feathers. All around us, like great flames quenched in the waters, the flamingos slowly came to rest again.

As day begins to fade, our eyes can better pierce the clearer, moister atmosphere. All around are the white recumbent forms of hundreds of birds preparing for rest. Little by little darkness hides them, until only the nearest are visible. Their piercing cries alone disturb the silence of the night, cries such as they utter during flight, only now their proximity makes them more intense and more discordant. This clamour of the entire colony does not cease from sunset to dawn, nor in the day-time either, if an intruder is near. The seemingly meaningless clamour may be designed to frighten off other creatures, an almost reflex action of defense against the outer world of foes. We cannot tell to what extent this infernal uproar may psychologically affect other predatory creatures that might venture, under cover of darkness, to approach the nests. It certainly has a depressing effect upon man.

During the night, these timid birds remain alert, anxiously mindful of the slightest change in their surroundings. On the first night we spent close to them, the rising moon behind our hide cast an unusual shadow. A sudden silence, more moving than any sound, broke the noisy clamour. In a moment, in a renewed uproar of cries and clashing wings, the mass of birds rose in confusion from its nests to seek the safety of the waters. It was long afterwards that they returned and began carefully sorting out their nests again. With long, drooping necks that swayed like trunks, they passed their great beaks over the surface of each nest. Perhaps it is a sense of smell that aids them in their search, at any rate, during the night, when lack of visibility would blind their eyes? But as they behave the same during the day-time, it seems that we must credit them with some instinct at present not revealed to us. . . .

Each bird, as it mounts its nest, shakes its feet clear of mud, without consideration for its neighbours' feelings. It arranges the egg with its

171

beak in a line with its body and folds its legs while its lightly spread wings cover the surface of the cradle. Then, as if by some atavistic instinct recalling a distant period when it laid more eggs than one, it rocks the single egg to and fro, fluttering its wings, like the larger gallinaceae.

(From *Flamingos of the Camargue*)

HELEN CRUICKSHANK

The King's Bar Rookery

The big ornithological find of 1937 was the great glossy ibis colony in Lake Okeechobee. Although no one before had ever seen more than forty pairs in a Florida rookery, it had been suspected that several hundred must be hiding their secret somewhere. Marvin Chandler, the Audubon warden, solved the mystery, and I was the first ornithologist to accompany him to the reedy reef far out in the lake where upwards of a thousand pairs were nesting. In subsequent years, by planting willow switches, Chandler induced the birds to change their residence to King's Bar where they could be more easily guarded. Marvin Chandler is now gone, but his nephew, Glenn Chandler, still watches over the birds of Lake Okeechobee and the Kissimmee.

Helen and Allan Cruickshank, who photographed the glossy ibis rookery several years later, have always had an especial regard for Florida where they now make their permanent home. Allan uses rather heavy camera equipment for his incomparable bird portraits while Helen has become very proficient with the Leica. Allan has a felicitous way with words on the lecture platform while Helen prefers to commit hers to paper. Together they complement each other like the two wings of a bird.

A NOTHER GLOSSY ibis nest near my blind has been broken up," Allan told me as he put his cameras in the boat and sat down with his feet dangling over the gunwales so the water could run out of his boots.

173

For several days he had been photographing and studying that rare bird, the eastern glossy ibis, in a rookery on King's Bar far out in Lake Okeechobee. The very first day when he built his blind he had found a dead ibis hanging from a nest in which there was a broken egg. In the days that followed he had found several other dead ibises on their nests.

Marvin was inclined to think the birds died of disease. To prove his point he skinned one of the dead birds and showed Allan the strange clotting of blood over the entire head. The eyes were rimmed with blood. He told us he had noticed the same condition on the heads of all the dead birds he had examined since the colony was established on King's Bar. But as Allan watched the same nests day after day and noted that whenever he found a dead bird, the eggs were missing, he came to doubt that disease was responsible for the deaths.

In the days that followed the glossy ibises showed no alarm and Allan's hopes for pictures were justified. However he was no nearer the solution of the robbed-nest problem than he had been the first day.

Finally he decided to let me spend a day in the blind while he searched for nests of the Everglade kites. This kite is among the rarest of all birds in the United States. . . . A few pairs nested in reeds on the end of King's Bar opposite the ibis rookery. Since very few photographs have ever been made of them, Allan was eager to make some.

Since Allan was to leave me behind in the glossy ibis blind, he warned that I might see a snake swim by "now and then." So eager was I to see the glossy ibises at close range, that I paid little attention to his casual remark about snakes. I had seen glossy ibises as they flew overhead or fed in distant marshes and they appeared to be completely black. Allan, on the other hand, had returned each day from his blind with enthusiastic accounts of the magnificent colors of the apparently drab birds.

In spite of my anticipation, I suffered a few qualms as I stepped overboard and into the warm black mud. The water plants clung like tangled strings to my legs, hampering each step. The water reached nearly to my hips and was covered with floating leaves. Nowhere could bottom be seen.

I was wearing sneakers and long socks, and the bottom of my dungarees were held closed by rubber bands in the hope that 'gator fleas would not bite. I was afraid if one of those flat, semitransparent

174

bugs did bite, I would disgrace myself, thinking it was a snake. 'Gator fleas give a vicious bite that feels like fire and hurts intensely for a few seconds. Marvin struck out ahead of me, quite unconcerned about possible unpleasant inhabitants of the bar while Allan walked behind me carrying my camera, tripod and notebook.

It is tiring to walk in water under any circumstances. But when mud sucks at the feet and the surface is covered by a tangle of clutching plants, when floating roots writhe like live things and the hidden space between the bottom and the surface might conceal sudden death, when rushes whip one's burning face, then half a mile seems like an interminable distance. I remembered another marsh where we had waded to take pictures of Ward's herons and in a narrow opening in the water weeds we looked down into the face of a great snapping turtle looking at us with its knifelike jaws gaping. If there were any steel-jawed turtles here we would be unable to see them. My sneakered toes quivered a bit as I pulled them out of the mud and shoved them forward. The sun blazed down on us and its rays bounced up from the water and seared our eyes. Occasionally we stopped to catch our breath and then plowed on. The sultry air was like a weight upon us. Once when we paused to rest while the thick, soupy water sloshed around our knees, I thought how much I preferred the crisp cleanness of steep mountain slopes to hot snake-and-insect-infested black marshes. But birds seem to prefer the marshes.

At last we came to the small willow thicket that Marvin had planted but two years before. The slippery roots with unexpected holes between them and branches lying beneath the surface made walking still more difficult though the water was shallow in that place. Beyond those young willows we passed through more reeds that towered high above our heads and shut out sight of everything but the closely pressing stalks and the blue sky above. Finally we glimpsed the blind ahead. Its artificial-grass cover blended almost perfectly with the green of the rushes. Best of all, to my eyes, was its floor lifted above the black water—water that floated a scum of algae and bits of decayed vegetation in the opening cleared in front of the blind.

I scrambled gratefully onto the platform and Allan pinned the blind opening securely. A row of nests was visible from the blind, some of them so low that they almost touched the water. From there they ranged upward to a height of perhaps four feet which was the greatest height possible in those flexible young willows. The ibis nests were

175

substantial affairs of stout twigs and lined with long marsh grasses. As soon as the camera had been focused on the nearest nest, Allan and Marvin left. Scarcely had the sound of their voices died away when I saw the sicklelike bill of a glossy ibis appear over the farther edge of a nest. Round black eyes peered at the blind. Then the ibis climbed up and settled on the large greenish blue eggs.

Although I had been pulling off my soggy clothes and hanging them over the blind framework to dry, I stopped to look at the bird in amazement. The glossy ibis that looked so drab from a distance was incredibly colorful! A bluish white band was drawn from the eyes around the lower mandible. A wider band was drawn across the upper mandible. Allan was so surprised the first time he saw the white faces that for a moment he thought they must be the western species: the white-faced glossy ibis. But soon he noticed that the bluish white area was in reality only the naked skin of the face and he decided that this whitish color was only a breeding-time decoration. As the days passed he found that the longer the birds incubated, the less pronounced the whitish face became. The bill was dull black, tinged with copper. Gunmetal gray spread over the forehead but in certain lights it glowed with an emerald sheen. Rich, coppery henna spread over the breast, shoulders and upper scapulars. Behind those burnished feathers a deep green gloss appeared on the wings. The back and tail were faintly touched with chestnut, green, purple and sometimes even blue and rose. In some lights the birds almost appeared to be covered with sequins. Sometimes the colors glowed with jewellike iridescence. Depending on the light, the colors occasionally became dull and almost disappeared. Only the breast and shoulders never seemed to lose their rich colors.

For some time I was so entranced by the changing colors that I could see little else. But their behavior was every bit as interesting. They repeatedly stood up on their bulky nests and shook their plumage until each feather stood out quite alone and looked as if it were made of shining metal. It was a very hot day and periodically the birds would hop off their nests and into the water. There they would shake water over themselves, take a drink and climb back to their eggs. In climbing about they are almost as agile as snowy egrets and use their wings even less than do those graceful birds. . . .

After having watched the noisy exchange of ceremonies of herons and egrets, it was surprising to watch that of the glossy ibis. An adult

176

would wander about behind the row of nests, apparently quite aimlessly and without purpose. In a few minutes one of the incubating birds would hop off into the water and join it. They would hold a brief low "conversation" during which their heads were lowered and their tails raised high. Then the newcomer climbed to the nest and took over incubation while its mate disappeared, perhaps to feed.

Suddenly I saw one bird hang its head, its long neck stretched to its greatest extremity. It was rigid except for its moving eyes. If you have ever looked squarely into the face of a bird rolling its eyes you will know why I laughed. But the laughter was cut short when I saw what the ibis was watching. A tannish colored young cottonmouthed moccasin was swimming beneath the nest. Then I saw another. Had Allan said I would see a snake just "now and then?" While I was still breathless from the sight of two poisonous cottonmouths at once, a brown water snake swam slowly towards the blind, swerved and climbed on some willow branches heaped at the right. I had not noticed those branches piled against the blind before and was not happy to see another snake that I could not identify already sunning itself there.

For a time photography and glossy ibises were forgotten. I moved quickly from one side of the tiny blind to the other, peering out and trying to see what all the snakes were doing. I did not want one to come behind me when I was not looking. I wrote a description of the snake I did not know (later identified as a black mud snake) and before I had finished, a banded water snake swam into view. Six snakes of four species in view at once was disconcerting. From then on I was uneasy in the blind. That heap of willow branches would permit a snake to come right into the blind if one chose to do so. Moreover the birds continually called attention to snakes. They looked odd indeed as they hung their long necks over the edges of their nests and rolled their eyes each time a snake swam beneath them. It was comforting to see that while they were interested, they were not particularly alarmed by the rookery visitors. But as more snakes swam by I shuddered to think that I must step back into the sinister-looking water with its festering slimy green things, its dirty bubbles, unexpected holes, and snakes. The long walk back to the boat was not one I looked forward to with pleasure. Several times I saw a huge dark shape move across the water far back in the willows, but though I stared intently I could see nothing that had more substance than a shadow and wondered if I had been mistaken.

177

It was half-past four when I heard the voices of Allan and Marvin as they splashed toward the blind. Allan is careful not to reveal his presence in a blind until the birds on the nests near him have been quietly induced to leave. Should one step suddenly from the concealment of a blind into the midst of a colony of birds, considerable damage might result. Eggs would be knocked out of the nests as the startled birds took off or they might actually desert. If one is patient in persuading the birds to fly, they show little or no fear and return quickly. In this case, Allan and Marvin had acted as "walk aways" so I silently waited for them to arrive. The ibises sensed their approach and one by one unhurriedly flew away. Peering through the blind cover, I saw Allan and Marvin appear beyond the protective screen of reeds. Then as I began to loosen the blind fastenings I saw Marvin, who was leading, stop suddenly and step backward. I heard him say softly to Allan,

"That's the biggest old cottonmouth I ever did see."

And then I saw it. The cottonmouth was lying right across the vague trail beaten down by Allan and Marvin on their daily trips through the reeds to the blind. Its great coils lay on a mat of water weeds as it sunned its sluggish, mottled, leaden gray length. Marvin was empty-handed. Allan carried a camera. Fear shook me as I looked at that silent reptilian barrier to my escape, a barrier that could spell death. For an instant I thought wildly that I never could leave the blind.

Marvin quickly took charge. With a whispered warning to keep still, to neither move nor speak, he withdrew so quietly that his movements were almost imperceptible. Once he reached a safe distance, he moved quickly, retracing his steps until he came to the young willow thicket through which we had passed on our way to the blind. There he cut as long and stout a stick as he could find. How fortunate that he had made a second planting of willows after the glossy ibis colony was established!

"There," I thought with horrified conviction, "lies the creature that moved like a shadow through the willows. It has been here all day."

The snake was still motionless when Marvin returned. A quick hard blow with the willow stick broke the snake's back. As Marvin struck the cottonmouth, it opened its mouth and in the gaping cavity was an expanse of snowy white tissue. Its long fangs shot erect. But the first stroke had done its work and the snake was quickly dispatched.

This was the only occasion I can recall when it was necessary for

178

one of us to kill to insure our safety. In any other location the cottonmouth would have been by-passed at a safe distance or frightened away. As we looked at this snake, there was no doubt in any of our minds that it was an extraordinary specimen.

"Ditmars says that something under five feet is the average length of cottonmouths," Allan exclaimed. "And just look at this fellow!"

The snake was five feet, eleven inches long. Later we talked with Ross Allan of the Reptile Institute and he told us he had collected six-foot cottonmouths in the Ocala region but around Lake Okeechobee he had never collected any that measured much over five feet.

As Allan looked at the bulging body of the snake, he believed the mystery of the destroyed nests was solved. With some string he tied the snake's head to the stick Marvin had used to kill it and dragged the snake back to the boat. There Allan took his knife and cut open the ugly reptile. Inside he found one glossy ibis egg and three Louisiana heron eggs which had been swallowed without breaking the shells. Strong digestive juices had eaten away the shell of another egg but its parchmentlike lining was still intact. Next Allan removed a very large young American egret. Last of all he pulled out an adult glossy ibis. It seemed almost incredible that one cottonmouth moccasin could hold so much.

With that concrete evidence there was little doubt that snakes were responsible for the loss of many of the eggs. Moreover the adults which showed the strange clotting of blood on the head were probably killed when they tried to defend their nests with their bills. Naturally even a sluggish cottonmouth would strike back if a fight developed and the bird's head would be the logical target. But it must be remembered that young cottonmouths form part of the diet of glossy ibises.

Allan continued his studies in the blind but I never went back. Perhaps there were no other cottonmouths as big as the one we examined but I preferred not to meet even a small snake in that fetid swamp.

(From *Flight into Sunshine*)

179

HERBERT BRANDT

Wild Turkeys at Bedtime

Audubon, whose turkey print commands the top price in his elephant folio, knew a great deal about this noble bird. It was undoubtedly his favorite, and his account in the "Biographies" has made subsequent writings about this species seem like pale reflections. It took a professional turkey raiser, Herbert Brandt, to add a chapter in the long bibliography of this bird that compares with that of Audubon. The following incident is excerpted from "Romance of the Wild Turkey," in Brandt's beautifully illustrated book, *Arizona and Its Bird Life*.

During the month of May, 1947, I was the guest of the author at his camp at Rustler Park in the Chiricahuas where he was studying a flock of sixteen gobblers and hens that roosted high in the Chihuahua yellow pines. One evening he decided to investigate the conduct of his turkey friends at bedtime. About five o'clock in the afternoon while the flock was still feeding in the iris-covered meadow we climbed the steep wooded slope to the ridge above Rustler's Park where the elevation is about 8,600 feet. Brandt brought his field journal, a light bedroll and a powerful flashlight. We knew approximately where the birds roosted in six tall pines, for their noisy synchronized gobbling at bedtime could be heard from the cabin. Selecting a spot on the steep slope opposite the trees we arranged a blind. While Herb lay comfortably on his sleeping bag, we covered him with newly cut pine boughs. My own army experience in the camouflage section of the Corps of Engineers came in handy, and when we had finished even the most suspicious turkey would have been deceived. But let Herb Brandt tell what he saw:

180

I<small>T WAS</small> fascinating to watch the change from day to night among the tree tops just at hand. A Red-shafted Flicker was especially noisy, and finally flew into a living pine directly in front of me. He uttered his loud "tick tick" call incessantly, until the light of day had dimmed to his preferred retiring illumination. The Long-crested Jay signed off earlier, while the several lesser birds all became quiet. . . .

Promptly at seven o'clock I caught a glimpse of three turkeys far below among the big trees. A large tom in full spread was slowly advancing, gobbling now and then. The light faded fast, and I began to wonder whether or not the birds were going to use their old roosting trees, when suddenly a huge gobbler appeared only five feet away from my face and, to my further surprise, walked on up the hill. By reason of the brush covering, I was in a position from which I could not follow his movements up the slope.

Suddenly a tremendous noise burst upon my ears, and just above me roared the big bird. As he passed over, the power of his rapid, fanning wings seemed to shake the very mountainside. Up he went, swiftly and directly with a gradual upsweep, finally landing as lightly as a feather on an upper limb of one of the large trees. To my surprise, this grand gobbler made no more ado about its bedtime flight than would any lesser bird. He shook himself a few times, then carefully started to preen; all at once he jumped to a higher limb, where he moved half way out toward the end and settled down.

Meanwhile, other birds of the flock gathered closely about me and then passed on up the slope. Each turkey, likewise, took off with the same display of violent power, only to sweep gracefully up to his chosen limb and always land without being the least out of balance. Before the take-off a bird did considerable stretching of neck, peering again and again in the direction of its roost, and in a low tone talking apparently about its flight. The hen, much more so than the tom, appeared to lack courage to make the flight, and would yelp several times, whereupon always a gobbler would answer her from up in the tree, as if to give encouragement. It seemed certain that each tom of a family group would be the first to go to bed. The hen, however, always

181

flew to a different tree from that whence the gobbler called, and invariably perched by herself. In fact, there was never more than one lodger on a limb, regardless of its length.

In every case the turkey alighted close to the trunk of the tree and then walked out from it or jumped to an adjacent higher branch. When finally it had chosen a spot to settle down, each bird spent a short time making its bedside toilet by preening itself industriously, and then settled down on the perch, with its tail pointing at an angle toward the ground. Its arched head curved gradually back in repose and later disappeared from my sight, usually being tucked under the wing, but of this I was not sure, since by that time the light was so dim as to make this observation uncertain.

From my cozy place of concealment the retirement procedure of the turkey was a thrilling, noisy affair. In all, I counted 14 birds which took to wing in the dusk, each going singly in its own clattering fashion. Evidently two females were incubating. The flock finally bedded down in the upper parts of four trees, with five birds going to roost in the one that had the most evidence below. Another tree held four, a third roosted three, while an especially large tree almost over my head had a tom and a hen, where, in the upper branches they seemed small indeed. It was a novel adventure to lie there at the keyhole to the bedchamber of these grandest of birds, and witness their retiring behavior. Through the pine plumes, as their inky forms outlined themselves against the starry sky, they became each an eerie black object with a long, snakelike, protruding neck, which occasionally uncurled upward in attention, or slowly cuddled down and disappeared.

Finally, everything in Turkey Town quieted down, the snaky necks coiled down into the dark bodies and the birds had truly gone to roost. Suddenly, close at hand, a Whippoorwill broke the silence in a lively tempo, and I concluded that my adventure was over for that evening, so as noiselessly as possible I wiggled out of my bushy hide and stood erect. Instantly, out popped all the long necks, but not a sound did the birds make. Then I flashed on the beam of the strong spotlight, and focusing it on each bird in turn, I received back, as I held the light in line with my eye, a glowing greenish yellow eye shine. It seemed as though each bird had two brilliant jewels of the first magnitude on its crown. While the turkeys were all astir, craning and peering and uttering occasional low alarm notes, not one rose to standing position, nor

182

did they as a group exhibit any fear, in spite of the fact that I flashed my light on them for several minutes. Finally, in the darkness I stumbled away and left the turkey hotel to the sighing pines and the close-in stars.

(From *Arizona and Its Bird Life*)

HENRY D. THOREAU

The Loon

No spot in America has been so lovingly chronicled as Concord, nor has any area in the New World been more continuously bird-watched. Some of Thoreau's notes go back to 1832 and since 1868 when William Brewster began to visit Concord the record is unbroken. We have more than a century of data which reveals much about the ups and downs of bird populations.

In Thoreau's time the loon stopped on Walden Pond; today it flies over Concord in migration, but very rarely alights.

IN THE FALL the loon came, as usual, to moult and bathe in the pond, making the woods ring with his wild laughter before I had risen. At rumor of his arrival all the Mill-dam sportsmen are on the alert, in gigs and on foot, two by two and three by three, with patent rifles and conical balls and spy-glasses. They come rustling through the woods like autumn leaves, at least ten men to one loon. Some station themselves on this side of the pond, some on that, for the poor bird cannot be omnipresent; if he dives here he must come up there. But now the kind October wind rises, rustling the leaves and rippling the surface of the water, so that no loon can be heard or seen, though his foes sweep the pond with spy-glasses, and make the woods resound with their discharges. The waves generously rise and dash angrily, taking sides with all water-fowl, and our sportsmen must beat a retreat to town and shop and unfinished jobs. But they were too often successful. When I went to get a pail of water early in the morning I frequently saw this stately bird sailing out of my cove within a few rods.

As I was paddling along the north shore one very calm October afternoon, for such days especially they settle on to the lakes, like the milkweed down, having looked in vain over the pond for a loon, suddenly one, sailing out from the shore toward the middle a few rods in front of me, set up his wild laugh and betrayed himself. I pursued with a paddle and he dived, but when he came up I was nearer than before. He dived again, but I miscalculated the direction he would take, and we were fifty rods apart when he came to the surface this time, for I had helped to widen the interval; and again he laughed long and loud, and with more reason than before. He manoeuvred so cunningly that I could not get within half a dozen rods of him. Each time, when he came to the surface, turning his head this way and that, he coolly surveyed the water and the land, and apparently chose his course so that he might come up where there was the widest expanse of water and at the greatest distance from the boat. It was surprising how quickly he made up his mind and put his resolve into execution. He led me at once to the widest part of the pond, and could not be driven from it. While he was thinking one thing in his brain, I was endeavoring to divine his thought in mine. It was a pretty game, played on the smooth surface of the pond, a man against a loon. Suddenly your adversary's checker disappears beneath the board, and the problem is to place yours nearest to where his will appear again. Sometimes he could come up unexpectedly on the opposite side of me, having apparently passed directly under the boat. So long-winded was he and so unweariable, that when he had swum farthest he would immediately plunge again, nevertheless; and then no wit could divine where in the deep pond, beneath the smooth surface, he might be speeding his way like a fish, for he had time and ability to visit the bottom of the pond in its deepest part. It is said that loons have been caught in the New York lakes eighty feet beneath the surface, with hooks set for trout,—though Walden is deeper than that. How surprised must the fishes be to see this ungainly visitor from another sphere speeding his way amid their schools! Yet he appeared to know his course as surely under water as on the surface, and swam much faster there. Once or twice I saw a ripple where he approached the surface, just put his head out to reconnoitre, and instantly dived again. I found that it was as well for me to rest on my oars and wait his reappearing as to endeavor to calculate

185

where he would rise; for again and again, when I was straining my eyes over the surface one way, I would suddenly be startled by his unearthly laugh behind me. But why, after displaying so much cunning, did he invariably betray himself the moment he came up by that loud laugh? Did not his white breast enough betray him? He was indeed a silly loon, I thought. I could commonly hear the plash of the water when he came up, and so also detected him. But after an hour he seemed as fresh as ever, dived as willingly, and swam yet farther than at first. It was surprising to see how serenely he sailed off with unruffled breast when he came to the surface, doing all the work with his webbed feet beneath. His usual note was this demoniac laughter, yet somewhat like that of a water-fowl; but occasionally, when he had balked me most successfully and come up a long way off, he uttered a long-drawn unearthly howl, probably more like that of a wolf than any bird; as when a beast puts his muzzle to the ground and deliberately howls. This was his looning,—perhaps the wildest sound that is ever heard here, making the woods ring far and wide. I concluded that he laughed in derision of my efforts, confident of his own resources. Though the sky was by this time overcast, the pond was so smooth that I could see where he broke the surface when I did not hear him. His white breast, the stillness of the air, and the smoothness of the water were all against him. At length, having come up fifty rods off, he uttered one of those prolonged howls, as if calling on the god of loons to aid him, and immediately there came a wind from the east and rippled the surface, and filled the whole air with misty rain, and I was impressed as if it were the prayer of the loon answered, and his god was angry with me; and so I left him disappearing far away on the tumultuous surface.

(From *Walden*)

LOUIS J. HALLE

Man-o'-War

On the 29th of September, 1492, Columbus' men on the Nina, the Pinta, and the Santa Maria saw their first man-o'-war bird. The mariners, close to mutiny, were given heart by the sight of this sable-winged bird which, though a seafarer, seldom wanders far from islands. In this respect it is quite unlike the albatrosses which seem to avoid all land except during their nesting. One can always see man-o'-wars in the Florida Keys, sometimes hundreds, hanging against the trade-wind cumuli on slim black sails, but they have never been known to nest nearer than the Bahamas. The man-o'-war has long been a favorite of Louis Halle. In *Birds Against Men,* for which he was awarded the Burroughs' Medal, he describes his first encounter with this frigate of the Caribbean.

I F SATAN should ever choose to incarnate himself as a bird he would find the man-o'-war cut to his measure. The power and beauty of his flight, his predatory habits, and his somber appearance are definitely satanic in the impression they make on the beholder. The first man-o'-war I saw, when at last I had my chance to travel, was all alone in a seascape that might have been designed to frame him. It was evening at the entrance to the Caribbean, and though we had just passed at a great distance, one tropical islet, no land was in view. As often happens when the sun is low, the horizon showed like a dark thread separating the sea from the sky. Some few clouds were reflected in a silver sheen over large areas of water across which leaden bars traveled in serene and endless succession. The clear sky, the binding

187

line of the horizon, the slumbering ocean, lent an air of suspense to the evening. It seemed to be ready and waiting for some act of creation. Then I looked up and saw him for the first time. At the very center of the picture, directly ahead, the great bird hung motionless, his wings crooked at the shoulders, his tail extended like a pikestaff, his rapacious beak turning from side to side without in the least disturbing the perfect equilibrium of the body.

I had been alert for the pirate all day, knowing that our ship was entering his waters, and here he was upon us as though he had taken the sky at one stroke of his wings. And he was simply gigantic. Having already familiarized myself with his person in the handbooks I should have been better prepared for his black immensity, but this apparition was totally unlooked for. He was the one dark, solid object between unbroken sea and unbroken sky; the whole setting seemed to reflect the majesty and dominion of his presence. It was impossible to doubt that the bird was a pirate. Seeing him for the first time I knew the quick thrill that every law-abiding mariner must feel when he first sees the approaching sail of a ship he knows to be outside the law. But our steam-propelled vessel, with that inhuman purposefulness of the machine moving in blind obedience to inhuman law, forged straight ahead through the sea till her forepeak was almost under the spread of the outlaw's wings. He hung over us like a fixture in the sky, his long, floating pinions resting loosely on the wind. Only the bony beak swung as the head moved to watch us. Having seen, the wings struck down, the body was jarred forward and began rocking to the strokes that followed in rhythmic succession. A moment later my first man-o'-war had diminished to a black speck in the eye of the setting sun.

(From *Birds Against Men*)

EDWARD WILSON

Adélie Penguins

Edward Wilson, the naturalist on Scott's Antarctic expeditions and his right-hand man, was destined to die with the great explorer on their return dash from the South Pole in March 1912. Days of driving blizzard pinned them down and prevented them from reaching their last depot only eleven miles distant.

Wilson had also been with Scott on the *Discovery* expedition of 1902-1903. It was on this penetration of the Antarctic that they surveyed the barrier cliffs, made soundings, discovered King Edward Island, Ross Island, and the Victoria Mountains—a mighty range that had previously been seen only from the sea. They discovered the great ice-cap itself, on which is situated the Pole.

Wilson filled many journals with his notes. A high point was the discovery of the first known colony of emperor penguins, the colony to which Cherry-Garrard was to return nearly ten years later on the "worst journey in the world." In his journal Wilson describes his meeting with the Adélie penguin.

O<small>N THIS</small> third day we were for the first time amongst the more extensive ice-floes, and these being far more closely packed, afforded an excellent opportunity for the inquisitive little birds to run long distances towards us, and with many halts to gaze and cry in wonder to their companions; now walking along the edge of a floe in search of a narrow spot to jump and so avoid the water, now with head down and much hesitation judging the width of the narrow gap, to give a little standing jump across as would a child, and running on the

189

faster to make up for its delay. Again, coming to a wider lead of water necessitating a plunge, our inquisitive visitor would be lost for a moment, to reappear like a jack-in-a-box on a nearer floe, where wagging his tail, he immediately resumed his race towards the ship. Being now but a hundred yards or so from us he pokes his head constantly forward on this side and on that, to try and make out something of the new strange sight, crying aloud to his friends in his amazement, and exhibiting the most amusing indecision between his desire for further investigation and doubt as to the wisdom and propriety of closer contact with so huge a beast. . . .

As we neared Cape Adare, we had Adélie Penguins in the water all around us, birds by hundreds dashing in and out like little dolphins, making very rapid travelling through the water, shooting into the air with heads drawn in and wings appressed, just clearing the water by a foot for a yard or more, and then in with the slightest little splash. When first seen, they may easily be mistaken for a school of fish. Under the water they wing their way with powerful strokes, often in a zig-zag course, especially if frightened, as a means, no doubt, of baffling the seals and Killer whales that are their terror. The feet and tail in this method of progression are used for steering only, but if the bird is at the surface, floating as he does low in the water, instead of the wings the feet will be used for propelling.

In landing on a shelving shore, the bird merely swims till he can stand upright and walk, but in landing from deep water on an ice-floe with its edge a foot or two above the water, he leaps like a salmon, with this difference, that instead of allowing his body to follow the curve of motion, he preserves the vertical position, and lands upon his feet, immediately running on a few paces or falling sometimes on his breast; and in this landing leap the stiff tail feathers must be of use in preventing any tendency to fall backwards.

In leaping from floe to floe across a crack of open water, they show no great athletic capabilities, and in crossing six inches or a foot, which is about as much as they ever dare attempt, their movements are exactly what one is wont to see if the same feat is performed by a child of three. If in their wanderings they come to a crack which is too wide to jump, and yet not wide enough for plunging into, they will follow the edge till they find a point more suited to their tastes; but it takes much time and many hesitations before they decide the thing to be possible for either.

190

Time, happily for them, is no object; but this at first sight one would hardly guess, their movements being always precise, busy, and pre-occupied. It is only when one has watched a little party hurrying along for full half a mile in a direct line, as though upon some urgent business, suddenly stop and all go to sleep, or suddenly turn and go off in another direction, or come back upon some equally urgent call, that one begins to realise that their business is not always so important as it looks.

On flat ice or snow they seem to prefer walking, balancing themselves with their flippers, and leaving between their footmarks a sinuous track made by the tail. If hurried or fatigued by soft snow they will fall on their breasts, the polished feathers of which form an excellent runner surface for toboganning. They then leave a track which takes the form of a straight smooth groove with foot and wing marks on each side, each working in alternation with the other.

On land, as, for example, in the rookeries, they progress as far as possible on their feet, and in making the longer journeys up the mountain sides, over very craggy rocks and really difficult steeps, they bring bills and wings into use as well as feet and nails, and blood stains in their tracks show that sometimes they must suffer in the process.

The pace at which these birds can travel in the water rivals that of many fish; on land they are of course not so fast, though their pace when toboganning on their stomachs is about as quick as a man can run on ice and snow, and a great deal faster than the birds can travel on their feet. . . .

The sooty-grey young ones in the third week of January were almost as big as their parents, and quite as active. Of these young birds there were literally thousands, and all were hungry, many very hungry. Moreover, each individual chicken acted upon the supposition that every old bird as it came up from the shore was full of shrimps. On this assumption the old bird had no choice but to run the gauntlet. Chased incontinently up and down the rookery by the importunate infants, the fond parent ran hither and thither with a keen eye open for the chicken it once had called its own. Driven at last to bay, it could only turn to swear and silence its persecuting followers for the moment with a vicious peck, but the moment its search again commenced it would be caught up and followed and worried in precisely the same way by a fresh relay of young ones, all belonging to someone else.

As we stood there and watched this race for food we were gradually

192

possessed with the idea that the chicks looked upon each adult coming up full-bellied from the shore, as not a parent only, but a food supply. The parents were labouring under a totally different idea, and intended either to find their own infants and feed them, or else to assimilate their already partially digested catch themselves. The more robust of the young thus worried an adult until, because of his importunity, he was fed. But with the less robust a much more pathetic ending was the rule. A chick that had fallen behind in this literal race for life, starving and weak, and getting daily weaker because it could not run fast enough to insist on being fed, again and again ran off pursuing with the rest. Again and again it stumbled and fell, persistently whining out its hunger in a shrill and melancholy pipe, till at last the race was given up. Forced thus by sheer exhaustion to stop and rest, it had no chance of getting food. Each hurrying parent with its little following of hungry chicks, intent on one thing only, rushed quickly by, and the starveling dropped behind to gather strength for one more effort. Again it fails, a robuster bird has forced the pace, and again success is wanting to the runt. Sleepily it stands there with half-shut eyes in a torpor resulting from exhaustion, cold, and hunger, wondering perhaps what all the bustle round it means, a little dirty dishevelled dot, in the race for life a failure, deserted by its parents who have hunted vainly for their own offspring round the nest in which they hatched it, but from which it may by now have wandered half a mile. And so it stands, lost to everything around, till a Skua in its beat drops down beside it, and with a few strong vicious pecks puts an end to the failing life.

(From George Seaver's *Edward Wilson—Nature Lover*)

ROGER TORY PETERSON

The Great Bustard

Pockets of wilderness have survived in Europe to this day. Scotland's St. Kilda, now untenanted except for the myriad seabirds, the Dutch islands and polders with their spoonbills and avocets, and the Camargue in the Rhone Delta, home of thousands of flamingos, are museum pieces in an over-populated continent. Surpassing even these spots in the wonder of its birds is an area in southern Spain, the broad Marismas with their surrounding plains and sierras. Here in Andalusia can still be found the grandest of all Europe's birds, the great bustard, now separated by more than a thousand miles from other remnant populations of its kind in northeastern Germany and on the Hungarian plains.

W HEN I found myself on the rolling plains of southern Spain last spring, I ruled out the great bustard as one of the birds I would be likely to see. The green corn was already too high and the hundreds of square miles of this grain (which is not what we call "corn") clothing the vast undulating plains of Andalusia made it seem a hopeless task to find the scattered bands. But our friend, Señor Don Mauricio Gonzales Diez, heir to the sherry empire which centers around Jerez, said, "Of course you must see the great bustard if you are to draw its picture for your book. I shall see to it." That afternoon he sent out an old poacher—"a reformed poacher," he assured us—to locate a flock.

Next day we drove to our base of operations, a hacienda a few miles

194

north of Jerez. While the old poacher, a little man with leathery visage and fierce deep-set eyes diverted us with stories of the Andalusian hemipode and other rare Spanish birds, Don Gonzales sent one of his horsemen into the rain to see if the bustards were on location. He returned after an hour or two, confessing no luck, and suggested we try the next hacienda. A *bandado,* or pack of bustards, had been seen there that morning. There in the great white-washed courtyard, while the tenant peasants gathered round, we self-consciously mounted our mules. The usual thing is for two men to ride on each mule, and believe me, these Spanish mules are most uncomfortable. You must almost do a split to straddle the broad saddle and projecting panniers. No wonder the peasants so frequently ride sidesaddle.

There were eight of us. Don Gonzales and the old poacher rode one mule—the tricky one. Etchecopar, secretary of the French Ornithological Society and my friend, Francois Hüe of Pezenas, mounted another. Guy Mountfort, secretary of the British Ornithological Union, had a mule to himself and so did I, so as to have more freedom for photography. Two Spanish horsemen on hybrid arabs went along to drive the bustards should we locate them.

Scarcely had we started when the skittish mule jumped a ditch unexpectedly, sending Don Gonzales and the old poacher into the mud in a tangle of arms and legs. Don Gonzales got up, but the poacher lay there in pain and finally rose with difficulty. The poor old fellow had broken his shoulder, so one of the horsemen took him back to the *posada.*

The skies were heavy with scudding gray clouds coming in from the sea but the rain had stopped. Pratincoles, those strange tern-like shorebirds, hawked for insects and everywhere could be heard the high *dzeep, dzeep, dzeep,* monotonously repeated by fan-tailed warblers cruising above the waving seas of corn. At one time we counted 22 black kites within sight. They seemed to be after grasshoppers.

After we had proceeded up one hill and down another for about four kilometers (2½ miles) the caballero out front halted and bade us bring our glasses to bear on a field of sprouting maize high on a hillslope. We could discern about a dozen tan objects. They could have been sheep, or anything else for that matter. But our binoculars showed them to be bustards, 14 of them, all males.

What magnificent creatures these *barbones* are. They strut about turkey fashion, trailing their wings and spreading their tails fan-like

195

over their backs. From their necks, swollen to abnormal thickness, flow bristling white beards. Even our wild turkey is scarcely as impressive, for a big *barbudo,* as the old bearded veterans are called, will exceed 30 pounds. The females are on their eggs in the corn, leaving the "bulls" to bluff and strut in their bachelor clubs or *toradas.* Sometimes a bird dragging its wings in display will get its stiff primaries so caked with balls of sticky mud that it cannot fly and so is caught. We saw one of these captives at Guy Williams' bodega in Jerez, where the proud thick-legged bird strolled about among the long rows of huge sherry casks.

We watched our flock for some time, scarcely daring approach closer (they were a quarter of a mile away) but we wished to see them fly. So while we dismounted and stationed ourselves behind one of the ancient draw wells which furnish the cattle their water, Don Gonzales sent forth the horsemen to drive the birds toward us. Setting off in a wide circle he was gone from sight for half an hour when we saw him appear over the crest of the hill behind the bustards. Alert, they stopped their strutting, stretched their necks and started walking, goose-like, with bodies horizontal and long necks erect. They looked most stately and dignified as they marched single file, and then, almost reluctantly, they spread their huge wings. This slow retarded take-off is said to account for their Spanish name of *Avetarda* as well as their French name of *Outard* and is suggested by their scientific name *Otis tarda.*

Never, with the possible exception of my first flamingos, have I been more impressed by a flock of birds in flight. They did not beat their wings rapidly, like gallinaceous birds, as I had expected them to do, but very, very slowly, more slowly than any goose, the great white wings contrasting with their golden bodies and the bright green of the maize and corn. They came on in single file and lit on the crest of the next small hill. Our rider pressed them again, whence they came by, into the wind, quite close this time, so that we could see them in their full glory. I can recall no experience in all my 30 years with birds that stirred me more.

What of the future of these birds in Spain? They are gone from most of Europe. . . . In Spain it is only because of the protection of the big landowners that the great bustard survives. Don Gonzales estimates that less than 50 are shot each year in the Jerez area, well within the natural reproduction, because few people can organize a bustard drive.

196

Poachers get a few more. He informed us that after the Spanish civil war, some army pilots would chase the flocks by plane, tire them out and slaughter them. The extinction of the birds was feared. When this became known, a stop was put to the practice.

(From *Audubon Magazine*)

ALFRED RUSSEL WALLACE

The Great Bird of Paradise

The theory of natural selection, credited to Charles Darwin by the man in the street, actually had two authors. Alfred Russel Wallace, traveling in the East Indies, arrived at his own conclusions about evolution quite independently; he did not know that Darwin was developing the identical theme. While lying ill with fever his ideas suddenly became crystal clear and upon his recovery he wrote them down and sent them to Darwin. The results of their collaboration are history.

Although Wallace visited New Guinea one hundred years ago he found that some of the birds of paradise which he had traveled so far to see were already becoming scarce. The Dutch officials, exploiting the plumes commercially, had formed a combine with coastal chiefs who got the birds at bargain rates from the hill savages. It was not until 1924 that the Netherlands government put an end to the traffic.

THE GREAT BIRD of Paradise (Paradisea apoda of Linnaeus) is the largest species known, being generally seventeen or eighteen inches from the beak to the tip of the tail. The body, wings, and tail are of a rich coffee-brown, which deepens on the breast to a blackish-violet or purple-brown. The whole top of the head and neck is of an exceedingly delicate straw-yellow, the feathers being short and close set, so as to resemble plush or velvet; the lower part of the throat up to the eye is clothed with scaly feathers of an emerald green

198

color, and with a rich metallic gloss, and velvety plumes of a still deeper green extend in a band across the forehead and chin as far as the eye, which is bright yellow. The beak is pale lead blue; and the feet, which are rather large and very strong and well formed, are of a pale ashy-pink. The two middle feathers of the tail have no webs, except a very small one at the base and at the extreme tip, forming wire-like cirrhi, which spread out in an elegant double curve, and vary from twenty-four to thirty-four inches long. From each side of the body, beneath the wings, springs a dense tuft of long and delicate plumes, sometimes two feet in length of the most intense golden-orange color and very glossy, but changing toward the tips into a pale brown. This tuft of plumage can be elevated and spread out at pleasure, so as almost to conceal the body of the bird.

These splendid ornaments are entirely confined to the male sex, while the female is really a very plain and ordinary-looking bird of a uniform coffee-brown color which never changes; neither does she possess the long tail wires, nor a single yellow or green feather about the head.

The Great Bird of Paradise is very active and vigorous, and seems to be in constant motion all day long. It is very abundant, small flocks of females and young males being constantly met with; and though the full-plumaged birds are less plentiful, their loud cries, which are heard daily, show that they also are very numerous. Their note is "Wawk-wawk-wawk—Wŏk, wŏk-wŏk," and is so loud and shrill as to be heard a great distance, and to form the most prominent and characteristic animal sound in the Aru Islands.

They moult about January or February, and in May, when they are in full plumage, the males assemble early in the morning to exhibit themselves in dancing-parties, in certain trees in the forest, which are not fruit-trees, as I at first imagined, but which have an immense head of spreading branches and large but scattered leaves, giving a clear space for the birds to play and exhibit their plumes. On one of these three a dozen or twenty full-plumaged male birds assemble together, raise up their wings, stretch out their necks, and elevate their exquisite plumes, keeping them in a continual vibration. Between whiles they fly across from branch to branch in great excitement, so that the whole tree is filled with waving plumes in every variety of attitude and motion. The bird itself is nearly as large as a crow, and is of a rich coffee-brown color. The head and neck is of a pure straw yellow above,

199

and rich metallic green beneath. The long plumy tufts of golden-orange feathers spring from the sides beneath each wing, and when the bird is in repose are partly concealed by them. At the time of its excitement, however, the wings are raised vertically over the back, the head is bent down and stretched out, and the long plumes are raised up and expanded till they form two magnificent golden fans, striped with deep red at the base, and fading off into the pale brown tint of the finely divided and softly waving points. The whole bird is then overshadowed by them, the crouching body, yellow head, and emerald-green throat forming but the foundation and setting to the golden glory which waves above. When seen in this attitude, the bird of paradise really deserves its name, and must be ranked as one of the most beautiful and most wonderful of living things.

This habit enables the natives to obtain specimens with comparative ease. As soon as they find that the birds have fixed upon a tree on which to assemble, they build a little shelter of palm leaves in a convenient place among the branches, and the hunter ensconces himself in it before daylight, armed with his bow and a number of arrows terminating in a round knob. A boy waits at the foot of the tree, and when the birds come at sunrise, and a sufficient number have assembled, and have begun to dance, the hunter shoots with his blunt arrow so strongly as to stun the bird, which drops down, and is secured and killed by the boy without its plumage being injured by a drop of blood. The rest take no notice, and fall one after another till some of them take the alarm.

The native mode of preserving them is to cut off the wings and feet, and then skin the body up to the beak, taking out the skull. A stout stick is then run up through the specimen coming out at the mouth. Round this some leaves are stuffed, and the whole is wrapped up in a palm spathe and dried in the smoky hut. By this plan the head, which is really large, is shrunk up almost to nothing, the body is much reduced and shortened, and the greater prominence is given to the flowing plumage. Some of these native skins are very clean, and often have wings and feet left on; others are dreadfully stained with smoke, and all give a most erroneous idea of the proportions of the living bird.

(From *The Malay Archipelago*)

DILLON RIPLEY

The Bower Bird

A long-standing predilection for the Orient caused Dillon Ripley to abandon thoughts of a business career when he graduated from Yale in 1936. Instead of setting up an office in Manhattan he sailed across the Pacific in a fifty-nine-foot schooner. Since then he has traveled and collected in the Marquesas, Tahiti, Samoa, the Solomons, the Dutch East Indies, Japan, Ceylon, India, and Nepal.

In New Guinea he ascended Bon Kourangen in quest of birds of paradise. Perhaps the most common kind was the *kourangen* after which the mountain was named, but his attention was inevitably attracted to a modest brown relative of these magnificent birds—a species of bower bird. During his stay on Bon Kourangen he found nearly a dozen of their curious little houses.

T HE BOWER BIRD is certainly one of the most ingenious birds in the world. Its behavior is so unbirdlike that one would think it had some type of rational intelligence. It seems impossible that an inherited pattern of instinctive action could be so complex. And yet even here there is an evolutionary process at work. Other species of bower birds make slightly simpler bowers. If these are carefully studied, it appears that there is a gradual trend from the simple to the complex and that this trend probably marks the phylogenetic relationship of the species comprising the family. The ancestral species probably had a simple little dancing place on the ground. The next step might have

201

been the erecting of a palisade of twigs around the edges of the spot. Further elaboration would result in the erection of a roof of twigs over this, and so on.

It was the following day, after collecting the first bower bird, that Saban and I found a bower. We had met along the trail and had gone on together for a distance, until we came to the place where the descent to the forbidden hinterland began. The sun was high overhead, but clouds were beginning to steal in among the trees. I sat down on a log to rest before going back. It was quite chilly in the shade. There was a sudden strange call from a little below us and Saban went off to investigate. I thought vaguely that it might be a tree kangaroo, simply because that was the most unlikely thing that I could think of. Fred and Charis had two pet tree kangaroos and neither of them had ever uttered a sound. The Karoon who was with us said, *"Damdom."* I knew then that it was a bird. The only Karoon I knew was that every bird's name began with the prefix *"Dam,"* not because the Karoon people were tired of birds or of me, but simply because that was the custom. There were days of rain and malaria when I was strongly inclined to agree with them.

Then I saw Saban's face. He was peering out at me from the under brush, and he seemed to be decidedly puzzled.

"Tuan, there is a bird here that makes a house."

He looked apologetic, but I didn't laugh at him, as perhaps he had expected. In a moment we had reached the spot. In one place on the gentle slope the undergrowth had been neatly cleared away from an area four feet square. The place looked as if it had been swept with a broom. At the upper end of this area was the "house." A small sapling had been used as a brace in the center. Around it had been woven an intricate framework of delicate stalks. They were small orchid stems, thin and yellow and shiny. The whole thing was shaped like a wigwam, about three feet tall and five feet broad at the base. In front was a rounded opening about a foot high, leading to an inner circular chamber with the solid base of the sapling as a central beam.

This curious structure fronted on the cleared area. The impression of a front lawn was heightened by several small beds of flowers or fruit. Just under the door there was a neat bed of yellow fruit. Farther out on the front lawn there was a bed of blue fruit. At the bottom of the lawn there was a large squarish bed of pieces of charcoal and small black stones. A few brownish fruits lay here also, some of them rather de-

202

cayed. Off to one side there were several big mushrooms in a heap, and near them were ten freshly-picked pink flowers.

The effect of all this was overwhelming. I had known vaguely that there were such things as bower birds in New Guinea, but I hardly expected to see anything as startling as this. It was much more as if, walking in the Catskills, I had stumbled over the handiwork of some of Rip van Winkle's small friends. How could a bird, unreasoning being that it is, ever contrive such an elaborate playhouse by instinct alone? I struck a match to light my pipe. Then I threw the match into the middle of the cleared ground. Saban and I withdrew a few yards until we were fairly well hidden in the undergrowth. We sat down to watch what would happen. After a short time there was another of those unfamiliar chuckling calls, and I spied one of the brown bower birds in a tree near the house. With a series of rather angular hops the bird sprang from branch to branch until it was on the ground. It looked about, apparently noticing my match, hopped over, picked it up, and with a toss of the head threw it out of the clearing. Then with a flirt of its tail, it leaped into the house and disappeared, making soft growling churring noises all the while. After a minute it came out and flew off again.

I walked about in the nearby undergrowth for a few minutes collecting flowers. There was a pinkish begonia that was common, and a vine with small yellow flowers. In one place I found a single very pretty red orchid growing on a tree. All of these I brought back and placed in the middle of the bower bird's front lawn. Again we drew off some distance and waited. After a time, a single bird reappeared, whether the male or female I could not be sure. This time it flew directly to the ground and hopped at once over to the pile. The yellow vine went first. Apparently these flowers were not at all acceptable. After some hesitation and a good many nods and looks and flirts of the tail, the begonias went the same way as the yellow vine. All were thrown out with an impatient twist of the head. Last of all, the bower bird picked up the pretty red orchid. This time it seemed to be in two minds. It would hop this way and that from one pile of fruit or flowers to another. Finally, with many darts and flourishes, the orchid was placed on top of the pink flowers. The two colors swore a bit, but under the circumstances it was certainly the best matching job that could be done.

For many days I took every opportunity I could to watch these fascinating birds. I even tried to trap some, knowing how valuable they would be to any zoo or research laboratory which might have facilities for studying their remarkable habits. But all my efforts were in vain. The bower birds, as might be expected, were far too sagacious for my snares. Malan knew how to make the typical Pauan snare, a loop of string attached to a bent stick. They can be very efficient. A well-made snare will spring up in a flash. But each time the bower birds were swifter. The nearest I came to catching one was when the noose slipped off the bird's bill as it rose up in the air.

After our first encounter with these strange birds, we found more bowers nearly every day. Ten days after arriving at Bon Kourangen I found the best one of all. It was rather near camp, but off on a steep hillside. I was looking for a ground pigeon which I had shot and lost when I came on the bower. There were several beds of fruit and a big one of charcoal, but in the center was the most astonishing bed of all. Right in the middle, in the place of honor, were six shiny used .410 shotgun shells. Evidently they had been picked up from all along the trails where Saban and I had gone shooting. They were bright red and had the usual polished brass butt ends, and of course were just the thing for a bower bird's garden. Nevertheless, the shells must have been a considerable burden for so small a bird.

(From *The Trail of the Money Bird*)

ALEXANDER HUGH CHISHOLM

Lyre Bird Revels

Australia and adjacent New Guinea have fallen heir to far more than their share of bizarre birds. The birds of paradise with their headquarters in New Guinea are generally conceded to be the most gorgeously adorned birds in the world, but their lesser relatives—the bower birds—make up for their comparatively modest appearance by building structures no bird of paradise can create—little "houses" with miniature "gardens."

The lyre bird, not related to the birds of paradise, is a plain brown hen-like bird until it performs; then no bird can match the breath-taking splendor of its lyrelike tail. Added to this, it is a mimic and vocalist without equal.

As WE SPED along the road from Melbourne to the Dandenong Ranges, on a Sunday fairly in the middle of winter, 1933, the thought arose that conditions in Australia at this period were much more genial than those of winter in most other lands. We knew that snow crowned some of the mountains not far away, but here the landscape was as clear and leafy as that of summer, and along the way birds sang or flashed joyously through the frosty air. It was amusing to recall that an old English essayist, writing in 1860, sympathized with "the unhappy Australians," who, he said, "live in a land where everything is topsy-turvy."

Soon, then—after a drive of perhaps twenty-five miles—we stood at the edge of the Sherbrooke Forest and saw a serried array of great trees, chiefly the mountain-ash and black wattle, growing to such heights that their crests appeared to be almost brushing the sky. Standing thus, looking and listening, we heard bird-voices of unusual power

205

and melody resounding through the forest. Australia's Lyre-birds, troubadours of winter, and the finest vocalists among the large birds of the world, were at their revels.

It was a fortunate thing for thousands of people that the Australian Broadcasting Commission had selected this day and this place for an attempt to broadcast the melody of Lyre-birds throughout the continent. Because of their shyness, and the fact that they are confined to heavy country (extending along the east coast from the vicinity of Melbourne to the vicinity of Brisbane) Lyre-birds are little more than a familiar name to Australians generally. It is true that my companion of the day, Mr. R. T. Littlejohns, had achieved both a sound-film and a gramophone record of the wonderful voice at this spot. Moreover, after many years of effort under difficult conditions, he had secured a motion picture giving glimpses of both the male and the female bird. But he knew, as I knew, that these mediums have their limitations, and thus we were anxious to have the melody filter throughout the continent on a "direct broadcast."

Whatever Mr. Littlejohns may have thought, I was dubious as to the complete success of the experiment. Experience further north, during many years, had taught me that Lyre-birds are temperamental artists, and are not inclined to sing to order. The most I expected was the capture of casual scraps of melody by any one of the four microphones that were hidden near four of the birds' display-mounds scattered throughout the undergrowth and rich soil of the forest. I was to learn that the Lyre-birds of Sherbrooke Forest are, so to say, a law unto themselves.

Sitting among shrubs and moss-grown logs in the dimly-lit forest, we heard, during the first half-hour, several glorious bursts of melody from unseen birds. The first impulse then was to say, "How like the gramophone record!" just as someone who heard the British Cuckoo for the first time said, "How like the clock!"

But, it may be asked, why should the voices of these Lyre-birds suggest the gramophone record any more than would the voices of Lyre-birds in other parts of Australia?

That question expresses the surprise that I felt on first hearing the record in question, for the song differed considerably from the melody of all other Lyre-birds I had heard. The basic qualities were akin, and there were just as many borrowings from the songs and calls of other birds; but the recorded bird-voice was less faithful in some of its imi-

206

tations, and was more given to adaptations, than were the voices of Lyre-birds in New South Wales and Queensland. Certain notes of the Grey Thrush, for example, were glorified far beyond the Thrush standard, and the laughter of the Kookaburra ran off into a wonderful ripple suggesting the sound of water bubbling and babbling over rocks.

All of the Sherbrooke Lyre-birds appear to use these distinctive notes. Were they developed by some master among the mockers of this tight little kingdom, and passed on from one generation to another? If so, why is it that Lyre-birds in other parts are resolute and faithful mimics, but are less inclined to adapt and improvise?

I do not wish to imply, however, that the Sherbrooke Lyre-birds depart from the originals in *all* their vocal borrowings. Much of their mimicry, indeed, is wonderfully exact. In that first half-hour we heard fantasias that contained brilliant imitations of almost every bird-voice of the neighbourhood.

How remarkable it was that these powerful voices could pass from the resounding crack of the Whip-bird to the soft chant of the Pilot-bird; from the wails of the Black and Gang-gang Cockatoos to the melody of the Grey Thrush and the churring of the Yellow Robin; from the laughing notes of the Butcher-bird to the tinkling chatter of a flock of Crimson Parrots! All the voices of the forest were caught into one throat. Listening keenly, we heard even the fragile chatter of the Scrub-Wren and Brown Tit—the voices of birds smaller than Sparrows faithfully imitated by a bird having a body as large as a domestic fowl!

Soon afterwards a warning "Hist!" ran round the small company gathered about the main broadcasting apparatus. Sitting tensely silent, we saw a fine male Lyre-bird stroll on to a mound twenty yards away, and fairly in front of a microphone. For a few seconds he stood in his small arena—a clearing perhaps three feet in diameter, with the soft soil gently elevated—and gazed at us appraisingly. Then the valour of song overcame discretion, and straightway fairy revels began.

What an exquisite performance that was! For the first half-minute or so the master stood at ease as he sang. The voices of a dozen birds of the forest fell easily from a plain brown bird with partly open beak. Pausing for a few moments, he began again; and this time we saw a bird transfigured.

Slowly, majestically, as though responding to the pressure of a secret spring, the great tail began to rise and spread. The two large outer

207

feathers fell away to each side, displaying a beautiful silver-white background and chestnut bars on the under-surface, together with a dainty black curl at the tip of each. Two long central feathers, grey, slim, gracefully curved, rose and were held at an angle above the back. A mass of fern-like plumes, appearing in an upright position from between the two large outer feathers, created a silvery fan for a moment, and then descended, like an elfin parasol, over the back and the head.

What an astonishing transformation was this! A plain brown bird, through the simple act of spreading and raising the tail so as to display the under-surface, had become beautiful beyond words.

Standing thus, and betimes causing the delicate feathers above the back to quiver and shake in a fairy shower, while the large feathers remained perfectly still, the artist poured out a stream of glorious melody, mingling his natural shouts and gurgles with a copious fantasia of stolen notes. There was no regular sequence in the various series. The talented creature merely took whichever voices occurred to his consciousness, in whatever order, and flung them forth in perfect harmony. But always he favoured that glorified Thrush call and the rippling melody born of the "laughter" of the Kookaburra.

Now came a variation in the fantasy. Swinging into a whimsical chuckle, while still the back and head were obscured by the gauzy filamentary feathers, the master began to "take up his dressing"—to shuffle from side to side. Pausing briefly again, he began a series of rhythmic notes, followed by a quaint little jumping dance.

"Ca-luck, ca-luck!" said the revelling bird.

Immediately on uttering these notes he gave two quaint jumps.

"Ca-luck, ca-luck!" he said again, and again the two jumps followed in perfect time.

"Oooooh!" whispered a small girl who was one of the fascinated audience, "he's skipping pepper."

So the bird proceeded, singing and chortling and dancing, and manifestly enjoying the performance as much as were the spellbound onlookers. As for the rest of Australia—alas! church services were in progress then, and a mere bird-melodist could not be allowed to break in upon the voice of a preacher! But this particular bird was thoroughly obliging; he repeated the performance an hour later and thus people all over Australia were enabled to hear the glorious medley of mockery.

(From *Bird Wonders of Australia*)

V *Birds in Far Places*

To APPRAISE wilderness values fully, one must also know the metropolis. Guy Emerson, who lives in a brownstone house in Greenwich Village but spends half his time away from New York, adheres to this view; and so does Joseph Wood Krutch, who explains his point so logically in *The Best of Two Worlds*. Many of our leading naturalists and biologists have lived at least for a while in large cities such as New York and London. Even John James Audubon lived for a few years in New York City (there is an Audubon Avenue, an Audubon Theatre, and an Audubon telephone exchange). If you peer through the iron gate of the little cemetery on 155th Street off upper Broadway, you will see the runic cross which marks his grave.

The environs of a large city such as New York are like a bird trap. Transients faced with the barrier of buildings are forced to drop into the parks and waste areas. If a lad in the Bronx cannot travel to the tundra, he may yet see a rough-legged hawk at Clason's Point on the East River. Or if he cannot go to the West Indies to see sooty terns, there is always a chance that a hurricane may strand one at Gravesend Bay in Brooklyn, only a subway-fare away—or, after a nor'easter, a dovekie from Greenland may be found on the beach at Coney Island. Some of the best naturalists I know were reared in crowded New York —Joseph Hickey, for example, now a professor of wildlife management, who as a boy climbed into the treetops near his Bronx home, the better to see the migrating warblers; and Allan Cruickshank who has photographed more than two-thirds of America's birds.

Given the opportunity, the city-bred naturalist leaves the metropolis (Hickey now lives in Wisconsin, Cruickshank in Florida), for birds infect a man with wanderlust. During the war years many young ornithologists had their first real opportunity to travel. Some sought assignments to army outposts on remote islands or in the jungle. Birds were the breath of life in their nostrils, while some of their fellow soldiers, lacking this consuming interest, almost went mad. At the close of the global conflict *Audubon Magazine* ran many articles by servicemen who had been in far places—North Africa, the South Pacific Islands, Hawaii, the Philippines, Java, and India.

Servicemen writing home were forbidden to mention just where they were stationed. Some got around this by listing in their letters the birds they had seen around camp. By a bit of detective work on the part of some ornithologist friend, the family could often pin-point the location of their son. This worked particularly well in the Pacific where no two groups of islands have precisely the same avifauna.

Great numbers of birds are always a stirring sight. I have not seen the fabulous guanays of Peru which Dr. Murphy writes about, but I doubt that they present a more awesome spectacle than the millions of seabirds that buzz around the thousand-foot cliffs of St. George in the Pribilofs. I have marvelled at a swarm of 190,000 sooty terns in the Dry Tortugas, and my eyes have goggled at 25,000 puffins around the Inner Farne off the Northumberland coast. The gannets of Bonaventure or of the Bass Rock in the Firth of Forth were worth traveling far to see.

Plane travel and longer vacations now bring other continents within the sphere of the footloose, but globe-trotting takes money, a great deal of money. However, there are always the writings of Darwin, of Bates and Wallace, of Abel Chapman, Murphy and scores of others to transport us to the world's Edens.

HENRY BESTON

Sea Birds on the Beach

Not long after the first world war, Henry Beston felt the need of a place where he could withdraw into monklike seclusion. He built himself a cottage on the dunes of outer Cape Cod, and here for a full year he lived a hermit's life, observing the cycle of the seasons, thinking deeply about nature and sharpening his beliefs. His chronicle, *The Outermost House*, became a literary classic, now in its twelfth printing.

The outermost house still stands on the dunes at Nauset. Bird watchers pass its door in late summer when they walk the sands of the great beach to the inlet where the shorebirds, sometimes by thousands, rest between tides on their passage.

M<small>Y BEACH</small> is empty, but not the ocean beyond. Between the coast guard station and Nauset Light, a "raft" of skunk coots is spending the winter. Patches of white on the forehead and the hind neck of the glossy black head of the male are responsible for this local name. The birds sit in the ocean, just seaward of the surf—the coast guardsmen say there is a shallow close by and shellfish—and the whole raft rises and falls unconcernedly as the swells roll under it. Sometimes a bird will dive through the oncoming ridge of a breaker and emerge casually on the other side; sometimes a bird will stand up in the water, flap its wings, and settle down again unconcernedly. There are perhaps thirty birds in this flock. In Thoreau's time, these rafts of coots formed a flock which was practically continuous the whole length of the

213

outer Cape, but to-day such rafts, though not at all rare, are but occasional.

Standing at the door of my house, I watch these winter birds pass and repass, flying well offshore. Now a company of a hundred or more old squaws pass, now a tribe of one of the scoter folk; now a pair of eiders come to rest in the ocean directly in front of the Fo'castle.

These birds practically never come ashore during the winter. They eat, sleep, live, and meet together at sea. When you see a sea duck on the beach, you can be sure something is the matter with him, so runs a saying of the Cape which I had from Captain Nickerson. The only way in which I can observe these winter folk is by using a good glass or by catching a specimen who has got into some kind of trouble and taken refuge on the beach. All these creatures are at a great disadvantage when ashore, and have a world of difficulty trying to launch themselves into the air; they make unwieldy jump after jump, the auks being practically unable to rise at all upon their wings. It was thrilling to walk the beach, and catch sight of a bird sitting solitary on the sands. What might it be? What had led it ashore? Could I possibly catch it and give it a careful looking over? The keynote of my strategy lay in the attempt to prevent the birds from getting back into the water, so between them and the surf I would rush—for the birds would begin to move down the slope to the surf the instant they saw or heard or felt me—and I soon learned that a brisk countercharge was worth all the ruse and the patient stalking in the world. Then began a furious game of tag, the alarmed bird skittering all over the beach, being gradually driven by me toward the dunes, till I manoeuvered him into the angle between the beach and the sandy wall.

My first prisoners were three unhappy little auks, *Alle alle,* who had dipped themselves in oil somewhere on their way down from the arctic —odd little browny-black and white birds about the size of a pigeon, who stood up on queer little auk feet, faced me, and beat little bent wings with a penguin look to them; indeed, the bird has much of an Adélie penguin air. On the Cape, these auks are known as "pine knots" —a term said to be derived from the creature's tough compactness—or as "dovekies." They have always been "aukies" to me. At the Fo'castle I gave them a generous corner floored with newspaper and walled in with boards and a chair. I tried to clean off what I could of the oil; I gave them what I could find of sea victuals, but all in vain; they would not eat, and I let them go just as soon as I saw that I could not possibly

214

help them and that Nature had best deal with the problem in her own way.

When they stood up almost perpendicularly and tried to walk about on their little legs set far aft—they are *pygopodes*—it was much as if an acrobat, standing on his head, were trying to patter about, using the length between his elbow and his finger tips as feet. These little birds used both wings and feet when trying to escape me on the beach. They ran and *rowed* the sand with their wings; the verb gives the precise motion. Moreover, what had taken place was beautifully marked upon the *tabula rasa* of the sand—little webbed feet running in a close chain, wing tips nicking the sand once in each stroke. Coming south from their distant arctic, these little auks do not fly above the ocean as do the more advanced birds; they "skitter" along just over the surface of the waves and keep well out to sea, even well out of sight of land.

One aukie I caught at night. I was on the beach walking north to meet the man coming south from Nauset, and, as I flashed my searchlight to see who the surfman might be, I saw an aukie coming toward me, fluttering along the very edge of surf, all sticky and a-glisten with fuel oil. Strange little fragment of life on the edge of that mysterious immensity! I picked him up; he struggled and then kept still, and I carried him back to the Fo'castle. The bird was small enough to be carried in one hand, and as I held him, his duck feet rested on my palm and his head and neck emerged from the fork between my thumb and index finger. At the Fo'castle he opened his beak, "chattered" with it (there is no word for that motion without sound), transformed his short neck into a surprisingly long one, and looked at me with a kind of "all is well but anything may be expected" expression in his eyes. Every now and then he rather solemnly winked, showing the delicate tan-coloured feathering on his lid. I put him in a corner by himself, and when I went to bed he had given up trying to pick himself free of the oil with his pointed, sparrowy bill, and was standing in his corner of shadow, facing the angle of the walls, for all the world like a small boy who has been naughty at school. The next morning I let him go at his own insistent request.

(From *The Outermost House*)

HENRY W. ELLIOTT

Birds of the Seal Islands

The climax of my odyssey around "Wild America" with James Fisher (1953) came in the Pribilofs. While standing on the bird cliffs I remembered an aquatint sketch that H. W. Elliott made eighty-one Julys earlier, a galaxy of oreels (red-faced cormorants), chikies (glaucous-winged gulls), baillie brushkies (paroquet auklets), canooskies (crested auklets), choochkies (least auklets), and arries (murres). All these had come to life in the seal islands.

As a boy I had read and reread Rudyard Kipling's "The White Seal" in *The Jungle Book,* but I did not know until later the famous old Smithsonian report, *The Fur-Seal Islands of Alaska,* written back in the seventies by Elliott who was then an assistant agent of the U. S. Treasury. It was this report with its topographical detail and place, animal, and man names and numerous drawings by Elliott himself that inspired Kipling's classic tale.

I N THE seasons of 1872-'73, respectively, throughout the ornithological breeding terms on St. Paul and St. George, I neglected no opportunities, as they occurred, to secure everything that was peculiar to the feathered life upon these islands. The dreary expanse and lonely solitudes of the North owe their chief enlivenment, and their principal attractiveness for man, to the presence of the vast flocks of circumboreal water-fowl, which repair thither annually. . . .

Over fifteen miles of the bold, basaltic, bluff line of St. George is-

216

land is fairly covered with nesting gulls, Rissa, and "arries" (murres), while down in the countless chinks and holes over the entire surface of the north side of this island millions of "choochkies" (least auklets), breed, filling the air and darkening the light of day with their cries and fluttering forms. On Walrus islet the nests of the great white gull of the north, Larus glaucus, can be visited and inspected, as well as those of the sea-parrot or puffin, shags or cormorants, and the red-legged kittiwake. These birds are accessible on every side, can be reached, and afford the observer an unequaled opportunity of taking due notice of them through their breeding-season, as it begins in May and continues until the end of September.

Not one of the water-birds found on and around the islands is exempted from a place in the native's larder; even the delectable "oreelie" are unhesitatingly eaten by the people, and indeed these birds furnish, during the winter season in especial, an almost certain source of supply for fresh meat. But the heart of the Aleut swells to its greatest gastronomic happiness when he can repair, in the months of June and July, to the basaltic cliffs of St. George, or the lava table-bed of Walrus islet, and put his grimy hands on the gaily colored eggs of the "arrie"; and if he were not the most improvident of men, instead of taking only enough for the day, he would lay up a great store for the morrow, but he never does. On the occasion of one visit, and my first one there, July 5, 1872, six men loaded a badarrah at Walrus islet, capable of carrying four tons exclusive of our crew, down to the water's edge with eggs, in less than three working hours.

During the winter months the birds are almost wholly absent, especially if the ice shall have closed in around about the islands; then there is nothing of the feathered kind save the stupid shag (red-faced cormorant), as it clings to the leeward cliffs, or the great burgomaster gull, which sweeps in circling flight high overhead; but, early in May they begin to make their appearance; and they come up from the sea overnight, as it were, their chattering and their harsh caroling wakes the natives from their slothful sleeping, which, however, they gladly break, to seize their nets and live life anew, as far as eating is concerned. The stress of severe weather in the winter months, the driving of the snow "boorgas," and the floating ice-floes closing in to shut out the open water, are cause enough for the disappearance of the water-fowl during the hymeneal season.

The position of the islands is such as to be somewhat outside of the

217

migratory path pursued by the birds on the mainland; and, owing to this reason, they are only visited by a few stragglers from that quarter, a few from the Asiatic side, and by the millions of their own home-bred and indigenous stock. One of these migratory species, *Strepsilas interpres* (ruddy turnstone), however, comes here every summer for three or four weeks' stay, in great numbers, and actually gets so fat, in feeding upon the larvae which abound in the decaying carcasses over the killing-grounds, that it usually bursts open when it falls, shot on the wing. A heavy easterly gale often brings a strange bird to the islands from the mainland; a grebe, *Podiceps griseigena* (red-necked grebe), was stranded on St. George in 1873, whereupon the natives declared the like of which they had never seen before; when I found a robin one cool morning in October, the 15th, the natives told me that it was an accident—brought over by some storm or gale of wind that took it up and off from its path across the tundra of Bristol bay. The next fair wind sweeping from the north or the west could be so improved by this robin that it would spread its wings and as abruptly return. Thus hawks, owls, and a number of foreign water-fowls visit the islands, but never remain there long. . . .

I am much divided in my admiration of the two great bird-rookeries of the Pribylov group, the one on the face of the high bluffs at St. George, and the other on the table-top of Walrus islet; but, perhaps, the latter place gives, within the smallest area, the greatest variety of nesting and breeding birds; for here the "arrie" and many gulls, cormorants, sea-parrots, and auks come to lay their eggs in countless numbers. The foot and brow of the low, cliff-like sea fronts to this island are occupied almost exclusively by the "arries" (murres), which lay a single egg, each, on the surface of the bare rock, and stand, just like so many champagne bottles, straddling over them while hatching; only leaving at irregular intervals to feed, and then not until their mates relieve them. Hundreds of thousands of these birds, alone, are thus engaged about the 29th of every June, on this little rocky island, standing stacked up together as tight as so many sardines in a box— as thickly as they can be stowed—each of them uttering an incessant, deep, low, hoarse, grunting noise. How fiercely they quarrel among themselves—everlastingly; and in this way thousands of eggs are rolled off into the sea, or into crevices, or into fissures, where they are lost and broken.

The "arrie" lays but one egg. If it is removed or broken she will soon

218

lay another; but, if undisturbed after depositing the first, she undertakes its hatching at once. The size, shape and coloration of this egg, among the thousands which came under my observation, are exceedingly variable. A large proportion of the eggs become so dirty, by rolling here and there in the guano while the birds tread and fight over them, as to be almost unrecognizable. I was struck by the happy adaptation of nature to their rough nesting; it is found in the toughness of the shell of the egg—so tough that the natives, when gathering them, throw them as farmers do apples into their tubs and baskets, on the cliffs, and then carry them down to the general heap of collection near the boats' landing, where they pour them out upon the rocks with a single flip of the hand, just as a sack of potatoes would be emptied; and then again, after this, they are quite as carelessly handled when loaded into the "bidarrah," sustaining through it all a very trifling loss from crushed or broken ones.

Those "arries" seem to occupy a ribbon in width, and draw around the outward edges of the flat table-top to Walrus island a regular belt, keeping all to themselves; while the small grassy interior from which they are thus excluded is the only place, I believe, in Bering sea where the great white gull, *Larus glaucus,* breeds. Here I found among the little mossy tussocks the burgomaster **building** a nest of dry grass, sea ferns, *Sertularidae,* etc., very nicely laid up and rounded, and in which it laid usually three eggs, sometimes only a couple; occasionally I would look into a nest with four. These big birds could not breed on either of the other islands in this manner, for the glaucous gull is too large to settle on the narrow shelf-ledges of the cliffs, as the smaller *Laridae* and other water-fowls do; and those places which would receive it might also be a hunting-ground and footing to the foxes.

The red-legged kittiwake, *Larus brevirostris,* and its cousin, *Larus tridactylus,* build in the most amicable manner together on the faces of the cliffs, for they are little gulls, and they associate with the cormorants, sea-parrots, and auks, all together; and, with the exception of the latter, the nests are very easy of access. All birds, especially the "arries," have an exceedingly happy time of it on this Walrus islet—nothing to disturb them, in my opinion—free from the ravenous maw of the foxes over at St. Paul, and from the piratical and death-dealing sweep of owls and hawks, which infest the Aleutian chain and the mainland.

(From *Fur-Seal Islands of Alaska*)

R. M. L O C K L E Y

Birds of Skokholm

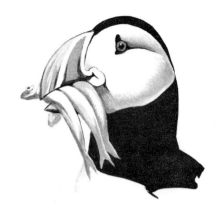

Islands and the birds that live on islands; these are the two recurrent themes of Ronald Lockley. His favorite island, if he had to choose from among the many hundreds of wave-lashed islets and islands that stud the offshore waters of England and Scotland, would be Skokholm. Here he lived for more than thirteen years, watched the birds and wrote several books, at least one of which, *Shearwaters,* is an ornithological classic. His fine prose is unequalled by any other naturalist writing in England today.

T HE CUCKLES is in," said John, warming his thin hands by the flame. "You'd best get out and enjoy 'em, for it's only on a dark night like this that you'll hear 'em at all. Did you hear tell of the young rabbit-catcher who wouldn't believe the islant was haunted? They put him ashore here one day in the late spring. The birds was back, but they told him nothing about the cuckles. It were just such another dark night as this. The cuckles came in by the hunner'-thousan'. They was screeching and howling about the house like the demons of hell. The poor fellow daresen't leave the room here. He huddled under the clothes, and they say that by morning he was as near demented as matters. . . ."

We left John with words still in his mouth, and went outside. The raft of "cuckles" had left the gathering place on the sea, and the birds were coming home to their burrows in twos and threes, dozens, and scores. Each bird seemed to try to out-scream the last. Imagine a pair of cocks crowing out of tune, and their heads being suddenly cut off near the end of the discordant duet. That is what the call of the shearwater is like. Yet no two calls are the same.

Out in the meadow they glided unseen about us, brushing past, even crashing into us, while from underground their mates, incubating the one egg deep in a rabbit-burrow, answered them with muffled crowing. The torch showed many shearwaters sitting on the ground at the entrances to the burrows, singly or in pairs, but these birds were dazed by the light, and refused to continue their natural business. They wriggled and bit vigorously when picked up.

The shearwater's wings are long and narrow, adapted for gliding low over the waves. On land these wings are a handicap, as they do not permit an easy take-off. Nor do the feet help; these are placed so far to the rear of the body that the breast falls forward to the ground. The shearwater blunders along on all fours so to speak, and it needs a fresh wind to enable it to get clear of the rough ground. That calm night many simply scrambled along until they reached the seaward slope. There they launched easily into the air and vanished in the darkness over the sea.

The screaming of the shearwaters became a regular bedlam soon after midnight. It did not prevent our hearing the sweeter, softer crooning notes of the storm-petrels, which were nesting here and there in the old hedge-walls, in the screes of the cliffs, and under boulders and stones. "Purr-rr-chikka! Purr-rr-chikka!" they crooned, and the torch, flashed into the crannies between the stones, showed this swallow-like bird brooding its one white egg. This Mother Carey's chicken of the sailor, foreteller of storm at sea, is a small sooty black bird. Even the fine legs and webbed feet are black, but the rump is pure white, and there is a smear of white under the wing. One came unintentionally to my hand as I lay with my ear to a crevice. Discovering its mistake, it opened its mouth and spat forth a shower of amber-coloured fluid. The warm, oily stuff dripping from my hand smelt no worse than musk. It was probably digested plankton, gathered at sea, which one bird would give to the other at the nest. I told the bird it was a wicked imp, and I let it go after I had turned it over in my hand and marvelled that such a frail-looking thing could withstand the great gales which sweep the north Atlantic Ocean in the winter. The storm-petrel is no bigger really than a large sparrow.

It was growing light as we moved home across the bluebells and the

221

bracken. There was a slight dew. The clouds rolled slowly away from the bright east, like shutters raised at daybreak. The last shearwaters called and were gone either down their holes or off to sea. The storm-petrels danced for the last time—we could dimly see them over their nesting crannies—then they vanished. The crooning from the stones ceased.

A puffin came out of its hole, yawned like a sleepy child, flapped its wings, then, seeing us, hastily dived back to earth. In the thicket by the spring the sedge-warbler rattled a few notes, challenging our passing as it had challenged the shearwaters all night, for the little brown bird will let no noise or movement pass without a word or two of scolding, and will lose its sleep in consequence on this island of noisy nights.

Next to sing was the wheatear. Its jumbled notes were answered by the hedge sparrows and pipits round the house. Before the sun appeared above the mainland in the east the blackbird rolled out its round notes: "Who told you so? I told you so!" The gulls took up their harsh mewing. The island day, just begun, had ended for us. We dragged our rugs into the sunlight and lay down to sleep in its warmth.

(From *I Know an Island*)

JAMES FISHER

The Dry Tortugas

In the spring of 1953 James Fisher and I started on our hundred-day grand tour of wild America, a journey that was to take us from Newfoundland to the Bering Sea by way of tropical Mexico. This was the first time my British colleague had ever set foot on this side of the Atlantic and I had the fun of seeing my continent again through fresh eyes. James Fisher, perhaps more than any other man living, has made his countrymen bird-conscious; his voice, over the BBC network, is known to every Englishman and his books now number more than a dozen. Scanning the titles, there is little doubt that his favorites are the sea birds. Most of the pelagic birds of the Canadian maritime provinces are the same as those one would see on the other side of the ocean. So are most of those which flock along the shores of New England or Long Island, but Florida, touched by the tropics, has novelties to offer. Here, off its southern tip, in the Dry Tortugas, several birds of the pan-tropical oceans make their headquarters. Two, the sooty tern and the noddy, nest nowhere else within the United States. In *Wild America* James Fisher gives his impressions of America's only coral islands.

Т HE SEVENTY MILES from Key West to the anchorage in the Tortugas went fast in the *Ungava,* in a close burning heat. Steve Briggs and his wife and Bob Allen—Floridians—simply looked brown and genial and enjoyed it. Roger and I enjoyed the company, the scenery, the birds, and the fishes, but not the heat. Both of us were reaching the stage where we had few layers of skin to lose, and it was a moot point whether the pressure of a shirt or the sun was more irritating. But we

223

soon forgot the heat in the contemplation of a succession of flying fish processions under our bows. I found my first flying fishes more amusing, prettier, and more powerful than I had expected; they zipped magically out of the water, glided an incredible distance; indeed before they entered the water again there seemed to be a hesitant moment in which they appeared not to obey the laws of gravity—and when they did touch the water by momentarily dipping their tails, they seemed to get a boost for a second short distance. All the way, as we passed other Keys (mangrove-covered Man and Woman, Boca Grande, and the Marquesas in the distance), these silvery flying fish fanned out from our bow. As our boat bore down upon them they flew races with each other, skittered, glided on, and plunged in with a final unequivocal dip beneath the surface of the tropical sea.

The sun was nearing the zenith when the Tortugas appeared on the shimmering horizon, first the tall light which stands guard on Logger-head Key, then the low massive fort on Garden Key. Close to the fort was another smaller key over which hovered a dusky smudge that grew larger, then smaller, constantly changing shape. Our glasses showed that this nebulous coronet was composed of myriad birds, thick as swarming bees around a hive—the famous sooty terns of Bush Key.

Four hundred and forty years before our visit Ponce de León, the discoverer of Florida, sighted this same swarm of birds. He called the islands "the turtles," and Las Tortugas they have been ever since; waterless islands where the sea turtles lay their eggs; the only coral islands in the United States. The Tortugas are one coral atoll, mostly submerged; at present the atoll breaks surface in seven different places (formerly ten), of which the three largest are Loggerhead Key, Bush Key, and Garden Key.

Garden Key, where we dropped anchor, is almost wholly occupied by one of the most extraordinary human artifacts in the New World, the slave-built, brick-built, hexagon-built Fort Jefferson, with its end-less wall, fifty feet high and eight feet thick, and the sites for 450 guns in its three stories and miles of galleries. This fort was started in 1846, primarily to guard the sea approaches to the Gulf of Mexico against the threat of British expansion; and for thirty years the work of build-ing went on. By the time it was nearing completion (at the cost, it is said, of a dollar for every one of its 42,000,000 bricks) the fort was defensively obsolete. It never fired a gun in anger, and the British never came, except as tourists! Subsequently it was used as a prison, as a coaling station, as a wireless station; now it has become a picturesque ruin, since 1935 a National Monument.

The Fort Jefferson National Monument, which embraces the whole archipelago is, through its very inaccessibility, a perfect sanctuary for the tropical seabirds that breed in thousands on the coral sands of Bush Key. For nobody can visit the Dry Tortugas unless he be self-supporting, with his own vessel, or with a vessel or seaplane he has chartered. There is a fine anchorage in the lagoon of the atoll, where the clear blue-green water laps the landing wharves of Garden Key. There the barracudas twitch slowly under the bows of anchored ships, and yellowtails, parrotfish, angelfish, and other tropical fish of coral colors dart about the incrusted pilings of old hurricane-wrecked quays.

It was here at the landing that we were greeted by John De Weese, the resident superintendent. We crossed the medieval-looking drawbridge across the wide moat where sharks once were kept, and followed our guide through the long dark galleries with their cannon emplacements, and up the spiral stone staircases from level to level. It was here, in this Bastille of the Gulf, that Dr. Samuel Mudd was wrongly imprisoned as an accomplice when he set the broken leg of Booth, President Lincoln's assassin, and here he redeemed himself by saving the lives of many men when an epidemic of yellow fever swept the fort. In the hexagonal parade ground within the fort grow graceful coconut palms and dates. Past residents had also planted tamarind, Jamaica dogwood, and gumbo limbo—there is good shelter here for little migratory birds. There are days, De Weese told us—particularly in April and in September—when the scattered trees in the enclosure and even the lawns swarm with tired passerine birds resting from their journey to or from Cuba or Yucatán. Although it was now nearly mid-May we spotted a few late migrant warblers, mostly females—magnolia, Cape May (new to me), black-throated blue, bay-breasted blackpoll, and redstart. They crept about the tops of the trees and we could watch them perfectly from the galleries above. There was a fine group of swallows hawking over the fortress walls—bank, rough-winged, barn, and cliff swallows. We also spotted a yellow-billed cuckoo and three hawks—marsh, pigeon, and sharp-shinned. De Weese showed us a barn owl sheltering in a hole in the ruined officers' quarters.

Tropical seas bathe the Dry Tortugas, even though they are over 80 miles north of the Tropic of Cancer, for the water heated by the

Caribbean's tropical sun circulates their way; everything about them is tropical—their coral, their shells, their fish, their bay cedars, coconut palms, cacti, moon-vines, and sea beans. But the most convincing sign of their utter tropicality is their seabirds, two of which, the sooty tern (black-backed with white underparts), and the noddy (smoky brown with a whitish cap), nest nowhere else in the United States. Two others, the brown booby and the blue-faced booby, wanderers from the West Indies, are seen here every year, but nowhere else in the United States.

During the heat of the day many of the unemployed noddies come across from Bush Key to sit on the ruined quay near the fort. We waded knee-deep through the limpid water (watching out for barracudas), to the rusted girders on which the birds sat; we could reach up slowly and touch some of them before they took wing.

When we rowed the dinghy across the channel to Bush Key later in the afternoon, a dark noisy cloud of sooties boiled up and squawked deafeningly at us, but soon they settled. They were very tame; it was not long before we could pick our way through their crowded ranks to the noddies on the bay cedars beyond without creating too much fuss. For hours we sat on the beach watching the sooties squabbling over the tiny territories round the scrapes which pass as nests. Bodies flexed, wings held out and slightly opened, necks arched, they squawked and crowed at each other. They bowed, like book ends opposing each other, touched bills, flared up in emotion, suddenly to break off and preen; they fiddled with their egg, billing it into a more comfortable position against the incubation patch. Some nibbled and struck at our intruding fingers, without rising from their egg.

The noddies nest mostly in the bay cedar, but also on *Opuntia* (prickly pear) cactus in the interior of Bush Key. Some of the nests, on the edges of bushes, overhung those of sooty terns below. They were loose and untidy and made of seaweed and little sticks; in some were lumps of shell. Some were dense and deep, built on the surviving structures of previous seasons. Not all appeared to have eggs (they lay single eggs normally, like most other tropical terns). In 1907 that pioneer student of terns, Professor J. B. Watson, found the first eggs on May 4; most were laid between the 11th and 16th of May. The season seemed to be about the same with us in 1953.

John James Audubon saw these tropical birds in 1832. He stayed in Key West that summer, and visited the Tortugas on the U. S. Revenue Cutter *Marion;* having already published over a hundred plates

226

of his immortal *Birds of America* he was now famous, and privileged to voyage in government ships. In Audubon's year there was clearly a ternery of immense size on the Tortugas. The first lieutenant of the *Marion* told him "both species were on their respective breeding grounds by millions"! We expect he took this with a pinch of salt. Indeed, these are the most populous terns of the tropical seas; on some islands in the Indian Ocean there *are* sooty colonies of over a million nests! But it is difficult to guess, from Audubon's account, just what numbers he found. Certainly in his time there were many more noddies than there are today. Bird Key, where Audubon found the big sooty colony, no longer exists. It started to sink in 1928 and disappeared entirely during the big hurricane of 1938. Since then the birds have used Bush Key, closer to the fort.

"At Bird Key," wrote Audubon, "we found a party of Spanish eggers from Havana. They had already laid in a cargo of about eight tons of the eggs of this (sooty) tern and the noddy. On asking them how many they supposed they had, they answered that they never counted them, even while selling them, but disposed of them at seventy-five cents per gallon; and that one turn to market sometimes produced upwards of two hundred dollars, while it took only a week to sail backwards and forwards and collect their cargo." A sooty tern's egg, Roger tells me, weighs thirty grams, or about fifteen eggs to the pound. Eight tons would come to nearly a quarter of a million eggs! If Audubon's figure was true, and the eggs had all come from the Tortugas (and none from the Bahamas and Cuba), then there must have been, since then, a spectacular decline in the only tropical tern population of the United States. No doubt this was primarily the work of the eggers. Uncontrolled, these people can undo a large population of social birds in a very few years. The turn of the century, with commercial persecution, was a terrible time for Florida's birds. Anyway in 1903, the first year for which we have any reliable information about the size of the ternery, there were only about 7000 sooties' nests and 200 noddies'. But slowly the sooty tern population climbed back, in the first quarter of the century, to 9000 or 10,000 nests. When the National Park Service took over in 1935, there were 15,000 nests; by 1937, 50,000. During the forties the number ran between 32,135 and 54,500, culminating in 95,438 in 1950, as censused by Willard Dilley.

Several times during our three days at this tropical atoll Stephen Briggs put us ashore on Bush Key for sessions with the birds. At the

228

suggestion of De Weese, we confined our operations to the morning and late afternoon when the sands were somewhat cooler than they were at midday. Our time was mostly devoted to watching, counting, photographing, even sound-recording. Clearly there was room on Bush Key, and on its neighbor Long Key, and their connecting spit, for the nests of even more sooties; the Tortugas were by no means full up, and it seemed quite possible that if the islands had been of about the same area in 1832, they could have supported enough terns to produce the eight tons of eggs that Audubon mentioned!

All over the beach, and among the sooty terns, were little holes in the firmer parts of the sand. A casual human invader of the sands sees no more than quick gray movements at these holes—unrecognized shapes scuttling in. But if he waits quietly, sits to watch *Ocypode albicans,* the ghost crab, comes out. This pallid wraith is the beach-comber of the Tortugas. In 1917 Paul Bartsch found that these crabs ate the eggs and probably killed the young of the least terns on Long Key. Certainly the quick scuttling crabs that rustle and click about the sands scavenge lost sooty tern eggs at the edge of the colony, though even the bigger of these crabs do not seem to try to put the sooties off their eggs as they did the least terns. These queer ghost crabs appeared to be the principal scavengers, except for some important birds. There were a few ring-billed and laughing gulls hanging about, and we saw a herring gull or two on our first day, but the real opportunists were the man-o'-war birds. The magnificent frigate birds (we can call them that) numbered about eighty, and made their headquarters in a row of tallish bay cedars at the edge of the noddy colony. There were always a dozen or more hanging in the wind over the colony and an-other half dozen perched like great marine vultures on the channel posts. They were ideal subjects for the camera gun. Roger found it no trick to hold them in the Nydar gunsight while he ran off film at 64 frames per second, which is the slow-motion speed. These long-billed, buoyant birds, with their seven-foot wingspread and long tail-streamers, are the most masterly soarers of all the seabirds; only the petrels and albatrosses can outdo them as sailplanes—and these do not soar and hang on the wind as continuously and skillfully. Dr. Frank Chapman once said that the man-o'-wars "perch on the air above their homes."

Man-o'-wars have never bred in Florida, but every summer a few thousands haunt the southwest coast, the Keys, and the Tortugas, their nearest nesting places are in the Bahamas and Cuba. At the Dry

229

Tortugas they lead their normal lives, never deliberately landing on the water (they quickly get waterlogged), but catching surface life, usually fish, with fast skillful dives and swoops. When the young terns hatch, the number of man-o'-wars goes up, for they apparently scavenge sickly, weak, and foolish young birds.

Between Garden Key and Loggerhead Light, four miles distant, are several large floating buoys. As we approached one of these in the *Tayto,* we saw sitting on it two large white birds. They were blue-faced boobies. Roger was astonished, because it was on this very same buoy, twelve years before, that he had photographed two blue-faced boobies —the first time, in fact, that these West Indian wanderers had ever been photographed in the waters of the United States. This time it was my turn to photograph them. When the boat, its motor cut off, drifted toward them, they bowed gravely in unison and waited until we were not fifteen feet away before they reluctantly abandoned their perch. On the wing they looked like small gannets but with more black in their wings. Perhaps they were the same two birds Roger photographed in 1941. Apparently they must be pretty faithful to their buoy; the fishermen say they are always there. . . .

When we last saw Fort Jefferson late the next morning it had a little crown of man-o'-war birds suspended above one of its towers, where air currents, deflected upward against the walls, had lifted them. But we did not see another sooty tern all the way back to Key West. Although, as Dr. Robert Cushman Murphy points out, these conspicuous black and white terns probably fly hundreds of miles every day and cannot rest upon the water, away from their populous colonies they seem to be swallowed up in the immensity of the ocean.

(From *Wild America*)

ARNOLD W. BOYD

Lake of the Swans

Arnold Boyd (A.W.B.), whose *Country Diary* has been a weekly feature in the *Manchester Guardian* since 1933, is "Cheshire born and Cheshire bred." Often when I have accompanied him on his favorite walks around Marbury Mere or in Delamere Forest he has lapsed from his proper Oxford tones into Cheshire dialect. A starling becomes a "shepster," a whitethroat a "smastray," and a magpie a "piannet." Colonel Boyd claims much credit for starting his nephew, James Fisher, on his career as one of Britain's great ornithologists. The following entry was written on one of his holiday excursions to Scandinavia.

THE GREAT Lake Vattern (or Wetter) in Central Sweden, with its rocky headlands and wooded shores, stony islets and wide expanse, is not such as can provide suitable resting-sites for birds that need big reed-beds and shallow stretches where they may feed at ease. On the rocky islands common gulls and common terns nest in plenty— as far from the sea as they can well be—and here and in other clear, deep lakes of the same kind red-breasted mergansers and black-throated divers find a home of their choice, not unlike those rivers and lakes in the Scottish Highlands where we know them so well. In the reeds in one shallow corner of the lake, where a green meadow ran down to the water's edge, we came across a flourishing colony of great-crested grebes; but it was necessary to visit another lake of an entirely different type to see water-birds breeding in any number.

We had heard of this lake, a comparatively small one, some seven

231

and a half miles long and two to four miles wide, but in a town only a
few miles distant we could learn little about it, nor could they tell us
how to approach it and get a boat. We knew that it was a place famous
for its swans, and, finding on the map a village called Svanhals, we
thought that this would make a good starting-place. Skirting the
marshes, we drove down a little lane where blue-headed wagtails
"chissick-ed" and whinchats flew from stump to stump; from the wet
marsh, as we passed, rose mallards and shovelers and teal in considerable numbers, with a few of the less plentiful garganey among
them; at the edge wood-sandpipers were feeding; and so on to Svanhals,
with the figure of a swan on the top of its church tower. From the
church we walked down a grassy lane to a vast meadow from which
we could look across the lake, but between it and us lay a bed of reeds
several hundred yards wide, and it was the lake that we had come to see.

The meadow, however, had its attractions. It had been flooded and
was still muddy in places, and in and out of the hummocks ran dozens
of ringed plovers and dunlins; some of the latter already had young that
could fly, for it was late in June, but on one tiny hummock, "teed up"
to escape the flood water, was a dunlin's nest with three eggs, from
which the old bird ran, its feathers puffed out and its head carried low.
It did not go more than two or three yards from us during the short
time we were examining the nest, but ran in and out of the tussocks of
grass like a feathered mouse.

Turning away from the church with the swan we drove on to a
bridge across a broad dyke, where three unclad flaxen-haired boys,
tanned all over a deep brown, were poling a punt through the reeds.
This dyke led towards the lake, and we walked along the bank hoping
to find a way down to the open water, but after a few hundred yards
the water had reached the top of my waders. Curlews were flying over
the low herbage crying noisily; a snipe "chippered" nearby, and in a
shallow pool two lovely dusky (or spotted) redshanks were wading together, birds I had never seen in their breeding haunts before, though
familiar with them on migration in Cheshire; pochards, too, were flying
up from the pools, where, doubtless, already their youngsters were
swimming.

We could go no farther, but on our way back we saw on the opposite
side of the dyke a farmer and his small son, who had brought their
cattle to water. We succeeded in explaining our wants, and into a little
ramshackle home-made punt we got with the boy. We passed slowly

along the dyke through a marsh for ever reminding us of the Norfolk Broads, a resemblance that seemed all the more real as a swallow-tailed butterfly flew over our heads. As we pushed our way slowly through yellow water lilies and greater spearwort a water-rail flew with dangling legs from under the end of the punt, and later, a blackish rail, which I took for a spotted crake, flew across our bows (if a punt can be said to have bows). Here were the nesting-places of the black-headed gulls; over the reeds there was an angry uproar, as a number of these gulls drove off a pale-headed marsh harrier which was quartering the ground where their fledged youngsters were hiding; here the reed-buntings stammered their song; sedge-warblers and then reed-warblers broke into song as we went deeper into the reeds, for a disturbance always makes them sing; at last, passing a great swan's nest, with an addled egg still in it, we reached the open water.

And then we saw the swans. Thousands of mute swans, the species so common in England in a semi-wild condition, stretching in line as far as the eye could reach. Here they live in a perfectly wild state, and who knows but that some of them occasionally find their way across the North Sea to reinforce their tamer relatives in England. Such a colony must take a lot of feeding, and it was not surprising that so late in the season we did not see duck in any great quantity on the open water; pochards were there, and tufted duck, and small groups of golden-eyes; coots both old and young were there by the hundred, and some of their nests still held eggs; and great-crested grebes with large youngsters or little ones riding on their backs were common, for a lake of this nature is their typical home. . . .

All had gone well, and our small boy wielded his punt-pole like a man, but some of the reeds on our way back were thick, and my additional weight on the pole was needed to push the punt through. A moment later my telescope was at the bottom of four or five feet of thick peaty water. During the search that followed, a long-threatened thunderstorm broke, and I was able to watch it in the comparative comfort of a warm bath from which only my head protruded. And how that small boy laughed, though he had recovered enough to say good-bye with a deep bow and a handshake a few minutes later.

(From *The Country Diary of a Cheshire Man*)

ABEL CHAPMAN
AND WALTER J. BUCK

Vultures in Spain

Twice have I tried to photograph griffon vultures at the edge of the broad Marismas in Andalusia where Abel Chapman birded at the beginning of the century. At the end of the long trophy-lined dining hall in the *palacio,* hunting lodge of Spanish kings and nobles, Guy Mountfort and I discovered a large decorative map which had actually been signed by the masters— Chapman and Buck.

We asked the *guardas* if they might locate a carcass with which to lure down the huge griffon vultures that patrolled the sky high over the cork oaks and cistus scrub. They produced the body of a deer which we placed at the foot of a gnarled tree skeleton. It was a perfect setting—one that Gustav Doré would have chosen for vultures, but though we waited an entire day in two expertly concealed blinds, not even a kite came to investigate.

Four years later, near the same spot, I tried a dead cow and although one Egyptian vulture came to investigate during my absence, I drew a blank with the griffons. Yet Guy Mountfort, setting up his blind near the completely stripped and sun-dried backbone of a deer, within twenty minutes focussed his lens on nine vultures of three species—griffon, Egyptian, and the rare black. There is no accounting for the feeding whims of vultures.

O N A HOT May morning we lay beneath the shade of palms and eucalypti in the garden at Jerez, watching the gyrations of Kestrels, Swifts, and Bee-eaters, and lazily listening to the soft bird-chorus—an infinite, space-filling refrain from myriad Nightingales,

234

Serins, and Goldfinches—to the spondee of Hoopoe and dactyl of Quail. Presently there appeared, far overhead, some half-dozen Griffon Vultures wheeling in immense circles, the huge birds dwarfed by the altitude to mere specks. Then another stratum, still higher, was detected, and afterwards a keen eye distinguished a third, and then a fourth, beyond the average range of human vision. How many more tiers of soaring vultures might yet occupy the regions of unseen space beyond, cannot be told: but the incident serves to illustrate the system on which Nature's great scavengers patrol the land. The lower strata we estimated at 800 to 1,000 yards altitude, and these only, it is probable, are on active service, the upper tiers merely standing by, ready to profit by the discoveries of all the working parties that may be in sight beneath them: for at the enormous elevations of the uppermost birds, it is impossible to suppose that even a vulture's eye could detect so small an object as, say, a dead goat on the earth.

There is something peculiarly impressive in the appearance of these colossal birds and in the automaton-like ease of their flight. Ponderous bodies appear suspended in mid-air without visible effort or exertion— the great square wings extended, rigid and motionless, filled with air like the wands of a wind-mill, enable them to rest on space, to soar for hours, as it were, by mere volition. How all the vultures manage to find subsistence is a problem, for even in Spain the earth is not strewn with carcases, as on a battle-field.

Towards a certain point of the evergreen plain of palmetto, there is a visible concentration of soaring forms: thither a string of creaking *carros* has conveyed to their last resting-place some dead horses, the victims of Sunday's bull-fight. Thither flock the vultures to hold high carnival: and a striking sight it is to watch perhaps forty or fifty, as they soar and wheel in as many opposing, concentric circles, gradually focussing themselves over the point of attraction. But as they fold their wings and gather in a seething mass around the carrion, all that was majestic and imposing disappears—as they tear open the flanks and, with spluttering growls and gurgles, and flapping of huge wings, dive their great bare necks into the innermost penetralia, the spectacle changes to the repulsive. Yet, as the only existing system of scavengers, they are performing a useful office. Quickly swells the crowd: from every quarter come more and more—the heavens seem alive with hurrying forms sweeping down to the banquet. As the earlier arrivals become satiated, they withdraw a few yards from the revels to enjoy

235

the state of rare repletion, perched on a neighboring tree or hillock, where they sit with distended crop, fluffed-out feathers and half-closed wings, gorged to the last mouthful, but making room for fresh comers, hungry as they had been before. Thus within a few hours the luckless horses have found a tomb, and when the Griffons have left nothing but bare bones, then another feathered scavenger appears, the Neophron, or in Spanish *Quebranta-huesos, i.e.,* the bone-smasher, who sets diligently to work to loosen the ligaments and tear the skeleton asunder. Then, one by one, the bones are carried off and broken by being dropped from a height upon the rocks, when the fragments are devoured: thus the earth is cleansed of corrupting matter.

Vultures, though found all over Spain—whether in mountain, marsh, or plain—breed only in the sierras. We have observed them in every province from Guipúzcoa to Galicia, and from Asturias to Mediterranean; but nowhere do they so greatly abound as in Andalusia, and especially in that wild mountain-region which forms the southernmost apex of Europe. Here they may fairly be said to swarm, and in our many campaigns in these sierras we have had abundant opportunities of observing them "at home." Here the Griffon Vultures build their broad flat nests on shelves and ledges of the crags, or in caves in the face of sheer walls of rock, many of which exceed 2,000 feet in vertical altitude. The little town of Grazalema is perched on the verge of one of these stupendous *tajos;* from the window of the *posada* one can drop a pebble to invisible depths, midway down which a colony of *Buitres* have had their eyries from time immemorial. The hill-villages of Arcos, El Bosque, Villa Martin, and Bornos all present similar instances—man seeking the highest apex, the vultures its middle heights, beyond reach of bullet from above or below. Ronda, too, has its *tajo,* but we do not recollect seeing any vultures breeding actually beneath the town.

The Griffons commence repairing their nests as early as January—we have watched them carrying claw-fulls of grass and cut branches from places where charcoal-burners had been lopping the trees, on January 21st; a single large white egg is laid in February, incubation lasts forty days, and a naked, blue-skinned chick is hatched early in April. The young vultures are of extremely slow growth, spending full three months in the nest. By mid-May they are as big as Guinea-fowls: ungainly-looking creatures, all crop and maw, with feathers beginning to show through the thick white down.

236

Once at that period (May) we were imprisoned in the Sierra de Ubrique, both our animals having fallen lame through loss of shoes, and it was with no small difficulty we eventually extricated ourselves from the heart of those rugged, pathless mountains. During four days and nights we were encamped in the wild pass of the Puerta de Palomas, whose crags were tenanted by numerous Griffons, and the strange growls made by them on returning to their eyries was often the first sound heard on awakening at daybreak, in our roofless bedroom among the boulders, mingled with the awakening notes of the Bluethrush and Alpine chough. These nests proved to be quite the easiest of access we ever saw—the cliffs being rather a chaotic jumble of big rocks and monoliths than crags proper; and by clambering over these we reached sixteen nests—many very slight affairs, with bare rock projecting through the scanty structure—of which only two held more than a single poult. The nests of the Griffon—albeit malodorous—are always cleanly. These vultures feed their young exclusively on half-digested food which they disgorge from their own crops—hence there is no carrion or putrefying matter lying about, as is the case at the nests of the Neophron and Lammergeyer. It is the *male* vulture only that, at this season, undertakes the lengthened journeys into the plains and low-lands, remaining absent for days together in search of supplies, and returning crop-full of unsavoury store. The vultures seen on the distant plains in spring are all males, the females remaining at or near their nests. . . .

Three of these eyries were situate on abrupt, detached stack of rock, so easily accessible that we almost "walked" into them. Some years afterwards, passing through this sierra on March 1st, we found the three stacks occupied as before, each nest containing a single egg.

During this scramble we came suddenly upon a pair of Eagle-Owls, solemnly dreaming away the hours in a deep cavern; but, being in an awkward position on the crag-face, could not spare a hand to secure them. These caverns were also occupied by Choughs and Rock-Martins, the latter sharing a cave with hundreds of bats.

Eventually, after dragging the lame beasts some twenty miles, we got clear of the sierra, but found that our absence had caused much anxiety at Jerez. On the outward ride, it had so chanced, we were present at a sad accident by which two men and their nine mules lost their lives, while attempting to cross the swollen Guadalete at the Barca Florida. Consequently we did not attempt the ford, and only reached the sierra

237

after a long detour: but news of the accident having reached Jerez, and our disappearance being unluckily attributed thereto, the curious result was that the first person we met on the *vega* of Guadalete was honest old Blas, all solemn and dejected, as he endeavoured, by watching the flight of the vultures, to discover our remains!

(From *Wild Spain*)

COLONEL
R. MEINERTZHAGEN

The Lammergeier

Leading my own list of "most wanted" birds in Europe is the fabled lammergeier. I have seen the beautiful wall-creeper with its crimson wings in the Swiss Alps and the great bustard—a flock of fourteen—on the rolling plains of Andalusia, but the lammergeier or bearded vulture has eluded me. Although apparently extinct in the Alps it can still be seen in the Pyrenees and also in the high Sierras of southern Spain. Legend has it that this great bird, shaped like a large wedge-tailed falcon, will swoop at an animal on a precipice or even a man, knocking him off balance. Colonel Richard Meinertzhagen once had an unnerving experience with one of these "bone-breakers" while crossing a moving scree in the mountains of Baluchistan. Sliding the slope he fetched up on a juniper stump to which he clung while the boulders whizzed past. A lammergeier, finding him in this difficulty, swooped so low that he could see its penetrating red eye, but the protecting juniper saved him from being struck. Colonel Meinertzhagen, an old British soldier who has studied birds for sixty-five years, knows a great deal about lammergeiers. He has lived with them in the Himalayas, in Crete, the Pyrenees, on Mount Kenya, and in Arabia.

I HAVE LITTLE respect for the lammergeier but have a great admiration for his grandeur, his poise and his magnificent flight. Two episodes, when I saw him at his best, remain indelibly engraved on my mind. Let me quote from my diary of 26th July, 1914, on the eve of the first world war, when I found myself in the mountains of Baluchistan:

The finest view I ever had of a lammergeier occurred today. I came on him but a few feet away silhouetted against a gold-red sunset, magnificent against an horizon stretching for miles and miles into golden infinity. He was quite unconscious of my presence. He sat on a rocky pinnacle facing the setting sun, wings slightly drooping and half-stretched head turned up towards heaven. Was this the phoenix of the ancients, Pliny's "bird of brilliant golden plumage around the neck, the throat adorned with a crest and the head with a tuft of feathers"? Was this lammergeier conscious of his sacred relationship with the sun? The phoenix of the ancients presaged peace everywhere in the land. What I saw this evening seemed to foretell war, a long, bloody war. It was the finest, most beautiful and yet most terrible, the most romantic view of any bird I have seen at any time anywhere.

The second episode occurred on Mount Sinai, where I spent the night alone in the small chapel on my fiftieth birthday. It had snowed all night, most of which I spent walking about to keep warm. Again, from my diary:

I felt lonely and detached from the world, longing for the break of day. At last it came, first a faint blush of grey light in the east, rapidly flooding with gold. As I paced up and down in the snow the most-soft horizon slowly revealed itself, and I felt I was living in a wilderness of spirits, lost and abandoned in the ghost-robe of dawn which enshrouded the earth. And when the sun rose over the deserts of Arabia the mist began to clear, revealing a crystal-clear ruby blaze over the eastern skies, and I looked down on one of the most beautiful sights I have ever witnessed: to the east I could see the Gulf of Aqaba and on the west I could see parts of the Gulf of Suez. On this holy mountain I felt very near to God. I turned to look at the chapel. On the small wooden cross sat a lammergeier, all hunched up in the cold but gloriously golden in the sunlight; and as I watched him, but a few yards off, his great wings spread out and he sailed forth into the gorges of those barren mountains searching for his breakfast, as his kind have done since the days of Moses.

(From *Birds of Arabia*)

240

MADELINE ALSTON

Birds at the Victoria Falls

In July of 1957, the first Pan-African Ornithological Congress convened at Livingstone near Victoria Falls in Rhodesia. Many Americans and Europeans who had long wanted to see the birds of the dark continent used this scientific gathering as an excuse to pack their bags and board the air transport.

Two things, primarily, lure the tourist to Africa; not the cities—cities are cities the world over—but the indigenous native peoples and the wildlife. The dark tribes, adopting European dress and ideas, are today less of a drawing card than the wildlife but soon, if the slaughter of the large mammals (in the name of progress and tsetse fly control) is not stopped, only the birds will remain.

AND, BY THE WAY, don't forget to look at the Falls!" was the parting shot of a relative as she saw me off. She was referring to my propensity for bird-watching, which relations sometimes find trying. That was why I went alone. I had been to the Falls before, but if you have once seen or heard anything beautiful you crave to hear or see it again, be it a cathedral or a sonata, a bird or a picture. But this time it was not so much the great waters that I wanted to see as the birds of the Falls at breeding-time—otherwise I should not have gone at the hottest season of the year, when the Zambesi was at its lowest.

Washed of the dust of the long railway journey, such fun it was to

241

look down on the famous bridge, over which hornbills and two eagles were flying, with oceans of bushveld, full of possibilities, melting into the horizon, and to see too the flamboyant tree in the hotel garden in full flower. One glory of the Victoria Falls is, among others, that you are free to come and go unmolested by would-be guides who spoil Egypt and other interesting places by their importunity. And the natural beauties of the surroundings are protected, and undisfigured by advertisements as at Niagara. You feel there is a proper spirit of reverence for the works of God.

Being alone, I did not have to waste time while other people were making up their minds what to do. This first morning, then, I decided to walk to the bridge, and, on my way, flying from tree to tree, I caught sight of a scimitar bill. This beautiful hoopoe, glossy purple and blue and black, with white on wings and tail, gets its name from its slender curved bill. It is not unlike the red-billed wood-hoopoe, but smaller and with legs and bill blackish instead of red. The scimitar bill, too, is always found singly or in pairs, never in small flocks like the wood-hoopoes. It has the most fascinating way of curving and creeping and twisting round the branches as it probes in search of insect food.

Golden-breasted buntings and blue-breasted waxbills were flying about and feeding on the ground, not at all shy. Everywhere in the bushveld one sees them. And there were Namaqua doves and laughing doves cooing and bubbling with gentle voice.

Then, approaching the bridge, two birds new to me, black and white and grey, with loud chattering cries, flew by and alighted on a tree, where, with the courage of Horatius guarding the bridge, they allowed me to come within a few yards and watch them for quite ten minutes. They were Smith's helmet shrikes. One feels one ought to apologize in the name of poetry—but I am not responsible for the name of these birds. I suppose some Mr. Smith once shot and stuffed one. Ornithologists will do anything in the name of science, including labelling innocent little birds with dull men's names. Not even Shelley could make a poem about a Smith's helmet shrike, or a Bradshaw's sunbird, or a Gurney's thrush. But I do not think anyone will want to make a poem about the Smith's helmet shrike, although they might want to make one about the Bradshaw's sunbird if it had a bird-like name. The Smith's helmet shrike has been given an absurd bunch of coarse feathers which flops over the beak, suggesting a distracted poet in need of a hairdresser. And the yellow eyes encircled by orange-coloured wattles add to the odd appearance. Does any other country have so many curious-looking birds as South Africa?

As I stood on the bridge another queer fellow, the trumpeter hornbill, flew over noisily within a few yards of me. This large crested bird, 27 inches in length, is black and white, with red eyes and a curious casque, like an additional bill, on top of the upper mandible.

And of course there were the ubiquitous go-away birds—grey louries —in plenty. As an instance of the inaccuracy of the casual observer, and also of the prevailing ignorance regarding South African birds, in a London paper the hornbills were identified with the go-away birds and described as a great nuisance as "they fluttered ahead of me with their alarm cry of 'go-away, go-away,' which disturbed the game in front." The hornbills are in no way related to the go-away birds, which are plantain-eaters, louries, or touracos.

Wandering towards the Eastern Cataract it was interesting to see the great walls of basalt over which the Falls leap partially bared by the lesser flow of water—yet not quite bare, for over them was spread a blanket of dry green moss which shone in the sunlight with the sheen of a sunbird—the very greens indeed of the little bifasciated sunbird.

Returning, I heard a voice reminding me of the tambourine dove, a voice gentle, and cooing in a descending scale. Following the voice I found it was the emerald-spotted dove, a beautiful creature with an emerald patch on its wings.

Bulbuls and the bubbling sounds of rain awoke me before sunrise next morning to a wet, sweet-scented tropical world. It was not yet light, but I did not mean to waste a minute, and as I stepped out through the passages of scrubbing and polishing natives (much too polite to appear to notice the unusual sight of an hotel visitor emerging from her room at such an hour), I felt as if I were embarking on some great adventure. And indeed I was, for I saw wonderful things that morning. The world was mine and the Victoria Falls might have been my private property, for not a human being did I see once I had left the hotel. On my way to the Devil's Cataract I stopped to watch some ruddy waxbills feeding, and with them were some little weaver-finches with a scarlet patch on each cheek. . . .

If the Zambesi was at its lowest the Devil's Cataract still tore and plunged like a thousand wild horses over the precipice with thunderous roar and clouds of spray. (I did *not* forget to stand and stare.) Walking along the banks of the river, where on my first visit I had met several natives carrying over their shoulders a dead python, and coming to an open view, my hungry eyes fell on an African openbill standing in a pool battling with a hard, round mollusc which, try as he might, he failed to crack, until eventually he flew with it to a hard rock and cracked it there. After some time, seeing me, he flew to a tree almost above my head, feeling, apparently, out of danger. This strange black stork measures about 37 inches. The remarkable thing about him is the bill with a great gap in the middle through which you can see daylight.

I stepped on to the rocks myself to watch the birds, a blue kingfisher flashing past tempting me. There were pied kingfishers hovering, with head and tail pressed downwards, and pied wagtails scurrying and flipping their tails, with quick, darting flights from pool to pool. There were two species of snipe, the double and the painted; and over my head, with loud screeching cries, flew an old friend, the giant kingfisher, familiar to me in my own home at the Cape, two thousand miles away. He alighted on an overhanging branch, his black and white and russet-red plumage merging into his surroundings in a wonderful way as he sat still as a stone for a time and then, with courage in his wings, he flew boldly right over the Devil's Cataract as if saying, "Do your devilmost!" Then I walked through the Rain Forest. I missed the maidenhair ferns I had seen before, but the forest was carpeted with scarlet hæmanthus flowers. I did not walk through with waterproof and rubber boots as I had seen people doing, but just made up my mind to get wet. How delicious it was, too, to walk through the rich greenness, in this region of perpetual rain, with the tumbling waters on one side, deafening, but not more deafening than the shrill screaming of the "Christmas beetles" (cicadas) on the other side, accompanied by the singing of the frogs—and some of our South African frogs have very musical voices. Emerging, a dripping woman, into the sunlight again, I was greeted by a scarlet-chested sunbird and a golden-breasted bunting, and, on the ground, was a flock of blue-breasted waxbills. It was a grateful and glad woman that returned to the hotel for bath and breakfast.

(From *Wanderings of a Bird Lover in Africa*)

JULIAN HUXLEY

A Voice in Africa

The bird watcher by his knowledge of bird voices may come by experiences denied to others, for we invest songs with many associations. A white-throated sparrow tuning up in migration brings memories of Maine woods; a skylark or a curlew in the sound track of a British film transports us to old-world meadows or moors. A familiar song heard in a distant land releases a rush of nostalgia.

ONE EARLY morning towards the close of last year, I was lying in bed, just awake, on the shores of the Victoria Nyanza, close on the equator in Central Africa. From my window, I could see the fronds of a tall palm-tree. At its foot, though the season was December, there were bright flower-beds and green lawns; and beyond there was a park-like stretch of grass, dotted with magnificent trees all in leaf, sloping down to the soft blue waters of the lake under the bright sun. Suddenly a song came from just outside the window—the song of a willow wren, a willow wren on migration three or four thousand miles from the place where it was hatched; and automatically, as I heard the fresh and delicate dying fall of the notes, they brought back to me all the other attributes and associations which give the willow wren its particular character—the slender, modest, green-brown body of the singer, the cool of an English spring, a piece of rough furzeland, with the leaves barely unfolded on the birch-trees, the bird prying about

245

for the few early insects. The willow wren is the antithesis of all that is tropical, an embodiment of freshness, delicacy, and northern spring-time; it was strange and even moving to hear it thus in the heart of Africa.

(From *Bird Watching and Bird Behaviour*)

J. J. TER PELKWIJK

Letter from the Indies

Joost Ter Pelkwijk, fresh from Holland, shyly introduced himself at a Tuesday night meeting of the Linnaean Society in New York. This lad of twenty-five was one of the most promising young field biologists I had ever met; he would have gone far—had it not been for the war.

"Pelk," as we nicknamed him, was rather clever at drawing birds and fish in a line and stipple technique. He begged to see how I tackled a bird painting, so one night after dinner while he sat at my elbow I painted a brown thrasher and a flicker for a *Life* magazine color spread. While I worked he told me of his plans to study the birds of Surinam. He had received a grant, and his father, the burgomaster of Utrecht, had supplemented this with enough extra money to see a bit of the United States before he continued his journey to South America.

Several weeks later, when young Pelk was traveling west (via Greyhound Bus, to conserve his dollars), the news broke that the Germans had invaded Holland. Days passed without word from his family. On opening the copy of *Life* in which my birds appeared, he was stunned to find a propaganda photograph, released by the Nazis, showing German parachute troops taking a Dutch airfield—the very field near his home! There in the corner of the picture was his family's summer home and the stream where he had studied the sticklebacks. And twenty round white spots—descending parachutes! Fortunately his family—even his aviator brother who was twice shot down—survived. But Joost himself would not be so lucky.

Contacting the colonial government he was assigned in a semi-military capacity to the Department of Fisheries in Java where he spent much of his time patrolling in small boats. Not many months after we had received the letter printed here, the Japanese started moving across the southwest

Pacific. Except for a Christmas card, that was the last we heard of our dear friend. He died on March 2, 1942, three days after his boat had been bombed and burned by Japanese aircraft. We recalled his words in an earlier letter:

Whatever happens, I will be grateful that I have had an opportunity to see so much of this beautiful world.

To my bird-friends, New York:

Dear Friends!

Would you like to go birding here? OK, take a bicycle and come along. A bicycle is here the best means of transportation and like everywhere the early morning is the best time for birding. Then the temperature is very pleasant too. We leave at half past five or quarter to six. My one-room house is in the garden city of Batavia. Batavia, a halfmillion city, is rather large and has the most unusual shape being nearly ten times as long as broad. Wherever you live, you are always relatively near to the fields. The city offers great variety of "Habitat" for human beings—and birds. The roads in the neighbourhood are excellent for bicycles, except after a shower, which comes nearly every afternoon. But then we will be home again. In the tops of the trees, as silhouets against the clear sky, small thrushlike birds are singing in chorus. These are golden-vented bulbuls (*Pycnonotus aurigaster*). They sing more or less like robins, and live everywhere near human dwellings. An other "city bird" is the gray-backed shrike (*Lanius shach*) very much like the California shrike, but with a nice orange-colored breast and very tame indeed. On a lawn in front of one of the larger houses, six or eight starlings are walking, pecking industriously in the grass. These rose-colored starlings (*Sturnogaster contra*) are perhaps one of the most popular cage birds, kept by the native population. Keeping of cage birds is an ancient tradition and no bird-protecting law has the power to deprive the people of their hobby. However the starlings are plentyful and tame, notwithstanding many are caught and sold. The other—may be still more popular—cage bird is a little dove (*Geopelia striata*). Nearly every native home has its "perquutut" in a dome-shaped cage sometimes attached to a long pole to give the little favorite a maximum of fresh air. A small woodpecker is making a terrific machinegun-noise in top of an antenna (*Dryobates analis*).

248

We are in the fields just after dawn. The air is clear and bluish green in color. Far away you see clearly the outline of two big volcanoes. In front, flooded rice fields. Early in the morning those fields remind of ancient church windows. All shades of colours from the rising sun are reflected in the separate parts of water, bordered by irregular narrow strips of black dikes, forming an interesting pattern over the scenery. In the water with its regular dots of bright green riceplants, hundreds of herons are fishing. During the flooded period the fields yield an additional crop of fish, but certainly not every little fish planted out will be found back afterwards! There are many different herons on Java and they are all rather common too. On a single trip you may see the great blue and purple herons, three egrets, night herons, bittern, and two little "pond herons" (*Ardeola*). It is a marvelous view to see a big heronnery in a huge Ficus-tree on the middle of the market place in a native village. Of course you may expect some rails in the rice fields. One of the most beautiful birds I know is the native coot (*Porphyrio albus*). Between the yellowish green of the rice you suddenly see a coot with a bright red bill and deep blue and purple all over.

Between the fields you see many little "woods." Please don't suppose these were tropical jungles! They are but villages with gardens of all kinds of fruit trees. The thing that fascinates me is that these trees look all the time as if it were spring. They don't have the dull green colors of our trees in summer, but look like oaks in early June. Some trees, or branches of trees however look very winter-like indeed. A flight of noisy paroquets (*Psittacula alexandri*) has stripped all the leaves. Many singing golden orioles make me think of my own garden in Holland. It was surprising to find a pale colored edition of the ordinary European coaltit (*Parus major*) here. They look like mounts that have been preserved for half a century or so in a show case, not far from the window. Two other interesting birds are the fantailed flycatcher (*Rhipidura albicollis*) and the magpy-colored Straits robin (*Copsychus saularis*), which however is certainly not named after your robin, but after the British one.

Real jungle may only be found here on the slope of the volcanos. Don't forget that Java is one of the most densely populated spots of the world. Over fifty million people live together in an area the size of Florida. If you realize that, it is surprising how much is left for a naturalist here. It seems unbelievable that tigers, rhinoceroses, wild

249

bulls and crocodiles can live in such an anthill of human beings. But they do, thanks to the rather well arranged nature protection and (if nothing unforeseen happens) they will be safe for an indefinite period of time. Along the coast however there is a strip of jungle like woods; partly flooded woods with trees on stilt-roots, partly a kind of secondary or tertiary jungle, that has a definite value as a producer of fire wood. We might just as well go to the mountain slopes to see wild orchids and rhinoceros birds, but we can do so a next time. In the coast-woods we are sure to see lots of my favorites: the birding is generally easier there. We have got to wade through brooks and swampy thickets. You may feel at home while hearing the rattle of the American kingfisher. However, the noise is produced by *Rhamphalcyon capensis,* the stork-billed kingfisher, who has about the size of the American and the brilliant colors of the European kingfisher. There are many kingfishers here and you see them near every little brook or stream. Some are bigger, others are smaller, but all have the most brilliant colors and colorpatterns. An other bright bird that we will see without doubt is the bee-eater, (not beef-eater, though that is a brightly colored animal too). They are considered to be migrants here though they stay all the year round. But nobody has ever seen them breeding and they will have to reproduce somewhere.

There are lots of migrants here: in winter from Asia and in summer from Australia. The barn swallows are leaving just now for China. All the time you hear the monotonous call of cuckoos. One of them has the disagreeable name of "brainfever" because of the sound (and the effect) of its call (*Caccmantis merulinus*). An other cuckoo, crow-pheasant (*Centropus sinensis*) is big and heavy and if he calls, it is as if a drum is beaten. It will not be long before we see the first monkeys. Sometimes you notice them far, far away because of their screaming noises. Often, especially at the middle of the day, you observe them suddenly overhead, sitting quietly and making faces at you. They are rather tame and will certainly stay, if you keep quiet. There are two kinds that are by far the most common: a gray one with a very human expression, and a slender black one (*Macacus cynomolgus* and *Semnopithecus maurus*). A remarkable creature that is quite common here is the "dragon," a little lizard that sails through the wood like a glider-plane on the skin, expanded between the ribs. There are many species of them and most have a very nice color. Between the roots of the trees all kinds of little noises are heard, produced by armies

250

of crabs. At the edge of a brook or in the top of a palm tree a group of birds, more or less sparrow-like, is flying about in a very busy manner. It is a colony of weaverbirds. There are three kinds of them here, all with different types of nests, the most remarkable being *Proceela hypoxanta,* a rather common zoobird I believe. The bright Java sparrow, the munias and field sparrow are the most common finches. They feed in huge numbers on the ripe rice fields.

Between the sea and the land often fish ponds have been laid out. They are more or less like the famous salt pans near Salinas (Monterey), only they are filled with brackish water instead of brine. All kinds of shore birds are to be found there—golden plovers (*Charadrius apricarius*), curlews (*Numenius phaeopus*), snipes (*Capella stenura*) and sandpipers (*Eriola ruficollis,* for instance) make you think of Long Island. In a sandy pool, however, a group of very official Adjutant-birds remind you to the fact that you are birding in the far east. Because of my job, I spend most of my time on or near the Java sea. Now you might think that I will have a fine opportunity for watching birds. It is a great shame that real sea birds are scarce here. Joe Hickey will be disappointed indeed for we don't have any gulls here to give them colored bands. He will have to spend all his time at peregrine falcons, that are only slightly different from the American ones. There are many more "hawks" here. Exceedingly common everywhere along the coast is a chestnut-colored Brahminy kite. Far from rare is a sea-eagle (*Haliaetus leucogaster*), that makes me think of your quarters and half dollars. They come down in the fish-markets to steal fish! But as a whole, the sea is rather desolate. Except for a few terns and one or two frigate birds or boobies, very little distracts my attention from the fishes. I wish that all of you, or at least one of you, will come here in the near future to go with me on a real bird-trip. I hope it will give you as much joy as birding around New York has given to me.

Sincerely yours,
PELK

(From *Deeze Mooie Wereld*)

CHARLES DARWIN

Unusual Tameness

Charles Darwin the great student of speciation was twenty-seven when the
Beagle, making its epic voyage around the world, dropped anchor at the
Galapagos Islands off the coast of Ecuador. It was here that he saw and
studied the black finches, *Geospiza,* which demonstrate so clearly the processes of evolution on islands.

Like every naturalist who has set foot on these islands he was impressed
by the incredible tameness of the birds. On other Pacific islands the seabirds—terns, albatrosses, boobies—often exhibit an extraordinary tameness, but here even the doves and hawks seem without fear. In spite of
more than two centuries of occasional visits by whalers and other predatory
seafarers the birds have retained to this day their seeming innocence of the
ways of men.

Darwin, some years after his voyage concluded "first, that the wildness of
birds, with regard to men, is a particular instinct directed against *him,* and
not dependent on any general degree of caution arising from other sources
of danger; secondly, that it is not acquired by individual birds in a short
time, even when much persecuted, but that in the course of successive generations it becomes hereditary."

I WILL CONCLUDE my description of the natural history of
these islands by giving an account of the extreme tameness of the birds.

This disposition is common to all the terrestrial species—namely, to
the mocking-thrushes, the finches, wrens, tyrant flycatchers, the dove,
and carrion-buzzard. All of them often approached sufficiently near to

252

be killed with a switch, and sometimes, as I myself tried, with a cap or hat. A gun is here almost superfluous, for with the muzzle I pushed a hawk off the branch of a tree. One day, whilst lying down, a mocking-thrush alighted on the edge of a pitcher made of the shell of a tortoise, which I held in my hand, and began very quietly to sip the water. It allowed me to lift it from the ground whilst seated on the vessel. I often tried, and very nearly succeeded, in catching these birds by their legs. Formerly the birds appear to have been even tamer than at present. Cowley (in the year 1684) says that the "turtle-doves were so tame that they would often alight upon our hats and arms, so that we could take them alive; they not fearing man, until such time as some of our company did fire at them, whereby they were rendered more shy." Dampier also, in the same year, says that a man in a morning's walk might kill six or seven dozen of these doves. At present, although certainly very tame, they do not alight on people's arms, nor do they suffer themselves to be killed in such large numbers. It is surprising that they have not become wilder; for these islands during the last hundred and fifty years have been frequently visited by buccaneers and whalers, and the sailors, wandering through the woods in search of tortoises, always take cruel delight in knocking down the little birds.

These birds, although now still more persecuted, do not readily become wild. In Charles Island, which had then been colonized about six years, I saw a boy sitting by a well with a switch in his hand, with which he killed the doves and finches as they came to drink. He had already procured a little heap of them for his dinner; and he said that he had constantly been in the habit of waiting by this well for the same purpose. It would appear that the birds of this archipelago, not having as yet learned that man is a more dangerous animal than the tortoise or the amblyrhynchus, disregard him, in the same manner as in England shy birds, such as magpies, disregard the cows and horses grazing in our fields.

(From *The Voyage of the Beagle*)

ROBERT CUSHMAN MURPHY

The Guanay
The Most Valuable
Bird in the World

Nowhere else on this earth—not even in the Pribilofs in the Bering Sea or on St. Kilda off Scotland—do the sea birds present such a mass spectacle as the guanay cormorants on the bird islands of Peru. The cold Humboldt current laving the desert coast of South America is the source of this abundance, for cold water has far more plankton—the minute floating plants and animals that populate the sea—than warm water. Plankton is the food base, the pasturage of everything that lives in the sea. The little fish thrive on it, and they in turn are gobbled up by the bigger fish and the birds.

Robert Cushman Murphy, our first authority on oceanic birds, visited the fabulous bird islands of Peru in 1919 and again in 1925.

Picture to yourself the shining, rainless coast of Peru, washed by ocean waters to which storms are unknown, where the swells surge northward, from month to month and year to year, before winds that blow regularly from a southerly quarter. On such an ocean dark flocks of guanayes form rafts which can be spied miles away. Slowly the dense masses of birds press along the sea, gobbling up fish in their path, the hinder margins of the rafts continually rising into the air and pouring over the van in some such manner as the great flocks of pas-

254

senger pigeons are said to have once rolled through open North American forests in which oak or beech mast lay thick upon the leafy floor.

At other times, when the guanayes are moving toward distant feeding grounds, they travel not in broad flocks but rather as a solid river of birds, which streams in a sharply marked, unbroken column, close above the waves, until an amazed observer is actually wearied as a single formation takes four or five hours to pass a given point.

Equally impressive are the homeward flights of these cormorants, after a day of gorging upon anchovies, when in late afternoon slender ribbons, wedges, and whiplashes of guanayes in single file twist and flutter, high in air, toward the rounded plateaus of white islands which gradually turn black as the packed areas of birds swell out from clustered nuclei toward the borders of the available standing room. . . .

At South Chincha Island in mid-October the breeding grounds were covered with just one year's accumulation of sun-baked guano, and the cormorants were getting ready to nest again. They stood in compact bodies, each comprising thousands of birds, on the flat top of the island, and, when a human being approached, all those on the nearer side began to stir—not *en bloc*, nor yet individually but in groups of a few hundred, each of which for the time constituted a unit. One group would move rapidly away, the birds carrying themselves bolt upright. Another group would advance toward the observer, so that this section of the army would gleam with white breasts instead of shiny, dark backs. Still another unit would rush to the right or to the left, so that both the dark backs and the white breasts showed at once, and the long bills and red nasal warts became conspicuous. Such closely huddled companies soon collided with others moving in different directions, producing much confusion about the margins. A few of the birds showed no fear at all, stolidly permitting a man to approach within a few feet. The greater proportion, however, frantically took to flight, rushing helter-skelter down a slope, and raising a cloud of dust with their whistling wings. The air became bewilderingly thick with birds as they circled overhead, but within a few moments the number returning to earth once more exceeded the number taking wing.

When an observer makes his way slowly and very quietly into the heart of a colony in which nesting has definitely begun, the guanayes gradually retreat, and one may sit down in a clear circle which is at first fifty or more feet in diameter. But almost imperceptibly the birds will edge in again, until the bare circle narrows to but three or four paces. From such a point of view it seems as though the ground were covered with as many pairs of sprawling webbed feet as there is room for, and yet new arrivals plump down by scores or hundreds every minute. Over the ocean, moreover, to the north, south, east, and west, one may commonly see endless black files still pouring in toward the island. The hum of wings is like the effect of an overdose of quinine upon the ears, and the combined voices seem like mutterings of the twelve tribes of Israel. It reminds one of all sorts of strange, oppressive roarings, such as the noise of railroad trains in river tunnels. The near-by voices, which can be distinguished individually, are merely sonorous bass grunts and screepy calls. It is the multiplication of such sounds by numbers almost too large to imagine that make the out-landish and never-to-be-forgotten babel.

Toward evening of such October days, most of the guanayes would be courting, after strenuous hours at sea during which all their energies had doubtless been devoted to winning the sustenance of life. Privacy does not enter into their notion of fitness, and while six or seven birds occupy each square yard of ground, the love-making antics are often in full progress.

These are in general not unlike the courtship habits of the closely re-lated antarctic cormorants. Two guanayes stand side by side, or breast to breast, and ludicrously wave their heads back and forth or gently caress each other's necks. The crests upon their crowns are frequently erected, and the feathers of the nape puff out so that the velvety necks appear twice their normal thickness. Cheeks and chin-pouches con-tinually tremble, and chattering bills are held wide open. Now and again one will bend its body forward and at the same time extend the head upside down along the spine and toward the tail, holding this curious, paralyzed attitude for several seconds. Sometimes the birds of a pair snap so much at one another that it is hard to judge whether they are making love or quarreling.

In the early stages of courtship it often happens that several cocks select the same female for their addresses. In one instance, five as-siduous suitors, all with necks expanded, were observed bowing around a single hen which crouched in their midst. But by no means all the birds are engaged in love-making at every moment, for they spend much time preening their feathers, frequently raising the coverts of the tail and thrusting the bill toward the oil-gland. Then, after combing

256

their heads and necks thoroughly with their claws—a real feat in balancing—they promenade in small troupes along the outer edge of the colony.

Visible actions, rather than unusual sounds, alarm the courting birds. A quick motion of the hand will start sudden pandemonium. Even when an observer rises to leave them as slowly, silently, and un-ostentatiously as possible, a small panic inevitably results, many of the nearer birds beginning to scamper about or to take flight. On the other hand, the firing of a gun straight into the air produces scarcely a stir provided the weapon is not brandished. The effect of human conversation is, however, most amusing. Whenever a man, sitting perfectly still, begins to talk to the guanayes in a loud voice, a silence falls over all the audience within hearing. Their mumbles and grunts die away, and they listen for awhile as if in amazement.

During the course of a few hours' resting on any island, the birds get much befouled with fresh guano, which hardens upon their plumage. They periodically rid themselves of this by flying some distance off the lee side of the island where they plunge and violently beat the water with their wings. Sometimes most of the inhabitants of a colony will make their toilet in this way at one time, producing a thunderous roar which can be heard from afar. It is often audible during morning fogs, when the flocks are invisible, and as a boat draws near such a gathering it is easy to mistake the sound for the dreaded crashing of waves upon unseen rocky shores.

Inhabitants of the Peruvian coast are agreed that the guanayes never spend the night upon the ocean, as the native pelicans often do, but that they return to their island roosting places even when the journey involves a flight which must continue long after dark. I have sometimes watched from two o'clock in the afternoon until nightfall, or for about five hours, while they streamed uninterruptedly homeward. A few piqueros often accompany them, as if filling honorary positions in the line, but fully 999 in every 1000 birds are guanayes.

The grandest sight of the day, when the homeward flight is at its maximum, usually comes during the hour before sunset. From some point far away the birds make a beeline for the center of their island, but, as they near their destination, they invariably skirt the shores so as to come down across the wind. The instinct of following a leader is evidently strong; if, for any reason, a file is broken, and the rear birds turn toward the left coast instead of the right, those behind will obey the signal and all swing into the new course. Close over gulches and ridges of their home island the oncoming streams of birds flow, the separate "rivulets" cutting across each other like the blades of scissors. At the same time these files also rise and fall in beautiful undulations which can best be seen from the crest of a hill above them. Sometimes three or more such lines will flow along for a while 10 to 15 yards apart, but sooner or later one of them will make leeway until two files interweave. Then the soft, humming swish of wings is interjected with sharp clicks as the quills of two guanayes strike together in air. When one beholds the endless mingling, the crossing and recrossing and tangling of the lines, it seems incredible that more birds do not clash.

(From *Bird Islands of Peru*)

GEORGE MIKSCH SUTTON

Faisán Real

Most North American birds have been painted dozens of times by latter-day Audubons, so George Sutton turned his back on the old familiars and set out to document Mexico's little-known avifauna. His Audubon-sized portraits are rich with life for he has drawn each one, not from skins, but from the fresh specimen. Even the plants on which they are posed were drawn as they grew in the filtered sunlight of the jungle.

Dr. Sutton, convinced of the soundness of W. H. Hudson's dictum that "a first sight is almost invariably the one that tells you most," has recorded in book form his first impressions of the birds of Mexico—impressions received on a trip through Tamaulipas, Nuevo Leon, and Coahuila. A high point of his Mexican travels was his adventure with the big black and white game bird, the great curassow—the *faisán real*.

NEXT MORNING I was to make another try for the *faisán real*. Rain or shine, I was to start for the big trees on the mountainside early enough to be there by daybreak. Following an arrangement made by Mr. Bensel, I was to call for Pepe on my way through the little village, just beyond the river.

Glad to have something to do aside from scratching tick bites, I rose in the darkness at about five o'clock, shook my damp clothes and shoes as a precaution against scorpions, and dressed. Determined to travel light, I took neither flashlight nor the fisherman's creel I usually carried for specimens. All I would need, I decided, were the binocular and gun.

The atmosphere was close, the fog heavy. Despite the semidarkness I had no trouble following the path past the horse corral, between the patch of tall cane and the palmetto thicket, and thence down a steep and slippery bank to the river bed. This route I knew fairly well. As for the other side of the river, the cart lane which led through the innumerable cornfields, the side road to the little village, and especially the path to Pepe's house, I could not be so certain.

As I waded the shallows a flock of Muscovy Ducks sprang from the water, wheeled heavily, and passed directly overhead. Though I was wholly unable to see them in the fog, I could actually feel the wind from their wings. Reaching the opposite shore, I kept to the water rather than trying to climb the precipitous bank, soon found the cut through which livestock were driven down for a drink, and made my way up to the cart lane. As I approached the village, I wondered how tolerant the dogs would be at this hour. Recalling that the dog at Pepe's house had been small and dirty and so nondescript as to be useless as a means of identifying the place, I cut a stout stick.

The fences, hedgerows, and thatched houses at either side of the lane were vague and two-dimensional. A monstrous apparition which loomed directly ahead turned out to be a bull. So placid was he that I did not even brandish my stick at him. I acknowledged his right to the middle of the thoroughfare, however, and walked around him discreetly. A dog barked. Three more dogs took up the cry. The canine population of the village, now thoroughly roused, welcomed this opportunity to voice its interest, alarm, and protest. Clutching my stick, I whacked at the grass and weeds. Let them come, the wretched curs, let them come!

Arriving at a sharp turn in the road, I thought I recognized the path leading off to the right. A pile of bamboo poles and a tethered pig assured me that I had chosen correctly. But nowhere did I see Pepe. Walking toward the hut, I looked closely for a small dog, but no dog appeared. Surely this was the place Pepe had pointed out! . . .

"Hi, Pepe!" I shouted, hoping to sound Mexican rather than American. My voice rang out through the fog, inciting the dogs to greater outcry, but no answer came from the hut. Realizing that it was growing late, that Pepe might be waiting for me elsewhere, above all that it was wholly up to me to find him, I called again. This time there was a grunt in response. "Now I've done it," I thought. "I've awakened the wrong household. These people won't know me, nor Pepe, nor Mr. Bensel, and they'll wonder what I want with anybody at this hour of the night."

260

Faisán Real

As for the *faisán* and my interest in getting one, the less said the better.

A hanging over the doorway moved slightly as a girl's solemn face peered out and a little hand waved. I waved back, hardly knowing whether I had been greeted or motioned to go away. Presently a barefoot man came forth, straightened up, and tightened his belt. On his head was a broad hat, in his hand a huge machete. I was so surprised that I failed to say good morning. The man, whoever he was, certainly was not Pepe. The only word which came to me, I spoke—*"Faisán!"*

At this the man smiled good-naturedly, motioned toward the mountain, shoved his feet into flimsy canvas-topped sandals, and started out the path. I followed, not knowing whether it was Pepe or the *faisán* we were going after. In either case, I thought, we were heading in the right direction. . . .

Though it was now past six o'clock, and considerably lighter, the fog had not lifted nor become less dense. My companion, who was not a young man, appeared to me to be inadequately dressed. Although a person of few words, he obviously knew what he was doing. I was glad enough to follow him, the more so when, turning directly right from the trail, we started up the mountain toward the forest of giant plum trees.

The sweet-voiced *perdiz* had wakened by this time and were whistling far and near throughout the river's flood plain. My guide seemed to realize that I was not after these birds, for he paid no attention to them. A gorgeous male trogon which flew up he dismissed with a brief *"Pajarito!"*—Mexican for "little bird." Recalling my hunt with Pepe, I said *"Ajol, no!"* by which I hoped to convey the idea that I did not want another Crested Guan. My companion seemed to understand me perfectly.

Within half an hour we had reached the great plum trees. Here we moved less rapidly, not only because we wanted to reduce the noise but also because the going was difficult. So dense was the fog that we could not see the treetops above us. Knowing that I might have to shoot at any moment, I stepped ahead of my companion. Frequently we paused to listen.

A low, throbbing oomh! sounded straight ahead, off in the fog. So indistinct was this dull booming noise that I had scarcely noticed it. My companion touched my arm and pointed up the slope. *"Faisán Real!"* he whispered. Then giving a faint whistle and a low *quit, quit,* he imitated the cries of the female bird. This he did not to attract the male,

261

which was repeating his oomh about once every ten seconds, but to acquaint me with other callnotes which I soon might hear.

The *faisán's* booming was a variable sound, sometimes loud, sometimes scarcely audible. Listening, I recalled how the hoots of Prairie Chickens on the Saskatchewan plains had varied with the direction and strength of the wind. Here, however, there was no wind. The heavy, wet leaves hung utterly motionless, as if they had been dipped in wax.

Slowly, as quietly as I could, and breathing hard from the excitement as well as the exertion, I picked my way over the rocks, wet vines, and slippery roots upward toward the booming sound. If only the fog would lift! If only the gray shapes about me would become less vague! Pausing to make certain that I was heading in the right direction, I wondered how far away the bird could be.

Suddenly, in a tree only a short way up the slope, a long bough shook, leaves swished and rustled, and a shower of big drops fell noisily. Though unable to see any part of the tree distinctly, I knew that some large-sized bird or beast had moved, was moving now. Taking a few steps forward, I sank to my knees. From this position I watched the gray ghost of a branch sinking lower, lower, lower, as if pulled earthward by invisible wires. Toward its tip some heavy creature was deliberately moving.

A projection at the end of the silhouetted branch attracted my attention. A slow movement there suggested power and muscle rather than the shaking of mere leaves. More clearly now I perceived that the projection resembled a grotesque, almost a malformed, bird with oddly humped back and erect, fantastically plumed tail. I looked at it with the glass, but the image became no clearer. If bird at all, it certainly could not be the *faisán,* for it appeared to be no larger than a pigeon.

Oomh! The sudden, sensuous sound beat at my eardrums as the fantastic projection wobbled, shook, sank lower, merged with the silhouetted leaves. The truth dawned at last: before me at the end of the sagging bough was the great *faisán* himself. The oddly shaped projection, which had called to mind a bizarre bird with plumed tail, was the *faisán's* incredibly crested head! There was no point in denying the sensation—I was tingling from head to foot. There we were, the *Faisán Real* and I, face to face at last, and my job was to kill the creature. The longer I deliberated, the more cordially I hated the thought. This opportunity to observe one of Mexico's most spectacular birds was, per-

262

haps, an opportunity of a lifetime. The *faisán* probably had not the faintest notion that I was close by, for no jay nor squirrel had sounded a note of warning. Were I to wait and watch, might I not see some wonderful plumage display, some courtship dance, perhaps the arrival of the female bird? The *faisán* suddenly moved again. The whole branch shook. Instantly sensing that my duty was to collect the specimen, to ascertain, at least, exactly what the *faisán* was, I raised the gun and fired. The heavy body plunged from the thrashing bough, struck the ground, and flopped down the slope.

Stumbling over the vines and wet rocks, I found my prize, a heap of black and white among the leaves. Fairly shaking with excitement, I lifted it from the ground. It was a Great Curassow (*Crax rubra*), a magnificent gallinaceous bird with big, broad tail, strong legs and feet, and muscular, powerful head. It weighed as much as a turkey.

I put it carefully down, and knelt to examine it. It was about three feet long. The prominent yellow knob, or wattle, at the base of the bill, the tousled crest of stiff, recurved plumes, the short, velvety feathering of the face: how striking all these were! Truly the bird was regal in size and beauty, truly it was a *Faisán Real!* Its plumage was blue-black all over, except for the pure white of the belly and under tail coverts.

Hearing a rustle I looked up, and there stood my Mexican friend, smiling diffidently. Rising, I shook his hand. "Bonito!" he said, expressing his admiration for the bird. . . .

Proudly I carried my specimen through the village, across the river, back at last to the Rancho. My friends there had not yet finished their breakfast. How their eyes shone as they examined this, by far our largest and most spectacular bird! How good that breakfast tasted! My mind was on the sketch I wanted to make of the *faisán's* tousled head, but I told my story with proper regard for the importance of every detail.

My guide, I learned, was Maclovio Rodríguez, Pepe's father. As for Pepe himself, and Pepe's nondescript dog, nobody seemed to know why they had failed to show up.

(From *Mexican Birds: First Impressions*)

LESLIE BROWN

The Bush

The forests of tropical America have been called "Green Hell," but to Leslie Brown, who spent some time in Trinidad, the large island off the coast of Venezuela, these jungles seem more like Heaven. Ever since he was a boy of nine in India, birds have been his ruling passion and they have dictated, I suspect, his global wanderings. Today he lives in East Africa, where he specializes on the dozen species of eagles that make Kenya their home. His *Eagles* is the finest book ever written about these birds of prey. He is now studying the flamingos that swarm on the soda lakes of the Rift Valley.

In the following selection from *Birds and I* he recalls impressions of Trinidad.

HIGH UP IN THE trees one would occasionally see toucans and trogons, true birds of the tropical forests in this part of the world. But I found most interesting a strange creature called the bell bird, and indeed it must sooner or later fascinate every ornithologist who visits Trinidad. Of its mode of life practically nothing is known, and yet it is a relatively common bird, heard throughout all the forest country and sometimes seen in some numbers. I usually spotted them perched on a fairly high branch—not necessarily *very* high—to which I had traced the note. This sound is like nothing else but the stroke of a hammer on an anvil, and it may be a single note of terrific vehemence, or it may be a series of softer notes as if the blacksmith was some distance away and regularly striking his iron. At close quarters the sound is startlingly loud and sharp, and the bird in producing it swells

264

or inflates its throat and sets its black pendant wattles wobbling violently. It is not an easy bird to see, but it is a fallacy to state (as many
do) that this is because it invariably or even regularly sits parallel to
the branch and not in the usual right-angles position. My experience is
that when at ease the bell bird sits on the branch in the same way as
other birds, that is, across it or at right angles to it. I have spent many
hours, when they were most vociferous, watching them and trying to
think where they could nest. . . . I wasted much time watching them,
but I do not want back the hours spent lying on my back gaping up at
that black and white bird making extraordinary sounds above my head.

After a while, when one gets to know it, the bush has great fascination for the nature lover, and towards the end of my time in the island
I used to go there often for the pure pleasure of following one of these
little mountain streams, whether or not there were any interesting birds
to be seen. There was absolute peace and quiet if one wanted it, and
yet teeming life all round if one wanted to look at that. It was not necessary to make any great effort to see birds—one had only to lie on one's
back on some comfortable log and whistle, and they would come. If
very lucky, as I was once, one might see otters; I saw parents and two
cubs one day when I was up there with Chenery. It was very delightful
to be there in the quiet, perhaps feeling fresh after a bathe in the clear
water, which was ten degrees colder than other water on the island. It
is to many people a great balm to go to some primeval place and there
sit quietly watching what goes on. Such habits are nowadays anathema-
tized, and the epithet "escapism" is applied to them. It might equally
well be applied to all novels, cinemas, plays, and in fact any amusement whatever. Although of course it is myself who am the odd and
eccentric one, I think it odd that more people cannot find pleasure in
some such place as the Trinidad bush.

Naturally, the place was at its best in the quiet of the evening, but
it was inadvisable to remain too long. In Trinidad there are two bad
snakes, the bushmaster and the fer de lance, which become active towards evening and of which I was afraid. I had a healthy respect for
such dangers, having been brought up in a snake-infested country;
this respect was not, I may say, shared by those who had never seen
anything worse than an adder. I used therefore to leave reluctantly
before it was really dark. At this time the various nightjars that lived
in the bush could be heard, and one could get a very good idea of their
relative numbers by listening and placing the calls. Most of them were

265

ground living birds about the same size as our British nightjar, and they made melodious calls that could be represented as "who-are-you", "chuck-will's-widow", and so on. But there was also one living in trees, the giant goatsucker, or, to give it its Trinidad name, the poor-me-one. This name means poor me all alone, and is derived from the bird's cry. It consists of six sad notes on a descending scale, the first two sharp and arresting—"poor me"—the next three equally spaced and perfect —"all-a-lone"—and the last is a kind of chuckling sigh. It is without exception the most perfect and moving sound I have ever heard produced, whether by a musical instrument or by the human or any other voice. To me only the sweet trilling of the curlew is worthy of comparison with it, and the nightingale, comparatively speaking, emits a harsh cackle. I have heard this call when lying in bed at night, and have forthwith risen and gone out to hear it better. It is a long way the most beautiful of all the beautiful things in the bush, and so long as it can be heard, and the lesser birds will answer to my whistling, I shall always wish to return and find them in the bush silence.

(From *Birds and I*)

266

LOUIS AGASSIZ FUERTES

Voices of
Tropical Birds

The name of Audubon will always live in the mind of the American public. His name has become a legend. But the strictly ornithological clan places Louis Agassiz Fuertes way ahead of Audubon as a bird portraitist. Those who really know birds insist there is more latent life in a Fuertes bird, composed and at rest, than in an Audubon bird wildly animated. The majority of younger men who paint birds today have been influenced indirectly by the genius of this man. We can truthfully say that there is a "Fuertes school" of bird painting, even to this day, a generation after his death.

Fuertes himself, for some unaccountable reason never wrote a book, although he illustrated many, and in fact, wrote very few articles except for a brilliant series of six on his "Impressions of the Voice of Tropical Birds" in *Bird-Lore* (1913-1914). He seemed to mistrust his ability with the written word.

IN THE TROPICS, as in more familiar scenes, the birdsongs of the fields are frank, pastoral, and prevalent. With us, the Meadowlark, Field Sparrow, Vesper, and Song Sparrows pipe often and openly, and, from May to October, their notes are almost constantly in the air. But the forest birds are more reluctant singers, and their rare notes are all mystery, romance, and reclusive shyness. The Field Sparrow will sit on a dock-stalk and sing, looking you in the eyes; the Veery will quietly fade away when your presence is discovered.

267

So it is, even to a more marked degree, in the tropics. In the open pastures and on the bushy slopes of the Andes, one hears the shrill piping of the "Fourwing" Cuckoo, the insistent *kekking* of the Spur-wing Plover, the dry, phœbe-like fret of the Spine-tails, the lisping insect-songs of Grassquits, and, from the bordering forest-edge, the leisurely whistling of Orioles.

But, enter the forest, and all is of another world. For a long time, perhaps, as you make your way through the heavy hush of its darkened ways, no sound strikes the ear but the drip of water from spongy moss-clumps on broad leaves. You feel yourself to be the only animate thing in your universe. All at once, perhaps far off through the forest, perhaps close behind you, you hear the strangely moving whinny of a Tinamou. I think no sound I have ever heard has more deeply reached into me and taken hold. Whether it is the intensity of feeling that a deep, silent forest always imposes; the velvet smoothness of the wailing call; the dramatic crescendo and diminuendo that exactly parallels its minor cadence up and down a small scale; something, perhaps the combination of all these, makes one feel as if he had been caught with his soul naked in his hands, when, in the midst of his subdued and chastened revery, this spirit-voice takes the words from his tongue and expresses so perfectly all the mystery, romance, and tragedy that the struggling, parasite-ridden forest diffuses through its damp shade. No vocal expression could more wonderfully convey this intangible, sub-duing, pervasive quality of silence; a paradox, perhaps, but not out of place with this bird of mystery.

Only less appealing are those other chaste singers in the cloud-forest, the Solitaires. It is, indeed, a strange sensation, in uncanny harmony with the unexpected familiarity one always feels in a tropic forest, when, thinking vaguely of Thrush songs, the silver note of a Solitaire crystallizes the thought. There are many kinds, and they have varied song-types beyond most similarly unified genera. The most typical is simply a lovely Hermit Thrush song, giving that effect of a private hearing so graciously done by our own Thrushes. For some elusive reason, it seems as if these birds always sang as the shy perquisite of the favored few, and thus, perhaps, it is that their songs never become common.

Our own Townsend's Solitaire has a very different melody, a blithe, Grosbeak warble, frequently given in lark-like flight, quite unlike any of the tropical species I have heard. These are all of the chaste, contemplative type, given from a perch part way up in the forest, and in frequent accompaniment of splashing water in mossy and fern fringed ravines. *Myadestes ralloides,* of the Andes, sings almost exactly like a Hermit Thrush, as does *Myadestes unicolor,* of Mexico, while *Myadestes solitarius,* of Jamaica, singing from the tree-ferns up on Blue Mountain, reminded me strongly of the Varied Thrush heard in the dark, cold spruce-flats of the Alaskan coast;—what a transposition! A vibrant, steadily crescendo note, as true as a violin, fading to nothing. Then another in a new key. A rich, descending broken scale followed, after a pause; then an exceedingly high trill, swelling and dying. These singers were common at about five thousand feet, and their choral chanting was an experience to be long remembered. *Myadestes obscurus,* of southern Mexico, has a song more spontaneous and overflowing than the other tropical species; I thought of a Bobolink when I first heard it. The song began high in the scale, and very loud; then through the rich progression of its bubbling cadences it gradually fell in pitch and lost volume till it died out, as with loss of breath. This is the "Jilguero" of the natives, while *unicolor* is known as "Clarin." Distinguished from these as "jilguero de la tierra" are the wrens of the genus *Leucolehis,* which have a way of singing at your very feet, hidden under the ferns and low-growing soft plants of earth. Theirs too, are violin tones, and, though the songs are not rare, the singer is seldom seen, however patiently you search or wait for him in the mosquito-ridden air of his dripping haunts. It has always seemed a mystery to me how these little birds of the cloud-forest keep dry. They are, indeed, the only dry thing you would encounter in a week's hunt, for overhead all is oozing water, all the leaves are shiny-wet, and under foot is soaking, rotting vegetable mold or deep muddy ooze, that frequently lets you in over your boot-tops.

In the same forests that shelter the Tinamou and Solitaire dwell the evasive and ventriloquistic Woodpartridges (*Odontophorus*). These are richly garbed in velvety, rotten-wood colors, with all the minute moth-like pattern of Whip-poor-wills. But wonderful as is their coat, it is their vocal performance that gives them real distinction, for besides the familiar Partridge clucking and pipping, heard only at close range and therefore seldom, they possess a loud rollicking call that may be heard a mile or more across the forested course of a mountain river. . . .

Perhaps it is a sort of statute of limitations that makes us constantly compare new birdsongs with familiar ones at home; perhaps it is the

269

paucity of our language that renders description almost futile. But occasionally a resemblance is so striking that no alternative suggests itself. Sweltering in the heat and glare of the Andean foothills, veins throbbing with the exertion of the climbing hunt, exhaustion screaming for a let-up, and temper getting thin, something turns over inside one when, of a sudden, comes the cheery, old-home "Bob-white" of the little crested *Eupsychortyx* Quail. Appearances would never suggest the close relationship, but this little fellow, three thousand miles from home, says "Bob-white" without a trace of accent, striking a primitive chord that does queer things, for the moment, to the inner *you,* caught unawares!

The principal sensation one gets in the tropical forest is the mystery of the unknown voices. Many of these remain forever mysteries unless one stays long and seeks diligently. I am very sure that many sounds I now tentatively attribute to certain birds really belong to others, though several are among the striking sounds.

The Toucans are all noisy birds, and for the most part they are all very boldly marked with strongly contrasting colors, all but the small green members of the genus *Aulacorhamphus* being brightly dashed with black, yellow, red, white, or blue, with bills as bizarre as they are huge. *Andigena* is commonly called the "Siete-color"—seven color— from his Joseph's coat of black, blue, red, yellow, chestnut, green, and white. *Pteroglossus,* as an entire group, is garbed in the most strikingly contrasting patterns of black, yellow, red, and green, with bills of enormous relative size and painted like a barber's pole. *Rhamphastos,* containing the biggest of all Toucans, with beaks like elongated lobster-claws, of all imaginable and many unimaginable designs in black and yellow, white, red, blue, green, or orange, are themselves principally black, trimmed with a yellow or white throat and breast, and lesser patches of red and white or yellow at the base of the tail. One would naturally suppose that with these flashy colors and their noisy habits and large size, Toucans would be among the easiest of birds to find; but this is far from the case. I think we all found them to be as hard to locate, after their calls had given us their general whereabouts, as any of the birds we encountered. The little green snarlers of the genus *Aulacorhamphus,* whose harsh voice seemed to me to sound like the slow tearing of a yard of oil-cloth, were in many places quite common; but only those whose movements disclosed them ever fell into our

270

hands, for it was about hopeless to discover them when they were sitting quiet among the leafage. The blue-breasted group, *Andigena,* we encountered only once or twice. The only one I saw I got from the steep trail in the Central Andes, and it was to the rattling accompaniment of horns of some fifty pack-oxen we were passing on the narrow road. The excitement the shot caused among the startled beasts gave me other things to think of, at the moment, and I do not now remember whether my "siete-color" had a voice or not. . . .

To our northern eyes, used only to green leaves seldom larger than our hand, the extravagant wealth of size, form and color in tropical vegetation offers quite as much wonderment and occupation as do the birds themselves; and here we have a diversion of the attention, however unconscious it may be, that certainly has its effect. Added to this, there are actual variations in the accustomed color of the foliage that repeat with greatest suggestiveness any red, yellow, blue, green, orange, or other color, that may be present on a bird. No Toucan's throat is yellower than the light shining through a thin leaf, and when leaf-forms are further complicated like those of the *Dendrophilum* creepers, by having great holes that let through patches of the dark background or the blue sky, no black-patched Toucan in the foreground looks more velvety than do these leaf-interstices. As for the bizarre bills, they only serve to make it harder; for they bear no resemblance to bill or bird, and simply merge their brilliancy with that of the whole picture they sit in. I don't know how many times I have searched and searched and scrutinized, to find the author of some raucous carping, only to see one of the large Toucans burst away from a perch in plain sight, where he had been all the time. This has happened to me so frequently that I am sure other students must have had the same experience. Perched on a dead stub above the sky line, Toucans, like everything else, are conspicuous in the extreme; sitting quietly within the shade of the forest cover, however varied their patchwork coat, they melt tantalizingly into their setting.

The big, black Toucans of *Rhamphastos* are generally called by the natives *Dios te de* or *Dios te ve*—meaning God will give to you, or God sees you. This is not a confession of faith on the part of the simple native, but a free and lilting transcription of the bird's call. It gives the rhythm and general shape of the sound fairly well. I could analyze it a little more closely by calling it a loud, hoarse whistle, with the words *Tios-to-to* or *Tios, to, to, to*. It has something of the queer quality of a

271

Yellow-billed Cuckoo's song, only, of course, it is much larger and louder. *R. tocard* is *the "Dios te de;"* but the name fairly well fits, and is generally applied, to the whole group of heavy-billed Toucans.

The only other group we encountered was the Aracari Toucans. These are small Toucans, all joints and angles, much given to going around in noisy troops, like Jays. Skilful and jerky acrobats, they are the very extreme of bow-legged angularity. Curious as Jays, they jerk and perk their way up into the branches of some dead tree, their great clumsy beaks and thin pointed tails complementing each other at odd angles. Toucans are all great tail-jerkers, and the Aracaris the most switchy of all. Their harsh mobbing-cries recall some similar sounds made by Jays, but are even louder and much more prolonged. Both are a great nuisance to the hunter, as they follow endlessly, their curious prying screeches and squawks effectually chasing out all the birds requiring more finesse in their approach. I should call their most characteristic noise a rattling, throaty squawk. In any case, it will not take a green hunter long to identify these birds, as they are restless and their motion will soon catch the eye. I strongly suspect all the Toucans of the habit and ability to slip noiselessly and rapidly away, in case their curiosity is satisfied or their fear aroused. They are capable of making long leaps from branch to branch with their wings closed, like Jays and Cuckoos, only more so. What with their looks, their noises, and their actions, no group of birds has more amusing and interesting new sensations to offer than the Toucans. . . .

Every student in the tropics hopes he may soon meet with Trogons, at once the most beautiful and the most mysterious of all the varied tropical birds. Nothing could exceed the richness of their contrasting blood-red underparts, white and black tails, and resplendent emerald-green heads and backs. The large *Pharomacrus* Trogons, of which the famed Quetzal is a type, with their delicate yet richly gorgeous and pendulous mantle of feathers, are, for sheer beauty, among Nature's truly great triumphs, and cannot fail to force deep appreciation from the most calloused or mercenary collector. *P. antisianus* has a loud, rolling call, which I put in my notes as *Whee oo, corre o,* done in a round, velvety whistle. When, after quite a long time spent in imitating the unknown note, in the soggy tree-fern forest at the ridge of the coast Andes, this magnificent ruby and emerald creature came swinging toward me in deeply undulating waves and perched alertly in full sight not far away, I found it hard to breathe, so great was my excitement and joy. We never found it a common bird and only three were seen in all our travel in Colombia. . . .

The curious racket-tailed Motmots have what I call the most velvety of all bird notes. It is usually a single short *oot,* pitched about five tones below where one can whistle. This note is very gentle, though fairly loud, and I think that some persons who do not hear low vibrations very well would often fail to notice it at a short distance. Most of the natives have sound-names for Motmots, and the Maya Indians of Yucatan call the brilliant little *Eumomota* "Toh," and, as an appreciation of the interest, he has come to nest and roost familiarly in the age-long deserted ruins of their former glory.

Indeed, these mysterious, gentle, shy, little birds came to me, at least, to be the living symbol of this great lost magnificence; for the present-day Mayas know naught of the art and history of their great fore-fathers, whose temples and beautiful buildings are now in utter oblivion and disuse, except as the shelters and dwellings of little "Toh," the Motmot, and his soft *hoot* is the only sound that ever issues from their carved portals.

(From *Bird Lore*)

HENRY WALTER BATES

Birds in the Jungle

We imagine the tropical jungles to be teeming with bird life, and at times they are, but more often these humid forests seem as empty as the tomb. Yet, if one hunted long enough—a few days or weeks—he might find many more kinds than he would in a northern woodland. This seeming paradox is because many tropical species are low in density, and cover more territory in their daily beat. In a more northern land the variety is less but the numbers of individuals of each sort are greater.

Bates, the associate of Russel Wallace, on his trip to the upper Amazon noticed the spotty distribution of birds in the forest; they ganged up in pods much like our little foraging parties of chickadees, nuthatches, and woodpeckers.

WHILE HUNTING along the narrow pathways that are made through the forest in the neighborhood of houses and villages, one may pass several days without seeing many birds; but now and then the surrounding bushes and trees appear suddenly to swarm with them. There are scores, probably hundreds, of birds, all moving about with the greatest activity—woodpeckers and Dendrocolaptidae (from species no larger than a sparrow to others the size of a crow) running up the tree trunks; tanagers, ant-thrushes, hummingbirds, fly-catchers, and barbets, flitting about the leaves and lower branches. The bustling crowd loses no time, and although moving in concert, each bird is occupied on its own account in searching bark or leaf or twig, the barbets visiting every clayey nest of termites on the trees which lie in

274

the line of march. In a few minutes the host is gone, and the forest path remains deserted and silent as before. I became in course of time so accustomed to this habit of birds in the woods near Ega, that I could generally find the flock of associated marauders whenever I wanted it. There appeared to be only one of these flocks in each small district; and as it traversed chiefly a limited tract of woods of second growth I used to try different paths until I came up with it.

The Indians have noticed these miscellaneous hunting-parties of birds, but appear not to have observed that they are occupied in searching for insects. They have supplied their want of knowledge, in the usual way of half-civilized people, by a theory which has degenerated into a myth, to the effect that the onward moving bands are led by a little gray bird called the Uirá-pará, which fascinates all the rest, and leads them a weary dance through the thickets. There is certainly some appearance of truth in this explanation; for sometimes stray birds encountered in the line of march are seen to be drawn into the throng, and purely frugivorous birds are now and then found mixed up with the rest, as though led away by some will-o'-the-wisp. The native women, even the white and half-caste inhabitants of the towns, attach a superstitious value to the skin and feathers of the Uirá-pará, believing the relics will have the effect of attracting for the happy possessors a train of lovers and followers. These birds are consequently in great demand, in some places the hunters selling them at a high price to the foolish girls, who preserve the bodies by drying flesh and feathers together in the sun. I could never get a sight of this famous little bird in the forest. I once employed Indians to obtain specimens for me; but after the same man (who was a noted woodsman) had brought me at different times three distinct species of birds as the Uirá-pará, I gave up the story as a piece of humbug. The simplest explanation appears to be this, that the birds associate in flocks from the instinct of self-preservation, and in order to be a less easy prey to hawks, snakes, and other enemies, than they would be if feeding alone.

(From *The Naturalist on the River Amazons*)

VI
There Is Often Adventure

O<small>RNITHOLOGISTS' WIVES</small> fall into two categories: those who share their husbands' interests and turn up at field trips and at gatherings; and those who do not. Like Elsa Allen, Florence Jaques, Helen Cruickshank, Eleanor Pettingill, and a number of other ornithologists' wives who are first-rate bird watchers in their own right, Grace Murphy has been able to go with her husband, Bob, on some of his expeditions to far places. In writing of her life as the wife of a world famous birdman she chose the title *There Is Always Adventure*.

As an ornithologist I would not go so far as to say there is *always* adventure. New birds are seen less often as the years pass, unless one leaves the country and plunges into a new avifauna. After a bit of that diversion, it is a pleasure to come home again and put the binoculars on a few cardinals, warblers, and other old familiars.

Most of our leading ornithologists—or at least those who cannot resist investigating nests—could tell of some close scrapes. As they grow older, they become more cautious, but Ralph Hoffman, author of *Birds of the Pacific States,* lost his life in a fall from a California seabird cliff. Herbert Brandt, in his mid-sixties, once suffered a heart attack while scaling an Arizona canyon wall to investigate a flycatcher's nest. The trembling handwriting of the late Arthur Cleveland Bent, author of the famous *Life Histories* was not due to his age, but resulted from a fall from a barred owl's nest. As he fell, his arm wedged in a crotch, saving him, but while he hung helpless, the nerves which controlled his fingers were permanently damaged. George Sutton, the bird artist, and Edward Howe Forbush of *Birds of Massachusetts* fame, also had close calls as related later. Oology is a dying hobby, but during its heyday, a few years ago, more than one egg-collector lost his life scaling cliffs. Once a group of falconers, peering over a duck hawk ledge on the Hudson were shocked to see a body sprawled below. They recognized it to be one of their despised competitors.

The era in which new species could be found on every tropical expedition—the day of discovery—is over. Undoubtedly there still are a few species—mostly obscure forms—to be described from little-known parts of the world. But even during my lifetime discoveries which fired the imagination have been made; the Congo peacock, the nests of the blue goose and bristle-thighed curlew; the rediscovery of the cahow in the Bermudas and of *Notornis* in New Zealand.

But the amateur birder feels himself no less a discoverer when his glass reveals, say, the first wood ibis for his state, or the first fork-tailed flycatcher. Birds have wings, therefore almost anything is possible. That is why bird watching is perhaps the greatest of all nature hobbies.

APSLEY CHERRY-GARRARD

The Weirdest
Bird-nesting Expedition

The emperor penguin is one of the most remarkable birds in the world. A male will tip the scales at eighty or ninety pounds. Little was known about these flightless giants until a sledge party of the British National Antarctic Expedition in 1902 looked down from an eight-hundred foot precipice at Cape Crozier and saw among the ice a number of small erect figures. This assemblage turned out to be the first breeding colony of emperor penguins ever seen by mortal eyes. There were no eggs, only well-grown young. But the date was October 18, which indicated that the eggs must have been laid in the middle of the Antarctic winter! Dr. Edward Wilson, naturalist of the expedition, was determined that one day he would secure eggs so that their embryos might be studied as a clue to the evolution of this remarkable species and of penguins in general. When, ten years later, Captain Scott again sailed for the Antarctic to make his fateful assault on the South Pole, Wilson went along as his right-hand man. Once down there, he begged leave to undertake the winter journey for emperor's eggs, choosing as his two companions Lieutenant Bowers and Apsley Cherry-Garrard. Later, Cherry-Garrard recounted the story of their terrible ordeal in his book *The Worst Journey in the World*.

The title of the book is not an exaggeration, for no one can fully appreciate the horrors of that journey; the three men reached the uttermost limit of human endurance. For nineteen days they hauled their heavy sledges in the eternal darkness from Cape Evans to Cape Crozier while temperatures dropped to forty degrees below zero and once went to seventy-seven below. On the return trip conditions were even worse but the three men had come to that point of suffering at which they did not really care if

281

only they could die without much pain. The trouble was to go on. Cherry-Garrard describes this journey as "the weirdest bird-nesting expedition that has ever been or ever will be."

W E SAW THE Emperors standing all together huddled under the Barrier cliff some hundreds of yards away. The little light was going fast; we were much more excited about the approach of complete darkness and the look of wind in the south than we were about our triumph. After indescribable effort and hardship we were witnessing a marvel of the natural world, and we were the first and only men who had ever done so; we had within our grasp material which might prove of the utmost importance to science; we were turning theories into facts with every observation we made—and we had but a moment to give.

The disturbed Emperors made a tremendous row, trumpeting with their curious metallic voices. There was no doubt they had eggs, for they tried to shuffle along the ground without losing them off their feet. But when they were hustled a good many eggs were dropped and left lying on the ice, and some of these were quickly picked up by eggless Emperors who had probably been waiting a long time for the opportunity. In these poor birds the maternal side seems to have necessarily swamped the other functions of life. Such is the struggle for existence that they can only live by a glut of maternity, and it would be interesting to know whether such a life leads to happiness or satisfaction.

The men of the *Discovery* found this rookery where we now stood. They made journeys in the early spring but never arrived early enough to get eggs and only found parents and chicks. They concluded that the Emperor was an impossible kind of bird who, for some reason or other, nests in the middle of the Antarctic winter with the temperature anywhere below seventy degrees of frost, and the blizzards blowing, always blowing, against his devoted back. And they found him holding his precious chick balanced upon his big feet, and pressing it maternally, or paternally (for both sexes squabble for the privilege) against a bald patch in his breast. And when at last he simply must go and eat something in the open leads near by, he just puts the child down on the ice, and twenty chickless Emperors rush to pick it up.

282

And they fight over it, and so tear it that sometimes it will die. And, if it can, it will crawl into any ice-crack to escape from so much kindness, and there it will freeze. Likewise many broken and addled eggs were found, and it is clear that the mortality is very great. But some survive, and summer comes; and when a big blizzard is going to blow (they know all about the weather), the parents take the children out for miles across the sea-ice, until they reach the threshold of the open sea. And there they sit until the wind comes, and the swell rises, and breaks that ice-floe off; and away they go in the blinding drift to join the main ice-pack, with a private yacht all to themselves.

You must agree that a bird like this is an interesting beast, and when, seven months ago, we rowed a boat under those great black cliffs, and found a disconsolate Emperor chick still in the down, we knew definitely why the Emperor has to nest in mid-winter. For if a June egg was still without feathers in the beginning of January, the same egg laid in the summer would leave its produce without practical covering for the following winter. Thus the Emperor penguin is compelled to undertake all kinds of hardships because his children insist on developing so slowly, very much as we are tied in our human relationships for the same reason. It is of interest that such a primitive bird should have so long a childhood.

But interesting as the life history of these birds must be, we had not traveled for three weeks to see them sitting on their eggs. We wanted the embryos, and we wanted them as young as possible, and fresh and unfrozen, that specialists at home might cut them into microscopic sections and learn from them the previous history of birds throughout the evolutionary ages. And so Bill and Birdie rapidly collected five eggs, which we hoped to carry safely in our fur mitts to our igloo upon Mount Terror, where we could pickle them in the alcohol we had brought for the purpose. We also wanted oil for our blubber stove, and they killed and skinned three birds—an Emperor weighs up to six and a half stones.

The Ross Sea was frozen over, and there were no seal in sight. There were only 100 Emperors as compared with 2,000 in 1902 and 1903. Bill reckoned that every fourth or fifth bird had an egg, but this was only a rough estimate, for we did not want to disturb them unnecessarily. It is a mystery why there should have been so few birds, but it certainly looked as though the ice had not formed very long. Were these the first arrivals? Had a previous rookery been blown out to sea and

283

was this the beginning of a second attempt? Is this bay of sea-ice becoming unsafe?

Those who previously discovered the Emperors with their chicks saw the penguins nursing dead and frozen chicks if they were unable to obtain a live one. They also found decomposed eggs which they must have incubated after they had been frozen. Now we found that these birds were so anxious to sit on something that some of those which had no eggs were sitting on ice! Several times Bill and Birdie picked up eggs to find them lumps of ice, rounded and about the right size, dirty and hard. Once a bird dropped an ice nest egg as they watched, and again a bird returned and tucked another into itself, immediately forsaking it for a real one, however, when one was offered.

Meanwhile a whole procession of Emperors came round under the cliff on which I stood. The light was already very bad and it was well that my companions were quick in returning; we had to do everything in a great hurry. I hauled up the eggs in their mitts (which we fastened together round our necks with lampwick lanyards) and then the skins, but failed to help Bill at all. "Pull," he cried, from the bottom. "I am pulling," I said. "But the line's quite slack down here," he shouted. And when he had reached the top by climbing up on Bowers' shoulders, and we were both pulling all we knew, Birdie's end of the rope was still slack in his hands. Directly we put on a strain the rope cut into the ice edge and jammed—a very common difficulty when working among crevasses. We tried to run the rope over an ice-axe without success, and things began to look serious when Birdie, who had been running about prospecting and had meanwhile put one leg through a crack into the sea, found a place where the cliff did not overhang. He cut steps for himself, we hauled, and at last we were all together on the top—his foot being by now surrounded by a solid mass of ice.

We legged it back as hard as we could go; five eggs in our fur mitts, Birdie with two skins tied to him and trailing behind, and myself with one. We were roped up, and climbing the ridges and getting through the holes was very difficult. In one place where there was a steep rubble and snow slope down I left the ice-axe half-way up; in another it was too dark to see our former ice-axe footsteps, and I could see nothing, and so just let myself go and trusted to luck. With infinite patience Bill said: "Cherry, you *must* learn how to use an ice-axe." For the rest of the trip my wind-clothes were in rags.

We found the sledge, and none too soon, and now had three eggs left, more or less whole. Both mine had burst in my mitts; the first I emptied out, the second I left in my mitt to put into the cooker; it never got there, but on the return journey I had my mitts far more easily thawed out than Birdie's (Bill had none) and I believe the grease in the egg did them good. When we got into the hollows under the ridge where we had to cross, it was too dark to do anything but feel our way. We did so over many crevasses, found the ridge and crept over it. Higher up we could see more, but to follow our tracks soon became impossible, and we plugged straight ahead and luckily found the slope down which we had come. All day it had been blowing a nasty cold wind with a temperature between 20° and 30° which we felt a good deal. Now it began to get worse. The weather was getting thick and things did not look very nice when we started up to find our tent. Soon it was blowing force 4, and soon we missed our way entirely. We got right up above the patch of rocks which marked our igloo and only found it after a good deal of search. . . .

We on this journey were already beginning to think of death as a friend. As we groped our way back that night, sleepless, icy, and dog-tired in the dark and the wind and the drift, a crevasse seemed almost a friendly gift.

"Things must improve," said Bill next day. "I think we reached bed-rock last night." We hadn't by a long way.

(From *The Worst Journey in the World*)

HARRISON MATTHEWS

The Wandering Albatross

Years before Harrison Matthews had become scientific director of the London Zoo he sailed in an old windjammer through the roaring forties to South Georgia. In this bird paradise at the edge of the windswept Antarctic he worked for three years with the Norwegian whalers who, not always in sympathy with his studies, preferred their albatrosses roasted. He undoubtedly had these shipmates in mind when, in his book, the *Wandering Albatross* he inserted this dedication:

"To Bird Lovers—especially those who love them piping hot, well-browned, and with plenty of bread sauce."

Once when he left his ship for the beaches at Kul Harbor near the north tip of South Georgia, where he was to see the astonishing courtship of the wandering albatross, a right whale, perhaps out of curiosity, followed his small landing craft. Rogue whales, of which "Moby Dick" was the prototype, are occasionally to be reckoned with, so there were some frantic moments before the dory grated on the cobble.

THE NEXT TIME the whale came up he was barely thirty yards astern, and we still had more than a hundred yards to the beach. He was very obviously following us. The two men at the oars increased their pace, and we all craned around to see where he would be next time.

There was no mistake about it then—next time he had cut the distance down to a bare ten yards, and the spray from his blow came down on us like rain.

286

Nils jumped up in the stern sheets, steadying himself on my shoulder as he wobbled at each stroke of the oars.

"Pull," he yelled. "Pull, you Christ-forsaken bastards, or he'll have us all in hell."

Suddenly there was a light green patch in the water beside us, and before we had time to think "Here he comes," an enormous mass of glistening black towered out of the foam and hung over our heads. In the half-second before it fell back I looked right into his little piggy eye not six feet away, and dead level with mine. Just above the corner of his mouth it was, and the curved line of his lip gave him an expression of tolerant amusement—a supercilious smile, but full of mildness. And as that eye slipped back below the surface I swear it winked.

A wave three feet high rushed at us, and I thought the pram was gone as the water curved in over the gunnel. We all lurched to one side, which made things worse, for the broken water following poured in as well when we swayed back. We seemed to be sitting in the sea, and I really thought for a minute that we should have to swim.

"My God," groaned Nils, baling like mad, "now we're done."

But we weren't; the rowers were splashing the water with the oars, trying to scare him away, and the moment that he went down they pulled as if driven by seven devils—they were surely scared.

Fifty yards to go, and up he came again. But this time he did not stick his head out. He blew right alongside, and then rolled over and caught the water a shattering blow with his flipper as he rolled back. There was a crash like a harpoon cannon going off, and the spray flew over our heads, soaking us as it deluged down all round. But he rolled away from us—had he rolled towards us we should surely have been engulfed. Nils was too busy baling to say anything; one rower was splashing, the other rowing, and between them they both nearly caught crabs.

The next we saw of him he was right beneath us, and for a moment it did look as though he was going to clout us out of the water with his tail-flukes. But no; away he went to our right with no harm done— and then we were in water too shallow for him to follow, and we grated on the pebbles. We pulled the pram well up the beach and unloaded the buckets and cases. Nils was again his usual self, and did not bother to give an answer when a sailor asked if he wanted another shirt.

The whale went back to the mouth of the bay and started cutting his capers again in the kelp where we had first seen him. When we were all

287

ashore and ready to go off egging one man took the pram back to the
ship for the others. But I noticed that he followed close-in to the shore
all the way round the bay to the place nearest to which the Sitka lay
before he pulled out across open water.

There were even more albatross here than on the hills at Kul Harbour—all the rising ground was covered with them. Although they do
not nest above the level of the foothills, they always keep to the
ground a hundred feet or so up, for they cannot rise on to the wing from
a level surface and must have at least a downhill run—preferably a
cliff edge—in order to take off.

Here most of the birds were paired, but I saw several groups of
dancers, and I had the impression that some of them were bachelor
parties—ballet without a ballerina. But not only were there hundreds
of adult birds everywhere, there was also a considerable sprinkling of
youngsters. Some of them even had tufts of down still sticking to their
feathers, though most of them had got rid of those signs of infancy.
They looked very forlorn, sitting deserted among the crowds who could
not be more indifferent to them—waiting, their feckless faces staring
without comprehension at the saturnalia all around them, waiting until
the spirit should move them to depart.

Strange as was the dance of the unmated groups, it was nothing to
the beautiful display of those who had chosen their partners. I walked
some way through the colony to a place where the birds had not been
disturbed by the egg-pickers. I watched pair after pair, and found that
the display was, on the whole, very similar everywhere. I sat down
close to a magnificent snowy and his wanderer—they were much too
taken up with each other to notice me.

They had not yet got their egg, nor was nest building finished. They
were building the nest, as is usual, on the stump of an old one of the
previous season, one of the old nests which had, by the time the new
pair took it over, been trodden down to about half its proper size by
the late occupant and its parents. The hen sat on the half-built nest
while the cock foraged round collecting tussac roots, fibrous mud, and
peaty moss, which he brought to her and laid on the edge of the mound.
As soon as each load was put down he bowed deeply to her, making a
low groaning noise as he did so; she half rose and returned the bow,
uttering a similar low groan. Then she picked up his load and arranged
it to her liking on top of the pile, shuffling round on her elbows and
pressing it down in place with her great webbed feet.

288

When the cock deposited his offering he did not immediately go off for more, but sat down close beside the nest and made a bubbling noise in the back of his throat; he then stretched his head upwards, opened his bill, and gave a loud bray. He repeated this several times, and the hen, who had now sat down again, answered him similarly. When they had done this two or three times they fell to caressing, gently nibbling the short feathers on each other's heads and necks, and appearing to take special delight in nibbling—and being nibbled—under the chin. Each time the partner's bill worked round to the region of the ear the one being nibbled stretched up its head so that the other could tickle its throat.

When they broke away they started bubbling and braying again, had another nibble, some more conversation, and then the cock stood up and went to gather more nesting material. When he came back the whole performance was gone over again, so that building went on at a very leisurely pace, for they seemed more interested in kissing and cuddling than in working. So much so that after every fourth or fifth journey their emotions got the better of them and they had a really elaborate display.

The cock brought a gathering and, after laying it down with the usual bubbling and braying, and the nibbling when the hen had tamped it down, they both stood up. The hen stepped down from the nest and stood facing him; they both stretched up their necks and, opening their bills widely, uttered a loud harsh bray. No sooner had they emptied their lungs than they turned their heads downwards, burying the tips of their bills in the feathers of their breasts while they made a much lower, softer note as they drew breath—an action that reminded me of the Sooties when they call.

Then they both leant forwards, reaching their necks out to each other until the tips of their beaks touched; immediately after the touch they inclined their heads a little upwards so that they were no longer in contact, and vibrated their bills very rapidly. This action made a most peculiar sound, for they did not use their voices, but gradually increased the rate of vibration drawing in their breath as they did so. Their chests acted as sounding boxes and gave a resonant effect, and the rattling, which had a slight musical ring, rose from a low note to a high one; as it went up so, too, did the tips of their beaks, which they tilted aloft while keeping their necks thrust out towards each other.

They did the rattling several times, after which the cock started walking round the hen, stepping sideways so that he faced her, and thrusting his head from side to side at each step; the hen moved round without quitting the spot on which she stood so that she, too, continued to face him. He stopped, and spreading his wings to the widest of their magnificent span, threw up his head, showing the full expanse of his snow-white breast, and rattled again. With his wings still widely open, their tips curved forwards, he bent towards the hen and repeated the trill, his neck thrust out and bill up-tilted. The hen replied by opening her wings, stretching out her neck to touch his bill tip, and then rattling that note with its ring of rising urgency.

One after the other they kept this up, first he then her, burying the bill-tip in the breast feathers after each phrase. Faster and faster it went, alternately stretching out to each other, touching, ringing, breasting; the excitement rising with the pace for a score or more repeats, until at last the hen sank down upon her breast and, fanning her tail turned it up over her back. The cock stepped forward and gently mounted, caressing her upturned face and nibbling her chin in ecstasy while he pressed his tail to hers for their brief consummation.

A sailor, climbing the ridge from a hollow behind me, stuck his head over the edge and made a ribald joke.

"Get out, you blasted fool; can't you see I don't want to disturb them?"

He was so surprised at my anger that he dropped silently out of sight.

The birds parted, and walking back to the nest, the hen climbed on to it and sat down. The cock sat alongside for a short time, bubbling, braying, and nibbling; then he rose and again started collecting material for the nest. Many times did they repeat the whole sequence of nest-building, caressing, and display; another round was just starting as I left.

(From *The Wandering Albatross*)

EDWARD HOWE FORBUSH

Edge of the Cliff

New England ornithologists schooled on the dependable granite of Maine's coastal islands sometimes find themselves in serious trouble on the crumbling sandstone of western sea-cliffs. Ralph Hoffmann, who left Massachusetts to devote his later years to western ornithology, lost his life in a fall from a California sea bird cliff. Edward Howe Forbush, author of *Birds of Massachusetts* was more fortunate—perhaps because he was younger—when a cliff-edge gave way beneath his feet in the San Juans. He described his unnerving experience in an article for *Forest and Stream* (1889), entitled "Five Days a Savage."

MOST OF THE islands that I visited on the coast of Washington and British Columbia were topped with scattering trees, and a few were wooded. In searching for birds' nests, my usual method of descending a cliff was to pass a rope around a tree trunk at the summit, throw the ends over, and go down holding both lines in my hands. On attempting sheer descents, I made one end of the rope fast, and let myself down hand over hand to some shelf.

On the last island of the group, which was treeless, I could find no point of attachment for a line, and as there were clefts in which sea birds made their home, I determined to try a descent without a rope. To see how this might be done, I lay down at the edge, and examined that portion of the cliff which could be seen from my position. The rock sloped irregularly downward for about twenty feet, and then as-

291

sumed the perpendicular. Along its visible portion there were occasional vertical fissures; also some horizontal and diagonal seams, with narrow projecting shelves which offered a precarious footing and handhold. Where the seams intersected the vertical fissures little caves were formed, and in these the birds were nesting. Some distance to my right was a cleft larger than the others. Projecting from it and overhanging the verge was a weather-beaten stump or snag, all that remained of a lone tree, which had once grown out of this miniature chasm. There the cliff overhung its base and was inaccessible from below.

Choosing a diagonal shelf for a foothold, and descending by thrusting my fingers into such crevices as happened to be within reach, I gained the first deep, vertical cleft. Inserting my head, arms and shoulders within, I secured a set of guillemot's eggs, but could reach no more, for they were far back out of sight in the very bowels of the rock. The next shelf was hardly five inches wide. I carefully let myself down to it, and finding such handhold as presented itself, crept cautiously on. I had almost reached the large cleft when an unexpected horror happened. The surface of the rock must have been undergoing disintegration, for the whole shelf gave way bodily beneath my weight. My feet shot out and down so unexpectedly, and my body followed with so sudden an impetus, that my hands were torn away from the cleft which my fingers just reached to clutch. In sliding past the place where the shelf had been, I involuntarily turned in the air, throwing my body toward the cleft and reaching downward for the snag on which my whole mind now centered. My hunting coat caught on the cliff and was dragged up over my shoulders. This may have checked my fall a little, but the only noticeable effect at the time was that my field glass fell out of my pocket, and my knife dropped from its sheath. Half falling half sliding down that steep and rugged slope toward that fearful verge, hurried toward certain destruction, I clutched at the snag in passing as a drowning man catches at a straw, reached it, and held on with a death grip. My whole soul went into that grip. The weeks of rowing, paddling, and cliff climbing that had hardened my muscles and strengthened my fingers served well their purpose. As my body, checked at arm's length, swung beneath the snag, it seemed as if the strain would tear my arms from their sockets. The snag bent and sank crackling downwards until it rested on the shelf at the bottom of the crevice. As I hung there and felt it give and splinter, the sound of rending wood sent a poignant shock through my every nerve. Still, all the time, I felt a thrill of delight that

292

hanging there on the brink of eternity I was able to hold on and defy death as long as the cracking wood should hold. I heard the clink of the knife as it struck far below, and the surge of the breakers on the rocks. It is said that at such moments all the events of one's life pass through the mind. No such thoughts troubled me. My whole attention was now concentrated in holding on till the last breath, or until the straining wood should part. But at last the old snag settled until it rested on the solid rock. Its roots were firmly anchored. It held! I was now hanging over the very verge of the cliff, with my legs dangling below the over-hang. There was no shelf for a foothold and it seemed that I must hang there until, strength failing, I fell into the abyss. But here my experi-ence as a lone hunter came to my aid. There are many compensations for such a life, chief among which is the spirit of self-reliance which it implants. I cast no despairing glance over that sailless sea, nor wasted breath in useless shouts for help. My eye ran over the face of the rock, while my fingers worked nervously in the effort to raise my body nearer the cliff. A little to my right was a widening of a small crevice, which I managed to reach with my right foot by working up the snag with both hands and then raising both body and limbs. It was a nerve-wracking task, for at every movement the wood creaked and crackled, sending thrills of agonized apprehension through my being. Having gotten the toe of my right shoe well into the crevice, and my body against the rock, I hung panting for breath, hopeful, yet fearing every instant lest the splintered snag should part. Having rested, I was able to hold my body against the rock with my left hand and right foot, and, unclasping my right hand from the saving wood, reach another crevice still higher up. From my right foothold a diagonal cleft led up the sloping rock toward the summit, which I managed in time to reach by clinging tooth and nail everywhere. Here I threw myself down on the brink, bruised, strained, exhausted, but happy, feeling the joy of a man who, standing on the scaffold, is saved at the last moment by a reprieve.

(From *Forest and Stream*)

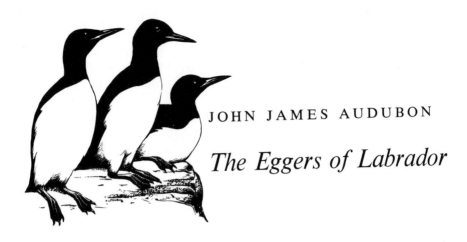

JOHN JAMES AUDUBON

The Eggers of Labrador

Audubon, anticipating that the readers of his five volume *Ornithological Biography* might weary of descriptive ornithology, introduced chapters of a general nature after every five articles on species. These off-hand essays were called *Episodes* or *Delineations of American Scenery and Character*. They relate mainly to events between 1808 and 1834. Today, a century and a quarter later, they are valuable documents, revealing what America was like before the invasion of Europe's surplus millions had drastically changed the face of the land. In Audubon's day there were about 26,000,000 people in the United States; today there are more than six times that number.

At one time the colonies of murres (or guillemots as the British call them) were probably far more populous in the North Atlantic. Until very recently they were regarded as game birds in Newfoundland and large numbers were shot annually. Today their colonies, guarded by Canadian wildlife officers, show signs of rebuilding to capacity.

THE DISTINCTIVE appellation of Eggers is given to certain persons who follow, principally or exclusively, the avocation of procuring the eggs of wild birds, with the view of disposing of them at some distant port. Their great object is to plunder every nest, whenever they can find it, no matter where, or at whatever risk. They are the pest of the feathered tribes, and their brutal propensity to destroy the poor creatures after they have robbed them, is abundantly gratified whenever an opportunity presents itself.

Much has been said to me respecting these destructive pirates before

294

I visited the coast of Labrador, but I could not entirely credit all their cruelties until I had actually witnessed their proceedings, which were such as to inspire no small degree of horror. But you shall judge for yourself.

See yon shallop shyly sailing along:—she sneaks like a thief, wishing as it were to shun the very light of heaven. Under the lee of every rocky isle some one at the tiller steers her course. Were his trade an honest one, he would not think of hiding his back behind the terrific rocks that seem to have been placed there as a resort to the myriads of birds that annually visit this desolate region of the earth, for the purpose of rearing their young, at a distance from all disturbers of their peace. How unlike the open, the bold, the honest mariner, whose face needs no mark, who scorns to skulk under any circumstances! The vessel herself is a shabby thing:—her sails are patched with stolen pieces of better canvas, the owners of which have probably been stranded on some inhospitable coast, and have been plundered, perhaps murdered, by the wretches before us. Look at her again!—Her sides are neither painted, nor even pitched; no—they are daubed over, plastered and patched with strips of seal-skins, laid along the seams. Her deck has never been washed or sanded, her hold—for no cabin has she,—though at present empty sends forth an odour pestilential as that of a charnel-house. The crew, eight in number, lie sleeping at the foot of their tottering mast, regardless of the repairs needed in every part of her rigging. But see! she scuds along, and as I suspect her crew to be bent on the commission of some evil deed, let us follow her to the first harbour.

There rides the filthy thing! The afternoon is half over. Her crew have thrown their boat overboard; they enter and seat themselves, each with a rusty gun. One of them skulls the skiff towards an island for a century past the breeding place of myriads of Guillemots, which are now to be laid under contribution. At the approach of the vile thieves, clouds of birds rise from the rock and fill the air around, wheeling and screaming over their enemies. Yet thousands remain in an erect posture, each covering its single egg, the hope of both parents. The reports of several muskets loaded with heavy shot are now heard while several dead and wounded birds fall heavily on the rock or into the water. Instantly all the sitting birds rise and fly off affrighted to their companions above, and hover in dismay over their assassins who walk forward exultingly, and with their shouts mingling oaths and execrations. Look at them! See how they crush the chick within its shell, how they trample

295

on every egg in their way with their huge and clumsy boots. Onward they go, and when they leave the isle, not an egg that they can find is left entire. The dead birds they collect and carry to their boat. Now they have regained their filthy shallop; they strip the birds by a single jerk of their feathery apparel, while the flesh is yet warm, and throw them on some coals, where in a short time they are broiled. The rum is produced when the guillemots are fit for eating, and after stuffing themselves with this oily fare, and enjoying the pleasure of beastly intoxication, over they tumble on the deck of their crazed craft, where they pass the short hours of night in turbid slumber.

The sun now rises above the snow-clad summit of the eastern mount. "Sweet is the breath of morn" even in this desolate land. The gay Bunting erects his white crest, and gives utterances to the joy he feels in the presence of his brooding mate. The Willow Grouse on the rock crows his challenge aloud. Each floweret, chilled by the night air, expands its pure petals; the gentle breeze shakes from the blades of grass the heavy dewdrops. On the Guillemot Isle the birds have again settled, and now renew their loves. Startled by the light of day, one of the Eggers springs on his feet and rouses his companions, who stare around them for a while, endeavoring to recollect their senses. Mark them, as with clumsy fingers they clear their drowsy eyes! Slowly they rise on their feet. See how the filthy lubbers stretch out their arms and yawn; you shrink back, for verily "that throat might frighten a shark."

But the master, soon recollecting that so many eggs are worth a dollar or a crown, casts his eye towards the rock, marks the day in his memory, and gives orders to depart. The light breeze enables them to reach another harbour a few miles distant, one which, like the last, lies concealed from the ocean by some other rock isle. Arrived there, they react the scene of yesterday, crushing every egg they can find. For a week each night is passed in drunkenness and brawls, until, having reached the last breeding place on the coast, they return, touch at every isle in succession, shoot as many birds as they need, collect the fresh eggs, and lay in a cargo. At every step each ruffian picks up an egg so beautiful that any man with a feeling heart would pause to consider the motive which could induce him to carry it off. But nothing of this sort occurs to the Egger, who gathers and gathers, until he has swept the rock bare. The dollars alone chink in his sordid mind, and he assiduously plies the trade which no man would ply who had the talents and industry to procure subsistence by honourable means.

296

With a bark nearly half filled with fresh eggs they proceed to the principal rock, that on which they first landed. But what is their surprise when they find others there helping themselves as industriously as they can! In boiling rage they charge their guns, and ply their oars. Landing on the rock, they run up to the Eggers, who, like themselves, are desperadoes. The first question is a discharge of musketry, the answer another. Now, man to man, they fight like tigers. One is carried to his boat with a fractured skull, another limps with a shot in his leg, and a third feels how many of his teeth have been driven through the hole in his cheek. At last, however, the quarrel is settled; the booty is to be equally divided; and now see them all drinking together. Oaths and curses and filthy jokes are all that you hear; but see, stuffed with food, and reeling with drink, down they drop one by one; groans and execrations from the wounded mingle with the snorings of the heavy sleepers. There let the brutes lie.

Again it is dawn, but no one stirs. The sun is high; one by one they open their heavy eyes, stretch their limbs, yawn, and raise themselves from the deck. But see, here comes a goodly company. A hundred honest fishermen, who for months past have fed on salt meat, have felt a desire to procure some eggs. Gallantly their boats advance, impelled by the regular pull of their long oars. Each buoyant bark displays the flag of its nation. No weapons do they bring, nor any thing that can be used as such save their oars and fists. Cleanly clad in Sunday attire, they arrive at the desired spot, and at once prepare to ascend the rock. The Eggers, now numbering a dozen, all armed with guns and bludgeons, bid defiance to the fishermen. A few angry words pass between the parties. One of the Eggers, still under the influence of drink, pulls his trigger, and an unfortunate sailor is seen to reel in agony. Three loud cheers fill the air. All at once rush on the malefactors; a horrid fight ensues, the result of which is, that every Egger is left on the rock beaten and bruised. Too frequently the fishermen man their boats, row to the shallops, and break every egg in the hold.

The Eggers of Labrador not only rob the birds in this cruel manner, but also the fishermen, whenever they can find an opportunity; and the quarrels they excite are numberless. While we were on the coast, none of our party ever ventured on any of the islands which these wretches call their own, without being well provided with means of defence. On one occasion, when I was present, we found two Eggers at their work of destruction. I spoke to them respecting my visit, and offered them premiums for rare birds and some of their eggs; but although they made fair promises, not one of the gang ever came near the Ripley.

These people gather all the eider down they can find; yet so inconsiderate are they, that they kill every bird that comes in their way. The eggs of Gulls, Guillemots, and Ducks are searched for with care; and the Puffins and some other birds they massacre in vast numbers for the sake of their feathers. So constant and persevering are their depredations, that these species, which, according to the accounts of the few settlers I saw in the country, were exceedingly abundant twenty years ago, have abandoned their ancient breeding places, and removed much farther north in search of peaceful security. Scarcely, in fact, could I procure a young Guillemot before the Eggers had left the coast, nor was it until late in July that I succeeded, after the birds had laid three or four eggs each, instead of one, and when nature having been exhausted, and the season nearly spent, thousands of these birds left the country without having accomplished the purpose for which they had visited it. This war of extermination cannot last many years more. The Eggers themselves will be the first to repent the entire disappearance of the myriads of birds that made the coast of Labrador their summer residence, and unless they follow the persecuted tribes to the northward, they must renounce their trade.

(From *Ornithological Biography*)

DONALD R. GRIFFIN

Sonar in Birds

Alexander Von Humboldt, exploring South America a century and a half ago, learned of a remarkable cave bird in the highlands of Venezuela. He visited the great cavern of the guacharos near the town of Caripe and reported that the guacharo ("one who cries and laments") was the size of a chicken and "had the mouth of a goatsucker and the bearing of a vulture." Its blue eyes were "dazzled by the daylight" for it was nocturnal, flying from its cave only at nightfall. Unlike the owls that feed on flesh, or goatsuckers that trap insects in their capacious maws, these strange night fowl with a wingspread of three and a half feet feed on fruit.

The brilliant young biophysicist Donald Griffin was much intrigued by Humboldt's description. If bats have a sort of radar—or rather, sonar—what about the guacharo or "oil bird"?

IT IS DIFFICULT to convey any idea of the frightful noise which thousands of these birds produce in the dark portions of the cavern. . . . The sharp and piercing sounds of the guácharos are reflected from the rocky vault, and the echoes reverberate from the depths of the cavern."

This part of Humboldt's account had intrigued me for some time. Here was a bird that flies about in dark caves uttering sharp cries. I had been working on the navigation of bats . . . and had demonstrated that it depends upon the echoes of the bat's high-pitched cries inaudible to human ears. Did the guácharo guide its flight in the darkness by means of a similar sonar-like system in the audible range?

299

I resolved to find out, and so a year ago I retraced Humboldt's footsteps to the Cavern of the Guácharos in Venezuela.

The trip was made possible by the generosity of William H. Phelps, Jr., the well-known ornithologist of Caracas. We took along a portable tape recorder and the same apparatus that we use to detect and analyze the high-frequency sound of bats. In 1953 we had a much more gentlemanly trip to the cave than that described by Humboldt in 1799. Humboldt and his botanist companion Aimé Bonpland had been obliged to climb through a heavy tropical forest, criss-crossing a raging torrent on the way up. We debarked from an airliner at an airport 50 miles from Caripe. Near Caripe was a pastel-tinted "Hotel El Guácharo." We were driven in an automobile up a gravel road to the very mouth of the cave. There we were greeted by a custodian and a crew of guides eager to lead us through the cavern. Indeed, we were told that electric lights were soon to be installed in the cave to save tourists the inconvenience of carrying flashlights.

The oil birds were still there in considerable numbers, now protected by the government. Our first concern was to determine the degree of darkness in which the birds could fly. We therefore walked deep into the cave, past a twilight zone full of nesting birds to a place where turnings in the passage shut out the daylight. Humboldt had described his penetration into the cave in the following words: "We had had great difficulty in persuading the Indians to pass beyond the anterior part of the cavern, the only part which they visit annually to gather fat. . . . The natives attached mystical ideas to this cave inhabited by nocturnal birds. They believe that the souls of their ancestors reside at the bottom of the cavern. . . . To go to join the guácharos is to rejoin one's fathers, is to die. . . . We walked in a thick mud to a point where we saw with astonishment the development of a subterranean vegetation. The fruits which the birds carry into the cave to feed their young germinate wherever they fall into the mould which covers the calcareous incrustations. Blanched stalks provided with some rudiments of leaves grew to a height of as much as two feet. . . . These traces of organization in the midst of darkness aroused a lively curiosity in the natives, otherwise so stupid and so difficult to excite. They examined (the blanched shoots) in silent contemplation inspired by a place which they seemed to dread. . . . The missionaries, despite their authority, could not persuade the Indians to penetrate farther into the cavern. As the roof of the cavern

300

became lower, the cries of the guácharos became more piercing. It was necessary to give in to the pusillanimity of our guides and retrace our steps."

We also found ourselves walking through a meadow of white shoots, just as Humboldt had described. About 2,000 feet from the entrance we arrived at a large chamber called *El Barrial,* which Humboldt apparently did not reach. Picking reasonably dry and comfortable rocks to sit down upon, we turned off all our lights and waited for our eyes to adapt to the darkness so that we could tell whether there was any natural light here. I also set up a camera facing the direction of the entrance, with its entire lens mount removed and its Super XX film directly exposed to whatever daylight might possibly penetrate to *El Barrial.*

Over our heads guácharos circled noisily and called back and forth to one another from ledges 75 to 100 feet high. We waited 25 minutes to assure complete dark adaptation of our eyes. I must admit that this wait in the clamorous darkness was an uneasy one, and I am sure more than one finger wandered wishfully toward a flashlight switch. I could only feel the deepest sympathy for the Indians of Humboldt's party and wonder what their reactions would have been if he had ordered them to extinguish their torches and listen to the guácharos in total darkness.

At the end of 25 minutes we were all agreed that no light was to be seen in any direction. Furthermore, the film, which had been exposed for nine minutes, later confirmed this by showing no evidence of light upon development. Our first question was thus conclusively answered: the guácharos did fly in total darkness.

Now we had to determine whether the squawks and shrieks the birds gave forth almost constantly were used for orientation. Bats employ very brief bursts of ultrasonic sound for their echo-locating system. Some of the sounds uttered by the guácharos were rather sharp, short clicks, but these clicks formed only a small part of the sounds we heard during our stay in the cave.

Phelps had noted on a previous visit that the birds made particularly striking noises as they flew out of the cave for their night's hunting. We therefore set up a microphone at the cave entrance. We had to place it on the pinnacle of a rock 15 or 20 feet high, because the birds generally flew near the ceiling some 75 to 100 feet above our heads. Lower down on this rock were arranged amplifiers, a vari-

301

able electronic filter, a cathode-ray oscillograph, a tape recorder, a 16-millimeter camera to photograph the cathode-ray traces and a storage battery plus vibrator to provide 60-cycle power.

At twilight the guácharos began to fly out. I could scarcely believe these were the same birds we had heard inside the cave that afternoon. For now there were no squawks, clucks or screeches. Instead there came out of the gathering darkness a steady stream of the sharpest imaginable clicks. Each click had a duration of only one to two thousandths of a second—about the same length as the ultrasonic signals of bats. Well into the night the stream of birds and the barrage of clicks continued undiminished. During the whole evening we heard no more than half a dozen of the longer calls and screeches that had predominated inside the cave during the day.

We still lacked any direct evidence that these clicks were actually emitted to locate objects in the birds' path by the echo. Perhaps the clicks were only call notes or symptoms of some other avian emotion the nature of which we could not guess. Accordingly we trapped three birds in a net and took them to an improvised darkroom to make further tests.

The first test was to plug their ears. When both ear canals were tightly stopped with absorbent cotton and cellulose acetate cement, the birds were completely disoriented. In the dark they banged into the walls whenever they took wing. But when the plugs were removed, they were again able to fly about in the dark room without colliding with anything. They also flew without difficulty when the light was turned on even if their ears were plugged.

Even these limited tests were sufficient to show that these birds, like bats, use clicks to avoid obstacles in the dark by echo-location. Unfortunately we were not able to carry the tests much further, and many interesting questions are still unanswered. For example, we do not know how small an object the bird can detect. Since the wavelength of its clicks (about five centimeters) is much longer than that of a bat's ultrasonic sounds (less than one centimeter), the guácharo must fail to detect obstacles which a bat could easily locate.

The oil bird's sounds have a frequency of about 7,000 cycles per second—well within the range of human hearing. The question arises: If the oil bird can use such sounds to guide it in the dark, could not a man develop the same skill? The highly perfected human hearing

302

apparatus would appear quite capable of achieving the type of sound analysis necessary for echo-location. . . .

The pragmatic experience of blind men, unconsciously using the taps of a cane, footsteps or other sounds to guide them, may already have produced as much skill in echo-location as the human auditory mechanism allows. But it might not be amiss to see what we can learn from the guácharo and other flying animals which have developed more precise systems of echo-location.

(From *Scientific American*)

PAUL ZAHL

Flamingo Hunt

Paul Zahl, a biologist distinguished for his cancer research, would rather spend his time photographing colorful subjects that swim, crawl, hop, or fly. He has a weakness for the long-legged glamour birds, particularly the pink and red ones—roseate spoonbill, scarlet ibis and flamingo—all of which he has documented in kodachrome. During the years between 1946 and 1949 he investigated the dwindling colonies of flamingos in the West Indies. His reports were so disturbing that the National Audubon Society delegated Robert Allen to spend three full years making a detailed study of these birds and their prospects for survival.

Several years earlier another part-time naturalist, Gilbert Klingel, had wrecked his boat on a reef off Inagua where he discovered the presence of a large breeding colony of flamingos. When Dr. Zahl made the rounds this was the only sizeable colony remaining in the Bahamas. The large Andros colony, unprotected during the war years, plagued by natives and buzzed by aircraft, had almost disappeared. Paul Zahl tells of his attempt to capture and band some large young flamingos, an attempt which became a near-disaster when he was all but trampled by a thousand panic-stricken birds.

B Y TEN O'CLOCK next morning we were two thirds of the way down the lake. John and I had separated and were proceeding parallel 100 yards apart. The idea was that of a two-man broadfront piston—as yet at a considerable distance, to be sure—forcing the pink line ahead of it. In my pocket was a pair of pliers, and over my

304

shoulder hung a small camera. In John's pocket was the ball of cord, and over his shoulder was a necklace of bird bands. The latter flashed in the sunlight, and he carried them as though never once doubting that we'd soon have plenty of flamingo legs in hand for banding. I wasn't quite sure of the plan, but John had everything figured out. We must concentrate the birds against the far end of the lake, he had said, then drive them along the north shore and into a bay there that tapered off like a funnel. How we'd actually catch the birds, once funneled, was still a mystery to me.

The herd sensed that something was afoot and, with the distance differential reduced to perhaps 300 yards, began to show signs of serious concern. Individuals spread loosely around the periphery of the mass hastened hubward. Ranks tightened, and before long the flock had retreated as far as it could, hard against the densely mangroved lake's end. All heads were high out of the water by this time, and from each periscope glinted a pair of hard, fierce, frightened eyes—all fixed in the direction of the two human figures moving clumsily down the lake but closing in inexorably. The flock had three possible routes of escape: between me and the north shore; between John and the south shore; or up through the center between us. Our aim was to prevent the latter two but to encourage the first. And yet we couldn't leave the favored north passage too wide, for then the birds might flee back up the lake past the bay entrance, out of our clutches. The whole thing was tricky and suspenseful and required a slothful balance of forces.

Except for their inability to fly and their lack of full coloration, these birds seemed like adults. Even as to size they were definitely not children. The correctness of this impression was borne out shortly when, under our increasing approach-pressure, several flame fragments ventured to make a break for it, pell-melling wildly away from the main solar body. Necks and heads pressed forward, legs slashed at maximum speed, wings beat with all the furious churning characteristic of frenzied adults. Sprinting toes skimmed the water, and the winging bodies rose almost clear. But the lift power was not yet enough; the birds' feet soon sank back into the water and down to the lake bottom for support. Each individual which failed to fly would turn hastily and dissolve back into the group. Two or three, however, did actually manage for the first time in their lives to get into the air. For a few long seconds their air-borne status was in doubt, then proved. This was probably more of a revelation to them than to us. With the sudden feel of flight their

305

wings seemed to beat all the harder as they swung up over the mangrove, bound at last for the free-ranging life of adulthood.

Soon we were within 100 yards of the knotted herd's front lines. The birds eddied this way and that; one felt the internal pressure would any second cause the boiler wall to give at its weakest point. But when I had reached a position just above the bay entrance John signaled me to stop. He continued, edging closer and easing the herd leftward, then gently goading them on uplake between me and the north shore. Beautifully according to plan they suddenly began oozing in the direction of what they thought was an escape hole. There was some crying and voicing, but not much; the birds seemed to direct their total energies into foot-and-swing action. A thousand pairs of sprinting legs made a sound suggestive of thunderless rainfall—one continuous wet murmur.

Why flightless flamingos are called "herds" by the natives was now clear: the movement was for all the world like that of a frightened herd of cattle. Even the dust was there—white spray from 2,000 legs slashing and splashing. From the air the flock would for a brief moment have resembled a lengthening teardrop. My presence just above the bay entrance left them no choice; into the bay they veered. By this time John was at my side, and we hurried in after so as to prevent any turnaround or retreat, although the word "hurry" to describe our movement across the lake swash is misleading. Our legs moved fast, to be sure, but mostly up and down; forward progress was anything but swift. The bay extended northward, but ever narrowing, a good quarter of a mile.

Now we had them, and as we closed in the herd dumbly crowded into the bay's mangrove-walled V. It had been my vague impression that John's plan involved thus kraaling the herd tightly into that V and there somehow fencing them in with the cord. Then we could catch them singly for banding and release. But when John came over, handed me one end of the cord and began giving instructions I realized I was wrong. It was evident now that he was up to one of the oldest tricks in the flamingo hunter's book, long since described to me by Robbie Ferguson and others. The classic technique is for two or more men to corner a group of pre-flight waders, then, with each man holding the end of a fishline or facsimile, force the birds to stampede out across it. The birds rush blindly through the space between the two men, who then pull the cord taut and begin sweeping it powerfully forward. Under the right conditions two good huntsmen can break the legs of dozens of flamingos within a few seconds and stun many more. These drop out

306

of the stampede and float helplessly on the water. Once the rush for freedom has begun, there is no stopping it. The birds will keep hurtling into the cord trap—some successfully hopping over, some successfully darting under, but many intercepting it squarely.

This plan is fine for native hunters in quest of fresh meat, but cruelly unsuited to a bird-banding mission. We'd have caught twenty or thirty birds, certainly, but half of them—legs or necks fractured—flapping great mortal flaps on the water . . . no, that was definitely not for us. Already I'd come to suspect that these adolescent birds were too wild and too nearly grown to be caught by any humane means. In bringing my 1,000 bands to Inagua I had envisioned a rookery with nestlings small enough to make their capture easy and harmless. That period had long since passed. Also, at the time of the first break I had been within close-up view of the fleeing birds. I had looked well at those tall pink toothpicks; their fragility had struck at the heart of me.

Unaware of my thoughts, John was unrolling the cord and preparing for the advance on the herd, which cowered, restlessly trapped, a couple of hundred yards before us. I called him back and, opening my camera case, said we'd go closer to take some pictures, but to forget about the banding. As best I could I explained that to band ten or twenty birds would be of no value whatever; and, even if it were, the capture would involve mortal injury to a prohibitively large number of others. These birds were definitely too old. It would be like trying to brand a herd of nearly grown range cattle.

John gave me an uncomprehending look: here after strenuous herding we finally had got a thousand of the quarry nicely bottled up; we had these lovely shiny rings and a pair of pliers with which to apply them; certainly no man in his right mind would pass up this wonderful opportunity.

But I wasn't to be persuaded; we were going in closer with only a camera. Before long we were within a few hundred feet of the pink picket fence. There was no place the birds could go now without first pushing us out of their way, and this I hoped to avoid by a careful, limited approach. Some had already tried the mangrove, only to trip, fall and get their wings, legs and necks entangled in the arches. Closer and closer. Now I was within good range and had the camera to my eye. I hoped to take pictures fast, then retreat. But just as I snapped the shutter it happened. The dam broke.

They came at us like the front of a tidal wave—heads down, necks

307

stretched out in front, wings beating wildly. Those horizontally held heads and necks resembled the down-spear charge of an ancient army, and it was this more than anything else that put the fear of God into me. To be trampled underfoot by birds seems like a silly thing, hardly possessing any element of danger. But these thousand wild creatures were nearly as tall as I and as dense as a solid wall.

John was about twenty feet to my left. I hastily glanced at him for a cue as to what to do. But just at that instant the tide hit us, obliterating John from sight. We were stones now on the shores of a raging pink sea. Suddenly my world was one of wings beating down and across my head and face, flamingo eyes and mouths inches from my own, necks spearing past. The first impact knocked me over, and I was knees-down on the ten-inch-deep bottom. Reflexively I turned my back on the stream and crouched with my head low. On and on they came, their webbed wet feet stamping up over my back, water from those alongside splashing up into my face. Out of the corner of my eye I could see only a speeding forest of pink bamboo.

The feeling swept over me that this could not be reality. It was so wholly removed from any other experience of my lifetime that for a moment I suspected my senses of deceit. Its duration was a year ten seconds long. Then it was over. I raised my head and saw the rear end of the herd tearing away in front of me. There was no lessening in speed until they were all across the bay and back into the primary lake.

Only then did I remember John and turn to where he had last stood. He was still there and most remarkably so. He too had stooped and turned his back to the flood. But, instead of being mentally stunned as I had been, he had worked. As the birds swept by he had reached and plucked one after another by its neck or its legs or even its wings. Now he stood there with a grin on his face and with nine flamingos somehow stuck to him. He held the necks of three in each hand, had another couple tucked under his arms, was holding one between his legs. They were quiet, beaten, subdued by his grasp.

I had managed somehow to keep my camera above water during the charge, and the first thing I can remember doing was snapping John's picture. Then I walked over. Several of the birds whose necks he was gripping in his big strong hands seemed limp and dead. I repeated that there'd be no banding, and why not release his catch? He saw I was serious and dropped the load. Six of the nine immediately galloped off. Three slumped into the water, stunned or half choked. I picked their heads up and held them above the surface. They were still breathing and would recover.

John stood awkwardly by. His fine banding plan had been vetoed, and he was still wondering why. On an impulse I told him to untie his necklace and remove three bands. Then I reached into my wet pocket and handed him the pliers. I lifted the leg of one of the flamingos and held it above the water. John's gloom evaporated. He quickly pliered open one of the aluminum rings. Then with the uncertain sureness of a bridegroom he placed the metal on the finger-thick flamingo leg and bent it back into circular shape. We did this to all three birds, which soon revived, stood up and loped away in the direction of the main flock. With each lope we could see the sparkle of something shiny.

There were at least eight birds stuck in the mangrove. We made our way to each of these and got them extricated. Placed back in the water, they too hurried along.

Three banded birds can have no scientific significance. But, should you ever run across a flamingo wearing a serial-numbered ankle brace-let, I'd certainly like to know.

(From *Flamingo Hunt*)

ROBERT PORTER ALLEN

*Last of the Louisiana
Whoopers*

On New Year's day in 1948, when Bob Smith, the Mississippi flyway
biologist, took me out over the vast coastal marshes west of the Delta in
his two-seated patrol plane, we invaded the lonely realm of the last of the
Louisiana whooping cranes. There had been a colony of ten prior to the
high water of 1940, then there were three. By 1942, only one remained.
As we flew west from the Rainey, Smith leaned back in his pilot's seat and
pointed ahead. Over his shoulder I saw a white speck against the golden
marsh, a huge white bird flying, not one of the numerous snow geese that
were scattered like white flakes among the blues. As our speedy little plane
shortened the gap we could see the great black primaries stroking the air
with the deft upward flip, so characteristic of cranes. We could even see
its bald red crown. The big bird towered and veered to the right and for a
brief moment we were flying not more than two hundred feet apart. I cursed
the broken lensboard of the graflex that rested idly across my knees. The
bird was bugling, for I could see its bill open, but the roar of our motor
drowned out its challenge.

This Louisiana bird never migrated, a circumstance that was of much
concern to Bob Allen who was studying the survival of this species. If this
individual did not mate it would have no influence on the vital statistics of
its race. Therefore, early in 1950 Allen decided to catch the bird and to
transport it to Texas where it would meet its surviving relatives which numbered about two dozen. The unique drama of its capture is unfolded in a
letter to John Baker of the National Audubon Society.

310

U SING A HELICOPTER, we caught the last wild whooping crane in Louisiana on Saturday afternoon, March 11, without disturbing a feather, and carried "him" to the Federal Aransas Wildlife Refuge in Texas that same night.

On reaching Lafayette I was met by John Lynch in his Stinson L-5. Next day we were joined by Nick Schexnayder, Superintendent of the Society's Rainey Wildlife Sanctuary in Louisiana, who was eager to take part in the capture. We went up in one of the helicopters and made a "dry run," landing near an imaginary crane, leaping out with our nets, etc. We finally arranged for Nick and me to ride in one ship and Lynch in another, from which he and Frank Lee could take photographs. We made numerous dry runs, Nick, who insisted on the honor of being the first out of the ship, trying his jump to pontoon and ground with the door open, door off its hinges, etc. We corrected details of sequence of action to start with nod from Mac when the pontoons were actually down, I to release safety belt, Nick to open door and leap to pontoon, from which he'd throw his net, I to follow on his heels with burlap, etc.

For two days Lynch and I rode the battered L-5 like hound dogs looking for a scent. No sign of the crane! You can imagine our thoughts —he was probably shot by this time! Then, early the next morning we found him! He was west of his usual haunts, in sawgrass near Black-fish Lake. . . .

A cold front was on its way down from Montana and the southerly breeze was picking up. Lots of clouds. We had a hasty conference and decided that it must be done that afternoon or not at all. Loaded Nick and me in the first helicopter and Lynch and Frank Lee in the other. Then followed a solid hour of frustration. We couldn't flush the bird. With our gas supply getting low (they carry only two hours in a tank) we were about to give up when Smith, Lynch's pilot, said casually, "What's that over there, an egret or the crane?" It was *him*. From our ship we saw the other helicopter gain air speed and tilt over toward the marsh. It was between Bleu and Blackfish, over the saw-grass. Then Nick, as tense as a drawn bowstring beside me, shouted,

311

"Look! To the right of them! That's him! That's him!" And there he was, streaking off to the north, flying low and making an air speed of just 45 m.p.h.

Mac "poured on the coal" and away we went. As we got on his tail, Smitty took his ship to 300 feet, keeping above and behind us as pre-arranged.

The crane turned off, rose in a beautiful *chandelle,* turned again and again. Finally we saw that he was going to land. His trailing feet dipped into the surface of a pond, his wings brushed the tops of the sawgrass. Nick and I made ready to jump. "This," said Nick, "is it!"

When the crane suddenly darted into an eight foot stand of dry saw-grass Mac stopped dead, hovered momentarily and set the helicopter down directly behind him, the right pontoon only 18 inches away. Nick was straining so hard on the safety belt that I had trouble releasing it. The door flew open and from the pontoon Nick leaped to the grass, with me behind him. Nets were unnecessary. In another second Nick was holding the crane's bill and wings and I had his legs and feet. We had him! . . .

We tied his legs loosely and slipped a burlap sack over his great wings. Then, laying him across our laps, and with Nick holding his head and talking to him soothingly, we started back to Abbeville, where the car waited for us to carry him to Texas. All night long we drove, the bird lying on the floor of the car, Nick stretched out beside him. Johnny and I took turns driving. In the middle of the night, between Galveston and Angleton, both Nick and John were snoring and at each sound the crane would answer with a low guttural talking note.

We slowed down at the other end so as to get Julian Howard out of bed (Sunday morning) at daybreak. He was one surprised refuge manager! . . . We hastily built a one-acre enclosure in a corner of a cat-tail marsh, with a pond of fresh water and a good natural food supply, and clipping the flight feathers of one wing, turned him loose. . . .

It was amazing to see how tame he became after a couple of hours in the new enclosure. Nick walked up and down with him, stroking his head and the glistening feathers of his back, talking to him while we finished the bracing of the fence. "Dr. Schexnayder," we would ask, "what sweet nothings are you whispering in that crane's ear?" And Nick would say, "Never mind, we understand each other, this bird and me, we understand each other."

(From *Audubon Magazine*)

313

GEORGE MIKSCH SUTTON

An Adventure with a Turkey Vulture

George Miksch Sutton, the bird portraitist, is living on borrowed time. Once as a young man of thirty, climbing to a raven's eyrie on a Pennsylvania ledge, he lost his hand grip and fell fifty feet to the talus, cracking seven ribs, tearing them loose from the spine, crushing the sides of the vertebrae, and springing his collar bones. During his weeks of convalescence he consoled himself with the thought that he was more fortunate than the young Indian brave who had been pushed off this same cliff by a rival. Less disastrous for George, but perhaps more terrifying, was a boyhood experience with a turkey vulture, recounted in his delightful book of reminiscences, *Birds in the Wilderness.*

Ι𝚗 Texas we lived in a big white house that stood on a hill southwest of the city of Fort Worth. About us stretched the rolling prairies, gay in Summer with red and yellow daisies and the tall spikes of blooming yucca, and studded with clumps of prickly pear cactus and feathery mesquite trees.

Not far to the south of us the Trinity River slipped through a dense, low woodland. Here I spent much of my time, eager to watch, and capture if possible, the strange and interesting creatures which lived thereabout. Flying squirrels built their globular nests of twigs high in the slender pecan trees. Chuck-will's-widows fluttered up from the leaves like gigantic moths. Raccoons and opossums searched for food along

314

the banks of the slow-flowing streams, leaving their neat lacy track-patterns in the mud.

In the pale far sky drifted wide-winged, sable-coated Turkey Vultures, their pinions motionless for hours at a time as they ascended in slow spirals, breasted the wind, or swung low to the level of the tree tops. I never ceased to marvel at their clean-cut outline, and at the ease with which they handled themselves in flight. I was all unconscious, in those days, of the probability that centuries, ages perhaps, had slipped by while the Turkey Vulture was learning to conquer the air. It did not occur to me then that thousands upon thousands of the gaunt creatures had perished in the eternal struggle for survival, that those dreamily swinging spots of ebon might enchant me for an hour! Drowsily, majestically, unceasingly they drifted about, many just above the low-hung fluffy cloud masses, some gently moving amid the ribbed cirrus of the dizzy sky plains. Lying on the warm earth, I watched them. I could hardly think; I only dreamed myself a sky bird, a playmate of the clouds. I was vaguely, sadly conscious, perhaps, that while my race had for ages been developing my brain into an organ of doubtful utility, it had at the same time been reducing the length of my forelimbs, solidifying my bones—in short, condemning me to four-score years and ten as a terrestrial being without the slightest glimmer of hope that I should one day spread my black wings and, rustling like heavy silk, mount to the blue. Never, never could I be a vulture!

I was roused from my reverie by the swish of dusky, stiff quills above me, as one of the vultures, made curious by my motionless, supine form, swung low. What a different creature! The naked head and pale bill were evil in appearance. There entered my mind the thought that, had I been a corpse, that white beak would have sought with its hooked tip the innermost chambers of my heart! The plumage of the drab fowl was rusty and ragged; its wing tips spread out like slender, heavily nailed fingers! The vulture, close at hand, was a revolting creature. I shuddered because the vile body and macabre pinions had cast their shadow across my face.

Walking one day in the depths of the woodland, near a stagnant pool, I came upon a huge, partly decayed, hollow log. Instinctively curious, I peered cautiously into the darkness, half expecting to discern the taut form of a wildcat crouched for a spring, or the lazy, pulpy coil of a water moccasin, white-mouthed and venomous. I could see nothing, though I strained my eyes. I went to the other end of the log, lay

315

upon my side, and peered through. From this position I could see light at the other end. The dim interior became more sharply defined. What was that strange shape? Was there a movement, just the slightest movement? Did I hear a noise? My back stiffened.

Then it dawned upon me that I was gazing at the silhouette of a Turkey Vulture—a mother bird, probably, sitting upon her eggs. Eager, fairly breathless, I dragged two large flat stones to one end of the log, closing the opening there, and instantly sprang to the other end of the log, half expecting to be greeted by a rush of wings. Assured that the bird was still within, I sat down. For a moment I pondered. The log was almost twenty feet long; I could not make the bird come to me by punching it with a stick, and there was danger of breaking the eggs. I could not smoke it out, because I had no matches and I doubted my ability to start a fire by twirling a pointed stick against a piece of wood. My course was plain. I would have to go through the log.

I entertained certain misgivings. Could I force my way through the dark, moist tunnel? What would I encounter there? Would the mother vulture try to pick out my eyes?

Nevertheless I started, to find at once that the aperture was not so large as it had appeared to be. Arms outstretched in front, hair and face scraping the musty wood, I inched forward, my toes digging doggedly into the earth. Within a short time the entire length of my body was inside the log. My face pressed against wet wood; my body ached with the strain of the unnatural position, but I could not bring my arms back because there was no room for such movement.

Perhaps, after all, I should not attempt this strange tunneling! In a panic I tried to back out, only to find myself powerless. It appeared that in my toes, which could push me forward, was my only propellent power. I was doomed to stay, or go ahead! I breathed hard, spent with exertion. There did not seem to be enough air in the place. My ribs were crowded. But I must go ahead! Digging my fingers in the soft wood, shoving forward with all the force of my feet, I made slow progress. A flake of wood somehow got into my eye. I could do little more than shed tears over this unfortunate happening, for my arms were so long that I could not reach my face with my fingers. And my handkerchief was in my trousers pocket!

I realized now, without question, that I should have not come into this log, that freedom of movement and plenty of fresh air were really all I had ever desired in the world. But I could not go back. Perhaps I

316

remembered, in that dark moment, certain lines of Joaquin Miller's poem on Columbus. At any rate I squirmed on. I heard dull sounds as the buttons of my shirt gave way. My trousers stayed on only because of the strength of the leather belt, the straps of cloth which held it, and the endurance of my pelvic bones. The slipping downward of my shirt did not improve matters any. Wads of the cloth seemed to be knotted all about my body.

I found myself wondering how much more an imprisoned, half-suffocated, tortured boy, miles from home, could endure, when suddenly I realized that the mother vulture and I were not the only inhabitants of this hollow log.

Tripping ever so daintily, his fine leg-threads just brushing the surface upon which he trod, came a grand-daddy longlegs, disturbed in his noonday sleep. A grand-daddy longlegs, considered impersonally, is an interesting creature. His legs are amazingly long and thin; his airy body is a strangely plump hub for those eight filamentous spokes which mince along so questioningly. I do not mind having a grand-daddy longlegs walk across my hand, in fact.

But to have a grand-daddy longlegs, and perhaps four hundred of his companions, suddenly decide to wander all over my face, neck and back is another story. The first tickle of the advance guard's feet upon my nose drove me fairly frantic. I plunged my face into the wood, crushing my adversary. The odor of his body was unpleasant. Already his companions were bearing down upon me. I writhed and shuddered in exquisite torture. By waiting a moment, then wiping my face deliberately across the damp wood, I could kill or disable whole squadrons at a time. The situation was not improved by the fact that I could see only imperfectly in the dim light and because of the bit of wood in my eye.

Gradually the queer spiders learned that they were safer when they moved toward the light. I could see their dancing, trembling forms slowly withdraw from me. Nervous, full of reproach for my foolhardiness, I tried to relax, to think of something besides the vise in which I was fixed.

Was this soft thing my hand felt a fluff of milkweed down? Was it a bit of silk, so oddly out of place in this nether world? It was the nest of a pair of white-footed mice—dainty, bright-eyed little creatures whose noses quivered with terror, whose bodies shook with dread, as they felt rude fingers upon their nest. Frantically they rushed forth. Instinctively they leaped for the darkest crevices they could find. Owing to the ef-

317

fective stoppage of my end of the log, these havens of refuge were naturally near me. Trim, sharp-clawed feet raced over my back, under my shirt, about my neck. Can mice run nimbly? Can they use their toes in holding on? Do they learn of the unknown in the darkness through touching objects with their silken whiskers? The answers to these questions, and to many more, I learned within our hollow log. I was half afraid the jewel-eyed gnomes would bite my face or that one of them would pounce into my mouth as I strove to get a deep breath of air. Could all this torture be actual? Was I having a nightmare? Would it never end? One of the mice crawled between my body and the wood. I gave my shoulder a frantic shrug; there was a tiny squeak, and the sharp nails which had been digging into my skin instantly went limp. The other mouse lodged himself somewhere in a fold of my trousers. Poor little creatures! They had sought only the safety of darkness. They could have harmed hardly a living thing. But I am sure they wrecked a thousand nerve cells in my quivering body.

Again shoving forward violently with my toes and digging my fingers into the soft structure of the tree, I pressed onward. The passageway became larger; I moved more freely. It was heavenly to be able to rest my weary body, and to breathe more deeply.

But I was yet to meet my most amazing, my most uncomfortable adventure! Suddenly the mother vulture stood up, hissed, coughed a little, and began vomiting decayed flesh she had eaten earlier in the day. I had somehow forgotten the vulture. I found myself wishing with all my heart that I had not sealed up the other end of the log. Summoning courage, and wriggling forward as rapidly as I could, I struck the great bird an awkward blow. She hobbled off, hissing hoarsely and leaving a new object exposed to view.

I could not see very well; but I had enough strength and interest in my strange expedition to permit me to realize that I was face to face with a lovely newborn creature—a baby vulture, no more than a few hours old. It was downy white, its legs and naked head were gray, its infant eyes had no expression. Breathing evenly, quietly, it rested beside a large egg which was of soiled white splotched with blackish brown.

The mother continued to cough and hiss, but she could not produce any more food. I was thankful that the digestive process in birds is so rapid that food does not, as a rule, stay long in the crop or gullet!

Lifting the young vulture as well as I could, and rolling the big egg

318

ahead of me, I wormed my way onward. The dusky parent retreated. At the end of the log I grasped her by the feet, pushed the obstructing stones away as well as I could, and breathed the fresh air in deep gasps. Nearly worn out, I trembled from head to foot. Most of my shirt was somewhere in the log; the underclothes which had covered my shoulders and chest were wound in tatters about my trousers. I was scratched up considerably, and bleeding in several spots. It must have taken me fifteen minutes to get out of the log, for the exit was small.

When I finally reached the outer air I sank to the leaves, awkwardly tied the vulture to a sapling, using a shred of torn underclothing, and panted and trembled as I picked grand-daddy longlegs from my hair, eyes, and neck, and a dead mouse from my clothing. The belt had dug deep into the skin and had worn raw grooves all about my waist. But I was free! I could breathe the air, the cool fresh air of heaven!

I hobbled over to the pool. In the rustic mirror I could see that I was no lovely vision. I washed my face and hands, smoothed back my hair, and pinned my torn clothing together with a thorn or two.

Then I returned to my captives. Somehow the little white baby seemed pitiably friendless in this bright world of the open. The eyes of the mother were hard and fierce and frightened. The egg was infertile. I could hear the liquid contents slopping about inside when I shook it.

Had I been less weary or had my predatory instinct been more keen, I might have killed the mother vulture and tossed her aside; or I might have carried her home. But I couldn't bring myself to take that woods baby away, or leave it there an orphan. I put it back in the damp shadow of the hollow log. I rolled aside the stones I had brought for sealing the opening. And then I put the mother back beside the cottony infant, which by this time was peeping faintly. The mother bird did not attempt to rush away. Mouth open, she eyed me impersonally. I moved off through the woods quietly, hoping that my retreat would not frighten her, or that if she did fly away she would return to her charge.

I was famished and exhausted when I reached home. I mounted the stairs to my room with stiff and weary feet. When I took off my trousers a bright-eyed mouse whisked out of a pocket and scampered behind the bookcase.

(From *The Atlantic Monthly*)

HAROLD PENROSE

Peregrine Saga

Harold Penrose, flying his little monoplane over the countryside of England and along the rocky coasts, has constantly been on the lookout for birds—swans, gannets, hawks, and waterfowl. Spotting them from his pilot's seat he can never resist an impulse to follow. A pilot such as Penrose knows the feel of the air beneath his wings; he comes to understand the way of a bird in the air, the mechanics of flight, the vagaries of wind and weather. Those of us who are earthbound can never attain full knowledge.

Of all the birds that cruise the skies, the peregrine is perhaps the most perfect flying machine. Swifts may be likened to small jet planes, the eagle to a bomber, the sparrow hawk to a hovering helicopter, but the peregrine is designed for pursuit and the lightning kill. It is rumored, though I have never had it confirmed, that during the war an interception unit of the RAF, patrolling the wildest parts of the English Channel, used fifteen peregrines to stop suspicious looking pigeons, some of which were carrying messages for the enemy's cross-channel spy service. On the other hand, some of the wild peregrines living on the chalk cliffs along the channel became such a nuisance, intercepting British pigeons, that they had to be shot.

OFTEN I HAD met him when I flew along the Dorset coast: and now he lay dead at my feet.

"Orders are to shoot every one of 'em," said the man with the gun. "You see, sir, they kill carrier pigeons."

I stared at the blood-stained bundle of feathers—the fearless eye closed, one of the great blue wings twisted under the barred body. And I remembered him in his pride, when, for years, he had swept the coast, from the Needles to Golden Cap, just short of Devon.

It was somewhere above Black Down, in Dorset, one summer day that we first met. Flying slowly at 2,000 feet, I was searching for those faint discolorations of the turf that are a trace of early man, when suddenly my gaze rested on the unmistakable, blunt-headed form of a tiercel, soaring seawards. The sun caught the blue of the sharply tapered wings, limning them like an anchor against the green of the downs.

My little monoplane closed on the bird all too rapidly, but it was not until I was within fifty yards that he seemed aware of the noise of my passage. With a quick twist of his dark head he looked upwards over his shoulder. The yellow cere and flange of his beak could be seen distinctly. For a moment he watched, almost with indifference; and then, merely extending his indrawn wings so that the tips changed from points to blunted emarginated ends, he turned slightly off his course and shot a hundred feet above.

Throttling back to reduce speed to stalling point, I gently turned, but even then the radius was too big and the peregrine was lost to sight. However, I had subconsciously noted the particular ground configuration above which he had been flying. Climbing, I made for this point again—and there he was, still soaring, but now three hundred feet below me. Steadily he swept across the wind, in a great curve westward, his wings once more retracted to fine points, and the wrist joint barely flexed. Such wing form gave the ideal low resistance for soaring at the flattest angle, and meant that he was about to glide off to some other site.

I tried to turn in station with him, but the best the machine could do was a wider curve, two hundred yards outside his. This time an eye was kept on the bird as I pivoted about him holding height. The Dorset landscape swung slowly around in a blur; downs gave place to water-meadows, to woods, a distant town, low hills, the sea in the distance, and once more the downs. In all that two mile circuit the bird made no more than a score of rapid wing beats, which may have given him impetus to cross a down-current a hundred yards wide. Two or three times he turned his head slightly, scanning the ground below, but not once did he look directly at my machine.

Perhaps the tiercel grew tired of the circling match—certainly he

321

showed no sign of fear—for suddenly he banked steeply away. As he dropped into a dive there was a fleeting glimpse of his wings being retracted to his sides although held normal to his flight path: quite clearly they were still bearing his weight, and he was in no sense dropping wingless like a bomb. For a few seconds I watched him magnificently slanting down, making an angle of 60° to the earth.

I never found him again at that spot, but later his eyrie was discovered on an overhung ledge pink with sea-thrift.

While walking the cliffs I had seen two gulls, low over the sea, excitedly diving, shooting up, and turning as they dived again. Their clacking screams had drifted to me as I watched, wondering why they played like this. And then, with a thrill, I had picked out the grey-blue of a peregrine that almost matched the sea. The wings flickered, the gulls were outdistanced, and the bird vanished seaward. A few minutes later came a faint, harsh *kak-kak-kak,* and, looking quickly round, I saw the great falcon shoot over a distant cliff edge—and a mournful clanging arose from the nesting gulls.

After that I often used to fly along the coast on the chance of finding the peregrines. On several occasions I was lucky. Once it must have been the falcon I watched as she went heedlessly skimming through a flock of rising and falling circling gulls. Another time the tiercel was hanging on the upward deflected air, eight hundred feet above the cliff. With head turned seawards he was watching intently. Jackdaws and pigeons were sallying from the cliff face, and wheeling back; gulls sailed the coast-line in steady procession. Two rock-pipits, distinctive in plan-form and with characteristic, rapid wing beat, passed abreast. Whether they were above or below the cliff top I could not judge, but the peregrine selected one and rocked over and down. As my aeroplane passed I just managed to see his stoop as he curved steeply to his target. I had a queer sense of foreseeing the pipit's end, the imminent quenching of his little flame of life . . . and pity for him.

But perhaps of greater interest, since it has a bearing on migration, was yet another occasion when I found a peregrine by chance.

It was at regatta-time, and, from the air, I had been watching the boats racing from Poole harbour. But though the Olympian view fascinates by showing every move, little boats seem to stay in one position a long time. So one flies away a while and then returns—like a kestrel quartering his hill. Thus I had dropped from fifteen hundred feet, and, at a discreet distance seaward, flew around the cliff tops—from the

322

shining chalk of Ballard to the dark rocks of Anvil. There had been nothing exceptional to see: the usual groups of gulls wheeling, two or three cormorants flapping fast as they skimmed the sea, but nevertheless each rock and wave and bird had a perpetual air of novelty through being viewed from the air.

Presently I turned, and there, showing clearly through the whirling disc of the propeller, was a peregrine racing seaward. I throttled back and crabbed sideways to lose speed and keep the bird in view. His wings beat rapidly, tirelessly, and he flew perhaps ten feet above the water. Straight as an arrow he went, for the short time I was able to watch, and, while I flew along at his level, there was nothing ahead but the endless sea. I pulled up to five hundred feet—and far away, dead on his course, were the bright cliffs of the Isle of Wight!

It may be affectation to believe that this was one of those birds I knew so intimately—for there were several pairs on the south-west coast—and it is the wildest imagination to think that the pair of peregrines I later saw near the Needles were our local Dorset birds. However, I like to believe it so. And it is good to remember how, from the cliffs of the Wight, I watched the tiercel playing with the raven who has lived there so long. The defiant *e-eep, e-eep* from the peregrine had been answered by a guttural *kronk*. As he came floating through the air, the raven slightly moved his great, black square wings and rolled on to his back, his terrible beak pointing at the peregrine whistling down on him. Again and again the tiercel had dived, until, tiring of the game, he zoomed away to join his falcon. The old raven had laughed hoarsely, practised a few more of his quick half rolls, and dropped to his favourite rock. So high above him that they were mere specks, the tiercel and the falcon began tumbling with each other. . . .

The voice of the man by my side broke into these thoughts. "Aye," he said. "Aye—they're no more than vermin," and contemplatively he turned the body of the peregrine with his foot.

(From *I Flew with the Birds*)

WILLIAM BEEBE

Asiatic Adventure

Among the world's great naturalists, few have had a life as adventure-packed as William Beebe. The general public perhaps knows him best for his descent to new ocean depths in the bathysphere, but the bird watcher associates him with pheasants. No man since the beginning of time has watched as many of the world's pheasants in their wild homes, nor will any man in the future know as many so intimately, for much of Asia is now closed to expeditions and one rare species after another—each the end product of millions of years of evolution—will be pushed to extinction by the swarming populations of the East. Beebe during his early years as curator of birds at the New York Zoological Park travelled for seventeen months in Ceylon, India, Burma, China, Japan, the Malay States, Borneo, and Java, and during the course of the expedition, we are told, nine men lost their lives. From Himalayan snow peaks at sixteen thousand feet to the tropical seashore of Java he gathered first-hand material for his sumptuous monograph on the pheasants which was published in a limited edition at $250 per set. Later it was reissued in a popular two-volume edition under the title *Pheasants—Their Lives and Homes.*

Of all the pheasants, Sclater's Impeyan (Sclater's Monal), living in the high ranges to the east of the Himalayas, is one of the least known. It is a stocky pheasant of rainbow hues with a relatively short white tail crossed by a russet band.

ONE OF THE greatest triumphs of my pheasant search came at the end of a cold, bracing day in early winter. I was camped upon the bare summit of a rounded knoll, and all through the night

324

there was heard the sound of the rushing waters which tumbled over the great boulders of the deep ravines on either side. Except for this, the nights were, as a rule, silent; the most startling sound being the frantic squeal of an unfortunate pig, pursued or caught by some beast of prey.

Waking in the early dusk, one heard only the soothing, distant roar of the streams, and now and then the footstep of the Ghurka sentry. Hardly had the jungle of the opposite slopes appeared through the cloud-drenched dawn, when the notes of a whistling thrush rose clear and sweet. A splendid, sturdy bird, making its home among the moss-hung oaks, more than a mile above the sea—its song was worthy of owner and place. Its blue-black coat was still wet with dew as its throat poured forth a series of penetrating flute-like tones. They rose above the roar of the torrent, and for a half hour jungle and mountain were silent, listening to this superb matin. Then, as suddenly as it began, the song ceased, and not a note was heard until at dawn the following morning.

Close upon the brightening of the dawn came another sound not of the wilderness and yet with a wildness hardly human—the pitiful wail of some insane Kachin child, which had awakened from its bitter sleep to its still more bitter daily life. It strove to put its poor deformed mind upon the task of gathering a few of the myriad sticks lying everywhere in the jungle, to carry them to the hut of some native— perhaps its parents who have discarded it—or of a strange Chinese, in exchange for a mouthful of rice. What heart could fail to be moved by the terrified sobbing of these poor creatures which haunted the forests about every village, where even the normal natives lived day and night in dread of the tiger-formed, evil "nats." Apart from nature as they were, one could not enter these regions without encountering these hopeless waifs, haunting jungle and trail.

The light now came quickly, and with it a multitude of birds' voices, and from the distant jungle the jubilant rollicking chorus of the jolly hoolock gibbons. Every creature here is a sun worshipper, for shade means the chill of death, and sun the bracing warmth which one can enjoy best only upon these high roofs of the world.

The sun had topped the great jagged barrier which led straight down from the heart of the unknown north, and on our sturdy little mountain ponies we crossed a foaming stream and began a stiff zigzag climb, the trail full of deep ruts and rolling stones. Now and then we came to a

325

ledge over which the horses scrambled on knees and hocks. At the last open field we dismounted and turned the ponies over to the Sikh. At an angle of forty-five degrees, we slid, scrambled, and scraped our way through the soft ground to the bottom of the ravine, where the cold shade of early twilight still reigned.

Here we separated, and I made my way slowly up stream, creeping over the great rounded boulders or wading through the rush of icy water. Every turn revealed new beauties. An enormous overhanging mass of quartz loomed up, draped with swaying vines, and, beyond, a little sandy bay was fretted with the tracks of pheasants, cats, and deer. In the spots of sunlight among the higher branches crimson butterflies flitted about, and white-fronted redstarts dashed ahead from stone to stone.

Stopping at a favourable opening, a half mile up stream, I began my laborious climb upward, first through a steep ascent of soft mould densely shaded by wild bananas. The undergrowth seemed scant, and as I brushed aside the first thicket of soft-leaved plants, I anticipated an easy first stage. But the gray down on the myriad green stems proved scorging whips of nettle which lashed face and hands at every step. There was no alternative, so I clambered painfully on, seizing hold of every cold, smooth-enamelled banana trunk as a haven from the merciless needles.

A small side ravine spread out into a broad, fern-filled bog, and the nettles were left behind. Then came more bananas and small evergreen trees with little or no undergrowth. Here was the feeding ground of the pheasants and deer. There was hardly a square yard of mould which did not bear the marks of the tiny hoofs of the barking deer or the strong claws of the birds. Now and then, I picked up a feather of some silver pheasant clinging to a bramble on the steep slope. The earth was crumbling, and again and again I fell headlong. Once I grasped a banana and brought it over upon me—a light, air-filled stem bearing streamers of old, crackling leaves, and a rosette of long, wavy, green ones. As I struggled, face and ears half covered with earth, my hand touched something which seemed to move. I turned my head and became suddenly sick with horror as I saw a king cobra crawling slowly out of the fallen debris, fortunately making its way to the other end of the prostrate banana stem. Its body was dull and brown, and trailing along, crackling like the dead palm leaves, were remnants of half-shed skin. My touch upon the sinuous body had seemingly not disturbed it.

326

If it had changed its course and turned toward me I could not have escaped from its path, half pinned down as I was by the mass of leaves and the stem. I watched the tapering point of the tail slowly disappear, and weak-kneed and trembling, crept slowly off in the opposite direction.

Fortunately, serpents of all kinds are rare, and this most fatal and irritable species is nocturnal. I had disturbed it among the roots of the palm by my awkward fall. During the past week it was not at all unusual to find king cobras in the deadfalls of the natives.

I had hardly crept five yards from the place of my ugly adventure when two feathers caught my eye, and straightway I forgot my fears. They were from the plumage of no silver pheasant, but brilliant, iridescent, changeable green and purple. I was at a loss to know from what gallinaceous bird they had come. A little way farther I found another. Later, while worming my way through a barking deer's tunnel at the roots of a perfect tangle of bamboo, I heard subdued chuckles and the rustling of leaves ahead. A few feet brought me to a deeply worn but steep sambur trail, along which I crept on hands and knees, without making a sound.

The rustling of leaves and of earthen pellets spraying down came more distinctly to my ears, and at last I rested for many minutes with my face buried in a clump of blue, sweet-scented pea flowers.

Inch by inch I then edged myself upward, digging with fingers and toes into every deepened hoof rut. A shower of earth fell upon me, and with joy I saw that a clump of soft-leaved, mintlike plants lay before me. I did not have to increase my numerous wounds by a slow penetration of either nettles or briers.

The revelation came sooner than I expected. Noiselessly plucking away leaves and stems one by one, to form a low tunnel, I pushed slowly and cautiously ahead. Never have I been "closer to Nature" than on this stalk. My trail was more like that of a snail or worm than of any vertebrate. Glints of light filtered through the green ahead, and I saw that a low, perpendicular bank of earth barred my way on each side. Then the forms of one or two birds appeared, and with a screen of leaves still intervening, I watched what was probably the first wild Sclater's Impeyan ever seen by a white man. A minute after I had reached my last position, one of the birds shook itself with all its might, sending down a shower of dirt into my eyes, while a feather or two floated off above me, down the hillside.

327

THERE IS OFTEN ADVENTURE

An inch nearer, another leaf cleared away, and I saw that there was but one bird, the appearance of the others being caused by several large mottled caladium leaves, waving about just behind the pheasant.

It was a splendid male, digging vigorously and almost continuously with its beak, working gradually around in a circle, so that I saw in turn its breast, sides, and back. I watched it for five minutes, when it turned, without apparent cause, but not from fright, and disappeared into the low, marshy tangle behind.

As quick as I could lift my arm and pull my gun up from where it was dragging behind me, I fired at the still moving stems, and listened for some hint of the effect. Not a sound came forth.

I clambered up to where the bird had stood, rushed into the underbrush, and almost stepped upon the pheasant as it lay six feet from the opening. As I leaned down, trembling with excitement, two living bombs burst from the ground a few feet away—a pair of hens, or young males—and in the fraction of a second were out of sight.

On the succeeding days, although I made inquiries everywhere, I could find no native who had ever seen or could give a name to this bird. The three which I blundered upon were doubtless strays from farther north, from somewhere in that mysterious land where no white man may go at present and live. Had I a yellow skin, slanting eyes, long hair, and a knowledge of the twanging words which came to my ears each night from my servants' camp fire, I might have followed these birds northward. As it is, strange people guard their haunts, neither Chinese nor Tibetans nor Kachins, but a mingling of the blood of all three, jealous of their useless land, living their bestial lives in filth and cold and squalor amid the howling winds of these heart-breaking steeps.

(From *Pheasants, Their Lives and Homes*)

JAMES P. CHAPIN

The Congo Peacock

Forty-odd years ago—in 1913 to be exact—James Chapin plucked a mysterious feather from the hat of a native at Avakubi in the Ituri Forest. Along with several other unknown feathers which were tied in a small bundle they were brought home to be classified later. All were eventually identified save the one puzzling quill. Rufous, barred with black, it matched the feather design of no known species.

Twenty-three years later, Chapin, known as "Congo Jim" to some of his associates, sailed for Belgium to continue his work in the Congo Museum a few miles from Brussels. One day, passing through a corridor which he had never before entered, his eye fell on two mounted pheasants on the top of a dusty show case. Had he seen them in any other museum he would have passed them by, but this museum housed nothing but African material —and no pheasants of any kind had ever been found in Africa! The pheasants as a family are Asiatic. Examining the cardboard label he found that the birds had been misidentified as young peacocks; that is why they were in the discard. But they were *not* peacocks. And what is more, some of the secondary wing feathers exactly matched the feather he took from the Congo native.

By a bit of detective work Dr. Chapin found that the birds had been given to the museum in 1914 by the Kasai Company, a trade monopoly in the Congo. But the Congo is huge, nearly a third the area of the United States. He could only guess at the districts where the birds might have originated.

Later that summer, Chapin, taking luncheon with a gold prospector he had known in the Congo, pricked up his ears when his host described a strange bird killed in the forest by a native hunter. He drew a sketch to show the bird's long vertical crest. This convinced Chapin that they indeed

329

were dealing with a great discovery—a pheasant living in the lower Congo.

From that point on, developments were rapid. An intensive search was made for the secretive bird and several specimens were soon secured by native collectors. Doctor Chapin describes, below, his own brief field experience with *Afropavo,* the ornithological discovery of the century.

Walking is not very difficult in the virgin forest of the Congo. It is often warm, but the heavy shade renders a hat quite unnecessary. We began by following the crest of the ridge back of de Braconier's house, and then investigated the slopes on both its sides. It was late in the afternoon of the 16th that I first caught a glimpse of the object of my search. The morning had been rainy, the afternoon was very dark, and at 5:20 we had just started homeward. We were ascending a slope when I saw something dark running through the low bushes ahead.

Anyasi saw it too, sprang ahead, spied it once more, and fired. Then followed a tremendous beating of wings as a male *Afropavo* rose from the ground, disappeared behind the leafy trees, and flapped its way out of earshot. Just as Anyasi dashed ahead I had heard another large bird rise from the ground on his right and make off in that direction. Neither bird did I see again.

It seemed to me that with dogs we should have a far better chance of finding our bird. I had seen long ago how much more apt the forest guinea-fowls are to take to trees when pursued by a dog. When on the 17th Anyasi saw another pair of "peacocks" dart off the path and we were unable to flush them, I urged him to bring his dogs along. He had two, not of the native race but of mingled European origins, and they became our constant companions.

Luck was with us these first few days. On the morning of the 18th we were hunting along a steep hillside when I saw Anyasi lower his gun and run forward. He had noticed that one of the dogs was chasing something, but the undergrowth was a little too dense to see what. Now came a bark, and we could hear two large birds take wing. One flew uphill past us, completely invisible. The other rose more vertically and seemed to have stopped in a tree. We pressed forward, looking upward. I saw nothing, but presently Anyasi fired two shots and I heard something fall. He brought me the bird before it was quite dead, an

330

immature male "peacock" in a plumage almost like that of the adult, but without spurs and its bristly crest only beginning to grow. The bare skin of its neck was already scarlet, as it is in old birds of both sexes.

This was the only example I had the good fortune to dissect myself. Its crop contained nothing but rather small green fruits which fall in numbers to the ground from one of the forest trees. But from a hasty examination of the crop of another bird prepared by Nkotiba in my absence I have reason to believe that the diet of *Afropavo* is as varied as that of the forest guinea-fowls.

During the five more days I spent at Ayena we never succeeded in flushing another "peacock." To the best of my knowledge only three had been killed there since the establishment of the camp.

Both natives and Europeans had assured me that these birds call loudly only at night. Mr. de Braconier wrote me a careful description of the noise, which begins with a deep "rro-ho-ho-o-a" and goes into a series of reiterated syllables like "gowé-gowah," which may continue with or without pause. Among the Wabali, Anyasi's tribe, these give the bird its name of "Ngowé." The hour when they are uttered varies. It may be soon after nightfall or at any time during the night, and several days may pass without their being heard at all.

Just before daybreak on July 19th, I was told, these cries were heard from two directions. Unfortunately I was not awakened. But during the night of the 20th I had better luck. A little after 10 o'clock I was aroused from my work table by a loud unaccustomed noise and stepped out on the verandah. From the forest to the southward came the "gowé-gowah" just as it had been described, repeated again and again. The "wé" syllable is higher in pitch than the "wah" syllable, otherwise there is little difference.

Later the sounds came from the valley to the north, and were repeated at least thirty times, with occasional interruptions. Again I had failed to hear the introductory notes. Mainly because of occasional irregularities in rhythm, I gained the impression that these loud calls were being uttered by two birds, probably a pair perching not far apart.

According to Anyasi, the best of my native informants, *Afropavo* feeds on the ground in pairs all day long. After sundown the pair flies up into the forest trees to roost. The calling is done from perches aloft. As proof of these observations I may add that Anyasi had killed one pair of the birds, after listening to them call in the evening, by locating them very early the next morning before they descended from their

331

roost. We tried to find the birds I had heard calling, for it seemed that they must be within four or five hundred yards. But all our efforts and those of the dogs were unavailing.

Often I have been asked how it happened that *Afropavo* escaped my attention and that of other ornithologists for so many years. The explanation is that its range seems restricted to a part of the Upper Congo forest where none of us ever did any systematic collecting of birds. Roughly speaking, this area extends from the southern edge of the equatorial forest in the Sankuru District northeastward to the country just south of Stanleyville, the vicinity of Bafwaboli, Batama, and Opienge. It may reach the base of the eastern mountains near Walikale. Because of its nocturnal calling, the natives must be acquainted with this bird wherever it occurs. While the real distribution may be somewhat more extensive than we yet realize, it certainly cannot reach the middle Congo near Lukolela, nor does it seem anywhere to touch the northern edge of the equatorial forest. I doubt very much if it now exists north of the Aruwimi or Ituri rivers, or in the Semliki Valley.

One possible explanation of this restricted range may be its extirpation from a large part of the forest by natives. Pygmies would find it relatively easy to shoot the birds with arrows from trees at daybreak, after locating them by their calls. Natives hunting with dogs during the day must often force them to take to the trees, where they are said to perch even more patiently than forest guinea-fowls.

If this be the case, there is all the more reason to hope that *Afropavo* will soon be given protection. Once the necessary specimens have been collected for the important museums of the world, I know that the Belgian Government will place it on the list of protected species. Whether this interesting pheasant can ever be completely protected from the forest-dwelling natives is a serious question, but we may be sure that it is still fairly numerous in the part of the country delimited above.

(From *Natural History*)

ARTHUR A. ALLEN

The Curlew's Secret

Why should the bristle-thighed curlew leave the warm luxurious shores of Tahiti and fly 5,500 miles over the open Pacific to nest on one of the most desolate stretches of tundra in North America? This pattern of life has meant security for the race, no doubt; in fact no human eyes beheld the eggs until 163 years had elapsed after the birds' discovery. To Arthur A. Allen of Cornell goes the credit for leading a National Geographic expedition in 1948 to the Yukon where the nest was found near Mountain Village. This large wader was the last of all the 800 North American species to give up the secret of its eggs.*

Although Dr. Allen was the expedition leader, his son David had the luck to find the first nest. Preceding his father to Alaska, he was flown out to the base camp with Henry Kyllingstad. The details of their discovery of the nest are quoted briefly from Dr. Allen's report in the *National Geographic.*

The four eggs were nearly as large as those of a domestic hen and, like the eggs of so many other waders, were handsomely marked with spots and dabs of gray and dark brown on a greenish background, perfect camouflage to match the tundra floor. The nest, tucked beside a low mat of Alpine azalea, was merely a scrape lined with reindeer moss.

The birds were excessively tame, perhaps because of the imminence of hatching, and a photographic blind proved quite unnecessary. Like so many birds of remote places they seemed to have little fear of men. Even Eskimos do not visit this almost inaccessible tundra with its bleak ridges.

A second nest was discovered later by another member of the party, Warren Petersen. Its clutch of four eggs had been reduced to one by op-

* Although the actual nest of the marbled murrelet has never been located, its egg is known. One was removed from the oviduct of a female shot by a Haida Indian boy.

portunistic jaegers, hawklike seabirds that are constantly on the lookout for eggs and unguarded chicks. So that the remaining egg would hatch, Dr. Allen, always resourceful, acted as midwife. For a "nest," he heated stones and wrapped them in a towel. All day he heated stones. At night he took the nest with him into his sleeping bag, protecting the fragile egg in a tin can. When the little bird cut through the shell wall with its egg-tooth, the good doctor helped it along with forceps. He wanted the egg-shell, undamaged if possible, for his museum.

To be the first to discover the nest of a species one must now turn toward the tropics. The northern world has yielded most of its secrets.

NAT BROWNE had delivered the two boys at the lake at 11 p.m. on Friday, June 11, and they had pitched camp in the afterglow of a sun that had just passed below the horizon. From the air they had seen the ridges behind the mountain and had decided to explore them the following day.

Next morning they were up early and climbed to the top of the ridge behind camp. David started south and Henry north, along the plateau behind the mountain, skirting the alders and scrutinizing all of the open areas.

Two hours from camp, when they were perhaps a mile apart, they heard, at about the same time, a peculiar whistle, somewhat like that of a black-bellied plover—"piu-wit"—and spotted a curlew flying toward David. Henry had heard the bristle-thighed curlew in previous years as it flew over Mountain Village; David was familiar with the Hudsonian curlew from Churchill on Hudson Bay. Neither one doubted they had found the long-sought bird. They froze in their tracks.

The curlew circled and set its wings for a plateaulike area a mile away. This area differed from most of the tundra in that it had some broken rock protruding and had numerous clumps of black lichen spotting its surface.

A couple of hours of intense watching with binoculars ensued. Meanwhile the watchers kept out of sight, but drew steadily closer. The curlew was plainly more interested in this one piece of several acres of tundra than in any other. Even after long sorties he kept coming back to it. Occasionally a parasitic jaeger would skim over the tundra. The curlew paid little attention to it until it approached a certain place. Then he would call excitedly and fly at the jaeger and drive him away. . . .

Gradually, as he watched the guardian curlew, David eliminated one spot after another until he felt he knew just about where the nest should be. Even so, it is not always easy to find the actual nest. Sometimes when a bird sees an enemy approaching, it will sneak off its nest and flush ostentatiously from a different spot. Again, the bird will freeze and rely upon its protective color to escape detection.

David had no way of knowing how bristle-thighed curlews would react. There is one technique, however, that is often effective when nothing else works—surprise. If a bird can be faced with an unusual situation suddenly, its reaction is likely to be less favorable to itself than if it has a moment's time. David removed his rubber boots lest they impede his actions, beckoned to Henry, who had now moved up to the same side of the promised land, and sprinted the 100 yards that intervened between him and the chosen spot. The reaction of the bird was as he had hoped, and the result is now history. She flushed 20 feet in front of him, and he found the curlew's nest!

(From The National Geographic Magazine)

WILLIAM BREWSTER

An Ornithological Mystery

New England's famous ornithological mystery of the last century is again up in the air. What is the "kicker"? Although William Brewster heard the "kicker" in the marshes near his home over a period of years he was never able to see it. He concluded that it was the little black rail.

Watchers of the succeeding generation did not accept this view. They decided it was the secretive yellow rail. In 1949, Ludlow Griscom in *The Birds of Concord* wrote: "Brewster, himself, guessed the bird might be the little black rail but this was later proven mistaken. There are now plenty of people who have heard both species on their breeding grounds."

Six years later Griscom reversed his stand. In *The Birds of Massachusetts* (1955), he states: "J. A. Hagar in a brilliant paper before the Nuttall Club (1954) concluded that the yellow rail never made any sound even remotely resembling that of the 'kicker'. . . . All published references to the yellow rail as nesting or heard calling in Massachusetts should therefore be cancelled and revoked."

What then, is the "kicker"?

IN THESE DAYS of multitudinous bird observers, when so many of the questions that both perplexed and stimulated the students of twenty-five or thirty years ago have been set finally at rest, it is refreshing to happen on an ornithological mystery; one, moreover, possessing no slight interest and importance since it concerns a bird

336

which is known to the ornithologists of eastern Massachusetts, as the Cuckoo was to Wordsworth, *only by its voice.*

At about six o'clock on the afternoon of June 7, 1889, I heard in Cambridge, among the dense beds of cat-tail flags which surround Pout Pond, some bird notes, rail-like in character but wholly new to me. They proved equally so to Mr. Walter Faxon and Mr. Bradford Torrey, whom I took to the place later that same evening. Together we listened to the bird for upward of an hour during which he was rarely silent for more than a minute or two at a time. As we were unable to obtain any clue to his identity, and as his song invariably began with a series of *kick-kicks* we christened him the "Kicker" by which name he has since been known among the Cambridge ornithologists.

In the course of the following fortnight, most of which Mr. Faxon and I devoted to searching for "Kickers," two more birds were heard in another part of the Fresh Pond Swamps, two in the meadows bordering Beaver Brook (one near the Waverly Oaks, the other in Rock Meadow, Belmont), one on the edge of Great Meadow, East Lexington, three in the Neponset River meadows near Readville, one on the banks of the Sudbury River just above Concord, and *five* in a meadow near the mouth of West Brook in Sudbury.

Most of the birds just mentioned were in very wet meadows or swamps, either among the wild grasses which grow so luxuriantly in such places, or in beds of tall rushes or cat-tail flags. We sometimes heard them in the early forenoon or late afternoon and once or twice at high noon, when the sun was shining brightly. As a rule, however, they did not begin calling before sunset and were seldom in full cry until twilight had fallen, after which their notes were uttered almost incessantly, at short, regular intervals, certainly far into the night and probably up to daybreak the next morning. From this it will appear that their haunts were similar to those of the Carolina and Virginia Rails and their periods of greatest activity to an even larger degree, nocturnal.

Their voices, also, were unmistakably rail-like. Their notes varied considerably in number—as well as somewhat in form and quality—not only with different birds but with the same individual at different times. The commonest forms were as follows: *"Kik-kik-kik, quèeah. Kik-kik-kik, ki-quèeah. Kìc-kic, kìc-kic, kìc-kic, kìc-kic, ki-quèeah."*

The *kic-kic* notes were very like those which the Virginia Rail uses to call together her scattered young, but they were at least thrice as loud. Although usually given in rather rapid succession they were sometimes divided by distinct if short intervals (indicated above by commas) into groups of twos or occasionally of threes. These pauses gave them the effect of being uttered with a certain degree of hesitancy or in a tentative spirit, as if the bird were clearing its throat or attuning its voice to exactly the right pitch before venturing on what was evidently his supreme effort, the terminal *quèeah*. . . . It was a shrill, slightly tremulous squeal or crow, given with exceeding emphasis and vigor and reminding us by turns of the rolling chirrup which a chipmunk makes just as he dives into his hole, of the sudden outcry of a half-grown chicken when it is pecked by one of its companions, or of the crow of a young rooster. . . .

That the notes just described constitute what, from the standpoint of the ornithologist, must be regarded as a true song seems obvious from the fact that they were uttered at such frequent and regular intervals, often for hours at a time. Indeed, the bird when engaged in producing them could not well have found opportunity for doing anything else. It is probable, however, that he often changed his position during his brief periods of silence, for his voice varied more or less in intensity or volume with successive utterances, the increase and decrease in volume being usually graduated but sometimes rather abrupt. . . . Perhaps the bird while singing faced in different directions, making a quarter turn after each series of calls, as the Woodcock does while peeping; or he may have been merely running about in the grass calling at times in open spaces, at others among or beneath herbage sufficiently dense to muffle the sound of his voice. The general effect of his song, while certainly far from musical, was not unpleasing and the terminal crow had a delightfully merry or rather joyous quality as if the bird, reveling in the rare June weather amid the lush grass of his favorite meadows, were altogether too happy to contain himself. Indeed, there were times when this note, rising above the croaking of innumerable frogs and the rustling of wind among the reeds, sounded like a shrill, exultant little cheer.

Needless to say we spared no efforts to get a sight of the bird while he was singing in the early evening twilight or, sometimes with the aid of a keen-nosed dog, to flush him by day from the rank vegetation of his difficult haunts, but all such attempts proved futile; and when his singing season waned and finally came to its close, about the end of June, we had obtained no definite evidence as to his identity.

So far as we know the "Kicker" has never since returned to any of

338

the localities above mentioned but I noted one at Falmouth, Massachusetts, in 1890, and in the extensive marshes opposite my camp on the Concord River (about two miles below the town centre of Concord) one was singing on the evening of June 22, 1892, and another nearly every evening from May 18 to June 12, 1898; while I heard at least three and I think four different birds in these meadows during the last week of June, 1901.

The Falmouth bird began singing shortly after sunset on June 25, near a house at which I had arrived late that afternoon. Whenever I was awake during the following night his merry little crow came distinctly to my ears through the open windows of my room, at the usual short, regular intervals. On the previous evening I had traced the sound to its source, and by a rough process of triangulation had fixed the position of the bird at about the centre of a fresh water meadow that lay just behind the beech ridge in the bottom of a bowl-shaped hollow surrounded by sandy, upland fields and pastures. Early the next morning I examined the place more carefully. The meadow scarce exceeded an acre in extent. Most of it was comparatively dry, and having been burned over the previous autumn or winter was covered only by a short and rather sparse growth of young grass but the course of a sluggish brook and the edges of some intersecting ditches which imperfectly drained it had escaped the fire and were bordered by fringes of tall grasses, weeds and cat-tail flags, representing the growths of several successive seasons. These belts of cover, although dense enough to be impervious to the eye, were so very narrow that it was an easy matter to search them thoroughly and I soon satisfied myself that they sheltered no nest of any kind, not even a sparrow's; after which I turned my attention to the open ground. I had scarce begun to scan attentively its level, brilliantly green surface when I saw, only a few paces away, a light yellowish object which I took, at first, to be the crown of an old straw hat, but which, on nearer inspection, proved to be a nest unlike any that I had ever before found. It was a domed structure, somewhat resembling that made by our field mouse but flatter and broader. . . .

I kept it under close observation for a week or more but although I was careful not to disturb it, even by tramping down the grass by which it was surrounded, it must have been deserted immediately after my first visit for no eggs were laid in it. Nor was the "Kicker" heard again in that locality.

(From *The Auk*)

339

THE BIRDER in his metamorphosis from looker or lister to full-fledged watcher traditionally passes through several phases. At first it is the joy of discovery. Soon it becomes a competitive game, to see how many birds he can identify in a day, to discover rare birds, or to record a bird a day or two earlier in the spring than anyone else, or a day or two later in the fall. Exhausting most of the possibilities at home (he can never completely do this), he plans trips to far places. But as he tears about the countryside, ticking off the birds on his checklist, he inevitably becomes interested in their way of life.

It gradually dawns on him that birds are not quite the gloriously unrestrained beings he had imagined them to be. They are bound by all sorts of natural laws. They go north and south almost by the calendar. They seem to follow certain routes between their summer and winter homes. A robin that lives in Connecticut this year will not think of going to Wisconsin next year. In fact, we are cautioned by some of the behaviorists against saying that birds *think*. We are told they are creatures of action and reaction, "releasers," and responses. Bird behavior is a baffling thing, but even Tinbergen and Lorenz admit that it isn't *entirely* mechanistic—thank heaven!

We learn early that most birds have "territory." The males hold down a plot of ground for their own—it may be an acre or it may be five. They are property owners just as we are—and song, instead of being only a joyous outburst, is largely a functional expression—a proclamation of ownership, an invitation to the female, a threat to another male.

Most thought-provoking of all is to discover the balance between the bird and its environment—the "balance of nature" (a swinging balance, it is true). Each plot of ground has its carrying capacity and predation only crops a surplus that otherwise would be levelled in some different way; putting up fences and shooting all the hawks and all the cats does not raise the number of redstarts or red-eyed vireos to any degree at all.

343

Birds then, are as earth-bound as we are. They have freedom and mobility only within prescribed limits. It can be downright disillusioning to read Tinbergen's technical papers on behavior, Kendeigh's studies of environmental factors, and Mathews' or Griffith's discussions of bird navigation. But the watcher who survives this phase has a more abiding interest. What had been a game becomes a philosophical pursuit, a key to eternal things.

Technical papers rarely make good reading, for the scientific worker has a way of making fascinating material seem extraordinarily dull. But some scholars, David Lack, Konrad Lorenz, Robert Cushman Murphy, and William Vogt, to name a few, have a very felicitous way with words. After addressing themselves to their colleagues in the more formal journals they frequently do a more graceful version for the lay public.

In a way, the amateur is in a better position than the professional to add to our knowledge of the living bird. The museum man is condemned to a life of inhaling paradichlorobenzine fumes from trays while he works out problems in taxonomy. The university professor teaches, and often becomes an armchair strategist, while his students, working for degrees, do the creative work.

Some amateurs settle on a favorite bird and try to find out everything they can about it. Lawrence Walkinshaw, a Michigan dentist, distinguished himself by becoming the top authority on the sandhill crane. Irving Kassoy, a jeweler, became fascinated by the barn owls that lived in the Bronx; while his friend, Richard Herbert, who lived a few blocks away, spent all his spare time going over to the Palisades to watch the peregrines. No falconer knows more than he about the prince of predators. One Brooklyn bird watcher, or, I should say, bird listener, specialized in thrushes' songs. When I met him in a wooded canyon near Salt Lake City he was looking for the willow veery, so that he might compare its song with that of the veery he knew in the East. Prentiss Baldwin, a Cleveland lawyer, had an elaborate system of bird boxes on his estate. Each box was wired electrically to charts and graphs in his laboratory. A wren could not make a move on the nest without Baldwin's knowing about it. Some say he knew more about a single species of songbird than any other man has ever known; others contend that this honor goes to Mrs. Margaret Morse Nice, a housewife who watched song sparrows for ten years while she raised a brood of four children of her own.

344

GILBERT WHITE

Barn Owls

The average Englishman even if he lives in the heart of London has a passionate curiosity about the outdoors and wild things. If the many bird programs of the BBC and the flood of nature books (a new bird book nearly every week) are indicators, the British must lead the world in their devotion to nature. This tradition can be traced back to a single source, Gilbert White, the little curate, who in 1788 published *The Natural History of Selborne,* the single great book by which he is known. Since its first appearance more than 150 editions have been issued and its readership must number hundreds of thousands if not millions. A contemporary of Linnaeus and the other pioneer systematists, White cultivated his amateur status by leaving the work of classification to the museum scholars while he spent his days carefully observing the living creatures. His series of letters to Daines Barrington on the swallows and the swift (in those days regarded as a sort of swallow) amounted to a brief monograph in itself.

In the little graveyard behind the church at Selborne we find Gilbert White's modest headstone, and we can imagine that the barn owls who live under the eaves must sometimes use it for a perch. Most certainly they sit in the ancient yew as their ancestors must have sat and their ancestors' ancestors, for this dark tree was probably a thousand years old when White walked in its shade. The big house across the street, "The Wakes," where the little curate lived, was recently saved as a national shrine by a committee which launched its drive with a letter to *The Times* in which I, a visiting American, appealed for action. The barn owls still fly from the church tower to perch on the gables of The Wakes, and perhaps extend their nocturnal forays on moonlit nights to the hill slope where White's switchback trail leads up into the beech hanger.

345

We HAVE HAD, ever since I can remember, a pair of white owls that constantly breed under the eaves of this church. As I have paid good attention to the manner of life of these birds during their season of breeding, which lasts the summer through, the following remarks may not perhaps be unacceptable: About an hour before sunset (for then the mice begin to run) they sally forth in quest of prey, and hunt all round the hedges of the meadows and small enclosures for them, which seem to be their only food. In this irregular country we can stand on an eminence and see them beat the fields over like a setting-dog, and often drop down in the grass or corn. I have minuted these birds with my watch for an hour together, and have found that they return to their nests, the one or the other of them, about once in five minutes; reflecting at the same time on the adroitness that every animal is possessed of as regards the well-being of itself and offspring. But a piece of address, which they show when they return loaded, should not, I think, be passed over in silence. As they take their prey with their claws so they carry it in their claws to their nest: but, as the feet are necessary in their ascent under the tiles, they constantly perch first on the roof of the chancel, and shift the mouse from their claws to their bill, that the feet may be at liberty to take hold of the plate on the wall as they are rising under the eaves.

White owls seem not (but in this I am not positive) to hoot at all: all that clamorous hooting appears to me to come from the wood kinds. The white owl does indeed snore and hiss in a tremendous manner; and these menaces well answer the intention of intimidating: for I have known a whole village up in arms on such an occasion, imagining the church-yard to be full of goblins and spectres. White owls also often scream horribly as they fly along; from this screaming probably arose the common people's imaginary species of screech-owl, which they superstitiously think attends the windows of dying persons. The plumage of the remiges of the wings of every species of owl that I have yet examined is remarkably soft and pliant. Perhaps it may be necessary that the wings of these birds should not make much resistance or rashing, that they may be enabled to steal through the air unheard upon a nimble and watchful quarry.

346

Barn Owls

While I am talking of owls, it may not be improper to mention what I was told by a gentleman of the county of Wilts. As they were grubbing a vast hollow pollard-ash that had been the mansion of owls for centuries, he discovered at the bottom a mass of matter that at first he could not account for. After some examination, he found it was a congeries of the bones of mice (and perhaps of birds and bats) that had been heaping together for ages, being cast up in pellets out of the crops of many generations of inhabitants. For owls cast up the bones, fur and feathers of what they devour, after the manner of hawks. He believes, he told me, that there were bushels of this kind of substance.

When brown owls hoot their throats swell as big as an hen's egg. I have known an owl of this species live a full year without any water. Perhaps the case may be the same with all birds of prey. When owls fly they stretch out their legs behind them as a balance to their large heavy heads; for as most nocturnal birds have large eyes and ears they must have large heads to contain them. Large eyes I presume are necessary to collect every ray of light, and large concave ears to command the smallest degree of sound or noise.

(From *The Natural History of Selborne*)

RICHARD JEFFRIES

Birds Climbing the Air

Born on a farm in the hamlet of Coate, near Swindon, North Wiltshire, John Richard Jeffries was destined to become one of the greatest of all English nature writers. Because he spent his days roaming the fields and day-dreaming, his neighbors insisted he was lazy. An early and improvident marriage stopped all that, forcing him to make a living in London with his only asset, his pen. Perhaps the reason both Hudson and Jeffries wrote so convincingly about nature while living in crowded London was because they were recalling more carefree days. The very best nature writing is often nostalgic.

Jeffries had no knowledge of thermals, those "winds which blow straight up," assisting the soaring of hawks, nor was he able to explain the aero-dynamics of a bird's wing, nevertheless his *Birds Climbing the Air* published in 1884 is perhaps the most vivid description of soaring flight to be found in the literature.

TWO HAWKS COME over the trees, and, approaching each other, rise higher into the air. They wheel about for a little without any apparent design, still rising, when one ceases to beat the air with his wings, stretches them to their full length, and seems to lean aside. His impetus carries him forward and upward, at the same time in a circle, something like a skater on one foot. Revolving round a centre, he rises in a spiral, perhaps a hundred yards across; screwing upwards, and at each turn ascending half the diameter of the spiral. When he begins this it appears perfectly natural, and nothing more than would necessarily result if the wings were held outstretched and one edge of the plane slightly elevated. The impulse of previous flight, the beat of strong pinions, and the swing and rush of the bird evidently suffice for two or three, possibly for four or five, winding movements, after which the retarding effects of friction and gravitation ought, according to theory, to gradually bring the bird to a stop. But up goes the hawk, round and round like a woodpecker climbing a tree; only the hawk has nothing tangible into which to stick his claws and to rest his tail against. Those winding circles must surely cease; his own weight alone must stop him, and those wide wings outstretched must check his course. Instead of which the hawk rises as easily as at first, and without the slightest effort—no beat of wing or flutter, without even a slip or jerk, easily round and round. His companion does the same; often, perhaps always, revolving the opposite way, so as to face the first. It is a fascinating motion to watch.

The graceful sweeping curl holds the eye; it is a line of beauty, and draws the glance up into the heights of the air. The darker upper part of one is usually visible at the same time as the lighter under part of the other, and as the dark wheels again the sunlight gleams on the breast and under wing. Sometimes they take regular curves, ascending in an equal degree with each; each curve representing an equal height gained perpendicularly. Sometimes they sweep round in wide circles, scarcely ascending at all. Again, suddenly one will shoot up almost perpendicularly, immediately followed by the other. Then they will resume the regular ascent. Up, like the woodpecker round a tree, till now the level of the rainy scud which hurries over in wet weather has long been past; up till to the eye it looks as if they must soon attain to the flecks of white cloud in the sunny sky to-day. They are in reality far from that elevation; but their true height is none the less wonderful. Resting on the award, I have watched them go up like this through a lovely morning atmosphere till they seemed about to actually enter the blue, till they were smaller in appearance than larks at their highest ascent, till the head had to be thrown right back to see them. This last circumstance shows how perpendicularly they ascend, winding round a line drawn straight up. At their very highest they are hardly visible, except when the under wing and breast passes and gleams in the light.

All this is accomplished with outstretched wings held at full length, without flap or beat, or any apparent renewal of the original impetus. If you take a flat stone and throw it so that it will spin, it will go some way straight, then rise, turn aside, describe a half-circle, and fall. If the impetus kept in it, it would soar like the hawk, but this does not happen. A boomerang acts much in the same manner, only more perfectly: yet, however forcibly thrown, the impetus soon dies out of a boomerang. A skater gets up his utmost speed, suddenly stands on one foot, and describes several circles; but in two minutes comes to a standstill, unless he "screws," or works his skate, and so renews the impulse. Even at his best he only goes round, and does not raise his weight an inch from the ice. The velocity of a bullet rapidly decreases, and a ball shot from an express rifle, and driven by a heavy charge, soon begins to droop. When these facts are duly considered, it will soon be apparent what a remarkable feat soaring really is. The hawk does not always ascend in a spiral, but every now and then revolves in a circle—a flat circle—and suddenly shoots up with renewed rapidity. Whether this be merely sportive wantonness or whether it is a necessity, it is impossible to determine; but to me it does not appear as if the hawk did it from necessity. It has more the appearance of variation: just as you or I might walk fast at one moment and 'slowly at another, now this side of the street and now the other. A shifting of the plane of the wings would, however, in all probability, give some impetus: the question is, would it be sufficient? I have seen hawks go up in sunny and lovely weather —in fact, they seem to prefer still, calm weather; but, considering the height to which they attain, no one can positively assert that they do or do not utilize a current. If they do, they may be said to sail (a hawk's wings are technically his sails) round half the circle with the wind fair and behind, and then meet it the other half of the turn, using the impetus they have gained to surmount the breeze as they breast it. Granting this mechanical assistance, it still remains a wonderful feat, since the nicest adjustment must be necessary to get the impetus sufficient to carry the birds over the resistance. They do not drift, or very little.

My own impression is that a hawk can soar in a perfectly still atmosphere. If there is a wind he uses it; but it is quite as much an impediment as an aid. If there is no wind he goes up with the greater ease and to the greater height, and will of choice soar in a calm. The spectacle of a weight—for of course the hawk has an appreciable weight—apparently lifting itself in the face of gravitation and overcoming friction, is a very striking one. When an autumn leaf parts on a still day from the twig, it often rotates and travels some distance from the tree, falling re-

350

luctantly and with pauses and delays in the air. It is conceivable that if the leaf were animated and could guide its rotation, it might retard its fall for a considerable period of time, or even rise higher than the tree.

(From *Life of the Fields*)

JOHN JAMES AUDUBON

Experiments with
Black Vultures

For many years a debate has raged about the olfactory abilities of vultures. Do they locate carrion by its odor, or must they always see it from the air? That their vision is extraordinarily acute has never been questioned. Ever since the convincing experiments of Audubon and Bachman in 1835 it has generally been conceded that these sable-winged undertakers are guided by sight alone.

Nearly a century later, Dr. Frank M. Chapman attempted some experiments of his own at Barro Colorado Island in the Panama Canal Zone. His trials with dead coatis which he hid in a shed and under burlap seemed to indicate that some of the time, at least, vultures were able to find their food by smell. Some critics, not convinced, point out that flies and other insects may have betrayed the hidden carrion.

W HEN I VISITED the Southern States, and had lived, as it were, amongst these Vultures for several years, and discovered thousands of times that they did not smell me when I approached them, covered by a tree, until within a few feet. . . . I assiduously engaged in a series of experiments, to prove to *myself,* at least, how far this acuteness of smell existed, or if it existed at all. . . .

My *First Experiment* was as follows:—I procured a skin of our common deer, entire to the hoofs, and stuffed it carefully with dried grass until filled rather above the natural size,—suffered the whole to become

352

perfectly dry, and as hard as leather,—took it to the middle of a large open field,—laid it down on its back with the legs up and apart, as if the animal was dead and putrid. I then retired about a hundred yards, and in the lapse of some minutes, a Vulture, coursing round the field tolerably high, espied the skin, sailed directly towards it, and alighted within a few yards of it. I ran immediately, covered by a large tree, until within about forty yards, and from that place could spy the bird with ease. He approached the skin, looked at it with apparent suspicion, jumped on it, raised his tail, and voided freely (as you well know all birds of prey in a wild state generally do before feeding),—then approaching the eyes, that were here solid globes of hard, dried, and painted clay, attacked first one and then the other, with, however, no farther advantage than that of disarranging them. This part was abandoned; the bird walked to the other extremity of the pretended animal, and there, with much exertion, tore the stitches apart, until much fodder and hay was pulled out; but no flesh could the bird find or smell; he was intent on discovering some where none existed, and, after reiterated efforts, all useless, he took flight and coursed about the field, when, suddenly wheeling round and alighting, I saw him kill a small garter snake, and swallow it in an instant. The Vulture rose again, sailed about, and passed several times quite low over the stuffed deer-skin, as if loth to abandon so good looking a prey.

Judge of my feelings when I plainly saw that the Vulture, which could not discover, through its *extraordinary* sense of smell, that no flesh, either fresh or putrid, existed about that skin, could at a glance see a snake, scarcely as thick as a man's finger, alive, and destitute of odour, hundreds of yards distant. I concluded that, at all events, his ocular powers were much better than his sense of smell.

Second Experiment:—I had a large dead hog hauled some distance from the house, and put into a ravine, about twenty feet deeper than the surface of the earth around it, narrow and winding much, filled with briars and high cane. In this I made the negroes conceal the hog, by binding cane over it, until I thought it would puzzle either Buzzards, Carrion Crows, or any other birds to see it, and left it for two days. This was early in the month of July, when, in this latitude, a dead body becomes putrid and extremely fetid in a short time. I saw from time to time many Vultures, in search of food, sail over the field and ravine in all directions, but none discovered the carcass, although during this time several dogs had visited it, and fed plentifully on it. I tried to go

353

near it, but the smell was so insufferable when within thirty yards, that I abandoned it, and the remnants were entirely destroyed at last through natural decay.

I then took a young pig, put a knife through its neck, and made it bleed on the earth and grass about the same place, and having covered it closely with leaves, also watched the result. The Vultures saw the fresh blood, alighted about it, followed it down into the ravine, discovered by the blood the pig, and devoured it, when yet quite fresh, within my sight.

Not contented with these experiments, which I already thought fully conclusive, having found two young Vultures, about the size of pullets, covered yet with down, and looking more like quadrupeds than birds, I had them brought home and put into a large coop in the yard, in the view of every body, and attended to their feeding myself. . . .

So accustomed to my going towards them were they in a few days, that when I approached the cage with hands filled with game for them, they immediately began hissing and gesticulating very much like young pigeons, and putting their bills to each other, as if expecting to be fed mutually, as their parent had done.

Two weeks elapsed, black feathers made their appearance, and the down diminished. I remarked an extraordinary increase of their legs and bill, and thinking them fit for trial, I closed three sides of the cage with plank, leaving the front only with bars for them to see through,—had the cage cleaned, washed, and sanded, to remove any filth attached to it from the putrid flesh that had been in it, and turned its front immediately from the course I usually took towards it with food for them.

I approached it often barefooted, and soon perceived that if I did not accidentally make a noise, the young birds remained in their silent upright attitudes, until I showed myself to them by turning to the front of their prison. I frequently fastened a dead squirrel or rabbit, cut open, with all the entrails hanging loosely, to a long pole, and in this situation would put it to the back part of the cage; but no hissing, no movement, was made; when, on the contrary, I presented the end of the pole thus covered over the cage, no sooner would it appear beyond the edge, than my hungry birds would jump against the bars, hiss furiously, and attempt all in their power to reach the food.

(From *Ornithological Biography*)

ALDO LEOPOLD

Sky Dance

Aldo Leopold once wrote: "There are two kinds of people: those who can live without wild things and those who cannot." All conservationists fit the second category but many of them find it difficult to explain their views. They feel deeply but grope for words which do not risk triteness. But Aldo Leopold was always articulate; more than anyone else in the wildlife conservation movement he was able, in translucent prose, to make clear his philosophy. As professor of wildlife management at the University of Wisconsin he had a profound influence on conservation thinking, an influence which his students, now teachers and technicians in their own right, have carried to every part of the land.

Many of the essays such as the following piece on the flight song of the woodcock, are concerned with what Leopold saw and did at his week-end farm in Sand County, Wisconsin.

I OWNED MY FARM for two years before learning that the sky dance is to be seen over my woods every evening in April and May. Since we discovered it, my family and I have been reluctant to miss even a single performance.

The show begins on the first warm evening in April at exactly 6:50 P.M. The curtain goes up one minute later each day until 1 June, when the time is 7:50. This sliding scale is dictated by vanity, the dancer demanding a romantic light intensity of exactly 0.05 foot-candles. Do not be late, and sit quietly, lest he fly away in a huff.

The stage props, like the opening hour, reflect the temperamental

355

demands of the performer. The stage must be an open amphitheater in woods or brush, and in its center there must be a mossy spot, a streak of sterile sand, a bare outcrop of rock, or a bare roadway. Why the male woodcock should be such a stickler for a bare dance floor puzzled me at first, but I now think it is a matter of legs. The woodcock's legs are short, and his struttings cannot be executed to advantage in dense grass or weeds, nor could his lady see them there. I have more woodcocks than most farmers because I have more mossy sand, too poor to support grass.

Knowing the place and the hour, you seat yourself under a bush to the east of the dance floor and wait, watching against the sunset for the woodcock's arrival. He flies in low from some neighboring thicket, alights on the bare moss, and at once begins the overture: a series of queer throaty *peents* spaced about two seconds apart, and sounding much like the summer call of the nighthawk.

Suddenly the peenting ceases and the bird flutters skyward in a series of wide spirals, emitting a musical twitter. Up and up he goes, the spirals steeper and smaller, the twittering louder and louder, until the performer is only a speck in the sky. Then, without warning, he tumbles like a crippled plane, giving voice in a soft liquid warble that a March bluebird might envy. At a few feet from the ground he levels off and returns to his peenting ground, usually to the exact spot where the performance began, and there resumes his peenting.

It is soon too dark to see the bird on the ground, but you can see his flights against the sky for an hour, which is the usual duration of the show. On moonlight nights, however, it may continue, at intervals, as long as the moon continues to shine.

At daybreak the whole show is repeated. In early April the final curtain falls at 5:15 A.M.; the time advances two minutes a day until June, when the performance closes for the year at 3:15. Why the disparity in sliding scale? Alas, I fear that even romance tires, for it takes only a fifth as much light to stop the sky dance at dawn as suffices to start it at sunset.

It is fortunate, perhaps, that no matter how intently one studies the hundred little dramas of the woods and meadows, one can never learn all of the salient facts about any one of them. What I do not yet know about the sky dance is: where is the lady, and just what part, if any, does she play? I often see two woodcocks on a peenting ground, and the

356

two sometimes fly together, but they never peent together. Is the second bird the hen, or a rival male?

Another unknown: is the twitter vocal, or is it mechanical? My friend, Bill Feeney, once clapped a net over a peenting bird and removed his outer primary wing feathers; thereafter the bird peented and warbled, but twittered no more. But one such experiment is hardly conclusive.

Another unknown: up to what stage of nesting does the male continue the sky dance? My daughter once saw a bird peenting within twenty yards of a nest containing hatched eggshells, but was this *his* lady's nest? Or is this secretive fellow possibly bigamous without our ever having found it out? These, and many other questions, remain mysteries of the deepening dusk.

The drama of the sky dance is enacted nightly on hundreds of farms, the owners of which sigh for entertainment, but harbor the illusion that it is to be sought in theatres. They live on the land, but not by the land.

The woodcock is a living refutation of the theory that the utility of a game bird is to serve as a target, or to pose gracefully on a slice of toast. No one would rather hunt woodcock in October than I, but since learning of the sky dance I find myself calling one or two birds enough. I must be sure that, come April, there be no dearth of dancers in the sunset sky.

(From *A Sand County Almanac*)

ERNEST THOMPSON SETON

*Dance of the
Prairie Chickens*

Young people of this generation miss a vivid experience by not growing up with the writings of Ernest Thompson Seton as did their fathers; a great pity, because Seton's writings are timeless and appeal to all ages. *Two Little Savages, Rolf in the Woods* and other novels by this great storyteller inspired many youngsters to identify themselves with Yan or Rolf. They became Seton Indians and tried their hand at woodcraft and wilderness living, even though the "wilderness" was just a small farm woodlot. It is almost certain that more copies of Seton's books have been read by Americans than those of any other naturalist, including John Burroughs. Total sales have exceeded two million copies. His most enduring monument is his several volume work, *Lives of Game Animals.* On first reading his autobiography, *Trail of an Artist Naturalist,* I pondered over his account of the prairie chicken, following, in which he describes dancing behavior in very young birds. This phenomenon has seemed more credible to me after I witnessed bill-clapping and so-called "courtship behavior" in nestling storks in Spain and in the Rhine Valley.

FAR TO THE south of my brother's farm at Carberry, Manitoba, some four miles away, the sand hills began; and two miles farther, the long black line of spruce forest. These were unexplored but most thrilling mysteries, sure to offer new kinds of life—birds and beasts. Like everything in the world about me, they were full of promise, full of joy.

358

Dance of the Prairie Chickens

One day in early spring, as I drove with my brother in that direction, we saw a flock of grouse skimming across the prairie. "There are the chickens," he said, "the prairie chickens. They are coming back from the bush now the snow is gone." We saw many of them; for they go into the timber to winter, but at this time were coming back.

Later on we saw a low mound on the prairie; and my brother, jerking his thumb toward it, said: "That's where they dance."

"Who?" I asked.

"The chickens," was the answer.

I did not know what to make of this. But my brother, taciturn and moody, made no further explanation.

On another occasion, a neighboring farmer made a similar remark about a low mound. When I asked for fuller details, he said: "Don't you know that the chickens have a regular dance in spring time? And that that's one of their dancing places?"

It certainly looked like it. The mound, for a space of fifty feet across, was bare of grass, apparently trodden down hard, and strewn with feathers and droppings.

Within a few days I saw, far off on a ridge, half a dozen prairie chickens rushing about, uttering a sort of cackling or crowing sound; and finally got something like a near view. But the birds flew away.

There could be no doubt, however, that I had got a glimpse of the chicken dance. That merely piqued my curiosity. I wanted a full, close view. And this is how I managed:

A mile from our shanty I found a dancing mound. So, taking hatchet and spade, in the afternoon, I took my blankets to the place, and camped in the hide.

About dawn I heard the whirring wings of the grouse, and one of them sailed out of the sky to alight on the mound. Others came; and when it was light enough to see, there were a dozen quietly walking about or sitting still. Then one of them suddenly lowered its head, spread out its wings nearly horizontally, and its tail perpendicularly, distended its air sacs on either side of the neck, and erected its feathers. Then it rushed across the "floor," taking the shortest of steps, but stamping its feet so hard and rapidly that the sound was like that of a kettle-drum. At the same time, it uttered a sort of budding crow, which seemed to come from the air sacs, beat the air with its wings, and vibrated its tail so that it produced a loud, rustling noise, and thus con-

359

trived at once to make as extraordinary a spectacle of itself and as much noise as possible.

As soon as one commenced, all joined in, rattling, stamping, drumming, crowing, and dancing together furiously; louder and louder the noise, faster and faster the dance became, until at last, as they madly whirled about, the birds were leaping over each other in their excitement. After a brief spell the energy of the dancers began to abate; and shortly afterward they ceased and sat down, or stood or moved about quietly, until they were again started by one of their number "leading off."

I lay there and watched them till sunrise. During that time they had at least a dozen set-to's. Then I came out of my hide; whereupon they scattered and flew in all directions.

Throughout May and June I found the chicken dance taking place; and later I learned that even in autumn, when feeling fat and fit, they assembled at the Dance Hall on fine days for a spiel.

But a more remarkable demonstration was in store for me.

In the summer of 1883, at Carberry, I had some fifteen baby prairie chickens hatched under a hen. When they were two weeks old, we were visited by a cold, driving storm of sleet. The chicks were in danger of perishing.

I brought the whole brood into the kitchen. Keeping the hen in a cage close by, I put the chilled and cowering little things under the stove, on the tin which protected the floor. Here, after half an hour, they were fully warmed. They recovered quickly, fluffed out their feathers, preened their wings, and began to look very perky.

Then the clouds broke. For the first time that day the sun shone brightly. It came through the window, down onto the stove, and partly under, on the assembled brood.

It seemed to stir them with some new thought and feeling of joy. One of the tiny things, no bigger than a sparrow, lowered his head nearly to the tin, with beak out level, raised high the little pimple where in time his tail should be, spread out at each side his tiny wings; then ran across the tin, crowing a little bubbling crow, beating his wings and stamping with his two pink feet so rapidly that it sounded like a small kettledrum.

The result was electrical. At once the rest of them leaped up and at it. Every one took the same position—head low, wings out, beating, tail stump raised and violently vibrated, the feet pounding hard—leap-

360

ing, bounding, stamping, exactly as is done by the old birds on the dance hill at love time.

For a minute or more it lasted; then they seemed tired, and all sat down for a rest.

In half an hour they were at it again; and did it several times that day, especially when the sun was on them, and they were warm and fed.

Then I found that I could start them, when the conditions were right, by rattling on the tin a tatoo with two fingers. They responded almost invariably; during the three days that I had them in the house, I started them dancing many times for myself or the neighborhood to see. A number of my friends made a buggy ride across country those days to come and see the tiny downlings "do their war dance" whenever I chose to start them beating the drum.

It is noteworthy that these chickens danced exactly as their parents do, without ever having seen those parents; therefore, the performance was wholly instinctive. All—and undoubtedly both sexes were represented—danced with equal spirit. It was not at the breeding season, and could not, in any sense, be said to have been sex urge. It was evidently and unquestionably nothing more or less than a true dance—a vigorous rhythmic, athletic expression of health and joy.

(From *Trail of an Artist-Naturalist*)

JULIAN HUXLEY

The Crested Grebe

Julian Huxley, grandson of Darwin's contemporary, Thomas Huxley, is one of the most productive of all living biologists as one may judge by the card file of his titles in any leading library. His range of interests is enormous, but bird behavior, particularly courtship, has always been one of his favorite themes. No mere recorder of details, he is never forgetful of the philosophical implications of what he sees.

TEN YEARS AGO I spent my spring holiday watching these birds [Crested Grebes] on the Tring reservoirs. I soon found out that their courtship, like the Herons', was mutual, not one-sidedly masculine as in Peacocks or fowls. It consisted most commonly in a little ceremony of head-shaking. The birds of a pair come close, face one another, raise their necks, and half-spread their ruffs. Then, with a little barking note, they shake their heads rapidly, following this by a slow swinging of them from side to side. This alternate shaking and swinging continues perhaps a dozen or twenty times; and the birds then lower their standards, become normal everyday creatures, and betake themselves to their fishing or resting or preening again. This is the commonest bit of love-making; but now and then the excitement evident even in these somewhat casual ceremonies is raised to greater heights and seems to reinforce itself. The little bouts of shaking are repeated again and again. I have seen over eighty succeed each other uninterruptedly. And at the close the birds do not relapse into ordinary life.

362

Instead, they raise their ruffs still further, making them almost Elizabethan in shape. Then one bird dives; then the other: the seconds pass. At last, after perhaps half or three-quarters of a minute (half a minute is a long time when one is thus waiting for a bird's reappearance!) one after the other they emerge. Both hold masses of dark brownish-green weed, torn from the bottom of the pond, in their beaks, and carry their heads down and back on their shoulders, so that either can scarcely see anything of the other confronting it save the concentric colours of the raised ruff. In this position they swim together. It is interesting to see the eager looks of the first-emerged, and its immediate start towards the second when it too reappears. They approach, rapidly, until the watcher wonders what will be done to avert a collision. The answer is simple: there is no averting of a collision! But the collision is executed in a remarkable way: the two birds, when close to each other, leap up from the water and meet breast to breast, almost vertical, suddenly revealing the whole flashing white under-surface. They keep themselves in this position by violent splashings of the feet, rocking a little from side to side as if dancing, and very gradually sinking down (always touching with their breasts) towards the horizontal.

Meanwhile, they exchange some of the weed they are carrying; or at least nibbling and quick movements of the head are going on. And so they settle down on to the water, shake their heads a few times more, and separate, changing back from these performers of an amazing age-old rite—age-old but ever fresh—into the feeding- and sleeping-machines of every day, but leaving a vision of strong emotion, canalized into the particular forms of this dive and dance. The whole performance impresses the watcher not only with its strength, but as being apparently of very little direct (though possibly much indirect) biological advantage, the action being self-exhausting, not stimulating to further sexual relations, and carried out, it would seem, for its own sake.

Further acquaintance with the Grebe only deepened the interest and made clearer the emotional tinge underlying all the relations of the sexes. This bird, too, has its "greeting ceremony"; but since, unlike the colonial herons and egrets, it makes every effort to conceal its nest, this cannot take place at its most natural moment, that of nest-relief, but must be made to happen out on the open water where there are no secrets to betray. If the sitting bird wishes to leave the nest, and the other does not return, it flies off, after covering the eggs with weed, in search of its mate; it is common in the breeding season to see a Grebe

363

in the "search-attitude," with neck stretched up and slightly forward and ear-tufts erected, emitting a special and far-carrying call. When this call is recognized and answered, the two birds do nothing so simple as to fly or swim to each other, but a special and obviously exciting ceremony is gone through. The bird that has been searched for and found puts itself into a very beautiful attitude, with wings half-spread and set at right angles to the body, ruff erected circularly, and head drawn back upon the shoulders, so that nothing is visible but the brilliant rosette of the spread ruff in the centre of the screen of wings, each wing showing a broad bar of brilliant white on its dusk-grey surface. In this position it swings restlessly back and forth in small arcs, facing towards its mate. The discoverer meanwhile has dived; but, swimming immediately below the surface of the water, its progress can be traced by the arrowly ripple it raises. Now and again it lifts its head and neck above the water, periscope-wise, to assure itself of its direction, and resumes its subaqueous course. Nor does it rise just in front of the other bird; but swims under and just beyond, and, as its mate swings round to the new orientation, emerges in a really extraordinary attitude. At the last it must have dived a little deeper; for now it appears perpendicularly from the water, with a slowish motion, slightly spiral, the beak and head pressed down along the front of the neck. I compared it in my notes of ten years ago with "the ghost of a Penguin," and that comparison is still the best I can think of to give some idea of the strange unreality of its appearance. It then settles down upon the water and the pair indulge in one of their never-failing bouts of head-shaking.

Two mated birds rejoin each other after a few hours' separation. Simple enough in itself—but what elaboration of detail, what piling on of little excitements, what purveying of thrills!

(From *Essays of a Biologist*)

LOYE MILLER

The Territorial Instinct

We usually associate Loye Miller with paleontology, for he was one of the first to glimpse the "small pit about the size of a piano box where someone had dug out some bones" at Rancho La Brea. He was to spend years excavating and cataloging the fossil deposits in these tar pits which are now surrounded by growing Los Angeles. In addition to bird bones of antiquity we associate this pioneer biologist of the West with bird song, for he would often entertain his classes at the University of California with his whistled imitations. The voices of owls are his specialty. In his book of recollections, *Lifelong Boyhood,* we find that he was not solely wrapped up in classification as were so many of his museum contemporaries, but also has a lively curiosity about the ways of living birds.

B<small>E IT ONLY</small> a treetop, there's no place like home. Yes, I'm sure the bird feels that way about his own particular treetop. I'm sure the desert rat has the same feeling for his own little patch of cholla cactus, the trout for his own pool, the toad for his particular tuckaway place in my garden, the cricket for his small crevice between the stones about my fireplace. Home is the spot to which each will return after a longer or shorter absence on whatsoever excursion far or near. All are moved by the same feeling that has stirred in man's heart since the time he claimed as his own some smoke-stained rock shelter which he defended against the cave hyena or the sabertooth tiger.

For many years the strong territorial behavior of the various owls has been a source of much interest and pleasure to me while on camp-

365

ing trips with students. Most of our southwestern owls are not definitely migratory, and hence the territory may be occupied during the entire year and thus become quite strongly fixed. A horned owl may lay claim to all the unwary wood rats in a certain bit of timber and will resent any encroachment by others of his kind, although the little pygmy owl may be stationed in the same area to pick up the grasshoppers, caterpillars, or small birds, all of which are given little attention by the larger owl. I have actually found both the great horned owl and his pygmy cousin in the same pine tree at Hume Lake in the Sierra Nevada. The little fellow has to be on the alert, however, for the big owl is not above using him as a first course at dinner time.

Our camp, one summer trip, was made among the yellow pines at 7,600 feet altitude in the San Bernardino Mountains. Shortly after sunset, I started hooting the horned owl's booming challenge to the local overlord. He was quick to respond from his daytime sleeping quarters about three hundred yards to the south of us. Soon he appeared atop the small pine beside our clearing. From tree to tree he moved about the circle, with call and answer, call and answer. Totally oblivious of us humans, he was looking for a feathered rival that was talking back to him. A mere man who "talked owl" was not comprehensible to his limited owlish brain. We played with him for some time just for the fun of seeing his confusion. Finally his mate came over to see what it was all about. She is notably larger than he is, but her voice is always higher in pitch and often is less fixed in its rhythm.

Our sleep that night was more or less disturbed by the very insistent owls. They sometimes came down within fifteen feet of us to sound their insistent challenge. As a result of their visits our camp was astir at a fairly early hour next morning and we started on a walk just before sunrise. The open and very gently sloping valley ran for several miles to the westward, clothed in fairly uniform, open pine woods. Our old owl, whom we called "Buho," had been quiet for some time. Perhaps he had decided to get his night's work done and get to bed before sunrise. Just now he was probably asleep in his customary tree, but with "one ear open" evidently, for it took only two hoots to bring him to life and response from the same spot where he had first started the night before.

In my notebook this point was called locality I. It is assumed to be about the central point of Buho's territory. As we walked from our campsite—station A—down canyon about two hundred yards' distance

366

we stopped at station B on the roadway and hooted again. Buho came gliding through the trees to perch in plain view answering and reanswering, first from one tree and then from another, about the spot where we were standing plainly visible in the middle of the road. But there was nothing that looked like an owl, stare as he would at the point from which my hoot came. . . .

After a few minutes at station B we moved on another two hundred yards to station C and repeated the performance. Buho came quickly to the new station in search of his elusive rival.

Another two hundred yards down the road, we stopped at station D and resumed calling. Buho promptly moved toward us, but remained well to the southward, refusing absolutely to come any nearer. We moved on again to station E and called persistently, but Buho remained at his latest post south of station D. The continued calling at station E, however, stirred up a second horned owl which we called "Tecolote," and he answered from his sleeping quarters at a locality we called II, about a quarter mile to the northwest. His voice was slightly higher in pitch than Buho's. Call and answer, call and answer, and finally we saw him glide through the trees in our direction; but he would not come quite all the way to us at station E. He stayed a short distance to the northwest. We therefore moved on down the forest road to station N.

It soon became evident that we had now crossed into Tecolote's territory, for he followed us to station N just as Buho had followed our call to stations A, B, and C. He occupied perches on the scrubby pines about us, first on this side, then on that, peering in the direction from which our hoots came but seeing no rival horned owl.

We repeated the play at stations O and P, with the same results. Then we went on down the valley and left him at station P. Buho in the meanwhile had lost interest and gone back to his sleeping quarters at locality I near our camp.

We were absent down the valley for nearly an hour, after which we started back to camp by the same roadway over which we had come. As we approached the region of station P, we resumed hooting, and Tecolote at once responded from his original position at II, north of the road, and we saw him come flying through the scrubby timber toward us where we stood on the roadway. The same performance was repeated here and at stations O and N, much as it had been enacted in reverse order an hour earlier.

367

I was greatly interested to see that the big owl was not molested by the small birds of the forest. Apparently they did not consider him an enemy and so made no attempt to mob him. On the other hand, only a short time before, we had sat under a tree whistling the note of the pygmy owl and had brought eight different species of small birds all scolding about us in search of this owl, their mortal enemy.

We played with Tecolote for a while at station P, then walked on to station O, and then to station N, hooting at each stop. Tecolote, following us, was completely puzzled at his inability to find his elusive rival.

When we went on to station E, however, the result was quite different. Hooting at this point stirred up Buho again and he answered from his original sleeping quarters at I, south of our campsite. This call from Buho roused in me a strong desire to apply the final test. Here was Tecolote, who had just followed me for nearly a mile up the road from the west, and there was Buho, answering from the eastward. Why not get the two birds together at station E?

We moved forward into a little glade which here ran through the forest, and called, and called, and called. Buho came readily toward us from the east, but stopped a hundred yards away. Tecolote came from the west, but he, too, stopped about the same distance away. Both owls were plainly visible to us at the same time, and both were much excited, but not a yard nearer would either one come. I hooted myself dizzy but to no avail. Finally, I saw Tecolote fly off through the trees, heading back to his sleeping quarters at II.

The little glade seemed to be about the dividing line between the territories of these two robber barons, and they had long ago settled their disputes. All the wood rats on one side paid tribute to Lord Buho, all those on the other were subject to Señor Tecolote, and neither hunter poached on the other's territory. We went on back to camp and to a late and much appreciated breakfast, leaving Buho and Tecolote to a peaceful day's sleep, each in his own pine-tree castle. I hope they are still good neighbors, and their international boundaries, settled by whatever means, held inviolate by mutual agreement. Would that men might be always as wise as those horned owls.

(From *Lifelong Boyhood*)

368

JOSEPH GRINNELL

Uphill Planters

Joseph Grinnell (1877-1939) was a born naturalist who had a profound influence on western ornithology. While director of the Museum of Vertebrate Zoology at the University of California he took time out from his administrative and research activities to conduct courses in the Department of Zoology. Many of our top zoologists today can say "I studied with Grinnell." He believed in field work, first-hand observation, and reflective thought. When a student once asked where he might go to study bird behavior he replied: "Just outside the door, on the lawn, you will find some Brewer's blackbirds. . . . They will do for a starter."

On the other hand, one of Grinnell's most brilliant papers, "The Role of the Accidental," gives much comfort to the incurable bird-lister who is forever being told by the pundits of zoology that rarities "don't mean a thing" and that the study of common species is more to the point. Grinnell maintained that accidentals "constitute sort of sensitive tentacles, by which the species keeps aware of the possibilities of areal expansion." It is by virtue of the continual activity of these pioneers that the species maintains itself. His favorite theme was the interplay between animals and their environment and the factors which limit their distribution. "Uphill Planters" is the concluding chapter in a posthumous collection of his writings.

THE SECOND WEEK of October, a year ago, found me nature-watching on the western slope of the southern Sierra Nevada. I was walking along the road which leads up to Sequoia National Park, when, as the morning sunshine began to increase the warmth and dry-

369

ness of the atmosphere, I began to note the sounds of falling and bouncing acorns. For, at the level where I was, about 5000 feet, the black oaks were just then yielding their annual crop of seeds. It would seem that these seeds are finally loosened from their cups, if not disturbed otherwise, when the air each day has reached a certain measure of dryness.

The mountain slope was steep, 25 to 45 degrees; and along about ten to eleven o'clock the sound and sight of descending acorns was impressive. They were even accumulating in appreciable windrows in places along the inside of the road next to the bank; now and then one, from source far up-slope, having gained extra momentum, bounced clear over the road and proceeded on its way toward the canyon bottom far below.

Acorns are smooth-shelled, heavy objects, and those of the black oak in particular are of rotund shape. These qualities make for insecurity of placement on any slope upon which they fall, until in their movements they reach some arresting crevice, or some sufficiently wide strip of level, or nearly level, ground on which to find lodgment.

It was clear to me that the direction of seed scattering from any one oak tree was here well-nigh directly down-hill. In that place and on that day I saw *no* acorn moving *up*-hill. Gravity alone was acting as the agency of distribution. There appeared no possibility that *wind* could serve as an agent of elevation, as with seeds of such trees as maple, cottonwood and willow. In the case of the oaks, it might therefore seem, the only possible direction of general forest spreading through time would have to be through the action of gravity and streams of water, always down-hill. But how, then, could forests ever have spread, naturally, so as to gain altitude on our many mountain sides?

The next two days, October 12 and 13, my companion, Dr. Eric Hill, and I spent seeking pocket-gophers down near Three Rivers, about 1000 feet altitude, in the valley of the lower Kaweah River. Here another kind of oak, the blue oak, abounded, and we observed that there was a fairly good crop of its acorns, though not borne as uniformly as those of the black oak in the life-zone above. Very many of the blue oaks had produced no acorns that season. Especially was this true of the trees far up the hillsides above the valley bottom. Some of the trees had produced a few acorns. Those trees which were bearing most heavily were those of larger, thriftier-looking condition, down toward the river bottom. Of certain possible bearing on our problem, this season was a dry one; and furthermore it was the latest of a series of dry years.

As we tended our trap-lines, run in all the different types of soil within reach, we became aware of the presence and especially the activities of California jays (*Aphelocoma californica*). These activities looked into, became of deep significance to us; for here, indeed, was the agency at this particular place, at this particular time, of transportation of acorns up-hill. The jays we saw to be centering their interest in those most abundantly fruiting trees down in the bottom of the canyon. There the birds were gathering the acorns and carrying them up the slopes, to be ensconced in various hidey-holes, some of them to be buried, after the well-known blue-jay tradition, in the ground of open spaces on the hillsides. From morning to evening, individual birds were almost constantly in sight when we looked out of the auto cabin where we worked, 150 yards from the river.

Every bird going up-slope bore an acorn lengthwise in its bill; every bird in return course was empty-billed. If I had only thought of it, here was a chance for counting birds, and their loads, in sight, during say, a three-hour period; and then computing the bushels of blue-oak acorns being elevated by the jays perhaps hundreds of feet each October day in that one valley.

In this same locality of observation, Dr. Hill and I saw "digger" ground squirrels busily gathering acorns that had fallen to the ground, carrying them in various directions (with these animals, however, irrespective of direction of slope) to their burrows or to their shelling stations. Twice we watched a ground squirrel climb up a blue oak to the larder of a group of California woodpeckers, filling its cheek pouches with the acorns they had gathered and stored, even though being attacked by the resentful birds. Then the squirrel would go precipitately down the trunk and off to its own cache in the ground.

Observations of the type just cited, gathered into notebook and memory from many parts of California, have led me to generalize concerning the paramount agency of vertebrate animals in the dispersal of trees, especially of oaks. My recollections bring into this credit column, not only California jays, woodpeckers, and ground squirrels, but also gray squirrels, chickadees, chipmunks and wood rats, and Steller jays and band-tailed pigeons. In reflecting upon this matter, we can see readily that the relationship is of reciprocal benefit; all of these animal

371

agents of seed dispersal are supplied, at least in part, by the oaks with food, or shelter, and (or) nursery sites. The trees produce crops of nutricious seeds—each seed nutricious either to the prospective oaklet or to the animal that eats it—in vast excess of immediate seeding needs. There is enormous seeming extravagance on the part of the trees, far and away greater production than would be needed to provide for persistence of the species, *if* the species were of fixed geographic position through time. Granting an individual longevity of 75 to 300 years for more or less mature oaks of one kind and another (I cite Jepson, *The Silva of California,* 1910, p. 57), perhaps one successful germination to only a million acorns would provide for mere forest replacement. Even this ratio is probably far too high. The point I wish to make is that in the long-time interests of the tree species, involving locomotion of the whole *forest,* there is value received upon this huge rate of production. It is not extravagance, but good investment, for the oaks to provide subsistence for a continuing population of animal associates.

Even in any relatively brief period of years, catastrophe may overtake the fortunes of the oak forest. Fire of great intensity may destroy all of the growths on a given slope clear to the top of the ridge. Then quick recovery—early repopulation by the oaks—will likely be dependent upon the survival and germination of acorns buried previously by animals, in open places, where the heat was least effective, as also upon the year-by-year marginal replanting process just described. I think especially of California's great erosion-guarding and water-conserving chaparral belt, of which the live oaks and scrub oaks of several kinds are prominent constituents—and their constant animal attendants, the California Jays, the chipmunks, and the dusky-footed wood rat.

Giving again to our scientific imagination fair rein, let us think of the oak belts of California in longest time vista—back through not only centuries, but millenniums. Also let us think of the, to us invisible, climatic boundaries which at any one time-level hem in those belts, each belt characterized by a different species of oak. And let us further think how these boundaries have shifted in past time spatially, as borne upon by changes in physical conditions affecting climate—those involved in repeated elevation and depression of the land surface, and in shiftings of prevailing air currents. We can then think of the oak belts, as slowly marching, through time, up hill and down dale, southward and northward, as their species have been driven by the gradually shifting exigencies of physical requirement which determine where new trees can not only sprout, but mature. Again, we must think, not of the individual tree up to 300 years old, but of the aggregate of trees involving long series of generations of their kind. Such time-space aggregation has been *forced* to move from place to place. It has literally *had* to keep up with the procession. It has *had* to provide ways and means of insuring transportation, or else be wiped out through complete failure at any one level of those favoring factors which have to do with the existence of each kind of oak in its own life-zone. Tree species have had to move their location from one period to the next or die in a struggle against oncoming adverse conditions.

Here, then, is where a certain portion of the associated animal life has come into the service of the oak species. In the present era, with life-zones probably advancing northward, and up-slope, we can think of the successive belts of valley oaks, blue oaks, golden oaks, black oaks, and huckleberry oaks, on our western mountain sides, as relying, most especially for that part of their dispersal comprised in elevation, entirely upon their bird and mammal associates. And there obtains that vital exchange of benefits to which I alluded. Plant-animal communities, eventually closely knit in their specific interrelationships, have been subject to evolutionary processes quite as definitely as discrete species.

(From *Joseph Grinnell's Philosophy of Nature*)

LEWIS WAYNE WALKER

Vital Struggle: Elegant Tern vs. Heermann's Gull

On islands off the desert coast of Mexico, particularly in the Gulf of Lower California—the Sea of Cortez—lives a lovely dark gull, white-headed with a coral bill. The bird watcher in the West sees Heermann's gull only after its nesting when the straggling flocks wander northward along the coast, some as far as Puget Sound.

Few men have visited the metropolis of Heermann's gull on Isla Raza in the Gulf of Lower California. Here Lewis Wayne Walker, the well-known bird photographer, found the elegant terns engaged in an intense struggle for survival in the midst of the gull colony.

ON ANY FORENOON during April, May, and June, the Heermann's Gulls blanket an area of the Gulf about 200 miles long, with Isla Raza at the center. They travel in bands of from 2 to 50 birds, and their focal points are the colony sites of pelicans, cormorants, and boobies. A few hours before dusk, however, the vagrant population diminishes as these birds that radiated from Raza at dawn start back to their tiny island home. Working toward this hub, singles converge with pairs, then with scores, and finally hundreds, until from an anchored boat the influx of birds makes Raza's coastline resemble a hive of swarming bees.

374

Vital Struggle: Elegant Tern vs. Heermann's Gull

As each returning bird drops to a waiting mate on their chosen plot of ground, the beaks open and gull-talk pours out. The sounds and scenes of home-coming are everywhere, and the island roars with the combined vocal utterances of thousands of birds.

Each sweeping wing lowered toward the ground swirls a small cloud of dust. The dust raised by a single bird is insignificant, but across the mile-square island every foot of ground has its agitator, each contributing its share to the yellow plume of haze that marks from a distance this home of the Heermann's.

Aside from a few depressions that are occasionally flooded at night tide, every spot that could possibly accommodate a nest is utilized, and the nests are spaced about two feet apart. This distance seems to be just right. It permits sparring without interruption of incubation and with only a modicum of damage.

During most of the daylight hours, the nest is tended by only one adult, but occasionally the other partner may be seen sharing some of the duties. Family chores are performed only under difficulties as the territory is crowded, and every time the extra bird moves more than a few inches from its incubating mate, the bill of another setting gull forces battle. Every time the "outside" bird moves around, a brand new adversary, fresh and willing, attacks from the new direction. Hence on flat ground, these couples rarely stay together for more than a few minutes. However, when the nest has a rock or bush near by that affords the protection of elevation, both of the birds not infrequently remain in attendance.

Diligent search about mid-April will usually locate a few chicks hatched by the gulls that nested early on Raza. These young seek the shade of rocks or bushes immediately after hatching and crouch there, blending with the ground, awaiting food from the parents. Thus, if the eggs of several adjoining nests hatch simultaneously, a bare plot of ground is left unguarded. This situation sometimes permits the mixed colonies of Royal and Elegant Terns to establish a nesting foothold.

If one of these vacated spots is selected by the terns, a milling mass circles constantly above, and occasionally an individual nervously alights in the clearing. As more screeching birds fill the air, more drop to the ground; and within a few hours their bodies completely blanket the earth. Terns on the outskirts of the packed ring are pushed and shoved by those within and forced into fights with Heermann's Gulls that are trying to save their nests.

This battle of attrition continues throughout the daylight hours and probably throughout the night, with the nesting gulls destined to be evicted. By morning, tern eggs at eight-inch intervals dot the chosen plot, and by sheer numbers the new colony continues to encroach into more occupied gull territory.

Until the laying of the first tern eggs, border gulls have to fight their own battles against superior numbers without help from others of their own kind. But now things are changed. Tern eggs are also gull food. Selfishly inclined reinforcements flock to the area and patrol just out of reach of the nesting newcomers. An egg left uncovered for an instant is devoured by a waiting Heermann's Gull, and by nightfall only a handful of last night's eggs remain. The next morning brings a new crop, several times the original number; but even though the raids of patrolling gulls make inroads, it is evident that the pulsating colony is gaining a permanent foothold. Three weeks later this shimmering blanket of birds covers an acre or more, and eggs in the exact center commence to hatch. Each day thereafter, concentric rings of new young hatch out progressively farther from the center of the colony.

Any estimate of the number of eggs laid by the terns and utilized by the waiting Heermann's would run into the tens of thousands. During the nesting season of the terns, a major part of the gulls' diet consists of these eggs and, later, of young hatched from eggs that survived. The final chapter of this annual battle of Raza places the terns in another predicament, this time one that is hopeless. The original pioneers in the exact center of the colony eventually complete their home duties and, in vacating, leave an expanding bull's-eye of bare terrain. Gulls flock to this unprotected clearing and wage simultaneous attacks from without and within. The tern colony assumes the shape of a doughnut, then a bicycle tire, and finally fades into oblivion in a disappearing act so rapid that its original formation seems slow by comparison.

(From *Natural History*)

DAVID LACK

Swifts at Night

"The swift question, which interests naturalists at the present time, is the habit of the bird, or of the males when breeding is in progress, of rising up higher and higher in the air at a late hour in the evening until they disappear from sight, and finally cease to be heard. It is supposed that these mounting birds, who are not seen to return, although it is possible that they do return after dark, spend the night at a vast height rushing or sailing about in the air, and that with morning they return." (W. H. Hudson, *Nature in Downland.*)

"The swift question" which Hudson wrote about apparently was not taken too seriously by the succeeding generation of British ornithologists, for *The Handbook* merely states that "on fine summer evenings a number will sometimes mount in circles to a great elevation till lost to view." But do they stay up there all night? *The Handbook* is silent on this point. In May 1952 from the walled citadel of Toledo in Spain I first witnessed this crepuscular performance. Hundreds of swifts circled and raced about the medieval walls and towers. At sundown many of the birds disassociated themselves from the milling mob and, as if taking advantage of the thermals, towered higher and higher until lost from sight in the waning light.

On a July day two years earlier, with my wife Barbara, I had climbed the ladder into the tower at Oxford University, where David and Elizabeth Lack were making their study of the nesting of the swift. Little wooden boxes open to our view from the dark interior of the tower revealed the activities of these slim-winged birds which are much larger and darker than our chimney swift. Dr. Lack had often wondered where the unemployed birds, the non-breeding yearlings, spent the hours of darkness. Often only one individual of a pair could be found in the boxes at night. When his book, *Swifts in a Tower*, finally appeared I eagerly thumbed through its pages for an opinion by this brilliant scholar.

377

O
N WARM AND still summer evenings, both in the city of
Oxford and in the surrounding villages, we have often seen swifts
circling and screaming fairly high in the air; as the light wanes, they
bunch more tightly together, fly with rapid beats, almost quivering the
wings, scream more shrilly and rise higher, then the breeding adults
break away and come down to enter their holes singly in the usual way,
but still there is a screaming party high up, which gradually rises higher
until finally the birds vanish from sight.

What happens to them? Various earlier observers claimed that they
came down again to their holes soon after dark. This is almost certainly wrong. Swifts roosting on their nests often scream and may even
scramble about after dark, and this noise has probably been mistaken
by the observers for the return of swifts to their holes after dark. The
question has been studied particularly by the Swiss observer Weitnauer.
He attached an automatic recording device to his nesting boxes and has
never yet registered the entrance or departure of a swift during the
hours of darkness, even on those evenings when night ascents have
occurred. He further pointed out that a swift finds it exceedingly hard
to enter its hole in fading light. . . .

What then happens to the birds last seen, still rising, at dusk? The
next step, clearly, was to watch in the early morning, and Weitnauer
as well as two other observers has now seen swifts descending from a
height down to the colony in the early morning, which strongly suggests
that they have stayed up in the air all night. To carry the matter further,
Weitnauer flew in an aircraft looking for swifts at dusk, and found
several parties high in the air, both later in the evening than the time
at which his breeding adults normally retire to their holes, and earlier
in the morning than the time at which they normally emerge. These
observations do not finally settle the matter, since the birds might con-
ceivably return to the ground (though not to their holes) when it is too
dark for them to be seen from an aircraft.

Fortunately, the matter can be carried further. Two reliable British
observers told me that, in Cyprus and French North Africa respectively, they on a number of occasions in summer heard swifts screaming above them in the air long after dark, under circumstances that

made it certain that the birds must have been in the air, not on or in high buildings. Recently, also, two Swiss observers have seen birds that were almost certainly swifts crossing the field of a telescope pointed at the moon on summer nights, though it is hard to be sure of the identification under such conditions. The birds were estimated to be in one instance at 7,000 feet and in the other at between 3,000 and 7,000 feet. Finally, there is one definite observation by a French airman in the 1914-18 war, an account which until recently was by most people dismissed as absurd. One night he was on a special operation on the Vosges front which involved climbing to 14,500 feet above the French lines and then gliding down with engines shut off over the enemy lines. "As we came to about 10,000 feet, gliding in close spirals with a light wind against us, and with a full moon, we suddenly found ourselves among a strange flight of birds which seemed to be motionless, or at least showed no noticeable reaction. They were widely scattered and only a few yards below the aircraft, showing up against a white sea of cloud underneath. None was visible above us. We were soon in the middle of the flock, in two instances birds were caught and on the following day I found one of them in the machine. It was an adult male swift." (Author's translation from French original.) . . .

I am convinced by Weitnauer's evidence that swifts do regularly spend the night on the wing in fine weather. He has often inspected his nesting boxes during the night after an evening ascent has occurred, finding the breeding swifts present on their eggs or young but the non-breeding yearlings absent. Clearly it is the birds without family ties that take part in the night ascents, and only rarely has a breeding adult gone with them. In May, however, before breeding has started, we have not infrequently found one and sometimes both members of a pair away from their box in the tower at night. Some individuals have been much more prone to do this than others.

While watching nightjars during a short visit to the Suffolk coast in 1952, we on 2nd July took an evening off to see an avocet; and chanced on something even more pleasing. At dusk, ten swifts flew high over us and out to sea. We supposed that they might be birds returning to the Continent . . . and did not follow up the observation. But two years later we again relaxed on our last evening, this time to see eight spoonbills, and again saw something more rewarding. As the light failed, thirty-three swifts stopped feeding over the marshes and headed out to sea, being lost to sight at the extreme limit of range of the field-glasses.

This second incident suggested that the habit might be regular, so we kept special watch for it during a month of the summer of 1955, and found that swifts not infrequently set off seawards at dusk, and in every instance they continued to fly away from the land until lost to sight. On a number of evenings, swifts were seen hunting for food above a belt of trees about half a mile inland bordering the coastal marshes. Shortly before it grew dark most of these birds flew off inland, presumably to their nests, but others sometimes stayed for about ten minutes longer, then turned and headed for the sea-wall, screamed once or twice as they crossed it, and flew on silently out to sea. They usually kept one or two hundred feet above the water, flying either directly or in small circles away from the land, and making no attempt to return. The number leaving together in this way varied from two to about a hundred.

On one evening in heavy rain, there was a more dramatic incident. Swifts were pouring south along the coast in a weather movement, at a rate of 1,500 in five minutes. As it grew dark the passage stopped, so abruptly that it seemed as though a referee had blown the whistle for "time". The swifts near to me, about 120 in all, circled several times over the beach, gaining a little height, and then set off out to sea through the driving rain. As no further swifts passed along the coast, similar parties were presumably leaving seawards at intervals all along it. On another evening there was a small passage down the coast, and again the movement stopped at dusk and those swifts near to me circled and went out to sea.

Night ascents from the breeding colonies take place only on fine and still evenings, the birds rising high in small circles, with rapid quivering wing-beats and intense screaming. In marked contrast, the dusk flights out to sea have taken place in all types of weather, on a calm and clear evening with a full moon, with a fresh wind and overcast sky, and in pouring rain. Further, the manner of flight has been normal, the birds did not rise much above a hundred feet, and were silent except for one or two screams at the moment of leaving the land. Clearly, the seaward flights have little in common with the night ascents inland, except that in both cases the birds presumably spend the night on the wing.

(From *Swifts in a Tower*)

ALEXANDER SKUTCH

Montezuma Oropéndola

The traveler in the Central American tropics cannot fail to notice the colonies of oropéndolas, their skillfully woven bags swinging like exaggerated oriole nests from the branch tips of the ceiba trees. The striking males, as large as crows, are deep chestnut shading into black on the chest and head; their outer tail feathers flash canary yellow. The summer of 1955 was a good season for these large icterids (blackbirds) on the Caribbean slope of southern Mexico where they do not seem to nest every year. I saw my first colony in a royal palm not far from the roadside. Later in a tall ceiba we watched a classic colony, forty nests suspended in an almost perfect circle around the perimeter of the tree. I spent an hour photographing the displaying males that swung upside down to the accompaniment of much wing flapping and loud gurgling noises.

They made a beautiful picture in the late afternoon light (it was five o'clock). The next morning, before nine, when we returned along the same road I sensed that something was missing; a mile or two later I had my delayed take—where was the ceiba tree? We went back and discovered that it had been chopped down. The big baglike nests lay sprawled on the ground and there were no signs of life. The big, wonderful birds, their colony ravaged, had fled.

In recent years a flood of American ornithologists has invaded Mexico; a few have investigated the other Central American countries. Most of them have been either collectors of specimens or collectors of lists. A few dedicated men like Irby Davis and George Sutton have inquired into the ways of the living birds. Alexander Skutch has gone one step further. Putting down his roots in Central America he has attempted to do for this virgin ground what Audubon did (in words, not pictures) for North America.

381

My MOST detailed study of the nesting habits of the oropéndolas was made in the Lancetilla Valley near the Caribbean coast of Honduras. It was late in April, 1930, when I returned to this narrow valley in the foothills and found the oropéndolas well advanced in their nesting in the same tree where they had reared their young the preceding year; for they flock each nesting season to the favored tree, as sea birds congregate from afar to lay their eggs on the same barren islet where they have nested for countless years. The tall, light-barked nest tree towered above an almost impenetrable thicket of low bushes and tangled vines which had taken possession of an abandoned banana grove. Here in May the large-leafed *Cornutia* lifted its great pyramids of lilac flowers. On one side of the narrow strip of thicket ran a well worn path that led to the natives' manacca shacks near the head of the valley, and on the other, beyond a little, grass-choked rivulet, a hillside pasture rose steeply to the west. Its slope offered the best point of vantage from which to view the tree, whose upper boughs were already laden with three-score pendant nests, clustered like great, gourd-like fruits at the extremities of the twigs. One unfamiliar with the habits of tropical birds would hardly have expected to see a big, chestnut-colored bird with a bright yellow tail emerge suddenly from near the stalk of the seeming fruit and fly with measured wing beats toward the steep, forest-covered mountains.

In these nests the incubation of the two white eggs was still in progress, or the young had already hatched and were clamoring to be fed. But a group of twenty-one birds, too eager to build close together, had crowded their twenty-one great nests among the twigs of one slender living bough. Things had apparently gone well with them until many had finished their nests and begun to incubate, when the branch, overladen by its heavy burden, snapped off at a point where it was two inches thick and came crashing down to the brink of the stream. This had happened a week or so before I arrived on the scene; and I found the foliage of the fallen branch already withered and the nests discolored by the dampness. Examination of the contents of these nests furnished no evidence that either parents or young had lost their lives in the crash. This accident gave me an opportunity to study and measure

382

the otherwise inaccessible structures and to watch the birds as they set about to build new nests.

The hens alone undertook the construction of the nests. Throughout the day they worked with tireless industry, although, like most birds, they built most actively in the early morning. The materials employed in weaving were chiefly long, pliant fibers ripped from beneath the midribs of banana leaves; slender green vines with foliage still attached and long, narrow strips of palm leaves were also used. The banana fibers were obtained in a small plantation across the path from the nest tree. Here the females went to gather them in small parties, usually accompanied by a male. I tried several times to watch the birds at this work; but the loud *cack* of alarm of the vigilant male, who stood sentry in a coconut palm or in some other commanding position, sent them hurrying away before I could see as much of the process of stripping the fibers as I desired. Still, through perseverance I discovered how this was done. Standing on the massive midrib of one of the huge leaves, the female, taking advantage of one of the transverse tears made by the wind in the broad blade, bent down and nicked the smooth lower surface of the midrib with her sharp bill, then pulled off a thin strand, sometimes as much as two feet long, from the fibrous outer layer. Then she doubled her harvest in her bill and returned to the nest, often with one end of the fiber streaming far behind her as she flew. The green midribs of the banana leaves were marked with long, brown streaks where the fibers had been pulled out, and many loose ends of fibers hung down beneath them.

The social urge of the oropéndolas was so strong that they crowded the new nests they were building in two compact groups close together on the same side of the tree, although an entire half of the spreading crown was left unoccupied. They had learned little from their recent calamity. The nests were sometimes attached to a slender, unbranched twig, but more frequently to a crotch, and sometimes to three branchlets which arose close together near the end of a bough. The twigs used for attachment had about the thickness of a lead pencil. They were always at the outside of the tree, never among the branches in the interior of the crown. Thus the nests were more easily reached by the oropéndolas and at the same time were less accessible to any climbing animal.

The first step in nest building was the formation of the anchorage, which was accomplished by wrapping many fibers around the arms of

383

the crotch, or around the single twig if this had been chosen for the support. The length of twig wrapped varied from eight to sixteen inches. The oropéndolas worked just as a man would if permitted to use only one hand in such a task, pushing the fibers under the twig and pulling them over, intertwining and knotting them carefully. The second step consisted in the formation of a loop, which was the real starting point of the pouch. As the mass of fibers encircling the arms of the crotch became thicker, the bird stretched strands across the space between them. When this weft had become sufficiently strong, on returning to work at her nest the female rested on these fibers instead of grasping the twigs themselves with her feet. Thus the strands were gradually forced downward, and as more fibers were stretched from arm to arm a pocket rather than a loop was formed. Then the bird gradually pushed apart the material in the center of the pocket and converted it into a sort of loop, which would later serve as the entrance to her nest.

The construction of the nests did not proceed without frequent discord on the part of the laboring hens. The most serious of these arose over the choice of the nest sites. Two birds often began their nests so close together that they were in each other's way as they worked, and they paused to express their annoyance in loud, high-pitched, irritated voices, like children who interfere with each other at their play. Sometimes completely losing temper, each menaced the other with open bill. Then, meeting face to face in the air, they went fluttering downward until their proximity to the foliage below warned them that it was time to cease their dispute; then they separated and flew up to continue their weaving side by side.

But what surprised me most in these generally orderly, industrious birds was the frequency with which they stole building material from their neighbors. A bird who was weaving could hardly resist the temptation to steal a fiber which hung loosely from the unfinished nest of another and incorporate it into her own. Sometimes, when the upper end of such a fiber was attached more firmly than she reckoned, the would-be thief, grasping it in her bill, hung with half-opened wings beneath the nest until the coveted strand gave way, or until the owner returned to drive her off. Sometimes an oropéndola discovered that the fiber she desired to take from a certain nest was too firmly attached to be torn away and then went straightway to another to attempt robbery there. In the end, I believe that this habit of thievery must be of a certain benefit to the colony, since it discourages careless construction. It

384

is not easy to pull out a fiber which has been well woven into the fabric of the pouch. Those birds which build most carefully and leave fewest loose ends are not often molested by their pilfering neighbors, and they finish the stronger nests.

The female oropéndolas outnumbered the bigger males by several to one. At the nest tree the males gave no indication of being mated to particular hens or groups of hens; they were ignored by the latter and mostly ignored them. While the hens were building, the males accompanied them on expeditions for foraging or collecting fibers, and at other times they strutted around on the branches of the nest tree with heads held high and pompous gait. Although they were idle, they never quarreled among themselves. The only disputes in the community were those in which the hens engaged over nest sites or building material. Sometimes one male dashed at another; but the latter usually retreated at once and thereby avoided a fight, since the pursuer was always quick to forget whatever cause of enmity he might have had.

At intervals the male oropéndolas delivered their far-carrying calls. Bowing profoundly, until the raised tail stood directly above the inverted head, lifting the spread wings above the back and fluffing all the body feathers, they uttered, or seemed rather to eject with heart-rending effort, an indescribable liquid gurgle. Heard from afar there is no sound, save possibly the ventriloquial call of the Short-billed Pigeon or the melodious wail of the Great Tinamou, which is to me more expressive of the wonder of the tropical lowlands; but close at hand the effect is marred by screeching overtones, as though the machinery which produces this inimitable song was badly in need of lubrication. The male oropéndolas did not worry the hens while they were building in the way the male Boat-tailed Grackles did; and their bows and gurgles were not addressed to individual hens so much as to the world at large.

The males were the watchmen of the flock. At the approach of danger, real or fancied, and not infrequently when there was no evident cause of alarm, they uttered a sharp, harsh *cack* which sometimes sent the whole flock dashing headlong into the nearest sheltering thicket; but at other times this was ignored by most of the community. The approach of a man was generally greeted by a few such *cacks* of alarm; but if the colony had not been persecuted, few or none of the building hens heeded the warning; and thenceforth the man might stand quietly in full view and watch all the activities of the colony without causing the least unrest. One or more male oropéndolas usually accompanied each

385

party which left the nest tree to forage or procure building materials, and it was extremely difficult to elude the keen eyes of these sentries. The birds were as shy away from the nest tree as they were bold and confident among its boughs; and when they were encountered afield the male's shout of alarm invariably sent them into instantaneous retreat.

Such was the patient applicat᾽ᴑᴨ of the hen oropéndolas that their great hanging pouches, which measured from two to four feet in length and from seven to nine inches in diameter near the bottom, were completed in an average time of ten days. One bird, who seemed to be in a particular hurry, finished her nest in only seven or eight days, but hers was considerably shorter than the others. The hen who had so much trouble in starting her loop on the unbranched twig finished last of all and took seventeen days in her work; while number 22, who was so greatly harassed by her thieving neighbors, required fifteen days to bring hers to completion. Most of the weavers took from nine to eleven days.

After the basket work was finished, the hens absented themselves for a day or two, during which courtship and mating probably took place off in the forest. Then they returned and labored assiduously for from three to six days longer, plucking dying or dead leaves from trees growing at a distance; tearing them between foot and bill into pieces an inch or two in length, and carrying them into the pouch. These formed a thick but loose and yielding litter in which the eggs rested and which probably served to prevent their rolling together and breaking when a strong wind rocked the swinging nest. Sometimes at first a bird brought fibers and leaves alternately, as though she had started to line the nest before she had quite finished the weaving. Even during the course of incubation, or while the nest contained young, a hen occasionally took pieces of leaf into it, or more rarely a fiber.

After the completion of the new nests the colony contained a total of 88, but not all were occupied.

(From *Life Histories of Central American Birds*)

KONRAD LORENZ

King Solomon's Ring

The modern science of animal behavior which has sent anthropomorphism into retreat has often been guilty of the equal intellectual misdemeanor of "mechanomorphism"—reducing the actions of animals to a mere set of reflexes. Konrad Lorenz of Austria, regarded unequivocally as the world's leading behaviorist, takes a more balanced view, for he admits that even though the psychology of animals cannot be honestly interpreted in terms of our own, and that much they do is automatic, triggered by "releasers," they are also endowed with individuality and may learn from experience.

It is to Lorenz that we owe our knowledge of the curious phenomenon of "imprinting," and in the following selection from *King Solomon's Ring* he tells us how he himself became imprinted on a brood of ducklings who regarded him as their parent. To explain the title: King Solomon, son of David "spake also of beasts, and of fowl and of creeping things, and of fishes."* This passage from Holy Scripture has given rise to a charming legend that with the help of a magic ring Solomon was able to talk to the beasts. Konrad Lorenz insists he is able to do so himself, without the aid of magic, black or otherwise.

O NE HOT DAY in early summer, when my friend and assistant Dr. Seitz and I were working on our greylag goose film, a very queer procession slowly made its way through this beautiful landscape, a procession as wildly mixed as the landscape itself. First came a big red dog, looking like an Alaskan husky, but actually a cross be-

* I Kings 4:33.

387

tween an Alsatian and a Chow, then two men in bathing trunks carrying a canoe, then ten half-grown greylag goslings, walking with all the dignity characteristic of their kind, then a long row of thirteen tiny cheeping mallard ducklings, scurrying in pursuit, forever afraid of being lost and anxiously striving to keep up with the larger animals. At the end of the procession marched a queer piebald ugly duckling, looking like nothing on earth, but in reality a hybrid of ruddy sheldrake and Egyptian goose. But for the bathing trunks and the moving picture camera slung across the shoulders of one of the men, you might have thought you were watching a scene out of the garden of Eden.

We progressed very slowly, as our pace was set by the weakest among our little mallards, and it took us some considerable time to get to our destination, a particularly picturesque backwater, framed by blossoming snowballs and chosen by Seitz to "shoot" certain scenes of our greylag film. When we arrived, we at once got down to business. The title of the film says, "Scientific direction: Dr. Konrad Lorenz. Camera: Dr. Alfred Seitz". Therefore, I at once proceeded to direct scientifically this, for the moment consisting in lying down on the soft grass bordering the water and sunning myself. The green water-frogs were croaking in the lazy way they have on summer days, big dragon flies came whirling past and a black-cap warbled its sweetly jubilant song in a bush not three yards from where I lay. Farther off, I could hear Alfred winding up his camera and grumbling at the little mallards who forever kept swimming into the picture, while for the moment he did not want anything in it but greylags. In the higher centres of my brain, I was still aware that I ought to get up and help my friend by luring away the mallards and the Ruddy-Egyptian, but although the spirit was willing the flesh was weak, for exactly the same reason as was that of the disciples in Gethsemane: I was falling asleep. Then suddenly, through the drowsy dimness of my senses, I heard Alfred say, in an irritated tone: "Rangangangang, rangangangang—oh, sorry; I mean—quahg, gegegegeg, Quahg, gegegegeg!" I woke laughing: he had wanted to call away the mallards and had, by mistake, addressed them in greylag language. . . . In the study of the behaviour of the higher animals, very funny situations are apt to arise, but it is inevitably the observer, and not the animal, that plays the comical part. The comparative ethologist's method in dealing with the most intelligent birds and mammals often necessitates a complete neglect of the dignity usually to be expected in a scientist. Indeed, the uninitiated, watching

388

the student of behaviour in operation, often cannot be blamed for thinking that there is madness in his method. It is only my reputation for harmlessness, shared with the other village idiot, which has saved me from the mental home. But in defence of the villagers of Altenberg I must recount a few little stories.

I was experimenting at one time with young mallards to find out why artificially incubated and freshly hatched ducklings of this species, in contrast to similarly treated greylag goslings, are unapproachable and shy. Greylag goslings unquestioningly accept the first living being whom they meet as their mother, and run confidently after him. Mallards, on the contrary, always refused to do this. If I took from the incubator freshly hatched mallards, they invariably ran away from me and pressed themselves in the nearest dark corner. Why? I remembered that I had once let a muscovy duck hatch a clutch of mallard eggs and that the tiny mallards had also failed to accept this foster-mother. As soon as they were dry, they had simply run away from her and I had trouble enough to catch these crying, erring children. On the other hand, I once let a fat white farmyard duck hatch out mallards and the little wild things ran just as happily after her as if she had been their real mother. The secret must have lain in her call note, for, in external appearance, the domestic duck was quite as different from a mallard as was the muscovy; but what she had in common with the mallard (which, of course, is the wild progenitor of our farmyard duck) were her vocal expressions. Though, in the process of domestication, the duck has altered considerably in colour pattern and body form, its voice has remained practically the same. The inference was clear: I must quack like a mother mallard in order to make the little ducks run after me. No sooner said than done. When, one Whit-Saturday, a brood of pure-bred young mallards was due to hatch, I put the eggs in the incubator, took the babies, as soon as they were dry, under my personal care, and quacked for them the mother's call-note in my best Mallardese. For hours on end I kept it up, for half the day. The quacking was successful. The little ducks lifted their gaze confidently towards me, obviously had no fear of me this time, and as, still quacking, I drew slowly away from them, they also set themselves obediently in motion and scuttled after me in a tightly huddled group, just as ducklings follow their mother. My theory was indisputably proved. The freshly hatched ducklings have an inborn reaction to the call-note, but not to the optical picture of the mother. Anything that emits the right quack

389

note will be considered as mother, whether it is a fat white Pekin duck or a still fatter man. However, the substituted object must not exceed a certain height. At the beginning of these experiments, I had sat myself down in the grass amongst the ducklings and, in order to make them follow me, had dragged myself, sitting, away from them. As soon, however, as I stood up and tried, in a standing posture, to lead them on, they gave up, peered searchingly on all sides, but not upwards towards me and it was not long before they began that penetrating piping of abandoned ducklings that we are accustomed simply to call "crying". They were unable to adapt themselves to the fact that their foster-mother had become so tall. So I was forced to move along, squatting low, if I wished them to follow me. This was not very comfortable; still less comfortable was the fact that the mallard mother quacks unintermittently. If I ceased for even the space of half a minute from my melodious "Qualig, gegegegeg, Qualig, gegegegeg", the necks of the ducklings became longer and longer corresponding exactly to "long faces" in human children—and did I then not immediately recommence quacking, the shrill weeping began anew. As soon as I was silent, they seemed to think that I had died, or perhaps that I loved them no more: cause enough for crying! The ducklings, in contrast to the greylag goslings, were most demanding and tiring charges, for, imagine a two-hour walk with such children, all the time squatting low and quacking without interruption! In the interests of science I submitted myself literally for hours on end to this ordeal. So it came about, on a certain Whit-Sunday, that, in company with my ducklings, I was wandering about, squatting and quacking, in a May-green meadow at the upper part of our garden. I was congratulating myself on the obedience and exactitude with which my ducklings came waddling after me, when I suddenly looked up and saw the garden fence framed by a row of dead-white faces: a group of tourists was standing at the fence and staring horrified in my direction. Forgivable! For all they could see was a big man with a beard dragging himself, crouching, round the meadow, in figures of eight, glancing constantly over his shoulder and quacking—but the ducklings, the all-revealing and all-explaining ducklings were hidden in the tall spring grass from the view of the astonished crowd.

(From *King Solomon's Ring*)

WILLIAM VOGT

Will and Kate

On Sundays, many years ago, William Vogt and I often birded with the small group of young men known then as the Bronx County Bird Club (Joseph Hickey and Allan Cruickshank also were members), and because they could not easily get rid of us they voted us into their club as the first non-Bronx members. It was Bill Vogt who talked me into writing my first *Field Guide* and to him I dedicated the volume. Acting in my behalf, he took the manuscript to six publishers before Houghton Mifflin Company saw its potentialities. Later he encouraged Joseph Hickey to write his *Guide to Bird Watching*. He was always promoting others; it was not until he wrote his runaway best seller, *Road to Survival,* that he came into his own.

The two extremities of his career seem to have little in common. When I first knew him, not long out of Bard College, he was a drama critic. To-day he is the national executive head of Planned Parenthood. But on re-viewing events there is a consistent thread that ties these unlikely occupa-tions together. Although the first outlet for his writing was as critic and editor, his interest in the outdoors led to a syndicated nature column in several newspapers. This brought him his chance to take over the director-ship of the Jones Beach Bird Sanctuary and from there it was a skip and a jump to the editorship of *Bird Lore* (now *Audubon Magazine*). As a full-fledged staff member of the National Audubon Society he distinguished him-self as a conservationist. It was during this period that he studied the willets and wrote *Will and Kate*. His knowledge of behavior and ecology made him the chosen candidate for a three-year research study of the guano cormorants of Peru for the *Administradora del Guano*. At the termination of this project, having acquired a background of Spanish and South Ameri-can living, he became chief of the Conservation Section of the Pan Ameri-can Union. His step from there to birth control was logical: his studies of

391

the population dynamics of wild creatures were transferred to man. Traveling throughout the Latin American countries had made him acutely aware of the dual dangers of depleted resources and explosive populations. His *Road to Survival* is a prophetic book, contested by some, but endorsed by nearly all conservationists who have any biological background.

M Y NEW NEIGHBORS in the southern New Jersey hamlet could see neither sense nor profit in settin' all day long on the meadows, as they call their wide marshes, watchin' birds. They concluded, therefore, that I must be doing it for the government, and their charges for various small services were accordingly raised. When I finally convinced them that I was actually watching the birds for my own pleasure, and that this was my chosen way of spending a vacation, they shook their heads hopelessly, but reduced their charges to a point where I felt as if I should be the one to blush at payment. Before I left, to return to a routine of desk and telephone, they had really become aware of the birds for the first time, and their interest was an embarrassment. My time was sharply restricted, yet a sizable section of it was given over, morning and night, to explaining, from one end of the single street to the other, what I expected to see during the day—and what I actually had seen. The front stoop, here as elsewhere, is the place where one sits to chew tobacco and interrogate passers-by. In a community where radios, without exception, blare from breakfast to bedtime, and where one can scarcely buy a nationally advertised product, Ethiopian massacres passed unnoted, and the local haul of fish and the local bird man were the news.

My first impulse towards this fishing village—one of the few places in the Northeast where the birds breed—came several years ago in one of those exalted moments that, for most men, justify their pursuits. A delicate nerve faultlessly excised by a surgeon—an "El" pillar missed a millimetre by a cab-driver—a batch of bonds unloaded on a bearish customer—three green-wings neatly dropped with a double gun—these are the things that make this world a better place than the parsons and the communists say it is. In my personal encounter with perfection, no element of my own skill was involved, nor could I claim any kudos, unless for having sense enough to spend an evening alone on a mosquito-ridden marsh pond.

392

The moon, hanging just over the ocean, was scarcely bright enough, in the dusk, to be notable except for its girth, vastly magnified by the atmosphere. There was still enough light in the West to show swimming black ducks as mud-lumps far out on the water. The swinish grunts of the males, and the hum of insects, were the only sounds, until there came a sudden wailing ka-a-a-ty. It was a stirring, reedy contralto that spoke for all the aeons of wildness on that coast.

Quickly I searched with my binoculars, and the powerful lenses picked up the birds and the moon at the same instant. The orb was at once greater and more candent. The light of the evening, concentrated by the glasses, brought the striking pattern of the wings into startling relief against the orange disc. Twice, still calling, they scaled like falling leaves across the moon, before they dropped into the shadowed limbo of the mud flats. The birds were Willets, and though I have watched their flashing pinions hundreds of times since, I have never seen them in such perfection of circumstance. In that instant the wings asked a question, and I have already spent several hundred hours seeking an answer. . . .

The Willet is a large American member of the shore-bird or snipe family and, as its long legs and bill indicate, is kin to the familiar teeter-tails of woodland waters. . . . As it probes along the shore line, or walks through marsh grasses, the Willet is one of the most nondescript of birds, a dun gray that seems the ultimate perfection of protective coloration. I have watched it, through glasses, on cloudy days, and had it vanish before my eyes, leaving not even a grin behind. But let it be stirred to flight or combat, and it becomes one of the most vivid creatures of the marshes and shores on which it dwells. Its long wings wear bands of broad black and white, more striking than the stripes of any zebra, and when the wings are open they flash a biological signal that has come down the ages.

The Willet is not common in the Northeast, but neither is it of extreme rarity. Its wing pattern has thrilled hundreds of observers, and it was not a novelty to me. But never until its black-and-white bands shone like filigree upon the rising moon, had my imagination been sufficiently quickened so that I realized this bird offered a clear-cut research problem. What is the value, to the bird, of this flash pattern? Has its chief function been that of intimidating enemies? Has it given the males the means of wooing reluctant and selective mates, and those mates a means of holding males through the long period necessary,

393

every year, to perpetuation of the species? Does it exist as a signal, to other Willets, which, in part at least, makes flock life possible? Does it serve, like war-time camouflage, as a "ruptive pattern" which, despite its brilliance, breaks the real outline and brings protection from stooping peregrines? These, and a number of other questions, began to ferment in my mind, and some years later, when a change of circumstances permitted, I went to live with the birds in the hope I might find the answers. . . .

During the weeks I spent with the birds, they ignored my presence and went their wild way within a few yards. They led me deeper into the fascinating cosmos of the marshes than I had ever been before, and showed me a minuscule of the truths that lie beneath the beauty of tangled sedges and gleaming mud flats.

Will and Kate were the names almost inevitably given them. The Willet, on its breeding ground, cries a ringing pill-will-willet, cries it over and over again, daylong, and even, occasionally, in the hot June night. I had been warned that I should become thoroughly wearied of the repetition, but as rehearing of a symphony increases understanding, it seemed that understanding of the birds' language could come only through a thousand hearings, in a thousand situations; and as I began to translate the few syllables they became, for me, the most exciting music in the world. I have found no Rosetta stone, to unlock the language, but I have discovered, among others, two of the most fundamental phrases in the whole long history of animal sound: proclamation of ownership, and invitation to love.

She, as well as he, cries pill-will-willet, and he also wails ka-a-aty. Indeed, most of the calls seem to be jointly used. The birds wear the same plumage. If it were not that Katy—the carrier of the eggs—is somewhat larger and acts quite unlike her belligerent husband, I should usually have been at a loss to know which was Will.

Many birds, like other lower animals, possess a Bourbon attitude towards private property; it is inflexible and unintelligent. Will and Kate were no exceptions. Once they had established control over a segment of marsh they were as intolerant of trespass as an English keeper. Let another Willet so much as fly across their territory—theirs merely by right of seizure—and a loud pill-will-willet would ring out to warn him off. Kate contented herself with scolding. Will, like as not, would take off in defense of his ownership of blue-sky rights, and see the interloper well away.

394

This rabid landlordism is a boon to the ornithologist. On a stretch of marsh where Willets nest over a score or more of miles, it means that the birds assort themselves. Out of hundreds of pairs, it is certain that pair A will spend most of the breeding season on the same few square rods of land, that they will not be permitted on the territory of pair B, and that pair B, in turn, will not be tolerated on A land. Thus, the observer, who is trying to learn their life history, has usually to watch only two birds at a time, and these two—despite their apparent identity of appearance—it is often possible to tell apart.

Bourbon-like, Will, in defense of his prerogatives, would become as belligerently defensive over a dummy threat as over a real danger. I had brought with me a Willet skin on which a taxidermist had worked his art. In some species, such a dummy, passively awaiting the will of the ruling male, will evoke an amatory response. But Will is not such a simple creature. He requires, from his mate, more than passive as-sent, and so far as his actions showed, there was no doubt that this strangely inert stranger was an unwelcome trespasser. A warning pill-will-willet having had no effect, Will sailed into the mount and literally made the feathers fly. He hammered it in the back of the head, he at-tacked it about the eye. From time to time, he shook his bill, as if the arsenic and alum with which the dead skin was preserved, were as bitter to him as quinine to human taste buds. There seemed little doubt that he would have torn it to pieces, had I not rescued it.

I put his animosity to severer test. I spread on his territory a great white square of mosquito net that obviously occasioned Will no little discomfort. He eyed it continuously and shunned it as we should shun a skunk. Then, one evening, when he and Kate returned from the dis-tant tide flats, the inert stranger stood spang in the middle of the cloth! Kate contented herself, as usual, with complaints.

Not so Will! He strode straight towards the dummy and, avoiding the square as though it were abomination, fluttered to the Dummy's back and, like the ghost of Queen Victoria that Archy saw with Lytton Strachey, "beaned him and beaned him and he never knew it." The dummy did fall to its side, however, and since presumably it no longer represented an intruding Willet, Will fluttered to the grass—still care-ful not to touch the cloth.

It was while trying to make some sense out of the territorial defense of the birds that I got a possible clue to the meaning of the wing pat-tern that had brought me to these marshes. One function of the song of familiar birds in our gardens is proclamation of territorial rights. The song sparrow that pipes up in February, the meadow lark that thinly cries in May, are serving notice on the avian world that the land and grass and shrubs about their singing-place will be defended against trespassers. Will and Kate had well-marked territorial limits. These were vigorously defended. To this extent their behavior was clearly like that of the song sparrow and the meadow lark. But they are not true "song birds," and they did not sing from an elevated perch. Was there analogous behavior?

Will and Kate, unfortunately, had taken up their land by the time I was able to leave New York—and they were already paired. How they had established their claim I could not surmise until, two territories away, I was able to watch a pair of Have-nots lop sectors off the territories of Haves as forthrightly as if they were Japanese warlords.

Parenthetically, I should explain how I was able to watch all these doings, to follow the different pairs, and to keep them separated. I had had built, before the Willets migrated from the South, a hide, or blind, whose floor was six feet above the flat marsh. It was merely a platform, four feet square, with a burlap shelter six feet high on top of it. Since it was part of the landscape when the birds arrived, they accepted it as readily as if it had been a clump of cattails, and fed and fought and carried on their love affairs almost beneath my feet. . . .

The Have-nots arrived with a fanfare of pill-will-willets. This clear cry, which cannot be imitated by the human voice or human instruments, can be heard over more than half a mile of marsh, and as the stranger male and female dropped onto an occupied territory they did not spare their syringes. The owners of the land responded with the same cry, and the males joined battle.

The conflict was sporadically renewed for several days, until the Haves gave up part of their land. But, as is so common in Nature, the dispute was a strangely conventionalized affair. Noise, display, and persistence seemed to be the principal weapons, and at no time did the birds give any indication of a serious impulse to injure one another.

The noise was a single cry—the pill-will-willet reiterated, by both Have and Have-not. I could detect no difference or variety in their notes. It was in the manner of the calling that I began to get my clue.

Have-not would fly to Have's territory and, shouting pill-will-willet over and over again, he would hang high in the air on still wings that moved through the narrowest of beats; indeed, on some windy days

397

he would occasionally soar on pinions that were as motionless as those of a turkey vulture. Slowly he would sink towards the earth, then he would climb again, all the time giving voice to his cry. Sometimes he would tower against the blue sky and piled cumulus clouds until he was five or six hundred feet above the earth.

And the whole performance might have been designed to display those wonderful wings! Wide-spread, with light piercing through to birds and man watching from the ground, vibrating through a few degrees of arc, they flickered like long tongues of black and white flame. As his mate, taking up the call and the flight, towered upward to fly just beneath the Willet, it was difficult for an excited ornithologist not to anthropomorphize the ceremony into ecstasy! But as the birds sank to earth, on Have's land, and as Have drove them off with fierce threats, and as Have went into the same display, curiosity reasserted itself, and the audience—at least the human audience—again assumed a role that was essentially critical. What does it mean? Why the call and why the display? What is its biological justification?

Will was frequently seen to engage in the same ceremony—it seems identical with what Julian Huxley calls a "ceremonial flight" in a European godwit—when repelling invaders, or immediately after they had left. Sometimes he would swing about the borders of his own territory, sometimes far out over the marsh, when the occupants of the lands he crossed would take up the performance, and the whole society of Willets would become one beautiful bedlam.

It was not until Will displayed his wings in a similar fashion, under markedly different circumstances, that I could begin to hope for an answer to the questions.

Will and Kate were a devoted pair. Whether or not the devotion outlasts a single season, I could not doubt its power during the weeks from April into July or August, when the young could fend for themselves. They spent virtually all their time together. Kate avoided the advances of unattached males, and Will was severely beaten in repelling one such Lothario. They fed together on the territory and off; together they sought the site of the future nest, and now one, then the other, would explore the possibilities of a tussock, their breasts shaping the predecessor of a grassy cradle. Together they shared the duties of incubating eggs, and the ceremony as he relieved her, or she relieved him, was as pretty as any ballet I have ever seen.

Here I was able to detect no difference between the behavior of Will

398

and Kate. Each was as cautious as the other, each as ceremonious; and each spoke as musically. If Kate had been warming the eggs for several hours, Will would feel some impulse, probably proceeding from inner, physiological compulsions, to take her place. As cautiously as though the lives of all Willet-kind depended upon it—as, indeed, they did—he would creep through the long grass, invisible except for the moments when his long neck would be raised, periscope-fashion, to permit a reconnaissance. The grasses stirred, as he walked, and it may be their rustling was perceptible to the superior ears of the birds; at least, when he was near the nest, he uttered a low clucking note, as though to reassure her.

He would circle the nest, with a meticulous care, and come to it across the little clearing on the edge of which it was placed. All this while, so far as I could tell, she gave no sign she was aware of his approach. Once, when crows were hunting eggs near-by, a nest relief that had already begun was abandoned with something of the air of, "We weren't doing anything, anyway."

When he stood directly in front of his mate, there came the climax of the ceremony. Will bowed low before her, his bill pointed towards the ground near her breast, and gave utterance to his ringing pill-will-willet cry. Still no sign from her. Then, very deliberately, he walked onto the nest, stepping over Kate, and as his breast touched her, she darted out beneath him and flew away, accompanying the flashing of her wings with a clear pill-will-willet that, certainly, would have attracted attention away from the nest she had left. Thus male gave way to female, or female to male, without exposing the precious eggs, for an instant, to cold or enemy eyes.

Once when he lost her in the grass he called her as plainly as could be; at least I could not interpret the cry in any other way, and a Dutch ornithologist has recorded the same circumstance in the closely related phalaropes. Altogether they were a model couple, but I have no doubt at all that, were it possible to transcribe Willet speech into equivalent English, we should find her addressing him as Mr. Will. Even in their most intimate moments the fine ceremoniousness persisted.

A neo-pagan poet would have been shocked at the lack of impetuousness in their love-making. At the slightest sign of negation from his Kate, Will would turn his attention to other matters (usually food). And as often as not she would put a period to his courtship by merely walking away three or four steps.

His manner of making his desires known was as exquisite a ritual as was the ceremonial flight. He would walk towards Kate, chipping slowly, and lift eloquent wings high above his back. At the same time the speed of the chips and the movement of the wings increased until he sounded like a cicada and wore, above his shoulders, a canopy of those same flickering black and white tongues of flame. He was now directly behind her, and her eyes, set wide on the sides of her head, were manifestly watching every flash of the wings. If she were willing, she would incline slightly forward—sometimes calling softly—and the beating wings would carry him lightly to her. Thus, in a manner that has been fixed by centuries of success, the seed of the future Willet race is sown.

Establishment and protection of territorial rights, and courtship, then, have one marked trait in common—rapid vibration of extended wings. In more than two hundred hours of field observations, the wing vibrations were observed under no other circumstances. What do these vibrations mean, and what do they tell us of the biological reason for that striking pattern?

Before a categorical answer can be given, much more research, probably requiring a number of years, must be done. Some way must be devised of trapping the birds, on their territories, and of dyeing the wings of some white, of others black, to destroy that pattern. Will it also destroy the ability of the bird to intimidate his territorial competitors—and to beguile his mate to an acceptance of love-making? The birds should be taken into some laboratory, or progressive zoo, and with hormone extracts induced to breed. Will staining of the wings, perhaps even trimming away the black tips, prove an obstacle powerful enough to counteract the internal chemistry?

This extraordinary feather pattern has presumably survived, along with the way in which it is used, for many centuries. The family to which the Willet belongs existed at least as far back as the Eocene period—and a pattern, either of plumage or behavior, does not become set for an entire wild species in a few generations. The fact that it has survived at all argues that it has been of value to the birds, and its prominence at the critical periods of territorial assumption and courtship is further evidence for that hypothesis.

If, as seems highly probable, the destruction of the plumage pattern would destroy the behavior pattern, the dependence of behavior on the signalling wings would be strongly indicated. Scientifically, they might be compared to the plumes of the heron that, returning to its nest, must use them as a token of its friendliness; otherwise it will be met, even by its wife, with hostilely slashing bill. More vulgarly, those wings might be compared to the red tie with which the Willie Baxters of this world indicate their intentions to the girl friend. If Willie lacks thirty-five cents for the tie, his life may be blighted—for a week, at least. (Possession of a second-hand car may be cynically, and not unjustly, described as a masculine, secondary sexual characteristic.) Were Willie closer to Nature, such matters would undoubtedly be taken care of for him.

To the casual human eye, the flickering Willet wing is a simple thing of beauty. To the naturalist it is more—it is a single perfect thread that belongs, somewhere, in the magnificent tapestry of life itself, a tapestry that can be understood and enjoyed only as one lovingly studies strand after strand. And the numbers of these strands, happily for the naturalist, are without limit.

(From *The Yale Review*)